Fundamentals
of
Population Study

FUNDAMENTALS

OF

POPULATION STUDY

T. Lynn Smith

*Graduate Research Professor of
Sociology, University of Florida*

J. B. LIPPINCOTT COMPANY

Chicago   *Philadelphia*   *New York*

Printed in the United States of America

Preface

THIS VOLUME WAS PREPARED for the specific purpose of aiding teachers to introduce the study of population matters to undergraduate students at colleges and universities throughout the United States. It is the culmination of almost thirty years of experience in teaching the introductory population course at five universities in the United States and one in Brazil. Because of the gradual way in which the writer's knowledge of demography has grown and developed, the general outline and frame of reference used in this book resemble rather closely those employed in the population sections of earlier works such as *The Sociology of Rural Life* (1940, 1947, and 1953) and *Brazil: People and Institutions* (1946 and 1954), and those used in *Population Analysis* (1948), *Introdução a Analise das Populações* (1950), and *The People of Louisiana* (with Homer L. Hitt, 1952). However, if one looks beyond the chapter headings, one will find innumerable modifications and extensions.

Sections dealing with genetics, the demographic aspects of economic development, the social consequences of population changes, and so forth, deliberately have been omitted in the preparation of this text. This is not because the writer depreciates the value of such fields, nor because he would not have population materials closely integrated with other aspects of sociological and economic analysis. On the contrary he believes that such subjects deserve places in the curriculum as separate courses, and he is convinced that demographic matters, considered both as independent variables and as dependent variables, must constitute an important part of any comprehensive and well-integrated system of sociological or economic analysis. Primarily, though, the limitations were imposed because of the belief, which this author shares with large numbers of others who have population courses as a part of their teaching loads, that a three-hour course for one semester is not too much time for the undergraduate major in sociology, economics, zoology, and so forth, to devote exclusively to the fundamentals of population study. Certainly even the most able of the students must concentrate at least to this extent upon demographic essentials if they are to master a few of the most fundamental population facts, to gain a knowledge of a basic frame of reference, to become familiar with the sources from which the materials are drawn, to acquaint themselves with even the most elementary techniques of population analysis, and to learn about the best-known relationships between demographic phenomena.

The teaching aids which accompany each of the chapters are those the author has used throughout the years, along with others suggested by friends and associates who also have had much experience with the population course. In the lists of suggested readings a variety of important works have been included to assist the teachers of the course in acquainting the students with alternative approaches to the various subjects, to supply the facts of publication about works that readily might be assigned for book reports, and to help the students locate the more basic sources that should be consulted in the preparation of term papers.

The author is indebted to many people for assistance in the preparation of this book. First and foremost of these is his wife, Louvina Jackson Smith, who has done so much to help create the proper surroundings and atmosphere for his scholarly activities; and ranking next are the hundreds of students who have participated in the work in his population classes. To several members of the administrative staff of the University of Florida, and especially to the late Dr. John M. Maclachlan (head of the Department of Sociology and Anthropology), Dr. Ralph E. Page (Dean of the College of Arts and Sciences), Dr. L. E. Grinter (Dean of the Graduate School), and Dr. J. Wayne Reitz (president of the university), appreciation is due for a favorable academic environment in which to work. Dean Grinter also provided the funds to pay two graduate assistants without whose help it would have been impossible to assemble and analyze the large masses of quantitative data on many of the topics. This work had to be done before large sections of many of the chapters could be written. Particular thanks also are due the John Simon Guggenheim Memorial Foundation and Mr. Henry Allen Moe, its secretary general, for the fellowships which have enabled the author to concentrate to a considerable extent since 1951 upon the study of the peoples and institutions of Latin America. Without this assistance the knowledge and experience needed in the various international comparisons attempted in this volume could not have been acquired.

The writer's colleague at the University of Florida, Professor Irving

L. Webber, read the entire manuscript and made innumerable suggestions which led to its improvement in substance and style. Much of any merit the book may have is due to his untiring assistance. Professor C. A. McMahan of the Louisiana State University Medical School, Professor John Van Dyke Saunders formerly of Mississippi State University and presently at the Louisiana State University, and Homer L. Hitt, vice-president of Louisiana State University in New Orleans read portions of the manuscript and made many helpful suggestions. Mr. Robert W. Nelson and Mrs. Barbara Meares Nelson, undergraduate students, and Mr. William M. Mauldin and Mr. Paul E. Zopf, Jr., graduate students at the University of Florida, assisted with the statistical compilations and analysis and with the preparation of many of the charts and maps which are used in the volume. Mrs. Louetta Young Holst, secretary of the Department of Sociology and Anthropology at the University of Florida, typed the manuscript in its final form. To all of the persons mentioned the author hereby expresses his most sincere thanks.

GAINESVILLE, FLORIDA   T. LYNN SMITH
NOVEMBER, 1959

Contents

Figures

Tables

Part One

THE NATURE AND DEVELOPMENT OF POPULATION STUDY

*The Scope and Method of
Population Study*

*Important Landmarks in the
Development of Population Study*

Chapter 1

The Scope and Method
of Population Study

THE MOST IMPORTANT THING in the world is the people. As people, you and I and billions of our kind spread over the face of the earth are at once the means and the end of all society's endeavors. Everything done in the fields of economics or industry, government or politics, education, religion, recreation, and all the rest is done by people and for people. Furthermore, the number of people involved, the manner in which they are distributed over the territory, the rate at which they are increasing or decreasing, and the extent to which they are young or old, male or female, married or single, rural or urban, in the labor force or out of it, of one race or ethnic group or another, literate or illiterate, native born or foreign born, and so on are of basic importance in nearly all of mankind's undertakings. For example those responsible for the military activities of a given country are avid for certain facts about the people of their own country and those of the potential enemy; and those in charge of educational programs want certain other information about the population just as badly. Dozens of other comparable needs for population facts might be listed, for virtually all questions of public policy have their population aspects. This is true at the local, state, national, and even international levels.

At the broad national level, information about the number of inhabitants, their characteristics, and recent trends with respect to each are basic in connection with the formulation of policies relating to agriculture and industry, immigration, education, social security, health insurance, taxation, and military service. At the state level, population facts and principles are of fundamental importance in connection with plans and policies relative to old age benefits and other welfare measures, the equalization of educational opportunities, construction of highways, apportionment of seats in the legislature, and

3

hospitalization. Even at the local level, the basic facts about the people involved are essential in the intelligent shaping of public policies. Questions such as those related to the location of schools, school construction and school consolidation, locating and building hospitals and other health facilities, and planning and improvement of roads and highways must all be studied in close relationships to population facts and trends. Thus, with much reason one might contend that comprehensive, tested materials about people, their numbers, and their characteristics are among the facts most useful to modern society. Certainly these matters deserve careful, objective, scientific study.

The prime objective of this volume is to introduce college and university students to the important and rapidly developing field of population study. In it an attempt is made to treat in a systematic manner all the major divisions of the modern field of demography. In preparing this introduction the author has felt it necessary to present in considerable detail relevant materials on each of the following aspects of the general topic: the systematized set of concepts, classifications, and principles, or the frame of reference, used by those who are most experienced in the field of population; the more important primary and secondary sources of information used in the study and analysis of each of the general topics included in demography; and various analytical devices and techniques which may be employed to extract meaningful results from vast masses of raw materials pertaining to the numbers, geographic distribution, characteristics, vital processes, migrations, and changes in human populations.

Scope and Content

The scope and content of population study or demography as developed in the United States and other parts of the modern world are fairly well agreed upon by those teaching the subject in colleges and universities and by most of those doing comprehensive research in the field. They may be set forth rather explicitly by means of a brief consideration of each of the principal divisions of the subject.

Number and Geographic Distribution of the Inhabitants

The number of its inhabitants is the most important demographic fact about any area, large or small. Therefore, the first task of the student of population is to determine as accurately as possible and to maintain as current and up-to-date as feasible the actual numbers of people in the various areas with which he is concerned (continents, nations, regions, congressional districts, counties, cities, boroughs, towns, villages, townships, wards, precincts, census tracts, and so forth). The taking of periodic censuses is the basic way, of course, of securing such information, but frequent post-census estimates also are a prime necessity. If the counts are properly tabulated and if the figures are given separately for each of the smaller units into which a given area is subdivided, the basis has been laid for significant study and analysis of the geographic distribution of the population. Thus, for a state such as Michigan or Mississippi, the tabulation of the data gathered in each census of the population, such as the ones made each ten years by the United States Bureau of the Census, should indicate clearly and exactly the number of persons in: (1) the state as a whole; (2) each of the counties of which it is composed; (3) each of the townships or other minor civil divisions into which the counties are subdivided; (4) every center of population (city, town, village, or hamlet), incorporated or unincorporated, in all of the counties; (5) every political subdivision (ward, precinct, and so forth) within each city, town, or village; and (6) for the cities in which the necessary preparatory work has been done, each census tract into which the urban or urbanized area has been subdivided. Given such tabulations the experienced student of population is enabled—by careful study and especially by means of various mapping devices—to extract and present facts and relationships of the utmost theoretical and practical importance.

Composition or Characteristics of the Population

A second fundamental division of demography is that relating to the composition or characteristics of the population. These two expressions are those commonly employed by census technicians and population analysts to designate the common and rather obvious, but highly significant, features which distinguish one person from another and which, therefore, are used as the basis for classifying human populations into the most fundamental categories. Each of these characteristics is mentioned briefly in turn. The first to be listed, however, are four (age, sex, rural or urban residence, and race or color) which are of greatest importance for purposes of demographic analysis. They are most basic in the sense that data about them should enter into the cross-tabulations with the materials on all the other characteristics. In a very real way they are the four principal threads in the "warp and woof" of modern census tabulations. Thus, for example, a meaningful table of data on the marital condition of a population should show the materials properly subdivided by age, sex, race, and residence so that a given column of figures will give the information for the white (or Negro), urban (or rural), male (or female) population in each age group.

Age, a little reflection will convince almost anyone, is the person's most important characteristic, the most fundamental determinant of one's behavior. For this reason, the data on the age distribution of the population is of the utmost significance in the field of demography. The extent to which adequate age classifications (those by five-year age groups are by far the most useful) are employed in combination with all the other subclassifications of population materials, determines to a high degree the ultimate value of the costly materials gathered by a nation's census and by its registration system. The student of population must exercise the utmost care in the study of this factor in order to insure that the other relationships and differentials he is seeking to test or to establish are not merely reflections of differences or similarities in the age compositions of the populations he is comparing.

Sex is the person's second most important personal characteristic; and the ratio of males to females in a given population rivals in demographic significance its age composition. As indicated above, proper classification of population facts according to the sexes of the persons involved is one of the principal threads in the warp and woof of modern census tabulations. The population analyst can make little headway until he is able to control through subsorting, or in other ways, the variations in the sex composition of the population he is studying.

Rural or urban residence is the third characteristic of a population that the student must have in mind constantly from the beginning to the end of his demographic endeavors. After long experience the technicians in charge of United States census tabulations use the rural-urban division of the population as the first of the highly elaborate sets of classifications employed in our decennial census reports. Table I in the national and state reports subdivides the population into the urban, rural-nonfarm, and rural-farm categories, and these categories wisely are retained throughout a large part of the tables that follow. This is because the demographic characteristics and processes of persons who live in the country are radically different from those of people who reside in cities. As will be abundantly clear throughout this volume, the classification of the population into rural and urban segments, or into various categories along a rural-urban continuum, is one of the primary concerns of the census that is manned by a professionally competent staff and one of the features most urgently needed by the population analyst.

Race or color is the fourth of the strands or threads that should run through all census tabulations and figure prominently in endeavors to understand and interpret demographic materials. From time immemorial human groups have attached significance to the differences in pigmentation, texture of the hair, and other distinguishing characteristics of *homo sapiens*. From the most remote times, also, these criteria have been used as a basis for establishing great categories of mankind, such as the white, the black, and the yellow races. It matters little that contemporary scientific findings and theories (in biology, psychology, anthropology, and sociology) give scant support to the belief that these physical characteristics are in any way related to native intelligence, innate capacities, or moral capabilities. As long as any considerable part of the members of a society *think* that such physical features are significant, they will continue to be the basis for fundamental divisions of the population. In the United States Census of population the classification of the inhabitants as white and nonwhite, with the latter subdivided into Negro and other races, is carried through a substantial part of the tabulations. Together, the materials on the four characteristics just discussed occupy, as properly should be the case, the bulk of the space in the voluminous reports of the decennial censuses of population.

National origins is another characteristic of considerable significance in countries, such as the United States, Canada, Australia, Argentina, and Brazil, which have received considerable numbers of immigrants. In our own country the classification of the population into native born and foreign born, with each of these categories further subdivided in various ways, gives valuable information on another important population characteristic. In the reports of many of our censuses, because of the high proportions of immigrants in the population of the United States and because of the pressures exerted by the organizations representing the various nationality groups, materials on this subject loomed very large. They are useful not merely in connection with the subject of national and ethnic origins *per se*, but also for endeavors to check upon conclusions relative to immigration and emigration that have been based upon studies of the records of the agencies responsible for administering our immigration laws.

The marital condition of the population is of tremendous sociological significance. The modern census of population includes queries relating to this characteristic and generally the replies to these questions are properly tabulated in relation to the characteristics already discussed and those to be considered below. Most censuses, including that of the United States, give elaborate data on this highly significant, demographic feature.

Occupation, industry, labor force, and employment loom large in the modern population census. Of course only the first of these, occupation, actually may be considered as a characteristic of the population, but its adequate study involves the other concepts as well. For this reason the occupations of those employed or seeking work fills a considerable part of most modern census reports. The student of population, though, has less of a monopoly on the study of occupational characteristics than he has on many other features of the composition of the population. This subject quickly leads into various other aspects of sociology and economics that go considerably beyond the proper range of demography.

Educational status of the population is a feature about which the modern census secures mountains of data. To date, however, this material has been studied very little, and such analysis as has been done was made, for the most part, by those who were working on other aspects of the composition of the population. Probably this is because the demographer, through his greater familiarity with the reports on the census of population, has most frequently been challenged by the comprehensive materials that have been collected on the subjects of literacy and illiteracy and the number of years of schooling completed by the various groups in the general population. The facts, relationships, and trends in this respect belong, of course, fully as much in the sociologist's study of educational institutions and the professional educator's analyses of the results of their efforts, as they do in demography.

Religious affiliations and preferences is another population characteristic of no slight importance. As a matter of fact, very frequently in historical times whether one was Christian or Jew, Catholic or Protestant, Moslem or unbeliever, and so on, has been by far his most important characteristic. No census of population in the United States has included queries on religious affiliations or preferences, but such questions are integral parts of many modern censuses, such as those made in Brazil, Canada, and Pakistan.

The Vital Processes

A third broad area encompassed within the field of demography is the study of the natural increase of population, that, is, of births and deaths and the resulting surplus or deficit that results when the one is weighed against the other. Births and deaths along with migrations are the only factors, of course, that can influence directly the size of a population or its geographic distribution. Hence, when one has a knowledge of birth rates and death rates, only materials regarding migrations are needed in order to account completely for all increases or decreases in the number of inhabitants and for all changes in the geographic distribution of population. This is the basic reason for postponing any discussion of the growth of population until after the rate of reproduction, the mortality rate, and migration have been studied.

Ordinarily the *birth rate,* the *rate of reproduction,* or the *fertility* of the population is the major element in the changing number and distribution of a given area. The study of this factor usually involves the keeping and systematic organization of detailed records of births in the population or populations being analyzed. Thus the basic data are not secured by means of a census but by entirely different procedures from those by which are obtained our fundamental information relative to the number, geographic distribution, and characteristics of the population. Registration, instead of enumeration, is the basic technique employed for the collection of data about births and also for the collection of information on the other of the vital processes, i. e., mortality or deaths.

Mortality, as just indicated, is the second of society's two vital processes. At most times and in most places, the death rate is considerably lower than the birth rate, thus producing a natural increase of population. As in the case of births an elaborate registration system is required in order to secure the detailed records of deaths, along with the characteristics of deceased persons, with which the student of population works. Since comprehensive morbidity or health statistics rarely are assembled, most of our knowledge of the health of various populations consists of inferences that are based on mortality data. For this reason it sometimes is difficult to determine exactly where the study of population terminates and that of health begins.

The number of births minus the number of deaths in a given population during a specified length of time (usually one year) gives the *natural increase* of population. This, in turn, is the primary element in the study of population growth and population redistribution. Ordinarily, however, attention is not focused upon natural increase *per se,* but the birth rate and the death rate are considered separately, along with migration, as the factors directly involved in the increase, decrease, and changing geographic distribution of a population.

Migration

The migration of persons from one country to another, or from place to place within a given country, is the fourth large area of study involved in the field of demography. As indicated above, this movement of persons from one area to another is the third factor (along with births and deaths) that must be considered before one can account for the growth or decrease of population or for changes in the geographic distribution of the inhabitants. As yet, however, the ways and means of securing the necessary data on migrations, especially those that involve movement from one part of a nation to another, have not been perfected; and much of what is known on the subject is inference based upon successive counts of the population and a knowledge of the other two factors involved.

Immigration and *emigration* are of concern to the student of population because they denote the international movement of persons from one society to another. The records kept by the national agencies concerned with the control of such movements and the naturalization of the immigrants are the basic sources of data for studies in this aspect of demography. They are supplemented, however, by the census enumerations and classifications of the population as native and foreign born and the various subclassifications of the latter category.

Internal or *intranational migration* remains the greatest unknown in contemporary population study, although for many areas the exodus or the influx of population is a major factor in the decrease or the growth of population. Few countries have anything remotely resembling an accurate system for accounting for the movement of population from one place to another, although many attempt rigid controls of such movements. In the United States the census of population has tried in various ways to secure partial information on this subject, but with only indifferent success. The problems involved are among the most serious with which the contemporary student of population is faced. Even such common and badly needed material as current estimates of state populations made regularly by the Bureau of the Census and various state and private agencies are subject to tremendous error for want of reasonably accurate data on the annual interstate migrations of the population.

The Growth and Geographic Redistribution of Population

The materials relating to the changing number and geographic distribution of the population is the fifth and final set of data with which the demographer is concerned. Studies of these subjects naturally lead to the making of estimates of future populations or population "projections," a commodity for which modern society seems to have an insatiable appetite. Naturally, successive census counts supply the substantial information needed for the determination and description of past changes, and the knowledge of recent trends and of the three factors involved in population growth or decline offer some basis for predicting the immediate future.

Population Problems and Policies

In addition to the scientific study, analysis, and interpretation of the data in the five general areas outlined above, the student of population may well carry his thinking to the point of indicating certain problems inherent in demographic situations and trends; and logically, too, he may try to formulate statements as to what national, state, or local population policies should be.

Sources of Data

The bulk of the data utilized by demographers are those secured, mainly for other purposes, in the periodic censuses of population which most nations conduct and from the registries of births, deaths, and immigration which they maintain. These are supplemented at critical points by materials the demographers themselves collect by means of surveys organized specifically for the purpose of filling some of the gaps in the essential statistical information. For this reason the student of population must be expert in the collection, testing, tabulation, manipulation, analysis, description, and interpretation of statistical materials. If he is working in the United States, he soon comes to know that the information gathered, tabulated, and published in the decennial censuses of population since 1790, plus the data on deaths registered since 1900 and on births registered since 1915, constitute one of the world's greatest repositories of social and economic facts.

Brief mention may be made of the specific sources in which the student will encounter a large share of the demographic information of which he may be in need. Nowadays it is relatively easy to secure the basic population facts about any nation as a whole, if they are to be had at all. These are readily available to all in the various editions of the *Demographic Yearbook* which the United Nations has published annually since 1948–49. The various issues of this indispensable compendium vary considerably, since each volume is devoted to a considerable extent to the presentation of detailed figures on just one of the major divisions of demography, such as mortality, fertility, or the growth of population. Since the Population Commission established by the United Nations secures directly from the nations involved, tabulates, and publishes these materials, by consulting the various issues of the *Demographic Yearbook,* the student may easily secure the more important demographic data for any or all of the world's nations, territories, dependencies, colonies, and so on, if such information is to be had at all. This is a remarkable improvement over the situation existing prior to 1948. If, however, one is in need of demographic information for the various national subdivisions, such as the states, provinces, or departments, he must consult the census reports, statistical yearbooks, and other sources published by the respective nations.

For the United States, there are two primary sources of demographic data. The first of these is the comprehensive reports of the censuses of population, which give the definitive tabulations of the data assembled each ten years since 1790. The latest of these enumerations, the seventeenth, was made in 1950, and most of the published results were available by the end of 1954. The second fundamental source is the annual publications issued by the National Office of Vital Statistics which give summary tabulations of the data on births and deaths. Departments of public health in most of the states also publish vital statistics data for their respective states, some of them slightly earlier and in somewhat greater detail than those given in the reports issued by the National Office of Vital Statistics.

It will require a considerable amount of time and effort for the student of population to inform himself adequately concerning the contents of the various reports of the Bureau of the Census and the National Office of Vital Statistics. For the serious student, however, the hours spent in this endeavor will prove highly rewarding.

The National Office of Vital Statistics also issues each year a series of *Vital Statistics—Special Reports* in which current and historical materials on births, deaths, marriages, and divorces are issued in a convenient form that makes this set of great value for reference purposes.

If only the more general demographic materials are needed, the *Statistical Yearbook of the United States,* issued annually by the Government Printing Office, is a convenient and thoroughly reliable source of information.

Population Index, a periodical issued six times a year by the Office of Population Research, Princeton University, is devoted almost exclusively to annotated bibliographies of population literature appearing throughout the world. The twentieth volume of this highly useful reference set corresponds to the year 1954. By consulting this periodical regularly the student may keep abreast of the more important surveys conducted in this and other countries and keep himself informed with respect to the most important current books and articles in the demographic field.

Method

The scientific method is the one employed by the population student or demographer in his endeavor to expand the frontiers of knowledge through intensive study of the materials in the areas mentioned above. In fact demography may be defined as the systematized body of knowledge that has been derived through the application of the scientific method to the study of population materials. This study includes the gathering, organization, manipulation, analysis, description, and interpretation of the data relating to the number, geographic distribution, characteristics, vital processes, and changing numbers and distribution of human beings.

Science itself should be thought of as one of the species of human knowledge, of which philosophy, history, and theology are other well-known varieties. From the standpoint of subject matter there is the utmost variety in scientific phenomena, ranging all the way from those studied by the astronomer to those which constitute the province of the social psychologist. The technical aids or devices employed by scientists working in the various subject matter fields also are of the utmost variety. Each branch of science develops and perfects its own, such as the telescopes of the astronomers, the microscopes of the biologists and the chemists, scales and vacuums of the physicists, and the schedules, tests, and interviewing techniques of the psychologists and sociologists. In these technical methods of science there is no unity.

But there is unity in the logical methods employed by those working in all parts of the realm of science, and it is this unity which makes it possible to think of science as a whole and not merely of the specific parts or disciplines of which it is composed.

Two types of mental activity are involved in the scientific method: (1) *observation* and (2) *inference*. Skill in securing unbiased, pertinent, and accurate observations and facility in making significant, logical inferences from these observations constitute the essence of the scientific method. Observation is "the act of apprehending things and events, their attributes and their concrete relationships," including the direct awareness of one's own mental experiences, whereas inference is the formulation of propositions (judgments, beliefs, opinions) based on these observations or as a consequence of other judgments already formed.[1]

Observation is of two types: (1) *bare observation* of phenomena subject to no control and (2) *experiment*. The importance of bare observation is generally overlooked since it is so commonplace, whereas the role of experiment is lauded by almost all of those who write upon the subject of scientific method. Indeed it is not unusual to encounter on the college campus the proposition that "science is experimentally verified knowledge," and it was upon this ground that many authorities for many years sought to exclude the social sciences from the general realm of science. The untenability of such a position is amply demonstrated by the mere mention of astronomy, universally recognized as the most highly perfected branch of science, which by its very nature must depend almost exclusively upon bare observation. Experimentation, or the control of all factors except the one purposely being varied, is a great aid to observation, but as mentioned above the various fields of science all have devices to facilitate the process of observation. In the field of population study the individual's powers of observation are

[1] A. Wolf, *Essentials of the Scientific Method* (New York: The Macmillan Company, 1930), pp. 17–18.

greatly aided by the schedules of questions prepared for use by census enumerators, the highly perfected forms employed by registrars of vital statistics, the tried and tested systems of tabulation, and the ingenious tables and charts designed for analytical purposes.

Inference, too, consists of two principal types, namely, *induction* and *deduction*. Induction, or reasoning from the particular to the general, is the process of formulating propositions that describe or assert some general regularity or uniformity among the phenomena that have been observed. Deduction, or reasoning from the general to the particular, is the process of postulating attributes of the specific from a knowledge of the general. As will be indicated below, both induction and deduction are indispensable parts of the scientific method. Induction supplies the generalizations that may be true, and deduction sets forth what should follow if such propositions are valid. Providing the proposition, or hypothesis, itself is of significance, the hypothesis is a good one if some of the consequences one deduces should follow may be tested empirically.

In the use of the logical scientific method, scientists in all disciplines are guided, consciously or unconsciously, by three fundamental characteristics of science, namely, (1) critical discrimination, (2) generality and system, and (3) empirical verification. *Critical discrimination* is the ability to be cognizant of the significant facts. One skilled at it is able to avoid being misled by mere appearances, preoccupied with the trivial, and bewildered by the multiplicity of insignificant details in which the fact of scientific consequence may be enmeshed. Critical discrimination of a high order was necessary before the whale was classified as a mammal instead of as a fish. It alone can prevent much purported scientific investigation from being merely an elaboration of the obvious. It is sadly lacking in the social scientist who spends years of his time manipulating masses of statistical data, expending enough time and energy to make himself the best informed man in the world on the topic, and then presents the reader with an elaborate set of statistical tables and a few statements to the effect that "the facts speak for themselves." Since the phenomena with which any segment of science must deal are infinite in number and variety, critical discrimination is the first requisite of all scientific endeavor; and this is especially true in demography, where the masses of raw materials that have accumulated over the years almost defy description.

Generality and system is a second requisite of all science, irrespective of the particular subject matter with which a given branch is concerned. Man would be unable to survive in a universe that was lacking in order and regularity. Therefore to discover, to describe, and to understand the order or regularity prevailing in nature is a chief task of man's intellectual endeavors, including those known as science. For this reason, since even the smallest part of nature is infinitely complex, the scientist must not be concerned with a phenomenon or a fact as such, but instead with the object or thing as a representative of many, as a specimen of an entire class of similar objects or things. For him the important facts are those that occur repeatedly in time and space; and the unique is of little value. He seeks instead individual objects and particular events merely as specimens of the types and classes his search for general uniformities and principles leads him to establish.

Finally, all science rests in a very special way upon *empirical verification*. In astronomy, physics, chemistry, zoology, geology, psychology, anthropology, sociology, and all the rest, every proposition sustained for more than temporary consideration must be based solidly upon the facts gained through sensory impressions. Every generalization must arise through induction from stimuli received through one or more of the senses; and, if it is anything more than a mere hunch or working hypothesis, the more critical deductions as to what should follow, providing it is valid, already must have been made and tested empirically. Such empirical tests involve the "look and see" procedures to determine if the things that should follow, providing the proposition is valid, actually do so.

Since systematized bodies of knowledge other than science, such as history and philosophy, also make use of observation and inference, and since they too require critical discrimination, generality and system, and empirical verification, it is well at this point to consider the distinction between science and one of the others, let us say philosophy. The essential feature distinguishing the two lies not in the nature of the cognitive processes employed but rather in the varying orders in which observation and inference appear in scientific endeavor and in philosophic inquiry. Philosophical endeavors may, and probably usually do, start with observation, just as do scientific activities. In both realms of thought, also, since the human mind has a tendency to leap forward from the observation of a few examples or cases to the formulation of some general rule or principle, induction generally follows immediately after a limited number of observations have been made.

At this point, though, the two mental disciplines may part company. The philosopher has the privilege of making his observations, inductions, and deductions in any order that suits his purpose, providing only that no internal conflicts are permitted in his line of reasoning. Thus he may proceed with observation—induction—deduction—deduction—observation—deduction, and so forth, or the three in any other sequence he may choose to utilize.

The scientist has no such freedom. For him after observation comes induction, or the formulation of some general proposition that may be true. At this point he must resort to deduction, to intensive reflection on the query, "If this generalization is true or valid, what consequences should follow?" Naturally, as he reflects upon the things that should follow, previous facts of observation in large numbers are brought to bear on the hunch or working hypothesis he is entertaining; and unless all these are in accord with the proposition, it is quickly discarded. The active scientific mind conceives and discards hundreds of such tentative propositions, for every one that merits more formal testing. In this stage, too, even for the generalization which is supported by the scientist's previously acquired knowledge, not all of the possible deductions as to what should follow are entertained for further empirical testing. In most instances the possibilities are far too numerous to allow for that. Rather the ingenious researcher asks himself, "If this proposition is not valid, under what circumstances is it most likely to prove defective?" In other words he attempts to resort immediately to the critical case. He seeks ways and means of making additional observations, under experimental conditions if at all possible, at the points of greatest significance. But under no circumstances, no matter how important the proposition he is seeking to test, may he proceed to further inferences, until after additional empirical tests have demonstrated that the results to be expected, providing the proposition is valid, actually do follow. Thus in the scientific method, in contrast with the philosophical method, the sequence is always as follows: observation—induction—deduction—observation—induction—deduction—observation and so on.

Order of Presentation

The order followed above in outlining the field of population study, or demography, is followed closely throughout this volume. Before commencing with the discussion of the number and geographic distribution of the inhabitants, which constitutes Part II of this book, however, a second introductory chapter is included. This was prepared to help familiarize students with various events that the present writer considers the principal landmarks in the development of population study. In selecting the items to be included the writer has been influenced heavily by the course of events in the United States and the needs of college and university students in this country. No separate chapters are devoted to problems of tabulation, map making, the construction of charts, the making and testing of indexes, and other methodological considerations. Instead such explanations as appear to be necessary are given in connection with the application of a given measure, index, or technique.

SUGGESTED SUPPLEMENTARY READINGS

Cox, Peter R., *Demography*. Cambridge: University Press, 1950, chapters 2–5.

Davis, Kingsley, "The Sociology of Demographic Behavior," in Robert K. Merton, Leonard Broom, and Leonard S. Cottrell, Jr. (Editors), *Sociology Today: Problems and Prospects*. New York: Basic Books, Inc., 1959, chapter 14.

Glass, D. V. *The University Teaching of Social Sciences: Demography*. Paris: UNESCO, 1957.

Hauser, Philip M., and Otis Dudley Duncan, *The Study of Population: An Inventory and Appraisal*. Chicago: University of Chicago Press, 1958, chapters 3–5.

Hillery, George A., Jr., "Towards a Conceptualization of Demography," *Social Forces*, 37, No. 1 (1958), 45–51.

Landis, Paul H., and Paul K. Hatt, *Population Problems: A Cultural Interpretation* (Second Edition). New York: American Book Company, 1954, chapter 1.

Statistical Office of the United Nations, *Demographic Yearbook, 1948*. Lake Success, New York: The United Nations, 1949, pp. 7–12.

Vance, Rupert B., and Nadia Danilevsky, *All These People: The Nation's Human Resources in the South*. Chapel Hill: University of North Carolina Press, 1945, chapter 1.

Willcox, Walter F., *Studies in American Demography*. Ithaca: Cornell University Press, 1940, appendix 1.

Wrong, Dennis H., *Population*. New York: Random House, 1956, chapter 1.

Chapter 2

Important Landmarks in the
Development of Population Study

INTEREST IN THE NUMBER of inhabitants and inventories of those with special characteristics arose very early in the history of civilization, but disinterested, objective attempts to determine relationships, trends, and principles seem to date from comparatively recent historical times. At least a search through contemporary compendiums of demographic knowledge reveals very few items in which contemporary scholars indicate that ancient and medieval intellectuals had any significant theoretical interest in demographic matters.

The Romans, of course, early used ingenious census procedures to determine for military and other practical administrative purposes the number, the geographic distribution, and a few of the most significant characteristics of the population. Servius Tullius (578–534 B.C.), sixth legendary king of Rome, is credited with the institution of the census. According to the ancient chronicler,[1] this monarch ordered his people to erect altars to the gods who were the guardians of the district and directed them to assemble once a year to honor these gods with public sacrifices. These occasions he made into solemn festivals, the Paganalia, and he laid down laws to govern the sacrifices. To cover the expenses of the sacrifices and festivities he ordered that all persons in a given district should each contribute a certain piece of money, the men paying with one kind, the women with another, and children with a third. Accordingly when these coins were counted, the number of the inhabitants, the sex distribution, and certain features of the age distribution of the population were known. Furthermore, in order to keep account of the number of inhabitants in the various cities, of births, of deaths, and of those arriving at manhood, he prescribed the type of coin that the rela-

[1] Earnest Cary, *The Roman Antiquities of the Dionysius of Halicarnassus* (Cambridge: Harvard University Press, 1939), II, 317–319.

tives should pay into the treasury at Juno Lucina on the occasion of a birth, that which should be paid into the treasury of the Venus of the Grove when a person died, and that to be paid into the treasury of Juvenatas for one who arrived at manhood. "By means of these pieces of money he would know every year both the number of all the inhabitants and which of them were of military age." Certainly for administrative purposes these data were much more complete, current, and accurate than those available to the heads of modern states, but there is little or no information available as yet that would indicate that they served any particular purpose for the kinds of abstraction and inference of which the science of demography is composed. If the Romans did secure and systematize such knowledge, modern scholars still must do the work of integrating it with contemporary systems. As yet the interesting activities of the Romans can hardly be cited as one of the principal landmarks in the development of population study.

The same is true of censuses and other concerns about population matters among the ancient Hebrews and other peoples of antiquity. As a result of the writings that were assembled to constitute the *Old Testament,* though, the peoples in much of the modern world long harbored a fear of any attempts to "number the people." The association in time between the census ordered by David and the pestilence which swept away seventy thousand men (II. Samuel, 24) gave rise to this fear. Modern demography was affected seriously by this case because the pestilence was attributed directly to God's anger over the taking of the census. This Hebrew tradition long made many Christian peoples fearful that similar results would follow any other attempts at census making.[1] Even now this fear lingers among some segments of the population in the United States. Aside from this, though, the census and other demographic efforts of the ancient Hebrews have affected modern population study little if at all.

In the pages that follow the effort is made to indicate and describe briefly the works of greatest importance in the perfection of scientific methodology in the demographic field, developing the necessary frame of reference and providing for the collection and systematic tabulation of essential data on the number of the inhabitants, their principal characteristics, and the three factors (births, deaths, and migrations) involved directly in population change. The development of population

---

[1] Cf. Clarence G. Dittmer, *Introduction to Social Statistics* (Chicago and New York: A. W. Shaw Company, 1926) , p. 5.

study in the United States was the primary consideration in the selection of items to be included.

John Graunt: Observations on the Bills of Mortality (1662)

The publication, in 1662, of *Natural and Political Observations Mentioned in the following Index and made upon the Bills of Mortality*, by John Graunt, Citizen of London,[1] certainly constitutes one of the great landmarks in the development of the science of population study. It is believed to be the first one sufficiently important to deserve listing in a summary account such as this. Others credit Graunt with being not only the founder of demography, but of statistics as well.[2]

Graunt's method was truly scientific. From the records of burial permits issued in the city of London, after the plague of 1592 gave rise to the practice of requiring such authorizations for interments of the deceased, Graunt carefully assembled the data for the years 1604 to 1661, inclusive. Wisely he included the materials for the surrounding districts, or "out-parishes," as well as the urban districts. These he supplemented with data on births taken from parish registers of christenings. For the years 1629 to 1659 he was able to get detailed information on causes of death, and for the period 1629–1660 he secured the data on all burial permits and christenings classified according to the sex of the persons involved. These materials he

reduced into Tables (the Copies whereof are here inserted) so as to have a view of the whole together, in order to the more ready comparing of one *Year, Season, Parish,* or other *Division* of the City, with another, in respect of all the *Burials,* and *Christnings,* and of all the *Diseases,* and *Casualties* happening in each of them respectively; I did then begin, not only to examine the Conceits, Opinions, and Conjectures, which upon view of a few scattered *Bills* I had taken up; but did also admit new ones, as I found reason, and occasion from my *Tables.*[3]

The observations, stated concisely in the "Index" and elaborated upon in the text, are 106 in number. The great majority of these propositions are genuine inductions, suggested as Graunt indicated by a

---

[1] Conveniently available in Walter F. Willcox (Editor), *Natural and Political Observations made upon the Bills of Mortality by John Graunt* (Baltimore: The Johns Hopkins University Press, 1939).

[2] See the "Introduction" by Willcox, *ibid.,* pp. iii-xiii, and the literature cited therein. Willcox himself concludes that Graunt, "more than any other man, was the founder of statistics," p. xiii.

[3] *Ibid.,* pp. 17–18.

study of various specific "bills" and tested by means of the comprehensive tables. Many of the demographic generalizations he formulated and stated on the basis of these studies are supported by the results of most inquiries made since he wrote and by the work of contemporary students of population. A few noteworthy examples are as follows:

1. There is a heavy migration of persons from the country to the city (observations 37, 46, 47, 58, 66, 89).

2. This migration is selective of "breeders," i. e., of persons in the reproductive ages (observations 46, 50).

3. The natural increase of population is higher in the country than in the city (observations 43, 44).

4. The rate of reproduction is higher in rural districts than in urban (observations 49, 50, 51).

Graunt also observed that the urban death rate was higher than the rural, a differential that has prevailed generally since he wrote and probably is still true in most parts of the world.

The First Census of Population of the United States: 1790

The United States Census of population, probably entitled to be called the first modern census, also has been called a political accident. This was because of the manner in which the conflict between the large states and the small states was resolved by the framers of the Constitution of the United States. In the early days of the new republic, as the work on the constitution progressed, the small states held out for equal representation in the Congress whereas the larger states insisted that they were entitled to greater representation in the legislative bodies. In the end a compromise was effected giving each state the right to send two members to the Senate and providing in paragraph 3, section 2, of Article I that members of the House of Representatives should be apportioned among the several states "according to their respective Numbers. . . ." This paragraph further stipulated that "the actual Enumeration shall be made within three Years after the first Meeting of the Congress of the United States, and within every subsequent Term of ten Years, in such Manner as they shall by Law direct."

In accordance with this constitutional provision the first census of the population of the United States was taken in 1790 and subsequent enumerations have been made each ten years from then to the present time. So began the work of assembling the vast store of concrete facts which today is fully entitled to be designated as the world's greatest repository of social and economic data. Even though decades were to pass before any considerable scientific study would be made of the rapidly accumulating mass of material, the beginning of the United States Census of population in 1790 is a prominent landmark in the development of population study. With the improvements made in 1800 it got well underway the procedures that supplied the all-important data on the number and distribution of the inhabitants.

Malthus: Essay on Population (1798)

The closing decades of the eighteenth century were marked by considerable interest in population matters, particularly in the rapidity with which human populations were increasing and of the economic effects of population increase. Both Benjamin Franklin and Thomas Jefferson devoted considerable time and thought to such subjects. The demographic event of greatest consequence in this period, however, was the appearance in 1798 of the first edition of the *Essay on Population,* published anonymously in England by a young Episcopalian clergyman named Thomas R. Malthus. A second edition of the work, tempered down and expanded considerably, appeared in 1803. The basic thesis of this volume, that the growth of population tends consistently to outstrip the increase in the means of subsistence, for decades was a chief bone of contention among those writing and debating upon social and economic questions. The pessimistic conclusions inherent in Malthus' propositions had much to do with economics coming to be known as "the dismal science." Even today it is not difficult to stir up an argument among sociologists and economists by raising a query relating to the validity of Malthusian theory.

Malthus wrote, of course, before modern censuses had yielded any considerable amount of reliable demographic data and before much in the way of analytical techniques had been perfected. Even so, to many he appears still to be the ultimate authority on all demographic questions. There are those, of course, with whom the present writer is inclined to side, who maintain that the Malthusian principles, and especially the extent to which debates over them have pre-empted the time and energy of those interested in population matters, may have hindered rather than helped the progress of demographic study and investigation. Still others take a more extreme view and maintain that the theoretical encumbrances of the economists working in the fields of labor, industry, and theory (scholars "still spellbound by the Malthusian and neo-Malthusian doctrines") are responsible for the fact that they "have been greatly lagging" in demographic matters.[1] Nevertheless, even today the demographer must have more than a passing acquaintance with Malthus' ideas, eloquent testimony that the publication of the *Essay on Population* constitutes an important landmark in the course of the development of population study.

Comprehensive Data on the Characteristics of Population: 1854

Most of the insight and organization needed to give value to census statistics on the characteristics of the population dates from the years 1853–1854 when J. D. B. DeBow served as superintendent of the United States Census. A native of South Carolina, DeBow moved to New Orleans, Louisiana, where he founded and developed to a point of greatness a periodical called *DeBow's Review*. This journal soon became the outlet for essays by its editor and others on numerous social and economic topics, including many of the first demographic treatises to be published in the United States. His vision, energy, and general leadership resulted in his appointment in 1848 to organize and direct a state bureau of statistics, the first such to be established in this country. The same year he also was appointed professor of political economy and commerce at the Tulane University. In these capacities he developed an outline for use in the study of Louisiana parishes (counties) and communities, which he then employed to stimulate leaders in various parts of the state to assemble, organize, and present in written form the more significant social and economic facts about their respective localities. Of the fourteen general topics included in his outline, the following dealt specifically with demographic matters:

1. Time of *settlement* of your parish or town; dates of oldest land grants; number and condition of first settlers; whence emigrating; other facts relating to settlements and history.

VI. Instances of *longevity* and *fecundity;* observations on diseases in your section; localities, healthful or otherwise; statistics of diseases; deaths; summer seats, &c.

VII. *Population* of your parish; increase and progress, distinguishing white and black; Spanish, French, American or German origin; foreigners, classes of population; number in towns; growth of towns and villages, &c.;

---

[1] Bernard D. Karpinos, "The Differential True Rates of Growth of the White Population in the United States and Their Probable Effects on the General Growth of Population," *American Journal of Sociology*, XLIV, No. 2 (1938), 252.

condition, employment, ages; comparative value of free and slave labor; comparative tables of increase; marriages, births, &c.; . . .[1]

Reports for about one half of Louisiana's parishes were published in *DeBow's Review*.

In 1853 President Franklin Pierce appointed DeBow as superintendent of the United States Census. At that time the work of enumeration and tabulation of the 1850 census had already been completed. Fortunately the schedules had been greatly improved, due mostly to the efforts of Mr. Lemuel Shattuck, of Boston. The new schedules made provision for the first time for recording the name and characteristics of each person enumerated. With the data thus subject to manipulation, DeBow—familiar with the work of Quételet and other European scholars, acquainted with the accomplishments of various European censuses, and driven by his own inquiring genius—proceeded to revolutionize the handling of the census materials and particularly those on the characteristics of the population. He also made detailed specific recommendations for the improvement of forms and tabulations in subsequent censuses. As a result many of the series of characteristics with which contemporary demographers deal in the United States can go back to the census of 1850. In addition the comprehensive *Statistical View of the United States,* cited above, which he prepared as a compendium of the results of the seventh and earlier censuses, both theoretically and practically must be regarded as one of the principal landmarks in the entire history of demographic studies. While he headed the Census Office, DeBow also was responsible for the first official attempts to assemble data on mortality and fertility of the population of the United States.

These accomplishments, to be properly evaluated, need to be reflected against those of the superintendents of the preceding six censuses, namely those from 1790 to 1840, inclusive. The first census secured only five particulars relating to the population: white males under sixteen, white males over sixteen, white females, slaves, and all other free persons "except Indians, not taxed." The second census, in 1800, improved this schema only by classifying white males and white females, separately, into the following age groups: under ten, ten to sixteen, sixteen to twenty-six, twenty-six to forty-five, and forty-five and over. Ex-

---

[1] J. D. B. DeBow, *Statistical View of the United States . . . Being a Compendium of the Seventh Census. . . .* (Washington: Beverley Tucker, Senate Printer, 1854), p. 19.

actly the same procedure was followed in the third census. In the fourth census the following innovations appeared: white males between sixteen and eighteen were classified separately, the numbers of unnaturalized foreign-born persons were indicated, and the free colored and slave populations were classified by sex into the following age categories: under fourteen, from fourteen to twenty-six, from twenty-six to forty-five, and over forty-five. In the fifth census (1830) white males and females were classified into five-year age groups up to the age of twenty, and into ten-year age groups from twenty to a hundred; the free colored and the slaves, of each sex, were classified by age into those under ten, those ten to twenty-four, those twenty-four to thirty-six, those thirty-six to fifty-five, those fifty-five to 100, and those of 100 and over; and the numbers of those born in another country who had not been naturalized were indicated. On population matters, the 1840 census followed exactly the preceding one. "These enumerations were published, within one, two, or three years, severally, from the time when they were made, but in such a manner as unfitted them for general use, understanding, or reference, and with very little tabular system and accuracy. A complete set of them does not exist in the public departments at Washington, and one or two are nearly, if not entirely, out of print." [1]

Unfortunately, DeBow's connection with the Census of the United States ended on December 31, 1854, when the work of the Seventh Census terminated, and, as was the practice in the censuses from 1790 to 1890, the Census Office was closed. When preparations for the Census of 1860 got underway, the same man DeBow had replaced in 1853 was again in charge of the Census Office established for the purpose of making the new enumeration.

International Resumé of Population Statistics: 1866

The publication of *Statistique Internationale (Population)*, by Adolph Quételet and Xavier Heuschling, presented to those interested in population study a comprehensive summary of population materials for most of the countries that had engaged seriously in the collection of demographic data. It is true that the compilation had comparatively little influence in the United States, but it deserves mention here because it did break the ground in this highly important part of population study and because even now the volume is of great value to those who desire to study demographic changes over a considerable period of time. Quételet was president and Heuschling secretary of Belgium's

[1] *Ibid.*, p. 11.

Commission Centrale de Statistique; and the book was published as Tome X of the *Bulletin de la Commission Centrale de Statistique,* Brussels, 1866. In its preparation they had the co-operation of the official statisticians of Austria, Bavaria, Denmark, England, France, Greece, Hanover, Italy, The Netherlands, Prussia, the two Saxonies, Spain, Sweden, Switzerland, the United States, and Württemberg.

The proposal for this compilation of primary international data developed in connection with various meetings of the International Statistical Association and crystallized at the fourth gathering of that body held in London in 1860. Here the Association acted favorably upon Quételet's proposal "for a conference of the official delegates to agree upon a common set of forms for use in their respective countries." Following this Quételet and Heuschling drew up plans for the compilation, which then were circulated among the others for criticism and advice. It was the consensus that the initial venture should concentrate principally upon "the number of inhabitants in each country, their distribution by sexes and by ages, and, wherever possible, upon mortality tables." In compiling and publishing the tabulations the authors wisely included information from as many census enumerations as possible, and the vital statistics for a series of years. Subsequently, important international compilations of population data were made by the French Ministère du Travail et de la Prévoyance Social,[1] and the International Institute of Statistics at the Hague.[2]

Following the organization of the League of Nations, the *Statistical Yearbook of the League of Nations,* beginning in 1927 and terminating with the 1942–1944 issue, presented current data on the number of inhabitants in various nations and territories. After the establishment of the United Nations, this body's Population Commission began issuing annually a *Demographic Yearbook,* but this represented such an important new step that it deserves mention below as another important landmark in the development of population studies.

Comprehensive Official Mortality Statistics: 1902

The struggle for comprehensive, reliable, official mortality statistics for the United States was a long one. It is somewhat difficult to establish precisely the time when the struggle was won, a victory surely en-

---

[1] *Statistique internationale du mouvement de la population* (Paris: Imprimerie Nationale, 1913) , 2 Vols.

[2] *Aperçu de la demographie des divers pays du monde: 1922, 1925, 1927, 1929, 1931, 1929–1936* (La Haye, 1923–1939) .

titled to a place in the list of outstanding landmarks in the development of population study in the United States, but 1902 is probably
the most appropriate year. This is when the Census Office was established on a permanent basis, renamed the Bureau of the Census, and
specifically charged with responsibility for making annual compilations and reports on mortality and birth statistics in the United States.
From an official report a few of the more salient facts relative to the
problem and the struggle may be extracted:

The United States until 1900 was the only civilized country of the occi-
dental world in great areas of which deaths and births were not registered.
This gap in American statistics was due mainly to the fact that registration
was, and still is, exclusively under State control. The Federal Government
has no authority to legislate about it and, before 1900, few of the States
maintained good registration laws and good administration of them. During
the second half of the last century the Federal Government asked of each
family at the time of a decennial census whether during the preceding 12
months a death had occurred therein or a child been born and died before
the enumeration. . . . But less than three-fourths of the deaths were thus
reported . . . the half century of experiment accomplished little more than
to set up a "no thoroughfare" sign against further effort to make a census
alone yield the information needed for vital statistics.[1]

The new Bureau of the Census chose to take 1900 as the year for
which its first compilation of mortality statistics was made. The registration area used in the beginning included only the six New England
states, four North Central and Middle Atlantic states (Indiana, Michigan, New Jersey, and New York), and 153 cities scattered throughout
the nation. Gradually this area was expanded until in 1933, with the
admission of Texas, the official death registration embraced all parts
of the continental United States. Thus from about 1930 on, students of
population in the United States had fairly adequate mortality data with
which to work; and this fact certainly was a major element in the phenomenal development of demography which took place in this country
during the second quarter of the twentieth century.

Essential Data on Population Fertility

Those interested in population study in the United States found the
procurement of adequate data on the fertility of the population even

[1] Walter F. Willcox, *Introduction to the Vital Statistics of the United States:
1900–1930* (Washington: Government Printing Office, 1933), p. 13.

more difficult and more delayed than getting the necessary material on mortality. The attempts between 1850 and 1900 to determine the birth rate of the population by use of the numbers of children under one year of age reported in the decennial censuses yielded little of value for the nation as a whole and nothing significant for its various subdivisions. Nor were the difficulties quickly overcome following the establishment in 1902 on a permanent basis of the Bureau of the Census, charged with the responsibility of preparing annual reports of the numbers of births registered throughout the country. The birth registration area was not established until 1915, and it did not cover the entire nation until 1933. Even then tremendous difficulties, far greater than those encountered in getting full coverage in the registration of deaths, had to be solved. Not the least of these was the length of time that had to pass before the emergence of an awareness on the part of those using the birth statistics that the data were not to be taken at their face value. The failure to register large proportions of the births, especially those occurring in rural areas and those to Negro parents, and the practice of registering births according to place of occurrence instead of according to the mother's place of residence long made the birth statistics of little or no value to any except the most skilled demographers. In fact, it was not until after 1950 that the official birth statistics for various parts of the United States were more or less adequate for use in comparative studies of the rate of reproduction of the population.

By the early 1930's, however, the ingenuity of American demographers had developed a substitute for the birth rate for use in the study of the rate of reproduction. As a result, since the publication of the results of the 1930 census, population study in the United States has been greatly facilitated by the demographer's ability to take that important factor into account. The ratio of young children to women of childbearing age, commonly known as the *fertility ratio,* is the measure to which reference has just been made. It is computed variously as the number of children under five per thousand or hundred women aged fifteen to forty-four, twenty to forty-four, fifteen to forty-nine, and so on.

Walter F. Willcox seems to have been the first to devise and employ this measure of population fertility. Following the census of 1900, he "attacked the problem from a different angle, abandoning the effort to obtain a true birth rate from census figures and studying instead the proportion of children enumerated under 5 years of age to women of child-bearing age." [1] As early as 1911 he presented a paper to the American Statistical Association describing his method and comparing fertility trends in the United States with those in France.[2] Others were slow to follow, however, and most of those writing on population matters in the United States used the birth statistics that soon thereafter became available, apparently blissfully unaware of their primary defects.

In 1931, though, the Bureau of the Census published a monograph entitled *Ratio of Children to Women: 1920* [3] prepared by Warren S. Thompson. For some reason, Thompson made no mention of the earlier work by Willcox, but the publication of his study almost immediately made the fertility ratio known and used by other students of population throughout the nation. This, in turn, represented a significant landmark in the development of population study in the United States.

Data for the Farm Population: 1930

From 1874 to the present time rural-urban classifications and analyses have figured prominently in population study throughout the United States. However, separate data for the rural-farm part of the rural population have played such an important role in the development of demographic studies in this country that the date on which it became generally available for use by men and women engaged in research work at the state agricultural experiment stations and other research centers deserves special mention. This is because detailed materials concerning the farm population in the various counties and other subdivisions of the state were a necessity, both practically and legally, before rural sociologists at such centers could devote any considerable amount of time to population study. As events transpired, though, such data became available just at the time Franklin Delano Roosevelt became president of the United States and just as the men working in this field were called upon for exceptional demographic activity in order to secure and analyze the materials needed to guide the federal relief and federal works programs.[4] As a result, population studies were the principal activity of the men working in the field as

[1] *Ibid.*, p. 56.

[2] *Ibid.*, p. 57.

[3] Washington: Government Printing Office.

[4] For details on this development, see, T. Lynn Smith, "Rural Sociology in the United States and Canada: A Trend Report," *Current Sociology*, VI, 1 (1957), 13–14.

rural sociology came to maturity in the years following 1930, and it continues today to receive more attention than any other branch of the subject. In turn the contributions by those who are employed as rural sociologists at the agricultural experiment stations, or who once were so employed, loom large in the whole field of demography. It must be stressed, therefore, that the provision of detailed materials on the numbers, distribution, and characteristics of the farm population deserves a place of prominence as one traces the course followed by the development of population studies in the United States.

Charles J. Galpin, well-known for his pioneering work in rural sociology, is the one entitled to the chief credit for this important innovation. In 1919 Galpin left the University of Wisconsin, where he pioneered the work in the study of the rural community, to become head of the Division of Farm Population and Rural Life in the newly established Bureau of Agricultural Economics of the U. S. Department of Agriculture. In his new position he was, of course, the one into whose hands eventually came the multitude of requests for data on the farm population which annually reached Washington from persons and agencies all over the United States. He quickly found that the materials for the rural population fell far short of meeting the needs of his clients in the forty-eight states. Those in charge of the U. S. Bureau of the Census, though, gave scant heed to his suggestions and requests that the materials about the rural population, then coming in from the 1920 census, be presented separately for the farm and nonfarm (then largely village) segments of which it was constituted. He did receive permission, however, to have one of his assistants sort by hand the pertinent information for eight selected counties distributed throughout the United States.[1] The reception accorded this fragmentary material was such that Dr. Leon E. Truesdell of the Bureau of the Census quickly had tabulated the necessary information for the entire United States and prepared a Census Monograph to make it available.[2] Then in the preparation of plans for the 1930 census the subclassification of the data for the farm and nonfarm portions of the rural

[1] Charles J. Galpin and Veda B. Larson, *Farm Population of Selected Counties: Composition, Characteristics, and Occupations in Detail for Eight Counties, Comprising Otsego, County, N. Y., Dane County, Wis., New Madrid and Scott Counties, Mo., Cass County, N. Dak., Wake County, N. C., Ellis County, Tex., and King County, Wash.* (Washington: Government Printing Office, 1924).

[2] Leon E. Truesdell, *Farm Population of the United States: An Analysis of the 1920 Farm Population Figures.* . . . Census Monograph VI (Washington: Government Printing Office, 1926.)

population became a basic consideration. As a result, in the reports of the 1930 and subsequent censuses, in the county tables, and to a certain extent in those for minor civil divisions as well, the materials on age, sex, race and nativity, educational status, occupations, and so forth, are given in most of the detail needed for administrative purposes; and in addition they constitute the basic facts that may be manipulated by demographers and other sociologists and economists in order to test empirically a large share of the working hypotheses they are able to develop. The present writer is of the opinion that the introduction of the rural-farm and rural-nonfarm categories as integral portions of the 1930 census tabulations constituted the most important innovation relative to all that has to do with the characteristics of the population since DeBow gave form to this all-important aspect of demography in the years immediately following the 1850 census.

Comprehensive Current International Demographic Data: "The Demographic Yearbook, 1948"

The Economic and Social Council of the United Nations at its fourth session, in 1947, recommended that the international organization publish a demographic yearbook "containing regular series of basic demographic statistics, comparable within and among themselves, and relevant calculations of comparable rates. . . ." The Statistical Commission and the Population Commission, to which the planning of the compilation was assigned, recommended forty-eight general topics for inclusion. These are as follows, with those selected for use in the first (1948) issue indicated with asterisks:

I. Area and population
　　1. Area*
　　2. Total population*
　　3. Population density*
　　4. Annual percentage rate of population change
　　5. Population of major cities
　　6. Population by age and sex—absolute numbers and proportions*
　　7. Population by age, sex, and marital condition—absolute numbers and proportions*
　　8. Population by urban and rural divisions*
　　9. Population by race and nationality (or citizenship)

  10. Population by age, sex, and literacy*

  11. Households—number and distribution by size*

  12. Women by number of children ever born and by number of children living*

 II. Economically active population

  13. Active population (labor force) by age and sex*

  14. Active population by industry*

  15. Active population by industrial status (class of worker) *

 III. International migration

  16. Emigrants by country of destination*

  17. Immigrants by country of origin and nationality*

  18. Emigrants and immigrants by age, sex, and occupation

 IV. Natality

  19. Total number of births*

  20. Crude birth rates*

  21. Births by month of occurrence

  22. Births by age of mother and father*

  23. Fertility rates by age of mother*

  24. Births by parity*

  25. Births by legitimacy

  26. Births by duration of marriage*

  27. Stillbirths*

  28. Gross and net reproduction rates*

  29. Ratio of children under five years of age to women aged fifteen to forty-nine years

 V. Mortality

  30. Total deaths

  31. Crude death rates*

  32. Deaths by month of occurrence

  33. Deaths by age and sex*

  34. Death rates by age and sex*

  35. Infant mortality rates*

  36. Deaths by cause

  37. Maternal (puerperal) mortality rates

  38. Life table death rates (q_x) *

  39. Life table survivors (l_x) *

  40. Mean expectation of life*

 VI. Morbidity

  41. General morbidity

VII. Marriage and divorce
  42. Total marriages*
  43. Crude marriage rates*
  44. Marriages by age of partners*
  45. Marriage rates by age and sex*
  46. Total divorces
  47. Crude divorce rates
  48. Divorces by duration of marriage and number of children

The first issue of the *Demographic Yearbook,* corresponding to the year 1948, appeared in 1949. As was to be expected, it contained a wealth of data such as never before had been available to the student of population. Another edition in 1951 gave materials through 1949 and 1950. Since then the volumes have been issued annually. All contain much of the more general data with the series brought up to date, but gradually the various issues have extended the time series into the past as far as possible. Furthermore, each number specializes to a considerable extent in a particular topic. Thus, for example, the 1949–50 issue featured marriage and fertility, the 1951 number mortality, the 1954 compilation natality, and the 1955 volume the statistics from censuses taken in the decade 1945–1954. Ready access to a complete set of these volumes is essential for the contemporary demographer.

The Census of the Americas: 1950

On June 7, 1943, Dr. Alberto Arca Parró, Director General of Statistics in Peru and chairman of the demographic statistics committee of the Inter-American Statistical Institute, proposed, in a letter addressed to directors of statistics in the other American countries, that all American nations take censuses of population in 1950. In his letter Dr. Arca Parró suggested the practical steps needed to make his proposal a reality, including the exchange of census documents and experiences, the determination of the queries to be included on the schedules in all of the countries (these to be amplified as each nation saw fit), and the preparation of necessary legislation in each of the nations. The Inter-American Demographic Congress, which met in Mexico City in October, 1943, considered and approved these suggestions, and formally requested the Inter-American Statistical Institute to take such steps as necessary to make the proposals effective. The Institute established a special committee for this purpose, and for a meeting in

September, 1947, it organized round-table discussions and plenary sessions of the Committee on the 1950 Census of the Americas. This meeting, held in Washington, D. C., was attended by almost 100 men and women representing twenty-two American nations. Even at this first session it was possible to secure agreement that the following items appear on the forms used in all of the countries: sex, age, place of birth, naturalization, and literacy.[1]

At about this stage the officials of the U. S. Bureau of the Census offered to supply to the other American republics technical assistance on censuses and vital statistics, and as a result specialists from this country worked closely with those from most of the others in the preparation of census plans, the making of the enumerations, and the tabulation of the results. Today Latin America must be considered as one of the great world areas for which population materials are most nearly adequate, whereas prior to 1950 it was among the portions of the world for which demographic materials were least available and most unreliable. This sudden change, secondary in importance for population students in the United States only to that for Latin American demographers themselves, ranks high among events in the development of the field of population analysis.

Certain of the Latin American countries, of course, have had a long and enviable record in the making of population censuses. This group includes such countries as Brazil, Chile, Cuba, Mexico, Panama, and Venezuela. For them participation in the Census of the Americas meant adding one more well-done enumeration to others taken periodically in the past. A second group of Latin American countries had taken occasional censuses prior to 1950, but in regularity of enumerations and quality of results they hardly were to be ranked with those just listed. This group includes Colombia, Costa Rica, the Dominican Republic, El Salvador, Guatemala, Honduras, and Nicaragua. Argentina, which took a census of population in 1947, the first since 1914, may belong in this group; and also Peru, for which the 1940 census was the first since 1876.

The third group is made up of those which either had had no previous census of population at all or in which the latest censuses were

[1] For a brief account of the background of the Census of the Americas, see Calvert L. Dedrick, "The 1950 Census of the Americas," *25th Session of the International Statistical Institute,* September 6–18, 1947 (Washington, D. C., Vol. III, Part A), pp. 17–23.

taken so long ago as to amount for practical purposes almost to the same thing. Ecuador and Haiti had never taken a census of population, and in Bolivia, Paraguay, and Uruguay, what technically may have deserved the name of a census was taken so long ago that its value was merely historical.

The final score relative to the Census of the Americas may be summarized as follows. All American countries, including Canada and the United States, participated except Peru, Argentina, and Uruguay. By a quirk of political circumstances, the country which supplied the initiative which led to the planning of the vast undertaking itself did not take part. Of course for Peru the excellent 1940 census is still of use to demographers. Argentina, as indicated above, had taken a census in 1947 and rightly felt it unnecessary to repeat. Uruguay, whose latest census is that for 1908, remains today the greatest demographic unknown in the Western Hemisphere. Canada and Colombia made their enumerations in 1951, Chile in 1952, and Cuba, in accordance with constitutional provisions, in 1953. All of the others made the enumerations in 1950. With the publication of the definitive results of these censuses, demographers of the Americas have available the richest store of materials with which students of population in the Western Hemisphere have ever been privileged to work.[1]

At Last—Minimum Essential Migration Data: 19??

As yet no event connected with the development of data on the important factor of migration nor its analysis deserves mention in this brief sketch of the major landmarks in the development of population study. The present stage of the science and its immediate needs, however, make it unlikely that this state of affairs can continue for many more decades. Probably within the twentieth century the Census of the United States will make the innovation that will represent another fundamental "break through" in population study. This is hardly likely in 1960, but it may come in the census of 1970. Before that time, too, vigorous leadership in some of the other countries may entitle one of them to credit for the next important landmark in the development of demography.

The need for adequate migration data is patent. Today, as in the centuries that have passed, most of what is known on the subject of

[1] For a brief outline of the development of census taking and the registration of vital statistics in Latin America, see T. Lynn Smith, "The Reproduction Rate in Latin America," *Eugenical News Quarterly* (1953), 64–67.

migration is based on inference from the data yielded by successive population counts and a knowledge of births and deaths, the other two factors involved directly in the changing number and distribution of the population. Only when an attempt is made to measure all three of the factors involved (births, deaths, *and* migrations), so that the student may then compare the net change indicated by the factors with the net change indicated by the successive counts, for a state, a city, a county, or other division, will there be any substantial improvement in the situation.

The absolute minimum of information needed could be secured if in the course of the decennial count, each person aged ten years or more were asked whether at the time of the previous census he was residing in the county in which he is being enumerated or in some other county and if each person of less than ten years were classified as being born in the county of residence, or in another county. These data should then be tabulated so as to indicate for each county the number of persons who had moved to it from another county during the intercensual period. Of course, other details, such as the sex, age, and other characteristics of the migrants, would add immensely to the value of the tabulations.

Once such an innovation is introduced by the U. S. Census of population, or that of another country, the attempt will have been made to account for all the factors in population change. Then if the difference between two successive census counts of the population of a county does not equal the net change indicated by subtracting the number of deaths during the interim from the number of births, plus or minus the number of migrants, it will follow that one or more of the figures (one or both of the census counts, the registry of births, the registry of deaths, or the reported migrations) is wrong. But the demonstration of such errors would be the first step in their correction. As indicated above, when they get these data on migration, students of population will be in a position to attempt to balance the equation. All of the other materials are now being assembled as a matter of course. The census that places the lacking data on migration in the hands of demographers will represent another fundamental contribution to the developing study of population.[1]

[1] The importance of this step was indicated at the 1954 meetings of the Population Association of America, *Population Index*, 20, No. 3 (July, 1954), 148; and in a report to the Rural Sociological Society. See T. Lynn Smith, "Levels and Trends in Rural Migration," *Rural Sociology,* 19, 1 (March, 1954), 80–81.

SUGGESTED SUPPLEMENTARY READINGS

Carr-Saunders, A. M., *The Population Problem: A Study in Human Evolution.* Oxford: The Clarendon Press, 1922.

Cox, Peter R., *Demography.* Cambridge: University Press, 1950, chapter I.

DeBow, J. D. B., *Statistical View of the United States . . . Being a Compendium of the Seventh Census; . . .* Washington: Beverley Tucker, State Printer, 1854.

Hauser, Philip M., and Otis Dudley Duncan, *The Study of Population: An Inventory and Appraisal,* part II. Chicago: University of Chicago Press, 1958.

Malthus, T. R., *An Essay on the Principle of Population or a View of Its Past and Present Effects on Human Happiness. . . .* Various editions and publishers.

Phelps, Harold A., and David Henderson, *Population in Its Human Aspects.* New York: Appleton-Century-Crofts, Inc., 1958, chapter 20.

Willcox, Walter F. (Editor), *Natural and Political Observations Made upon the Bills of Mortality by John Graunt.* Baltimore: Johns Hopkins University Press, 1939.

Willcox, Walter F., *Studies in American Demography.* Ithaca: Cornell University Press, 1940, chapters 4, 13, 17, and 24.

Part Two

NUMBER AND DISTRIBUTION OF THE INHABITANTS

*The Number and Geographic
Distribution of the Population*

Chapter 3

The Number and Geographic
Distribution of the Population

THE NUMBER OF PERSONS in the populations of various geographical units and their distribution with respect to area are among the most important facts of demography. This is to say that the number of its inhabitants is the first population fact called for with respect to a given nation, state, city, county, or any other political subdivision, and that the number of persons per given unit of area is the second. In fact, as a general rule first judgments with respect to the size and importance of a nation or other political unit are based on these two indicators. Fortunately, both are thoroughly objective items, and their magnitudes are subject to accurate quantitative measurement. Moreover, where abundant demographic information is available for study and use, the facts relating to the number and geographic distribution of the population generally will be among the most reliable.

The essential facts about the number and geographic distribution of the inhabitants are not only of intrinsic value, but in contemporary society they also are the population facts most commonly needed for various research and administrative purposes. Thus sociologists must have the facts relative to the numbers of inhabitants in various areas before they can compute indexes of criminality, juvenile delinquency, marriage, and so on; administrators must have them in order to determine how state and federal funds for education, agriculture, road construction, and so on, are to be apportioned among the counties, states, or other political divisions with which they are concerned; and economists must have exact information on the numbers of persons involved before they can determine the ratios that constitute the units employed in so many of their analyses. Even demographers themselves find that reliable facts about the number and geographic distribution of the population are among the basic elements needed for almost all the other facets of their discipline, such as the study of the characteristics of the population, the analysis of fertility, and the investigation of mortality or the expectation of life. For these reasons it is well to begin the systematic study of demographic phenomena with a consideration of fundamental matters relative to the number of inhabitants and their geographic distribution.

Basic Concepts and Indexes

A concise understanding of the meaning and significance of several specific concepts and indexes is essential in the study of the number and geographic distribution of the population. In the first place, perhaps, it is advisable to explain why the modifier "geographic" is used instead of merely saying "the distribution of population." The simpler construction would be preferable in many ways. However, in recent years some demographers have been including under the heading of "distribution of population" such matters as "age distribution," "distribution by sex," and so on. These are matters which probably should be treated under the general topic of the composition or characteristics; nevertheless in order to avoid any possible ambiguity the expression geographic distribution is used consistently throughout this volume.

Our principal sources of information about the number and geographic distribution of the population are derived from the periodic enumerations, or *censuses* of population, made officially by governments throughout the world. The term *census* comes from the Roman word that designated the practice of registering adult males and their property, a procedure that has little in common with the modern census. Its object was to provide the basis for administering programs of military service and taxation. In modern demography, however, a census is a count of the population effected through direct visitation to all the households in the political unit involved. Strictly speaking the United States Census could satisfy constitutional requirements merely by enumerating the population of the various states every ten years. Actually, the modern census invariably includes a long list of items on the characteristics of the population, housing, income, and various other social, cultural, and economic matters.

As set forth in the *Demographic Yearbook of the United Nations, 1955*,[1] a population census "may be defined as the total process of collecting, compiling and publishing demographic data pertaining, at a

[1] New York: Statistical Office of the United Nations, 1955, p. 1.

particular time, to all persons in a defined territory;" and its five most essential characteristics are as follows: (1) universality—it should include every person in the area, without omission or duplication; (2) simultaneity—all census facts should refer to one specific point of time; (3) individual units—the data are recorded separately for each individual; (4) defined territory—the coverage should be of a precisely defined territory; and (5) compilation—"the compilation and publication of data by geographic areas and by basic demographic variables is an integral part of a census."

Despite the length and complexity of the schedules of questions used in the modern census, its primary task is still that of ascertaining the number of the inhabitants or the population of the unit under consideration. Since this is the most elemental demographic fact, it is necessary to ask, what is a *population?* The applicable definition of population given in the second unabridged edition of *Webster's New International Dictionary* is "the whole number of people or inhabitants in a country, section, or area." But this omits one basic consideration. In modern times there is a vast difference between the persons who actually are in a state such as New York or Florida on April 1 of a census year and the persons who for legal or social reasons may be said to belong there. Likewise at the time of the census in Brazil, Canada, or France, to mention only three nations, many nationals of these countries are abroad, whereas tourists, businessmen, diplomatic and consular personnel, and mere transients are present in each in goodly numbers. This raises the question as to whether the population of a given town, city, county, state, or nation includes the persons *found* there at the time of the census or whether it includes all those who *belong* there. In attempts to resolve this issue, those in charge of modern censuses usually decide upon one or the other of the two following alternatives. In Great Britain, for example, the *de facto* approach is employed, i. e., all persons found in a given area the day the census is taken are included in the population. In the United States, on the other hand, the *de jure* approach is used, i. e., the attempt is made to assign to their usual place of residence all persons enumerated in areas other than the one in which they customarily reside. In still other countries, of which Brazil is a good example, the attempt is made to prepare certain of the tabulations on both the *de facto* and the *de jure* bases.

The assumption that each person has one and only one usual place of abode, heretofore implicit in the procedures of the U. S. Census of population, is becoming increasingly invalid with the passage of each decade. Millions of men and women are in the armed forces, large numbers of them stationed abroad; and not only they themselves but the members of their immediate families are shifted from one place to another with considerable frequency. Hundreds of thousands of persons maintain legal residences in states or counties other than the ones in which they actually reside, a phenomenon that is particularly acute on the part of those who live and work in the District of Columbia. Additional hundreds of thousands actually have two residences and spend approximately one half of the year in states such as Florida, Arizona, or California and the other half elsewhere. Finally, the mobility of the population in general is increasing by leaps and bounds, and the elements in the population that have no fixed residence are becoming more numerous year by year. Under these circumstances the definition of population on the *de jure* basis is becoming more and more unsatisfactory.

Census procedures also vary with respect to the time allowed for the making of the enumeration. In the United States the census of population is taken as of April 1 of the census year. This is to say that the enumerators begin the task of counting on April 1 and continue for four or five months until all households have been visited; and on the schedules the information for the members of each family is entered as though all the interviews had been conducted on April 1. In many other countries, only one day is allowed for the enumeration. In these cases large numbers of workers are employed and everyone else is required to stay indoors throughout the day until all the visits have been completed and the all clear signal has been given.

Several concepts used in connection with the geographic distribution of the population also require brief specific mention. As indicated above, any population figure has reference to the number of persons found in or classified as belonging to a given portion of the earth's surface, such as town, city, county, state, or nation. If the ratio between the number of the inhabitants and the area of the unit is calculated, so as to determine the average number of persons per square mile, per square kilometer, and so forth, one has an index of *density of population.*

The *center of population* is a second concept of importance in the study of the geographic distribution of the population. Its nature may be indicated as follows: Suppose that it is desired to assemble all the inhabitants of a nation (state, county, or other geographic unit) at one given spot. Then the center of population will be the point at which all could gather with the minimum total amount of direct air line travel.

Tabulations of census data for the various divisions and subdivisions of nations, states, cities, counties, and minor civil divisions, are the raw materials for the study of the geographic distribution of the population. For many years the tables prepared and published by the U. S. Census of population have been fairly adequate on this score insofar as the rural population is concerned. Only recently, however, with the development and use of the concept of the *census tract,* has it been possible to do very much analysis of the geographic distribution of population within the limits of a city or in the suburban fringe which surrounds it. Analysis of the rural materials has been facilitated because established legal subdivisions of a state include not only the counties, but also minor civil divisions (designated variously as townships, commissioners' districts, wards, beats, precincts, and so forth in the several states). Therefore, when the Bureau of the Census has prepared and published the population data showing for each state the number of inhabitants in each county and (with the materials further subdivided) the number of persons in each minor civil division and population center (village, town, or city) within the county, the demographer has the materials he needs for the study of the geographic distribution of the rural population. The minor civil divisions are small in area and the vast majority of such units contain fewer than a thousand inhabitants.

Similar procedures, however, are far from adequate for supplying the information needed for study and analysis of the geographic distribution of the population in a city and the built-up area surrounding it. The wards or other political subdivisions of a city may be small in area, but they invariably are large in terms of the numbers of inhabitants. The city has no minor civil divisions corresponding in size (as measured by population) to those which the division of the counties into townships, precincts, and so forth automatically supplies for the rural portions of the nation. For this reason sociologists in many of the nation's larger cities have cooperated with the Bureau of the Census in dividing the urban area into small and fairly homogeneous units.

Census tracts are small areas, having a population generally between 3,000 and 6,000, into which certain large cities (and in some cases their adjacent areas) have been subdivided for statistical and local administrative purposes, through cooperation with a local committee in each case. The tract areas are established with a view to approximate uniformity in population, with some consideration of uniformity in size of area, and with due regard for physical features. Each tract is designed to include an area fairly homogeneous in population characteristics. . . . The tracts are intended to remain unchanged from census to census. . . .[1]

Tables and maps of various kinds are indispensable in the study of the geographic distribution of the population in any area, but these will be introduced and described in the following pages as the occasion arises.

The Number and Geographic Distribution of the World's Inhabitants

The number of people on the earth has never been known with any degree of exactitude. In some of the more densely populated parts of the world there has never been anything deserving the name of a population census. Furthermore, there is little uniformity in the years selected as census dates so that the counts made in some populous nations are out of date before those in others get underway. Finally, there is a considerable margin of error in all enumerations that are made. For these reasons any total figure arrived at is at best an approximation of what actually is the number of the earth's inhabitants.

During the last century, though, there has been a notable increase in census activities throughout the world, so that our present knowledge of the number and geographic distribution of the earth's population is far superior to what it has been in the past. Thus, according to the information assembled in the 1955 issue of the *Demographic Yearbook* [2] in the decade ending about 1870 only around 200 million persons were covered by the census enumerations made in the ten-year period. This figure rose to approximately 800 million for the decade ending in 1910, and to some 1.9 billion for the decade "around" 1950. Even so, however, since the same source estimated the total population of the world in 1950 at about 2.5 billions, it is evident that only about three-fourths of the earth's inhabitants were included in the territory in which censuses were taken during the decade in the middle (1945–1954) of

[1] U. S. Bureau of the Census, *U. S. Census of Population: 1950.* Vol. I, *Number of Inhabitants* (Washington: Government Printing Office, 1952) , p. xxxvi.
[2] *Op. cit.,* pp. 1–2.

the twentieth century. In the period 1855–1864, according to the same authority, censuses were conducted by only twenty-four sovereign countries, of which seventeen were in Europe, four in North America, two in South America, and one in Asia and Oceania. This figure rose to forty-four for the decade 1895–1904, and the total included twenty-three countries in Europe, seven in North America, seven in Asia and Oceania, five in South America, and two in Africa. For the period 1945–1954 the total was sixty-five, including twenty-eight countries in Europe, fifteen in Asia and Oceania, twelve in North America, eight in South America, and two in Africa. These compilations include a reported census of China for 1953, but the materials relating to the last decade do not include those for the U.S.S.R., since its most recent census was taken in 1939.

In an attempt to give as concisely as possible the most essential facts pertaining to the number and geographic distribution of the world's inhabitants, Table I has been prepared. For each country, territory, or dependency having as many as 10,000 inhabitants on the globe, it gives the date of the latest census, the population enumerated, the area in square kilometers, estimates of the population in 1955, and the density of population. For all countries or territories with 1955 populations of 10 million or more, the percentage each country or territory contains of the total world population also is presented. The materials in this table are by far the most complete and accurate ever available to students of population relative to the number of inhabitants of the earth and their geographic distribution, but even so those in charge of the preparation of the *Demographic Yearbook* did not total them, along with the figures for the few small areas they omitted, in order to obtain the figure they publish as that for the total population of the world. This total, along with regional and continental subtotals, includes allowances for under- and over-enumeration wherever such were possible. Even so, however, the totals as given for the various continents have been included in Table I.

The estimate of total world population in 1955, as given in the 1956 issue of the *Demographic Yearbook,* is 2,691 millions. That for 1950 was 2,476 millions. In each case 5 per cent is given as the "possible error" in the total. Not until about 1963, after a large share of the nations in the world have published the results of censuses taken in 1960, will it be possible to make another equally reliable estimate of total world population.

Table I. Population, Area, and Density of Population for Each Country and Territory of the World: Latest Census and Midyear Estimates for 1955

Country or territory	Latest census Year	Latest census Population	Population 1955 (Midyear estimates in thousands)	Percentage of world population	Area (Square kilometers)	Density 1955 (Persons per sq. kilometer)
Africa	...	....	223,000	8.3	....	7
Egypt	1947	19,021,840	22,934	0.9	1,000,000	23
Ethiopia and Eritrea	...	....	20,000	0.7	1,184,320	17
Liberia	...	....	1,250	..	111,370	11
Libya	1954	1,091,830	1,105	..	1,759,540	1
Morocco						
Former French Zone	1952	7,442,110	8,495	..	390,800	22
Former Spanish Zone	1950	1,010,117	1,045	..	19,656	53
Tangier	...	....	183	..	349	524
Sudan	...	....	8,900	..	2,505,825	4
Tunisia	1956	3,782,480 [1]	3,745	..	155,830	24
Union of South Africa	1951	12,667,759	13,669	0.5	1,223,409	11
Territories and Dependencies						
Belgian Congo	...	....	12,600	0.5	2,343,930	5
Algeria (France)	1954	9,368,665 [1]	9,620	..	2,191,464	4
French Equatorial Africa	...	....	4,680	..	2,510,000	2
French Somaliland	...	....	63	2.3	22,000	3
French West Africa	...	....	18,729	0.7	4,633,985	4
Madagascar (France)	...	....	4,776	..	590,000	8

Réunion (France)	1954	274,370	278	..	2,511	111
Angola (Portugal)	1950	4,145,266	4,280	..	1,246,700	3
Cape Verde Islands (Portugal)	1950	148,331	172	..	4,033	43
Mozambique (Portugal)	1950	5,738,911	6,030	..	783,030	8
São Tomé and Principe (Portugal)	1950	60,159	58	..	964	60
Spanish Possessions in North Africa	1950	141,302	143	..	213	671
Spanish Guinea	1950	198,663	208	..	28,051	7
Spanish West Africa	1950	51,922	83	..	300,375	0
Basutoland (U. K.)	1956	634,000 [1]	627	..	30,344	21
Bechuanaland (U. K.)	1956	327,335	324	..	712,200	0
British Somaliland (U. K.)	..	....	640	..	176,120	4
Gambia (U. K.)	..	....	285	..	10,369	27
Gold Coast (U. K.)	1948	3,735,682	4,191	..	204,097	21
Kenya (U. K.)	1948	5,405,966	6,048	..	582,646	10
Mauritius (U. K.)	1952	501,471	549	..	1,865	294
Nigeria, Federation of (U. K.)	1952–53	29,730,874	31,254	1.2	878,447	35
Rhodesia and Nyasaland, Federation of (U. K.)	..	....	7,609	..	1,262,986	6
Seychelles (U. K.)	1947	34,632	39	..	404	97
Sierra Leon (U. K.)	..	....	2,050	..	72,326	28
Swaziland (U. K.)	1946	185,215	223	..	17,364	13
Uganda (U. K.)	1948	4,958,520	5,508	..	243,411	23
Zanzibar and Pemba (U. K.)	1948	264,162	278	..	2,657	105
Trust Territories						
Cameroons (British)	1952–53	1,440,509	1,500	..	88,270	17
Cameroons (French)	..	....	3,146	..	432,000	7
Ruanda-Urundi (Belgian)	..	....	4,280	..	54,172	79
Somaliland (Italian)	1931	1,021,572	1,280	..	461,541	3

Table I. Population, Area, and Density of Population for Each Country and Territory of the World (Continued)

Country or territory	Latest census Year	Latest census Population	Population 1955 (Midyear estimates in thousands)	Percentage of world population	Area (Square kilometers)	Density 1955 (Persons per sq. kilometer)
Tanganyika (British)	1948	7,447,677	8,324	..	939,361	9
Togoland (British)	1948	382,768	429	..	33,776	13
Togoland (French)	..	......	1,080	..	57,000	19
South West Africa	1951	417,928 [1]	458	..	823,876	1
North America	..	......	241,000	9.0	......	9
Canada	1956	16,080,791	15,601	0.6	9,960,547	2
Costa Rica	1950	800,875	951	..	50,900	19
Cuba	1953	5,829,029	6,075 [2]	..	114,524	53
Dominican Republic	1950	2,135,872	2,404	..	48,734	49
El Salvador	1950	1,855,917	2,193	..	20,000	110
Guatemala	1950	2,790,868	3,258	..	108,889	30
Haiti	1950	3,097,304	3,305	..	27,750	119
Honduras	1950	1,368,605	1,660	..	112,088	15
Mexico	1950	25,791,017	29,679	1.1	1,969,367	15
Nicaragua	1950	1,057,023	1,245	..	148,000	8
Panama	1950	805,285	910	..	74,470	12
United States	1950	150,697,361	165,271	6.1	7,827,976	21
Territories and Dependencies						
Greenland (Denmark)	1951	24,118	26	..	2,175,600	*
Guadeloupe (France)	1954	229,120	230	..	1,780	129
Martinique (France)	1954	239,130	240	..	1,102	218

Netherlands Antilles	1930	71,769	182	..	961	189
Bermuda	1950	37,403	41	..	53	774
British Honduras	1946	59,220	79	..	22,965	3
British West Indies						
Bahama Islands	1953	84,841	94	..	11,396	8
Barbados	1946	192,800	229	..	431	531
Jamaica	1943	1,237,063	1,542	..	11,424	135
Leeward Islands	1946	108,838	128	..	1,094	117
Trinidad and Tobago	1946	557,970	721	..	5,218	141
Windward Islands	1946	251,771	313	..	2,139	146
Alaska (U. S.)	1950	128,643	209	..	1,518,775	*
Canal Zone (U. S.)	1950	52,822	53	..	1,432	37
Puerto Rico (U. S.)	1950	2,210,703	2,263	..	8,897	254
Virgin Islands (U. S.)	1950	26,665	24	4.6	344	70
South America		....	125,000		....	7
Argentina	1947	15,893,827	19,111	0.7	2,778,412	7
Bolivia	1950	2,704,165	3,198	..	1,098,581	3
Brazil	1950	51,976,357	58,456	2.2	8,513,844	7
Chile	1952	5,932,995	6,761	..	741,767	9
Colombia	1951	11,548,172	12,657	0.5	1,138,355	11
Ecuador	1950	3,202,757	3,675	..	270,670	14
Paraguay	1950	1,341,333	1,565	..	406,752	4
Peru	1940	6,207,967	9,396	..	1,249,049	8
Uruguay	1908	1,042,686	2,615	..	186,926	14
Venezuela	1950	5,034,838	5,774	..	912,050	6
Territories and Dependencies						
French Guiana	1954	27,863	28	..	91,000	*
Surinam (Netherlands)	....	....	225	..	142,822	2
British Guiana	1946	375,701	485	..	214,970	2

Table I. Population, Area, and Density of Population for Each Country and Territory of the World (Continued)

Country or territory	Latest census		Population 1955 (Midyear estimates in thousands)	Percentage of world population	Area (Square kilometers)	Density 1955 (Persons per sq. kilometer)
	Year	Population				
Asia [4]	...	....	1,481,000	55.0		55
Afghanistan	...	....	12,000	0.4	650,000	18
Bahrain	1950	109,650	120	...	598	201
Bhutan	...	....	623	...	50,000	12
Burma	1941	16,823,798	19,434	0.7	677,950	29
Cambodia	...	....	4,358	...	175,000	25
Ceylon	1953	8,098,637 [1]	8,589	...	65,610	131
China, Mainland	1953	582,603,417	582,603 [2]	21.7	9,700,327	78 [2]
China, Taiwan	1956	9,863,264	8,907	...	35,961	248
India	1951	356,879,394	381,690	14.2	3,288,375	116
Indonesia	1930	60,412,962	81,900	3.0	1,491,564	55
Iran	1956	18,944,821 [1]	21,794	0.8	1,630,000	13
Iraq	1947	4,566,185	5,200	...	444,474	12
Israel	1948	716,678 [4]	1,748	...	20,678	85
Japan	1955	89,275,529	89,100	3.3	369,813	241
Jordan	1952	1,329,174	1,427	...	96,610	15
Korea	1944	25,120,174	28,000	1.0	220,792	127
Republic of Korea	1955	21,526,374	21,256	0.8	93,634	230
Kuwait	...	....	203	...	15,540	13
Laos	...	....	1,425	...	237,000	6
Lebanon	...	....	1,425	...	10,400	137

Maldive Islands	1946	82,068	89	...	298	299
Mongolian People's Republic	1918	476,506	1,000	...	1,531,000	7
Muscat and Oman	...	...	550	...	212,380	3
Nepal	1952–54	8,431,537	8,432[5]	3.1	140,753	60[4]
Pakistan	1951	75,842,165	82,439	0.8	944,824	87
Philippines	1948	19,234,182	21,849	...	299,404	74
Qatar	...	...	35	...	22,014	2
Saudi Arabia	...	...	7,000	...	1,600,000	4
Syria	...	...	4,145	...	181,337	23
Thailand	1947	17,442,689	20,302	0.8	514,000	39
Trucial Oman	...	...	80	...	83,600	1
Turkey	1955	24,121,778[1]	24,122	0.9	776,980	31
Viet-Nam	...	...	26,300	1.0	329,600	80
Yemen	...	...	4,500[6]	...	195,000	23[5]
Territories and Dependencies						
West New Guinea (Netherlands)	1930	314,271	700	...	412,781	2
Macau (Portugal)	1950	187,772	200	...	16	12,500
Portuguese India	1950	637,591	644	...	4,194	154
Portuguese Timor	1950	442,378	469	...	14,925	31
Aden Colony (U. K.)	1955	138,441	140	...	207	676
Aden Protectorate	...	...	650	...	290,080	2
Brunei (U. K.)	1947	40,657	65	...	5,765	11
Cyprus (U. K.)	1946	450,114	520	...	9,251	56
Hong Kong (U. K.)	1931	840,473	2,340	...	1,103	2,310
Malaya, Federation of (U. K.)	1947	4,908,086	6,058	...	131,287	46
North Borneo (U. K.)	1951	334,141	370	...	76,112	5
Sarawak (U. K.)	1947	546,385	614	...	121,914	5
Singapore (U. K.)	1947	939,010	1,213	...	742	1,635

Table I. Population, Area, and Density of Population for Each Country and Territory of the World (Continued)

Country or territory	Latest census		Population 1955 (Midyear estimates in thousands)	Percentage of world population	Area (Square kilometers)	Density 1955 (Persons per sq. kilometer)
	Year	Population				
Gaya Strip	....	......	325	..	202	1,609
Ryukyu Islands (U. S.)	1955	801,065	798	..	2,196	363
Europe [3]	....	......	409,000	15.2	......	83
Albania	1945	1,122,000	1,394	..	28,748	48
Austria	1951	6,933,905	6,974	..	83,849	83
Belgium	1947	8,512,195	8,868	..	30,507	291
Czechoslovakia	1950	12,338,450	13,093	..	127,819	102
Denmark	1950	4,281,275	4,439	..	42,936	103
Faeroe Islands	1950	31,781	34	..	1,399	24
Finland	1950	4,029,803	4,241	..	337,009	13
France	1954	42,843,520	43,274	1.6	551,208	79
Germany	1946	64,457,489	70,134	2.6	353,702	198
German Democratic Republic	1950	17,199,098	16,794	0.6	107,459	156
Federal Republic	1950	47,695,672	49,995	1.9	245,359	204
Greece	1951	7,632,801	7,973	..	132,562	60
Hungary	1949	9,204,799	9,805	..	93,030	105
Iceland	1950	143,961	158	..	103,000	2
Ireland	1956	2,894,822	2,909	..	70,283	41
Italy	1951	47,158,738	48,016	1.8	301,226	159
Liechtenstein	1955	14,861	15	..	157	96
Luxembourg	1947	290,992	309	..	2,586	119

	Year					
Monaco	1956	20,422	22	0.4	1	22,000
Netherlands	1947	9,625,499	10,751	..	32,450	331
Norway	1950	3,278,546	3,425	1.0	323,917	11
Poland	1950	24,976,926	27,278	..	311,700	88
Portugal	1950	8,441,312	8,765	0.6	92,200	95
Romania	1956	17,489,794	17,000	..	237,502	74
Saar	1951	955,413	992	1.1	2,567	386
Spain	1950	27,976,755	28,976	..	503,486	58
Sweden	1950	7,041,829	7,262	..	449,681	16
Switzerland	1950	4,714,992	4,977	1.9	41,288	121
United Kingdom	1951	50,225,224	51,215	1.7	244,016	210
England and Wales	1951	43,757,888	44,623	..	151,113	295
Northern Ireland	1951	1,370,921	1,394	..	14,139	99
Scotland	1951	5,096,415	5,198	0.7	78,764	66
Yugoslavia	1953	16,927,275	17,628	..	255,395	69
Territories and Dependencies						
Channel Islands (U. K.)	1951	102,776	102	..	195	523
Gibraltar (U. K.)	1951	23,232	25	..	6	4,167
Isle of Man (U. K.)	1951	55,253	56	..	588	95
Malta and Gozo	1948	305,991	314	..	316	994
Oceania	....	....	14,600	0.5	....	2
Australia	1954	8,986,530	9,201	..	7,704,159	1
New Zealand	1956	2,174,062	2,136	..	268,231	8
Territories and Dependencies						
French Oceania	1951	62,678	69	..	3,998	17
New Caledonia (France)	1951	20,947	63	..	18,653	3
Cook Islands (New Zealand)	1951	15,079	16	..	229	70
British Solomon Islands	1931	94,066	103	..	29,785	3

Table I. Population, Area, and Density of Population for Each Country and Territory of the World (Continued)

Country or territory	Latest census		Population 1955 (Midyear estimates in thousands)	Percentage of world population	Area (Square kilometers)	Density 1955 (Persons per sq. kilometer)
	Year	Population				
Fiji Islands (U. K.)	1946	259,638	339	...	18,234	19
Gilbert and Ellice Islands (U. K.)	1947	36,000	41	...	956	43
Tonga (U. K.)	1939	34,130	54	...	697	77
American Samoa	1950	18,937	22	...	197	112
Guam (U. S.)	1950	59,498	36	...	534	67
Hawaii (U. S.)	1950	499,794	560	...	16,636	34
New Guinea (Australia)	....	......	1,254	...	240,870	5
Pacific Isles (U. S.)	....	......	64	...	1,779	36
Western Samoa (New Zealand)	1951	84,909	95	...	2,927	32
New Hebrides (U. K. and France)	....	......	54	...	14,763	4
U.S.S.R.	1939	170,467,186	200,200	7.4	22,403,000	9

SOURCE: United Nations, Demographic Yearbook, 1956 (New York: Statistical Office of the United Nations, 1956), Table 1. States or territories having less than 10,000 inhabitants are omitted. (* Less than one person per square kilometer.)
[1] Provisional.
[2] Author's estimate.
[3] U.S.S.R. given separately.
[4] Jewish population only.
[5] 1954.
[6] For 1949.

Observation and study of the substantial data given in Table I enable one to draw many important conclusions concerning the geographic distribution of the world's inhabitants. Note, in the first place, that the inhabitants of Asia make up well over one-half of the human race, even with those living in the Asiatic part of the U.S.S.R. not included. Europe, also without the corresponding portion of Russian territory, is second with about 15 per cent of the earth's population, and North America third with approximately 14 per cent.

Communist-controlled China alone has almost one-fifth of the world's total population, followed by India with about one-seventh. Between 7 and 8 per cent of the inhabitants of our planet live within the 1955 limits of Soviet Russia and slightly over 6 per cent in the continental United States. The six other most populous nations are Japan, Pakistan, Brazil, the United Kingdom, the German Federal Republic, and Italy.

The number of persons per square kilometer of land surface ranges from only two in Oceania, due largely to the inclusion of huge and sparsely populated Australia in this world division, to eighty-three in Europe. Asia's teeming millions make for an index of fifty-five for the continent. Neither of these figures includes the appropriate portions of Soviet Russia, for which the density of population is computed at nine per square kilometer, the same index as that prevailing for the North American continent. In Africa and in South America there are only seven persons per square kilometer of territory.

Because of the large numbers of people involved, the indexes of density of population in Japan, India, China, and Pakistan command especial attention. They are 241, 116, 87, and 78 persons per square kilometer of territory, respectively; the corresponding figure for the United States is only 21. However, it should not be overlooked that there was in 1955 an average of 331 persons per square mile in the Netherlands, 295 in England and Wales, 291 in Belgium, and 204 in the German Federated Republic. Puerto Rico, with 254 persons per square kilometer of territory, Haiti with 119, and El Salvador with 110, claim particular attention in the Americas.

The Number and Geographic Distribution of the Inhabitants of the United States

In the United States significant study of the geographic distribution of the population may be made with a minimum of trouble and wasted effort. This is because all of the essential data and materials are readily available to the student. Fairly current and highly reliable data are supplied in detail by censuses taken only ten years apart; and the indispensable maps showing boundaries of all major and minor civil divisions are kept up to date and are obtainable at a nominal charge. In addition, for most of the nation's major cities the data are tabulated for units; the census tracts, which are much smaller than any administrative entities, and maps are published showing the location and boundaries of all these small areas in each city. In many other parts of the world, however, it is difficult or impossible to secure population counts for small areas, and even if these are available, very frequently maps showing the boundaries of the corresponding units are long out of date if indeed they are available at all. The comparative stability of the boundaries of counties and minor civil divisions is another advantage enjoyed by demographers using data for the United States over those who work with materials for many countries throughout the world.

Tabulations concerned with the number and distribution of the inhabitants are given a primary place in the publications of the United States Census of Population. Counts of the number of persons are presented not only for each of the forty-eight states and for the District of Columbia, but for each county, minor civil division (township, ward, beat, etc.), incorporated center, and unincorporated place of a thousand inhabitants or more in each of the states. In addition special tabulations for "urbanized areas," "standard metropolitan areas," "state economic areas and economic subregions," and, for most of the larger cities, the census tracts, greatly facilitate the study of many aspects of the geographic distribution of the inhabitants.

The seventeenth decennial census, taken as of April 1, 1950, enumerated a total of 150,697,361 persons in the continental United States. As may be noted from Table I, this figure is equal to approximately one-sixteenth of the population of the globe. There will not be another rather exact determination of the number of inhabitants in this country until the first results from the 1960 census are published late that year or early in 1961. Even then only the data on number and distribution will be available, and several years more will have to pass before the comprehensive materials on the characteristics of the population have been tabulated and published. In the meanwhile, the Bureau of the Census is publishing estimates annually, and for the nation as a whole the calculations probably are fairly accurate. The present writer states this even though estimates made in the years prior to the 1950 census were considerably lower than the number eventually enumerated, for he believes that significant improvements in population estimation have been made since the close of World War II. Even so, however, it would be unwise to put too much trust in the estimates for the later years of the intercensal period, even for the United States as a whole, and substantial independent testing should be carried out before reliance is placed upon those for any state. The estimates of 170,293,000 for July 1, 1957, and of 173, 260,000 for July 1, 1958, will need considerable revision after the definitive counts are made in 1960, and that for July 1, 1959, is likely to contain an even larger margin of error.

A broad idea of the general geographic distribution of the inhabitants of the United States is given by a consideration of the numbers and proportions of the population residing in the four major regions in the nation, as these regions are delineated by the Bureau of the Census. As indicated by the 1950 census the bulk of the population lives in the North, 39,477,986 (26.2 per cent) in the Northeastern States and 44,460,762 persons (29.5 per cent) in the North Central States. The South, with a total of 47,197,088 inhabitants, accounted for 31.3 per cent of the total; and the West, with 19,561,525 residents, for 13.0 per cent. In line with these differences in the populations of the respective regions are the indexes showing the average number of persons per square mile. In comparison with the figure of 51 persons per square mile in the continental United States as a whole, the indexes of density of population in the various regions are as follows: Northeast, 241; North Central, 59; South, 54; and West, 17. These differences in the density of population are reflected in popular thinking with respect to the congestion in the Northeast and the "wide open spaces" of the West. The middle sections of the country, on the other hand, both in the North and in the South, are those in which the number of persons per square mile most nearly approach the mean for the nation.

Further understanding of the distribution of population in the United States may be obtained through careful study of the data given in Table II and of the map which is presented as Figure 1. That New York, California, and Pennsylvania ranked in that order in 1950 as the three most populous states in the Union is fairly well known, even

Table II. Number, Geographic Distribution, and Density of Population in the United States, 1950

Division and state	Population 1950	Per cent of national population	Rank in population	Population per square mile
Continental United States	150,697,361	100.0	. .	51
New England	9,314,453	6.2	. .	148
Maine	913,774	0.6	35	29
New Hampshire	533,242	0.4	45	59
Vermont	377,747	0.3	46	41
Massachusetts	4,690,514	3.1	9	596
Rhode Island	791,896	0.5	37	749
Connecticut	2,007,280	1.3	28	410
Middle Atlantic	30,163,533	20.0	. .	300
New York	14,830,192	9.8	1	309
New Jersey	4,835,329	3.2	8	643
Pennsylvania	10,498,012	7.0	3	233
East North Central	30,399,368	20.2	. .	124
Ohio	7,946,627	5.3	5	194
Indiana	3,934,224	2.6	12	109
Illinois	8,712,176	5.8	4	156
Michigan	6,371,766	4.2	7	112
Wisconsin	3,434,575	2.3	14	63
West North Central	14,061,394	9.3	. .	28
Minnesota	2,982,483	2.0	18	37
Iowa	2,621,073	1.7	22	47
Missouri	3,954,653	2.6	11	57
North Dakota	619,636	0.4	42	9
South Dakota	652,740	0.4	41	9
Nebraska	1,325,510	0.9	33	17
Kansas	1,905,299	1.3	31	23
South Atlantic	21,182,335	14.1	. .	79
Delaware	318,085	0.2	47	161
Maryland	2,343,001	1.6	24	237
District of Columbia	802,178	0.5	36	13,151
Virginia	3,318,680	2.2	15	83
West Virginia	2,005,552	1.3	29	83
North Carolina	4,061,929	2.7	10	83
South Carolina	2,117,027	1.4	27	70

Table II. Number, Geographic Distribution, and Density of Population in the United States (Continued)

Division and state	Population 1950	Per cent of national population	Rank in population	Population per square mile
Georgia	3,444,578	2.3	13	59
Florida	2,771,305	1.8	20	51
East South Central	11,477,181	7.6	..	64
Kentucky	2,944,806	2.0	19	74
Tennessee	3,291,718	2.2	16	79
Alabama	3,061,743	2.0	17	60
Mississippi	2,178,914	1.4	26	46
West South Central	14,537,572	9.6	..	34
Arkansas	1,909,511	1.3	30	36
Louisiana	2,683,516	1.8	21	59
Oklahoma	2,233,351	1.5	25	32
Texas	7,711,194	5.1	6	29
Mountain	5,074,998	3.4	..	6
Montana	591,024	0.4	43	4
Idaho	588,637	0.4	44	7
Wyoming	290,529	0.2	48	3
Colorado	1,325,089	0.9	34	13
New Mexico	681,187	0.5	40	6
Arizona	749,587	0.5	38	7
Utah	688,862	0.5	39	8
Nevada	160,083	0.1	49	2
Pacific	14,486,527	9.6	..	45
Washington	2,378,963	1.6	23	36
Oregon	1,521,341	1.0	32	16
California	10,586,223	7.0	2	68

SOURCE: Compiled and computed from data in *U. S. Census of Population: 1950*, Vol. I, *Number of Inhabitants* (Washington: Government Printing Office, 1952).

though California was only in fifth place in 1940 and very likely will occupy first place in population in 1960. Less well known is the fact that Illinois, Ohio, and Texas ranked fourth, fifth, and sixth, respectively; and not many persons are aware that Michigan, New Jersey, Massachusetts, and North Carolina, in the order named, completed the list of the ten most populous states. It is well known that Nevada is not only the most sparsely populated but also the least populous state

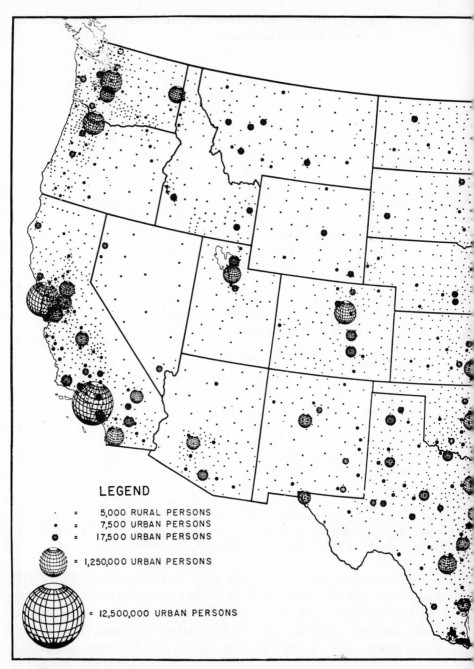

LEGEND

- · = 5,000 RURAL PERSONS
- • = 7,500 URBAN PERSONS
- ⬤ = 17,500 URBAN PERSONS

🌐 = 1,250,000 URBAN PERSONS

🌐 = 12,500,000 URBAN PERSONS

Figure 1. Distribution of population in the United States, 1950.

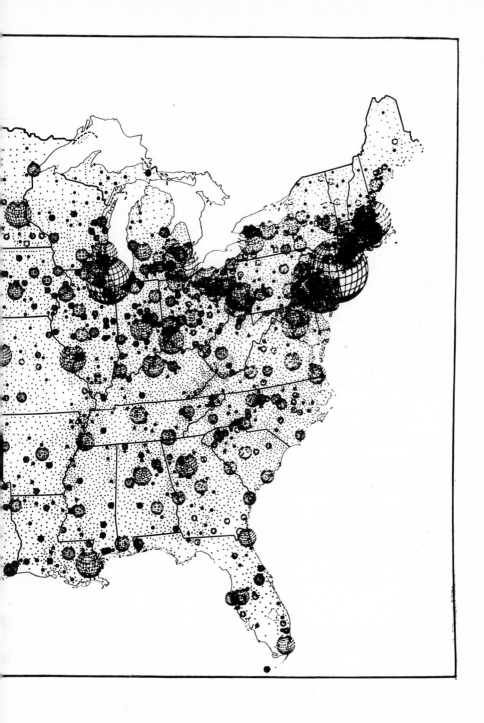

of the Union, and that it is most closely rivaled in this latter respect by
Wyoming and Delaware. All three occupied the same positions in
1940. At the time of the 1950 enumeration, the other seven of the ten
least populous states, in ascending order of the number of inhabitants,
were as follows: Vermont, New Hampshire, Idaho, Montana, North
Dakota, South Dakota, and New Mexico. Between 1940 and 1950
Montana and South Dakota supplanted Arizona and Utah in the list
of the ten states having the smallest populations.

More useful for many purposes than the tabular materials to which
reference has just been made is the map showing the geographic
distribution of population throughout the United States. In its construction the dots represent the rural population and the volumetric
spheres represent population centers of various sizes. The combination of the two is the only satisfactory manner so far devised for representing simultaneously on the same map both urban and rural populations in an area in which the density of population varies so greatly
as it does in the United States. A study of Figure 1 will prove highly
rewarding to one who wishes to know the essentials about the geographic distribution of population in the United States; and the construction and study of comparable maps for the various regions and
states will prove highly informative for those who wish more detailed
information for one or more of the important divisions of the nation.

In 1950 the center of population in the United States was located in
Denver township, Richland County, Illinois, about eight miles from
the small city of Olney. (See Figure 2.) Ten years earlier it was forty-
three miles to the east in southwestern Indiana, and in 1790 it was near
Baltimore, Maryland. At every census, from the first to the seventeenth,
the center of population in the United States moved steadily westward,
with the progress between 1830 and 1840, 1850 and 1860, and 1870
and 1880 being especially marked. The distance spanned in the latest
intercensual period was considerably greater than that during any other
decade since 1910. Because of recent tremendous gains in population
in California and other western states, and those in Florida, Texas, and
other states far to the south and the southwest, by 1960 the center of
population may be expected to be still farther west and somewhat to
the south of its 1950 location.[1] Although the concept of the center of

---

[1] Alaska and Hawaii are not taken into account in these statements.

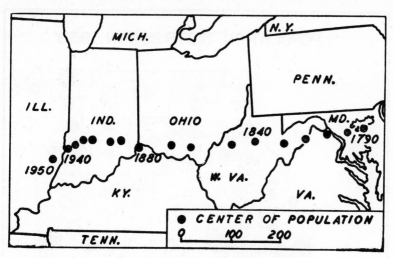

Figure 2. The westward march of the center of the population in the United States, 1790 to 1950.

population is of some use in the study of the geographic distribution of the population, its utility is not sufficient to make its determination of primary concern to those largely concerned with the demographic study of a given state or region.

The density of population, or the ratio of people to land, serves many useful purposes in the study of the geographic distribution of the population. As indicated above, there was in 1950 an average of fifty-one persons per square mile of territory in the United States. This index stood at forty-four in 1940 and forty-one in 1930. As may be seen from Table II, tiny Rhode Island, with almost 750 persons for each square mile of territory, was by far the most densely populated state in the Union, followed most closely by New Jersey (643 persons), Massachusetts (596 persons), and Connecticut (410 persons). At the other extreme stood Nevada with only two persons per square mile, followed by Wyoming (three persons), Montana (four persons), New Mexico (six persons), and Arizona and Idaho (seven persons). Density of population in Florida, fifty-one persons per square mile, was exactly equal to the average for the United States as a whole; and Iowa, Mississippi, Missouri, New Hampshire, Georgia, and Louisiana also were characterized by densities of population closely approximating the average for the nation.

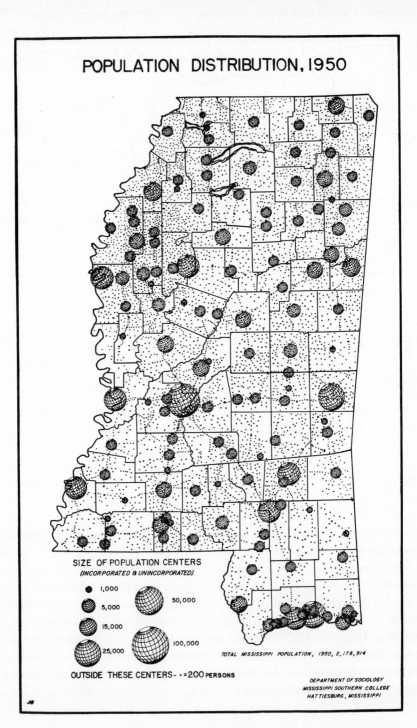

POPULATION DISTRIBUTION, 1950

SIZE OF POPULATION CENTERS
(INCORPORATED & UNINCORPORATED)

- ● 1,000
- 5,000
- 15,000
- 25,000
- 50,000
- 100,000

TOTAL MISSISSIPPI POPULATION, 1950, 2,178,914

OUTSIDE THESE CENTERS-·=200 PERSONS

DEPARTMENT OF SOCIOLOGY
MISSISSIPPI SOUTHERN COLLEGE
HATTIESBURG, MISSISSIPPI

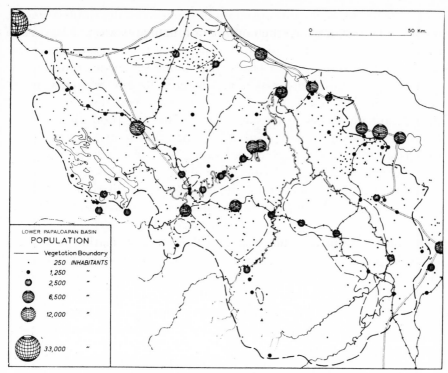

Figure 3. Distribution of population in Mississippi (on page at left) and in the Papoalpan Valley of Mexico (above), 1950. (Courtesy of Dr. John N. Burrus and Dr. William W. Winnie, Jr., respectively)

Some of the Uses of Data on the Geographic Distribution of the Inhabitants

The materials relating to the geographic distribution of the population make up the portion of demographic information that is most directly applicable for a host of social and economic purposes with the least expenditure of effort and the minimum of analytical skill and experience. Indeed from the time the population counts made in the census of 1790 were used to apportion the seats in the House of Representatives among the thirteen original states to the present, the tabulations showing the numbers of inhabitants in the various states, counties, towns and cities, and minor civil divisions have been used increasingly in myriads of useful ways. During the second and third quarters of the twentieth century, for example, rarely has the Congress of the

United States made an appropriation of funds to be distributed among the several states in which the number of inhabitants was not a primary factor in the formula by which the share going to each state was determined. Indeed, since the 1930's this fact alone has made accurate estimates of the populations of the various states for postcensual years of critical importance, especially for the combined federal-state programs in the most rapidly growing states. Today, the self protection and interest of every state in the Union demands that it make every effort to see that full counts of the population are made in every census and that the postcensual population estimates are as accurate as possible.

Similar uses of the materials on the geographic distribution of the population, in the form in which the data are organized and published in the census reports, are made on a large scale in each of the forty-eight states. In this case, however, it is the material relating to the distribution in the counties of a segment of the population, namely the children of school age, which figures most largely in the apportionment of state tax funds. Nevertheless, the number of inhabitants in any political subdivision and the proportion this constitutes of the state's total population are primary considerations in its contemporary fiscal policies. In 1957, for example, the officials of the City of New York risked $1.5 million, the fee charged by the U. S. Bureau of the Census, on a special census in the belief that the increased number of inhabitants, since 1950, would entitle the city to additional sums of state funds greatly in excess of the cost of the enumeration. State law at the time provided for an annual distribution of state funds to each city at the rate of $6.75 per person, based on federal census population counts. The officials reasoned that by January 1, 1957, the population of New York City was about 200,000 greater than it was in 1950, and that if this higher figure could be established they would be entitled to an annual increase of approximately $1.4 million of funds from the state.[1] As so frequently is the case when Chamber of Commerce estimates of population are matched with the results of census enumerations, however, the estimates proved to be highly inflated. The city's financial interests were best served by continuing to use the 1950 population counts. But the case does illustrate the application in contemporary affairs of current and reliable information on the number and geographic distribution of the population.

[1] See the publicity given the census drive in the *New York Times* for March 24, 1957, and in various other issues.

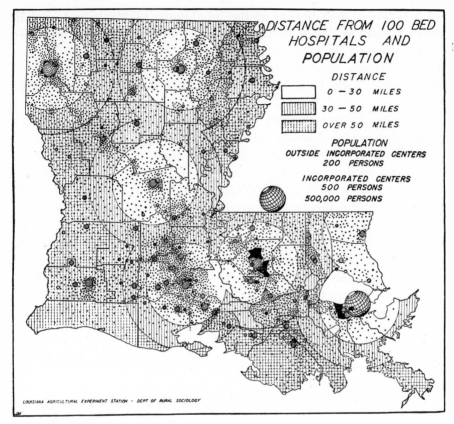

Figure 4. Distribution of population in Louisiana, 1940, in relation to the location of hospitals having a hundred or more beds, 1945. (Reproduced from Homer L. Hitt and Alvin L. Bertrand, "The Social Aspects of Hospital Planning in Louisiana," Baton Rouge: Louisiana Agricultural Experiment Station and the Office of the Governor, 1947)

For many modern uses the data on the geographic distribution of the population must be processed to a considerable extent before they can be brought to bear upon policy decisions and other matters. For example, the maps prepared by the demographer showing the distribution of the population within a city, county, or district, along with those showing recent changes, are widely employed by those who must determine the locations and attendance areas of new schools. At the state level, too, the maps prepared by population specialists, of which some of the best examples are those presented in Figure 3, showing the geographic distribution of the inhabitants in Mississippi, and in the Papoalpan Valley in Mexico, have great utility. When, as in Figure 4, such a map of the geographic distribution of the population was correlated with one showing the location of and zones about hospitals of various sizes, some basic facts needed in the planning of Louisiana's program of hospital construction were immediately apparent to all.

By far the most important use of the data showing the number of inhabitants in the various subdivisions of a nation, a state, a city, or a county, however, is in the computation of the various rates and ratios which play such an important role in demographic, sociological, economic, and other study and analysis. An accurate count or estimate of the population of the area involved is absolutely essential before such indexes as the crime rate, the rate of juvenile delinquency, the marriage rate, the divorce rate, the death rate, the birth rate, per capita income or expenditure, per capita wealth, and a host of other important indicators can be computed. One hardly need mention that indexes of these types are indispensable for the understanding of and conduct of modern economic and social affairs.[1]

SUGGESTED SUPPLEMENTARY READINGS

Bogue, Donald J., *The Population of the United States*. Chicago: The Free Press, 1959, chapters 4–5.

Davis, Kingsley, *The Population of India and Pakistan*, part I. Princeton, N. J.: Princeton University Press, 1951.

Knox, John Ballenger, *The People of Tennessee*. Knoxville: University of Tennessee Press, 1949, chapter 8.

Lorimer, Frank, *The Population of the Soviet Union: History and Prospects*. Geneva: League of Nations, 1946.

McMahan, C. A., *The People of Atlanta*. Athens: University of Georgia Press, 1950, chapter III.

Orleans, Leo A., "The 1953 Chinese Census in Perspective," *Journal of Asian Studies*, XVI, No. 4 (1957), 565–573.

Siegel, Jacob S., *The Population of Hungary*, U. S. Bureau of the Census, International Population Statistics Reports, Series P-90, No. 9. Washington: Government Printing Office, 1958, chapter IV.

[1] See *Life*, September 9, 1957, pp. 49–50, for an illustration with respect to crime rates and trends and the anomalies introduced by the lack of adequate data on the sizes of various populations.

Smith, T. Lynn, and Homer L. Hitt, *The People of Louisiana*. Baton Rouge: Louisiana State University Press, 1952, chapter II.

Taeuber, Conrad, and Irene B. Taeuber, *The Changing Population of the United States*. New York: John Wiley & Sons, 1958, chapter 1.

Taeuber, Irene B., "China's Population: Riddle of the Past, Enigma of the Future," *The Antioch Review*, Spring, 1957 issue, 7–18.

Zelinsky, Wilbur, "Recent Publications on the Distribution of Population in the United States," *Annals of the Association of American Geographers*, 48, No. 4 (1958), 472–481.

Part Three

THE CHARACTERISTICS
OF THE POPULATION

Rural or Urban Residence

Race, Color, Ethnic Stock,
  and Nativity

Age Composition

Sex Composition

Marital Condition

Occupational Status

Educational Status

Chapter 4

Rural or Urban Residence

LOGICALLY, ANY ONE OF FOUR chapters might very well be the first in this section on the composition or characteristics of the population. This is because, as was indicated in chapter 1, the factors of rural or urban residence, race and nativity, age, and sex constitute the warp and woof of modern census tabulations. Through sorting and subsorting of the data, it must be possible for the population student to control all four of these before he can go very far in the analysis of any other demographic phenomenon. Therefore, the treatment of any one of them would constitute a suitable point of departure. Since the U. S. Bureau of the Census regularly makes its first classification of the materials on the basis of residence, this subject is placed first in this volume. The other three are treated in the chapters that follow immediately.

As is stressed both in the study of the sociology of urban life and in the study of the sociology of rural life, a person's residence in a rural or in an urban area is among his most distinguishing characteristics. Whether one lives in the city or in the country, or in the shadowy area between the two made into a reality of considerable magnitude by the transportation facilities of the twentieth century, determines in a general way what he does and the conditions of life under which he lives. Thus rural society presents a sharp contrast to urban society, and this is true even in the United States during the early decades of the atomic age. Outstanding in rural society is the preponderance of the agricultural occupations, low density of population, small population aggregates or communities, and a high degree of ethnic and cultural homogeneity. The farmer still lives in an environment that is vastly different from the one surrounding the typical urban resident. In general, nature in all its benevolent as well as its malevolent aspects impinges directly upon the people who live in the country, whereas the inhabitants of the city have placed a thick shield of manmade culture or environment between themselves and the natural environment. The farmer has relatively few social contacts with others, and those he does have are restricted to more limited geographical and social spheres.

The sum total of all these and other dissimilarities determines that the country person and the urban man are surrounded and conditioned by radically different natural, cultural, and social environments. The urban environments in turn form and shape urban personalities and behavior patterns in ways that are considerably different from those the rural environment gives to those conditioned by it. Consequently, the resident of an urban center is distinguished from the one who lives in the country by a long list of important social, cultural, and economic differentials. Fortunately, this is fairly clear to most of those who have continued responsibility in planning and administering broad state and national policies in connection with health, welfare, education, and other services. From the demographic point of view, sizeable differences between the rural and urban segments of the population with respect to age distribution, sex composition, incomes and economic resources, morbidity, mortality, and rate of reproduction are facts of life with which the successful administrator must be acquainted.

This has been particularly true since the federal treasury became the source of support for significant proportions of the funds used to support health programs, agricultural activities, educational services, welfare measures, hospital development and construction, and so on. Apparently the time has passed when Congress would appropriate for a given program equal amounts of money to each of the states, regardless of the size and composition of their populations. Such was done, however, in the first federal grants for highway construction and agricultural research. More and more the funds are being apportioned on a per capita basis, and frequently the formulas used specify that certain definite segments of the population, such as the rural or the rural-farm categories, shall be the ones to figure in the computations. Nowadays, before they can vote intelligently on many bills awaiting action, members of the Congress must know well the distinctions between the urban, rural-nonfarm, and rural-farm populations. In these and many other ways knowledge of the basic facts concerning the rural or urban residence of a given population now has considerable application.

Definitions and Classifications

Sociologists have difficulty in making a satisfactory distinction between rural and urban society, for the reason that the great society is not sharply divided into two clearly differentiated parts, one urban and the other rural. Instead society in general resembles a spectrum in which the elements most clearly identifiable as rural are concentrated at the one extreme, and those most indisputably urban at the other, with the two gradually changing in relative importance as one moves from one end to the other. From the standpoint of the size of the community, the relative importance of agriculture and stockraising activities, the degree of social differentiation, or any other criterion that may be employed to distinguish between rural and urban, the rural features become less important and the urban features more so as one passes from the single farmstead to the homes and other buildings clustered at a crossroads, to a rural hamlet, to an agricultural village, to a village trade center, to the town, to a small city, to a large city, and to a great metropolitan center. In addition, somehow one must fit into this continuum situations representing the various degrees of urbanization or its opposite that are represented by the more remote sections of the metropolitan area, the heterogeneous situations that constitute what is known as the rural-urban fringe, and many other combinations of the rural and urban patterns of living. The vast majority of communities are neither purely urban nor purely rural, but rather they are localities in which the rural and urban features are combined in varying proportions. In spite of all this, however, sociologists are pretty well agreed that for census and other statistical purposes it may be necessary to take one, and only one, criterion, such as the size of the community as measured by the number of its inhabitants, as the basis for classifying the population into rural and urban categories. Such is the position of the present writer. As a sociologist he sets forth nine basic differences between the rural and urban worlds that should be understood by the one who would differentiate the rural from the urban.[1] But as a demographer he is well content when the census of a given country classifies as urban all of its inhabitants living in communities having more than a

[1] Cf. T. Lynn Smith, *The Sociology of Rural Life* (Third Edition), (New York: Harper & Brothers, 1953), pp. 18–37; T. Lynn Smith and C. A. McMahan, *The Sociology of Urban Life* (New York: The Dryden Press, 1951), pp. 42–58; and T. Lynn Smith, "Rural Sociology: A Trend Report and Bibliography," *Current Sociology*, VI, No. 1 (1957), 5–7.

stated number of inhabitants and as rural the remainder of the population.

Even though allowance is made for a necessary difference between definitions that are best for logical purposes and those that are practicable in census classifications, there is no agreement throughout the world as to where to draw the line between urban and rural populations or even upon the criteria that should be employed in separating the two categories. The French procedure of making the division arbitrarily at a given place on the population scale is used in many countries, including Mexico, New Zealand, and the United States. (See Table III.) But some nations count as urban, population centers which for some reason have been "elevated" to a certain rank, received distinctions which authorize them to designate themselves as towns or cities, or have come to enjoy other social, political, or administrative distinctions over other places of equal size and importance. Perhaps the situation today, as evidenced by the material in Table III, is even more confused than once was the case. After France selected (in 1846) the numerical criterion of 2,000 inhabitants as the point for separating the rural from the urban portions of the population, the practice spread rapidly throughout Central Europe. This type of criterion was recommended by the International Institute of Statistics in 1887.[1] Nevertheless today there still remains almost complete lack of comparability between the residential classifications employed in the census publications of various countries throughout the world. Indeed, so much individuality is expressed in this respect that much effort and ingenuity must be employed before any accurate comparisons may be made of the degree of urbanization in two or more countries. Even more labor is needed if one would attempt a comparison of trends.

The definitions of urban and rural currently in use for census purposes fall into several fairly clear categories. The first of these is employed in the countries which follow the French pattern and classify as urban, inhabitants of all population centers which have more than a specified number of inhabitants. Indeed the actual criterion applied by the French, that is to consider as urban the persons residing in communes having 2,000 or more inhabitants, is rather widely used in Europe. The slight modification of this procedure that long has been

---

[1] Cf. Adna Ferrin Weber, *The Growth of Cities in the Nineteenth Century* (New York: Columbia University Press, 1899) , p. 14.

standard in the United States, which sets the basic division between rural and urban at 2,500 inhabitants, also is used by several other American countries. Other nations employ variations of essentially the same criterion, and use such criteria as 250, 1,000, 1,500, 5,000, 20,000 and 40,000 as the number of inhabitants required before a given population center is classified as urban.

A second category of rural-urban classifications consists of those in which various towns and cities have been given charters or other privileges and distinctions which entitle them and them alone to status as urban centers, whereas all places lacking such honorific titles are classed as rural. Such bases for the rural or urban classification of the population prevail for the United Kingdom, Romania, and elsewhere in Europe.

Somewhat related to this procedure is that rather widely used throughout Latin America which designates as urban those population centers which serve as seats of local, state or departmental, and national government, and as rural all other localities, irrespective of their size. Various American countries, too, are experimenting with the use of other urban characteristics, such as the provision of municipal water systems (Guatemala), or the existence of municipal lighting, water, and sewage-disposal systems (Panama).

A new and promising approach to the problem of rural-urban classification was employed in Brazil's 1940 and 1950 censuses. Since this procedure may point the way to considerable improvements elsewhere, it deserves detailed description. During the preparatory work for the 1940 census a decree was issued making the prefect of each *município* (or county) responsible for having drawn and deposited with the Regional Geographic Office a map of his *município,* prepared in accordance with instructions supplied by the National Geographic Council. Among the instructions was one requiring each map to contain inserts showing the plan of the seat of the *município* and of the seats of all the *distritos* of which it was composed. The instructions also stipulated that "the urban and suburban areas of each *vila* (district seat) together shall include at least thirty dwellings; the urban area of the *cidade* (seat of the *município*) shall include a minimum of two hundred dwellings." It was provided, however, that all existing *cidades* and *vilas* should be mapped even though they did not meet the minimum requirements. Additional instructions were as follows:

Article 8: The determination of the urban part of the seat, whether of *município* or *distrito,* shall consist in the clear and simple description of a line, easily identifiable on the ground, surrounding the center of the greatest concentration of houses, in which, as a general rule, are located the principal public edifices and where the commercial, financial, and social life of the seat is manifested most intensely, and where, in many cases, there is the imposition of special taxes, as for example the urban tenth.

Single Paragraph—The said line of delineation of the urban area shall describe preferably, a polygon, made of sraight lines, which follows closely the periphery of the above-mentioned center of concentration of the houses in the seat.

Article 9: The delineation of the suburban portion of the seats (of *municípios* or *distritos*) shall consist in the clear and simple description of a line, also easily recognized on the ground, embracing an area that surrounds, at a variable distance, the urban section, an area into which the expansion of the urban zone is already proceeding or to which, due to its favorable topographic conditions, this expansion is naturally destined. The boundary line of the suburban zone should circumscribe as rigorously as possible, the area that really corresponds to the present or future expansion of the urban center, it being prohibited to delimit under any pretext whatsoever that may be invoked, even that of regularizing the form, a suburban perimeter which is removed in distance and confrontation, from the area of expansion mentioned above.[1]

Thus it is evident that the territory of each *município* is divided into three residential categories, namely, one or more urban areas, one or more suburban zones, and the remaining rural territory. This division was used in the 1940 and 1950 censuses for classifying the population into the urban, suburban, and rural categories. As will be indicated below, somewhat analogous procedures were used in the 1950 census of population in the United States for determining zones about cities of 50,000 or more inhabitants that were to be placed in the urban category and in delineating the boundaries of unincorporated centers of a thousand or more population.

United States Census Definitions and Classifications

More than fourscore years elapsed between the taking of the first census of population in the United States and the official inclusion of a classification of population according to rural or urban residence. How-

---

[1] Conselho Nacional de Geografia, *Resolução N. 3, de 29 de Marco de 1938* (Rio de Janeiro: Directoria de Estatística da Produção, 1938) , pp. 7–8.

ever, the importance of the deficiency was recognized by J. D. B. De-Bow who during the short interim in 1853 and 1854, when he served as Superintendent of the Census, salvaged the results of the seventh census and did so much to plot the course of development for the modern census. Consider the understanding and vision expressed in some of his comments on the subject:

The Census does not furnish material for separating the urban and rural population of the United States, so as to admit of a statement showing the extent of either. Such a table to each of the States would be very valuable, and it is much to be regretted that it can be deduced from none of the census publications.

So imperfect is the Census of 1850 in this respect that hundreds of important towns and cities in all parts of the country, and especially in the South and West, are not even distinguished on the returns from the body of the counties in which they are situated, and therefore their population cannot be ascertained at all. Again, slaves are often included in the towns, simply because their owners reside there. But what is of more importance and the greatest cause of embarrassment is the fact that in New England and the Northern States, what are returned as cities, and towns, often include whole rural districts. If the information in regard to town and city population is ever to be correctly ascertained, there must be explicit instructions to separate upon the returns, distinctly, all places having an aggregation of over fifty or a hundred persons, with a store, tavern, blacksmith shop or school house and post office, or some or all of these, and to include within such village, town, or city, no person not resident within its limits proper. It would not be difficult to frame suitable instructions upon this point.[1]

It is readily evident that if DeBow had participated in planning the 1860 census, the necessary improvements would have been made at an early date.

As it was, however, the first appearance of the rural-urban classification of the population came in 1874 with the publication of the *Statistical Atlas of the United States,* prepared under the supervision of Francis A. Walker.[2] At this time the division between rural and urban was placed at 8,000; persons living in cities having that many or more inhabitants were placed in the urban category, and all others in the rural. In this volume the data for all the previous censuses were re-

[1] J. D. B. DeBow, *Statistical View of the United States . . . Being a Compendium of the Seventh Census. . . .* (Washington: Beverley Tucker, Senate Printer, 1854), p. 192.

[2] Washington: Government Printing Office, 1874.

classified, and the numbers of urban people so defined were tabulated for all the decennial censuses through 1870. There is no way of knowing to what extent or in what manner the basic difficulties pointed out by DeBow were overcome. With primary interest still focused upon the urban group, the census of 1880 employed the criterion of 4,000 inhabitants as the dividing line between the rural and urban segments of the population.

Attention was shifted somewhat to the rural segment of the population in the 1890 census, when all persons living in aggregates of 1,000 or more inhabitants were classed as rural. Ten years later the 4,000 criterion again was employed to define the lower limit of the urban category, with the remainder of the inhabitants being divided into two subclasses: the semiurban, those residing in incorporated centers of less than 4,000 population, and the rural, those residing in unincorporated territory.

In 1910 the line of demarcation between rural and urban was set at 2,500; and this continues to be the basic element in the classification of the population into the rural and urban categories. However, those who use the results of the 1950 census of population should be familiar with the "new" definition of urban employed in connection with that enumeration:

According to the new definition that was adopted for use in the 1950 Census, the urban population comprises all persons living in (a) places of 2,500 inhabitants or more incorporated as cities, boroughs, and villages, (b) incorporated towns of 2,500 or more except in New England, New York, and Wisconsin, where "towns" are simply minor civil divisions of counties, (c) the densely settled urban fringe, including both incorporated and unincorporated areas, around cities of 50,000 or more, and (d) unincorporated places of 2,500 inhabitants or more outside any urban fringe. The remaining population is classified as rural.[1]

They should understand, though, that the cities of 50,000 or more specified in the definition include only those having populations of that size in 1940 or in some other official enumeration made prior to 1950.

For many purposes the student also must be acquainted with the "old" definition of urban employed for comparative purposes in the

---

[1] U. S. Bureau of the Census, *U. S. Census of Population: 1950*. Vol. I, *Number of Inhabitants* (Washington: Government Printing Office, 1952), p. xv.

1950 census and the only one used in the still highly important 1940 and 1930 enumerations.

According to the old definition, the urban population has been limited to all persons living in incorporated places of 2,500 inhabitants or more and in areas (usually minor civil divisions) classified as urban under special rules relating to population size and density.[1]

As indicated above, for many purposes the simple rural-urban dichotomy is inadequate, and the concept of the continuum is much more satisfactory. Therefore, it is fortunate that the Bureau of the Census employs subdivisions of both the urban and the rural categories in the majority of its basic tabulations, and that special compilations of data enable the student to determine many of the demographic variations that occur as one passes from the most highly rural to the most highly urban portions of the population.

The urban category is the one for which, from the standpoint of the population analyst, the data are tabulated and published in the most satisfactory manner. The category as a whole is employed, or the facts for it may be obtained by subtraction, in nearly all the state and county tables; and in addition fairly complete information is given separately for every city of 100,000 or more inhabitants, rather plentiful materials for each place having between 10,000 and 100,000 residents, and considerable data for each smaller center. Furthermore, in the 1950 census tabulations a wealth of demographic detail was published for each of 157 *urbanized areas* that had been delineated, as well as for each of 168 *standard metropolitan areas* scattered throughout the nation.

As defined for census purposes, "an urbanized area is an area that includes at least one city with 50,000 inhabitants or more in 1940 or later according to a special census taken prior to 1950 and also the surrounding closely settled incorporated places and unincorporated areas that meet the criteria listed below." The boundaries of the urbanized areas were fixed "after careful examination of all available maps, aerial photographs, and other sources of information, and then were checked in detail in the field by trained investigators to insure that the criteria were followed and that the boundaries were identifiable." [2] The portion of the urbanized area lying outside its central city or cities was designated as the *urban fringe*. This zone embraced the following types

[1] *Ibid.,* pp. xv–xvii.
[2] *Ibid.,* p. xxvii.

of area if they were "contiguous to the central city or cities or if they are contiguous to any area already included in the urban fringe":

1. Incorporated places with 2,500 inhabitants or more in 1940 or at a subsequent special census conducted prior to 1950.
2. Incorporated places with fewer than 2,500 inhabitants containing an area with a concentration of 100 dwelling units or more with a density in this concentration of 500 units or more per square mile. . . .
3. Unincorporated territory with at least 500 dwelling units per square mile.
4. Territory devoted to commercial, industrial, transportational, recreational, and other purposes functionally related to the central city.

Also included are outlying noncontiguous areas with the required dwelling unit density located within 1½ miles of the main contiguous urbanized part, measured along the shortest connecting highway, and other outlying areas with one-half mile of such noncontiguous areas which meet the minimum residential density rule.[1]

Those phrasing the census definitions further inform us that "the urbanized area can be characterized as the physical city as distinguished from both the legal city and the metropolitan community." Urbanized areas are smaller than the standard metropolitan areas and usually are embraced within the limits of the latter.[2]

The standard metropolitan area, as the concept was employed in the 1950 census for the purpose of giving detailed tabulations of information for the 168 most highly urbanized segments of the United States, "is a county or group of contiguous counties which contains at least one city of 50,000 inhabitants or more." In addition to the county or counties containing the city or cities of this size, the standard metropolitan area includes the contiguous counties which were judged to be socially and economically integrated with its metropolis. The criteria of integration employed are somewhat involved, but they include consideration of such factors as the following: (1) the numbers and proportions of nonagricultural workers in the outlying county; (2) the proportion these workers constituted of all nonagricultural workers in the standard metropolitan area; (3) the percentage of the workers in the outlying county who were employed in the county containing the central city; (4) the percentage of the workers employed in the outlying county who

[1] Ibid.
[2] Ibid., p. xxxiii.

lived in the county containing the metropolis; and (5) the ratio of telephone calls between the central and outlying county to the number of telephone subscribers in the latter.[1]

The *rural population* as given by the 1950 census, as is evident from what was said above relative to the definition of urban, consists of all persons who neither resided within the limits of a center of 2,500 or more inhabitants nor in the "urban fringe" of a city of 50,000 or more inhabitants as shown by the 1940 census or in a special enumeration made prior to 1950. It is divided into two principal subcategories, and the data for each of these figure in most of the state and county tables. In order to appreciate the fundamental distinction between these two segments, it is necessary to know that the 1950 *farm population* includes all persons considered as residing on tracts of land that were classified as farms, irrespective of their occupations.[2]

Those living on what might appear to be farm land, however, who paid cash rent for the use merely of a house and yard, were not included in the farm population. Virtually all farms in the United States are located in rural territory, hence the *rural-farm population* as classified by the 1950, 1940, and 1930 censuses is almost synonymous with the farm population.

The *rural-nonfarm population* is the residual group. It includes all persons who were classified neither as urban nor as rural-farm. Therefore it is a hodgepodge embracing some of the most widely divergent segments of the entire population. The village population, i. e., those living in centers of less than 2,500 inhabitants, and the people living just outside the corporate limits of towns and cities of less than 50,000 population make up two of the most important groups in this category. But it also embraces a wide variety of nonagriculturists (miners; trappers; woodsmen; fishermen; filling station operators and attendants; the personnel engaged in the operation of motels, tourist courts and re-

---

[1] *Ibid.*, p. xxxiii.

[2] The definition of a farm employed in the 1950 census is as follows:

A farm.—For the 1950 Census of Agriculture, places of 3 or more acres were counted as farms if the value of agricultural products in 1949, exclusive of home gardens, amounted to $150 or more. The agricultural products could have been either for home use or for sale. Places of less than 3 acres were counted as farms only if the value of sales of agricultural products in 1949 amounted to $150 or more. . . .

All the land under the control of one person or partnership was included as one farm. Control may have been through ownership, or through lease, rental, or cropping arrangement. [U. S. Bureau of the Census, *U. S. Census of Agriculture: 1950.* Vol. I, *Counties and State Economic Areas* (Washington: Government Printing Office, 1952), p. xii.]

sorts; the keepers of stores, bars, beer parlors, and fish camps; and so forth) dispersed throughout the countryside.

In addition to the rural-farm and the rural-nonfarm categories, for which the data are presented with all detail that reasonably may be expected, the census reports also give the more important data for each incorporated center of less than 2,500 inhabitants and each unincorporated center having from 1,000 to 2,499 inhabitants. If, in addition to the materials supplied in 1950, in future tabulations the Bureau would consolidate and publish the data for all such rural population centers in each state taken collectively, the work of those engaged in the study and analysis of the rural population would be greatly facilitated.

Indexes and Scales of Urbanity and Rurality

Very frequently there is need of an index showing the points on the rural-urban continuum at which the various counties and minor civil divisions of a given state are located. Such need arises principally, of course, where it is desired to include this variable in the analysis of demographic interrelationships or trends and particularly where correlation analysis is essential. Many demographers, sociologists, economists, and political scientists, when confronted with the problem, have found it difficult to devise a satisfactory index. The proportion of the total population that is classified as urban frequently is suggested and employed. However, in practice this turns out to be highly unsatisfactory because so many of the counties in a given state, and an even larger percentage of the minor civil divisions, contain no urban populations whatsoever. For example, the student attempting to correlate the degree of urbanization with one or more other factors in the state of Kentucky, and using the percentage of urban population in the total population as an index, would discover that in 1950, 67 of the 121 counties in the state contained no urban centers; or if Colorado were the state for which the analysis were to be made, he would find that urban populations were lacking in 35 of the 63 counties in the state. Since the logic of correlation analysis breaks down completely when any considerable number of the items have a value of zero, the measure that at first glance appears to be the most appropriate is entirely unsuited for use in these cases. Similar is the situation in many other states; and the defects are even more pronounced if minor civil divisions are the units employed in the analysis. Also frequently encountered is a very sparsely populated county, far removed from metropolitan centers and slightly exposed to direct influences from the city, but in which is a town of more than 2,500 inhabitants. Indeed counties of this type may contain extremely high proportions of persons classified as urban. This is another reason why the proportion of urbanites in the population in a county is a very poor indicator of the degree to which such a county is urbanized. What are the alternatives? After considerable exploratory study, it would appear that the best readily available index for use in the type of problem under discussion is the proportion of the population in the county, or in the minor civil division, that is resident in places (incorporated centers of all sizes and unincorporated places having 1,000 or more inhabitants) for which separate tabulations are prepared by the Bureau of the Census. If in the 1960 and subsequent censuses, the data are published separately for unincorporated centers of less than 1,000 inhabitants, this index will be even more satisfactory as a measure of the degree of urbanity of the various counties and minor civil divisions in a given state.

Frequently the population student needs more than a simple division of the population into the rural and urban categories, and this is the case especially when he desires to relate to other factors populations according to the size of their communities of residence. The need in this case is for a series of categories that will reflect the various grades or degrees encountered as one moves from the most rural to the most urban situations or populations. Usage in this respect is not standardized, and the terminology employed frequently is confusing. Substantial progress was made, however, in connection with the 1950 census of population when the population living on the outskirts of cities of 50,000 or more was included in the urban category and the data published for each such urbanized area as a unit. The value of the information so assembled was greatly enhanced by the publications for the nation as a whole of data on selected items, based on a 3.5 per cent sample of the population separately, for the total area, central cities, and fringes of urbanized areas of the following sizes: 3 million inhabitants or more; 1 million to 3 million; 0.25 million to 1 million; and less than 0.25 million. To complete this valuable compilation, comparable information was included for the population living outside the localities designated as urbanized areas of the following sizes: places of 25,000 or more inhabitants; places of 10,000 to 25,000; places of 2,500 to 10,000; and places of 1,000 to 2,500, with this class further subdivided into the farm and the nonfarm categories.[1] The smallness of the sample did not permit comparable classifications of the populations of the various states, a feature that would be even more useful than the national data that are available. Under these circumstances the present writer has found the following arrangement or scale of considerable use.

Size of Community			
	Rural	Open country	Less than 100 inhabitants
		Hamlets	100 to 249 inhabitants
		Small villages	250 to 999 inhabitants
		Large villages	1,000 to 2,499 inhabitants
	Urban	Small towns	2,500 to 4,999 inhabitants
		Large towns	5,000 to 9,999 inhabitants
		Small cities	10,000 to 99,999 inhabitants
		Large cities	100,000 to 999,999 inhabitants
		Metropolitan centers	1 million or more inhabitants

Some International Comparisons

Prior to 1949 it was almost impossible for the student of population to secure any comprehensive and reliable information about the absolute and relative importance of the rural and urban populations in most parts of the world. Anyone vitally interested in the matter could easily spend weeks or months in the endeavor, only to discover eventually that all his efforts were fruitless.[2] Fortunately, this was one of the first items to which the Population Commission established by the United Nations turned its attention, and comprehensive tabulations of such data as could be secured appeared in the first issue of the *Demographic Yearbook*.[3] More recently a second, much more inclusive tabulation was included in the 1955 edition of this magnificent source of information.[4] From this second compilation the materials presented in Table III have been taken.

The lack of uniformity in the definitions of rural and urban makes

[1] See, U. S. Bureau of the Census, *U. S. Census of Population: 1950.* Vol. IV, *Special Reports,* Part 5, Chapter A, Characteristics by Size of Place (Washington: Government Printing Office, 1953.)

[2] Cf. T. Lynn Smith, *Population Analysis* (New York: McGraw-Hill Book Company, 1948) , p. 28.

[3] *Demographic Yearbook: 1948* (Lake Success, New York: United Nations, 1949) , pp. 18, 213–229.

[4] *Demographic Yearbook: 1955* (New York: The United Nations, 1955) , pp. 185–197.

it impossible to make fair comparisons between most of the countries; and even if the definitions were uniform one could by no means be sure that a place of a given size in one country was equally urban, or equally rural, with one of the same size in another. For example, both the United States and Mexico employ 2,500 inhabitants as the point at which the line is drawn between the rural and urban portions of the population. But in Mexico the agriculturists commonly reside in villages and towns from which they commute daily for work on their lands in the surrounding territory; whereas, in the United States farmers generally live on their lands amid their fields. For this reason in Mexico a population center of three or four thousand inhabitants is likely to be largely agricultural, while in the United States a village of no more than one thousand inhabitants generally is highly commercial and it may be industrial as well. Again, a population aggregate of three thousand people in England or Belgium is almost certain to represent a much higher concentration of urban traits and practices than is one of comparable size in Spain or Bulgaria, not to mention towns of this size in India, China, and many other parts of the world.

For these reasons it is likely that many of the variations in the extent to which various nations in the world are rural or urban are even greater than might appear at first glance from the data which have been assembled in Table III. Even so there can be little doubt that Israel, Scotland, England and Wales, Western Germany, Belgium, and the Netherlands are the most highly urbanized countries in the world. They are most closely rivaled in this respect by Denmark, East Germany, France, and Sweden in Europe; Argentina, Canada, and the United States in America; and Australia and New Zealand.

The most outstanding fact to be obtained from Table III, however, is the extent to which the world's inhabitants still reside in highly rural territory and are conditioned by rural influences and ways of life. Note that more than four-fifths of India's teeming millions fall in the rural category, undoubtedly highly rural from the qualitative standpoint as well. Were the data available for China, the degree of urbanity hardly could be much higher. In all of Asia, as a matter of fact, Israel is the only nation in which the urban population is larger than the rural, and in no other part of this densely populated continent does the proportion of urban in the population reach 40 per cent. Likewise in the Americas, where the data are most complete, only Argentina, Canada, Chile, the United States, and Venezuela are in the group in which the

Table III. The Absolute and Relative Importance of the Urban Population in Each Country or Territory Having 1 Million Inhabitants or More for Which Data Are Available

Country	Year	Total population	Urban population	Per cent urban	Definition of urban areas
Africa					
Algeria (French)	1948	7,787,091	1,838,152	24	Agglomerations of 2,000 or more inhabitants that are administrative centers of self-governing communes.
Egypt	1947	18,966,767	5,711,761	30	Governorates and chief towns of provinces and districts.
Kenya (U. K.)	1948	5,405,966	271,156	5	Towns of natives having 3,000 or more inhabitants, plus 50 towns and municipalities of non-natives.
Morocco (French)	1952	7,442,110	1,375,830	19	Municipalities and other agglomerations of 2,000 or more inhabitants.
Morocco (Spanish)	1950	1,010,117	232,883	23	Localities constituted as municipalities.
Rhodesia and Nyasaland (U. K.)	1950	1,816,000	247,000	14	Nine main European towns. (African population only.)
Tunisia (French)	1946	3,230,952	965,489	30	Centers having status of communes.
Union of South Africa	1951	12,667,759	5,396,644	43	All centers having some form of urban local government.
North America					
Canada	1951	14,009,429	8,628,253	62	Population centers having 1,000 or more inhabitants and suburban parts of metropolitan areas.
Costa Rica	1950	800,875	268,286	34	Administrative centers of cantons.
Dominican Republic	1950	2,135,872	508,408	24	Administrative centers of communes and municipal districts.
El Salvador	1950	1,855,917	677,167	37	Administrative centers of departments, districts, and municipios or counties.

Country	Year	Total population	Urban population	Percent urban	Definition of urban
Guatemala	1950	2,790,868	696,458	25	Population centers of 2,000 or more inhabitants and places of 1,500 or more if running water is provided for homes.
Haiti	1950	3,097,220	377,355	12	Administrative centers of communes.
Honduras	1950	1,368,605	424,453	31	Administrative centers of districts and *municípios* or counties.
Mexico	1950	25,791,017	10,983,483	43	Population centers of 2,500 or more inhabitants.
Nicaragua	1950	1,057,023	369,249	35	Administrative centers of departments and *municípios* or counties.
Panama	1950	805,285	289,697	36	Population centers of 1,500 or more having essentially urban characteristics.
Puerto Rico (U. S.)	1950	2,210,703	894,813	41	Population centers of 2,500 or more inhabitants.
United States	1950	150,697,361	96,467,686	64	Population centers of 2,500 or more inhabitants and suburbs of cities of 50,000 or more inhabitants.
South America					
Argentina	1947	15,893,827	9,932,133	63	Population centers of 2,000 or more inhabitants.
Bolivia	1950	3,019,031	1,013,350	34	Administrative centers of departments, provinces, and cantons.
Brazil	1950	51,944,397	18,782,891	36	Administrative centers of *municípios* or counties and districts. (Includes population classed as suburban.)
Chile	1952	5,941,750	3,561,450	60	Population centers having definite urban characteristics contributed by public and municipal services.
Colombia	1951	11,545,372	4,186,885	36	Population centers of 1,500 or more inhabitants which are seats of *municípios* or counties.
Ecuador	1950	3,202,757	913,932	29	Capitals of provinces and cantons.
Paraguay	1950	1,328,452	459,726	35	All municipalities.
Venezuela	1950	5,034,838	2,709,344	54	*Município* or county seats having 1,000 or more inhabitants.

Table III. The Absolute and Relative Importance of the Urban Population (Continued)

Country	Year	Total population	Urban population	Per cent urban	Definition of urban areas
Asia					
Ceylon	1946	6,657,339	1,023,042	15	Municipalities, urban council areas, and local board areas.
India	1951	356,879,394	61,875,123	17	Municipalities and towns, i. e. centers of 5,000 or more inhabitants possessing definite urban characteristics.
Iraq	1947	4,816,185	1,627,762	34	Not indicated.
Israel	1948	686,837	576,207	84	Predominantly nonagricultural centers: towns, urban settlements, and urban villages.
Japan	1950	83,199,637	31,203,191	38	Municipalities (*shi*) most of which contain agglomerations of 30,000 or more inhabitants.
Jordan	1952	1,329,174	501,072	38	Not given.
Korea (South)	1949	20,188,641	3,962,203	20	Incorporated cities of 40,000 or more inhabitants.
Malaya, Federation of (U. K.)	1947	4,908,086	1,301,376	27	Towns and villages of 1,000 or more inhabitants.
Pakistan	1951	75,842,165	8,663,320	11	Not indicated.
Philippines	1948	19,234,182	4,630,758	24	Chartered cities and administrative centers of municipalities.
Thailand	1947	17,442,689	1,734,767	10	Population centers of 2,500 or more inhabitants.
Turkey	1945	18,790,174	4,687,102	25	All administrative centers of provinces and districts and other agglomerations having 5,000 or more inhabitants.
Europe					
Austria	1951	6,933,095	3,410,842	49	Communes of 5,000 or more inhabitants.

Country	Year				Definition
Belgium	1947	8,512,195	5,339,726	63	Communes of 5,000 or more inhabitants.
Bulgaria	1946	7,022,206	1,730,655	25	Population centers legally established as urban.
Czechoslovakia	1947	12,164,095	5,935,433	49	Communes of 2,000 or more inhabitants.
Denmark	1950	4,281,275	2,881,990	67	Agglomerations of 250 or more inhabitants.
Finland	1950	4,029,803	1,302,427	32	Population centers legally established as towns or boroughs.
France	1954	42,734,445	23,899,131	56	Communes of 2,000 or more inhabitants.
Germany					
East Germany	1946	17,180,407	11,240,339	65	Communes of 2,000 or more inhabitants.
West Germany	1950	47,695,672	33,930,037	71	Communes of 2,000 or more inhabitants.
Greece	1951	7,632,801	2,807,905	37	Municipalities and communes with agglomerations of 10,000 or more inhabitants.
Hungary	1949	9,207,286	3,180,178	35	The capital, 13 autonomous cities and 46 county towns.
Ireland (Republic)	1951	2,960,593	1,227,393	42	Towns of 1,500 or more inhabitants.
Netherlands	1947	9,625,499	5,251,149	55	Administrative municipalities of 20,000 or more inhabitants.
Norway	1950	3,278,546	1,054,820	32	Incorporated towns.
Poland	1946	23,625,435	7,424,589	31	Communities having urban administrative organization.
Portugal	1950	8,441,312	2,634,869	31	Communities of 2,000 or more inhabitants.
Romania	1948	15,872,624	3,713,139	23	Cities and towns established by law.
Spain	1950	27,976,755	16,935,306	61	Communities of 2,000 or more inhabitants (includes semiurban).
Sweden	1950	7,041,829	3,342,603	48	Administrative towns, not including market towns and other municipalities.
Switzerland	1950	4,714,992	1,720,057	37	Communes of 10,000 or more inhabitants.

Table III. The Absolute and Relative Importance of the Urban Population (Continued)

Country	Year	Total population	Urban population	Per cent urban	Definition of urban areas
United Kingdom					
England and Wales	1951	43,757,888	35,361,797	81	Boroughs and urban districts classified as such for local governmental purposes.
Northern Ireland	1951	1,370,709	728,215	53	Cities, municipal boroughs, and urban districts.
Scotland	1951	5,096,415	4,226,803	83	Cities, burghs, and villages of 1,000 or more inhabitants.
Yugoslavia	1948	15,751,935	2,555,638	16	Administrative units governed by City People's Committees.
Oceania					
Australia	1947	7,560,755	5,206,507	69	Capital cities of states and territories and other agglomerations classified as urban for census purposes.
New Zealand	1951	1,933,594	1,184,672	61	Cities and boroughs regardless of size.

SOURCE: *Demographic Yearbook, 1955* (New York: The United Nations, 1955), Table 7, pp. 185–197.

urban population is more numerous than the rural. In Africa by far the highest proportion of urban among the inhabitants is in the Union of South Africa, and there the percentage is only forty-three. Even in Europe, fifteen of the twenty-four countries for which data are available are more rural than urban, and this is so only when East Germany and Western Germany, England and Wales, Northern Ireland, and Scotland are all counted as separate countries.

Trends

A world-wide tendency for populations to concentrate in towns and cities was one of the outstanding developments during the first half of the twentieth century, and the same highly significant tendency continues unabated since 1950. The importance of economic and social effects of this trend can hardly be over-estimated. The demographic data which have a bearing on this subject leave a great deal to be desired: many countries lack adequate rural and urban classifications of the population; and for many of those that do, the radical changes in national entities and national boundaries which have occurred in recent decades have made it practically impossible to determine the changes taking place during intercensual periods. In addition to those for the United States, which will be given later, there are available, however, fairly reliable and comparable materials for thirty countries spread throughout the world. An analysis of the trends in these should be sufficient to make the general tendency sufficiently clear.

To begin with, in nine of these countries during the latest intercensual period substantial increases in the urban population were accompanied by actual decreases in the rural population. Interestingly enough two American countries, Chile and Venezuela, are found in this category, and the latter in particular includes in its vast dominions extensive acreages that still await transformation into productive fields and pastures. Little Iceland, too, recently has seen all of the natural increase of its rural population and part of the "seed stock" as well leave the country for the town or city. The other six are all European countries, namely, Belgium, Denmark, Finland, Ireland, Norway, and Scotland. As a result of these changes during the latest intercensual period the proportions of urban people in these countries rose as follows: Chile, from 52 per cent in 1940 to 60 per cent in 1952; Venezuela, from 30 per cent in 1941 to 54 per cent in 1950; Belgium, from 61 per cent in 1930 to 63 per cent in 1947; Denmark, from 65 per cent in 1945 to 67 per cent in 1950; Finland, from 25 per cent in 1947 to 32 per cent in 1950; Iceland, from 61 per cent in 1940 to 73 per cent in 1950; Ireland, from 38 per cent in 1946 to 42 per cent in 1951; Norway, from 28 per cent in 1946 to 32 per cent in 1950; and Scotland, from 80 per cent in 1931 to 83 per cent in 1951.

Only slightly less striking is a second category of countries in which substantial increases in the urban population were accompanied by numerically insignificant increases in the rural population. Five of the thirty countries belong in this group, and their names and distribution seem especially significant. These countries, the intercensual periods involved, and the numerical increases in urban and rural populations, respectively, are as follows: Union of South Africa, from 1946 to 1951, 1,247,820 and 1,590; Canada, from 1941 to 1951, 2,375,837 and 135,937; Japan, from 1945 to 1950, 11,180,858 and 20,675; France, from 1946 to 1954, 2,790,437 and 95,826; and Western Germany, 1946 to 1950, 3,956,492 and 33,891. As a result during the interims indicated the proportions of the population classified as urban rose as follows in the various countries: Union of South Africa, from 36 to 43 per cent; Canada, from 52 to 62 per cent; Japan, from 28 to 38 per cent; France, from 53 to 56 per cent; and Western Germany, from 69 to 71 per cent.

Those countries in which the numbers in both the urban and rural populations rose substantially, but in which the rate of increase in the former far exceeded that in the latter may be placed in a third group. The ten countries included, the intercensual periods involved, and ratio of the rate of increase in urban population to that in rural population are as follows: Egypt, 1937 to 1947, urban 3.8 times as high as the rural; Cuba, 1943 to 1953, urban 1.8 times that of the rural; Dominican Republic, 1935 to 1950, urban 2.8 times that of the rural; Honduras, 1945 to 1950, urban 2.0 times that of the rural; Mexico, 1940 to 1950, urban 3.7 times that of the rural; Brazil, 1940 to 1950, urban 2.7 times that of the rural; Colombia, 1938 to 1951, urban 3.4 times that of the rural; Greece, 1940 to 1951, urban 3.5 times that of the rural; England and Wales, 1931 to 1951, urban 2.2 times that of the rural; and Switzerland, 1941 to 1950, urban 5.0 times that of the rural.

This leaves only six of the thirty countries for which fairly reliable comparisons are possible. Of these, three (Portugal, Northern Ireland, and New Zealand) are cases in which the rate of growth of the urban population is higher than that of the rural, but not as much as 1.5 times as high; and three are those in which the rate of growth of the rural population exceeded that of the urban. Among the latter, the rates of growth of the urban populations expressed as percentages of those for the rural populations are as follows: El Salvador, 1930 to 1950, 70 per cent; Panama, 1940 to 1950, 84 per cent; and Sweden, 1945 to 1950, 12 per cent.

Were data available for India, Pakistan, China, Soviet Russia and her various satellites, the many countries recently achieving national status, and various "underdeveloped" sections of the world, the tendency for the population to concentrate in towns and cities would probably be seen to be equally as strong as it is in the parts of the earth mentioned above. Indeed the urbanization of the world and the contemporary dominant position of urban values and philosophies must be considered as among the most potent forces shaping civilization during the second half of the twentieth century.

The Rural and Urban Populations of the United States

Of the 150,697,361 inhabitants of the United States, as shown by the census taken as of April 1, 1950, a total of 96,467,686 (64.0 per cent) were classified as urban and 54,229,675 (36.0 per cent) as rural. This is on the basis of the "new" definition of urban employed for the first time in 1950. Using the same definition of urban as was employed in 1940 and other preceding censuses, only 88,927,464 (59.0 per cent) were classed as urban. Thus the change in the definition had the effect of transferring almost 8 million persons from the rural to the urban category. Since the bulk of this change was due to the inclusion in the urban population of inhabitants of the thickly populated zones adjacent to cities of 50,000 or more, nearly all of the transfer was from the rural-nonfarm category. In 1940, 56.5 per cent of the national population was classed as urban and 43.5 per cent as rural. Thus in the interval between the 1940 and the 1950 enumerations, irrespective of which of the definitions of urban is employed, the urban population increased much more rapidly than the rural, on the relative basis as well as the absolute. The number of urban centers in 1950 totaled 4,741, using the new definition of urban, or 4,023, if the old definition is employed. In 1940 the corresponding number was only 3,464, and in 1930 it was 3,615. The change during the last decade represents the net influence of adding centers that passed the 2,500 mark in population between 1940 and 1950, subtracting a few that had populations above 2,500 in 1940 and under that figure in 1950, and adding all unincorporated places and all newly incorporated centers having more than 2,500 inhabitants in 1950.

The rural population of the United States, in 1950, consisted of 31,-181,325 persons (20.7 per cent of the national total) classified, on the basis of the new definition of urban, as nonfarm, and 23,048,350 (15.3 per cent) classified as rural farm. Employing the old definition of urban, 38,693,973 (25.7 per cent) are placed in the rural-nonfarm category and 23,076,539 (15.3 per cent) in the rural-farm group.

Population by Size of Place

The numbers and proportions of the population of the United States residing in places of stated sizes as shown by the 1950 census, with comparable data for 1900, are shown in Table IV. In 1950 almost 40 per cent of the people in the United States were residing within the corporate limit of large cities, i. e., those having populations of 100,000 or more. In addition a very large share of the 20,871,908 persons (13.9 per cent of the total) residing in the urban fringes of cities of 50,000 or more also should be included in this category, but it would be difficult or impossible to determine exactly how many. One may reasonably maintain, however, that in 1950 at least 50 per cent of the population of the nation were residents of urban communities having more than 100,000 inhabitants. In 1900 the comparable figure was less than 20 per cent.

The second big mass of the nation's citizens is composed of those who live either on farms, in other portions of the open country, or in unincorporated villages and hamlets of less than 1,000 inhabitants. Almost 30 per cent of the population is in this category. Such a distribution makes it clear that the resident of the large city is the typical American and that the person living on a farm has the second best claim to such a distinction. Those who live in the nation's "Littletowns" and "Middletowns," on the other hand, definitely are in third position in this respect. This point is further emphasized by an examination of the data for the urban places lying outside of the "urbanized areas." Collectively the 3,253 places in this category contained only 27,218,538 inhabitants, or 18.1 per cent of the nation's population. Of this total the proportions corresponding to these smaller urban centers of various sizes are as follows: places of 50,000 or more, 0.8 per cent; places of 25,000 to 50,000, 3.9 per cent; places of 10,000 to 25,000, 5.5 per cent; places of 5,000 to 10,000, 4.1 per cent; and places of 2,500 to 5,000, 3.7 per cent.

Table IV. Numbers and Percentages of the Population of the United States Residing in Places of Stated Size, 1950 and 1900

Size of place	Number of places		Number of inhabitants		Percentage of inhabitants	
	1950 [1]	1900	1950 [1]	1900	1950 [1]	1900
Total	18,548	10,668	150,697,361	75,994,575	100.0	100.0
Urban	4,741	1,737	96,467,686 [2]	30,159,921	64.0 [2]	39.7
1,000,000 or more	5	3	17,404,450	6,429,474	11.5	8.5
100,000–999,999	101	35	26,907,167	7,778,873	17.9	10.3
10,000– 99,999	1,156	402	29,605,049	9,848,215	19.6	12.9
2,500– 9,999	3,022	1,297	14,629,002	6,103,359	9.7	8.0
Under 2,500	457	.....	577,992	....	0.4	....
Rural	13,807	8,931	54,229,675	45,834,654	36.0	60.3
1,000–2,499	4,158	2,128	6,473,315	3,298,054	4.3	4.3
Under 1,000	9,649	6,803	4,031,148	3,003,479	2.7	4.0
Other rural territory [3]	.....	.....	43,725,212	39,553,121	29.0	52.0

SOURCE OF DATA: Compiled and computed from data given in, U. S. Bureau of the Census, *U. S. Census of Population: 1950*, Vol. I, *Number of Inhabitants* (Washington: Government Printing Office, 1952), pp. 6–7.

[1] The "new" urban definition is used.

[2] In 1950 about 5.4 per cent of the population lived in those portions of the urban fringe that were made up of incorporated places of less than 2,500 inhabitants or unincorporated territory.

[3] Unincorporated places of less than 1,000 inhabitants and the open country.

Regional and State Differences

As is well known, within the United States the relative importance of the urban, rural-nonfarm, and rural-farm portions of the population varies tremendously. (See Figure 5.) Whereas in New Jersey 86.6 per cent of the population in 1950 was classified as urban, in New York 85.5 per cent, in Massachusetts 84.4 per cent, and in Rhode Island 84.3 per cent, in North Dakota, Mississippi, Arkansas, and South Dakota less than one third of the inhabitants were placed in the urban category, the exact percentages being 26.6, 27.9, 33.0, and 33.2, respectively. California (80.7 per cent) ranked fifth from the top in percentage urban, and North Carolina (33.7 per cent) fifth from the bottom in this respect. With the exception of Indiana, all of the states from Illinois to Massachusetts were more than two-thirds urban, and Florida and Utah, each with percentages slightly above 65 barely failed to qualify for inclusion in such a category. In general the southeastern states, with the exception of Florida, and the northern plains and mountain states, along with Iowa, make up the most highly rural parts of the nation, whereas the northeastern area, except for the northernmost part of New England, California, and peninsular Florida, constitute the most urbanized sections. (On these points it also is well to consult Figure 1, presented in an earlier chapter to portray the geographic distribution of the population.) The seven most populous states in the nation also are the seven having the largest urban populations, and their rank is exactly the same in each case. Together in 1950 they contained 52 per cent of the urban population. These states and the urban populations of each are as follows: New York, 12,682,446; California, 8,539,420; Pennsylvania, 7,403,036; Illinois, 6,759,271; Ohio, 5,578,274; Texas, 4,838,060; and Michigan, 4,503,084.

As indicated above, the net effect of the change in the definition of urban, introduced in the 1950 census, was to transfer approximately 7.5 million persons, who would have been classified as rural on the basis of the criteria employed in preceding censuses, from the rural-nonfarm to the urban category. Even so, in 1950 the rural-nonfarm group was considerably larger than the rural-farm group, and totaled 31,181,325 or 20.7 per cent of the nation's population. In West Virginia 44.9 per cent of the 1950 population fell in the rural-nonfarm class, and it was most closely rivaled in this respect by Vermont (42.1 per cent), and Maine (35.0 per cent). In none of these states were cities of 50,000 or

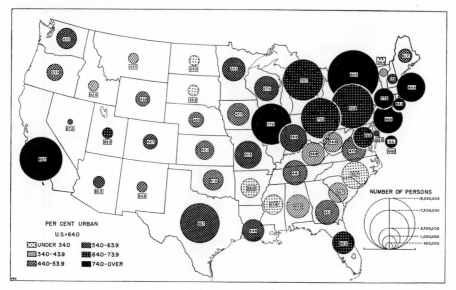

Figure 5. Variations in the proportions of the population classified as urban, by states, 1950.

more inhabitants sufficiently numerous to result in the inclusion in the urban category of large numbers of persons residing in the urban fringes. At the other end of the scale, however, the situation was quite different. The list of the states with the smallest proportions of their populations in the rural-nonfarm category is that of those with populations most highly concentrated in large cities and the areas adjacent to them. Thus, in 1950, the states with the lowest percentages of the population classified as rural-nonfarm were as follows: New York, 10.6; New Jersey, 11.2; Illinois, 13.7; Massachusetts, 13.9; California, 14.0; Rhode Island, 14.4; Missouri, 16.6; Michigan, 18.4; Ohio, 19.1; and Connecticut, 19.2. In this connection it is pertinent to observe that the urban populations were larger and the rural-nonfarm populations smaller in 1950 than they would have been, had it not been for the change in definition, by the following numbers of persons: California, 1,440,254; New York, 793,438; Michigan, 404,077; New Jersey, 338,-436; Ohio, 305,068; Illinois, 272,598; Connecticut, 271,825; and Missouri, 142,566. Other significant changes in the definitions employed were involved insofar as Massachusetts and Rhode Island are concerned, which precludes including them in the comparison. As a matter of fact, in previous censuses the proportions of urban persons in the

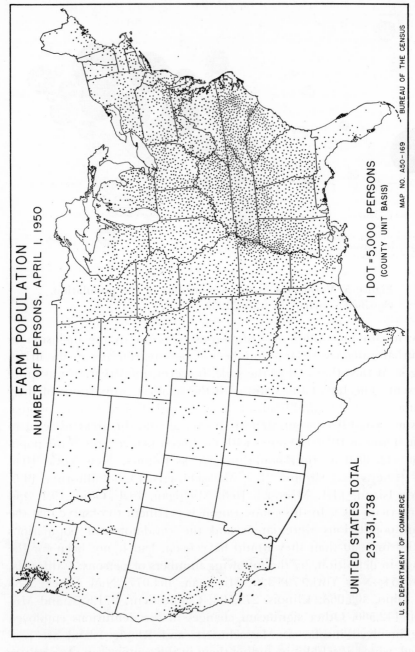

Figure 6. Distribution of the farm population of the United States, 1950.

population of these states had been inflated by census procedures to the extent that each of them had smaller urban populations in 1950 than would have been the case had the old criteria been employed. It seems fair to generalize that the change in definition was effective in getting the portions of the urban population residing on the outskirts of the nation's major centers out of the rural and into the urban category, but that the task of a comparable transfer of those in the fringes of the smaller cities and towns remains to be done. Be that as it may, twelve states taken together accounted for 51 per cent of the rural-nonfarm population of the United States in 1950. These are as follows: Pennsylvania, 2,389,769; Texas, 1,580,867; New York, 1,570,092; Ohio, 1,515,-265; California, 1,478,572; North Carolina, 1,317,268; Illinois, 1,189,-709; Michigan, 1,173,940; Virginia, 1,026,604; Indiana, 909,874; Georgia, 922,696; and West Virginia, 900,143.

In 1950 the rural-farm population of the United States totaled 23,-048,350 and made up 15.5 per cent of the nation's inhabitants. The manner in which they were distributed throughout the country is shown in Figure 6. Note the high concentrations in certain parts of the South, the rather heavy and regular distribution throughout the Midwest, and the sparsity of farm residents in the Great Plains, the Rocky Mountain area, northern New England and New York, and in Florida. The relative importance of the farm population, mapped on a county basis, is given in Figure 7. The percentages are especially high in many sections of the South and in the northern plains. Only in Mississippi, Arkansas, North Dakota, South Dakota, and North Carolina did the rural-farm population make up more than one-third of the inhabitants. Twelve states taken together contained 51 per cent of the 1950 rural-farm population of the nation. They are as follows: North Carolina, 1,376,560; Texas, 1,292,267; Mississippi, 1,097,207; Tennessee 1,016,204; Kentucky, 974,170; Georgia, 962,435; Alabama, 960,493; Missouri, 863,496; Ohio, 853,088; Arkansas, 801,827; Iowa, 782,650; and Illinois, 763,196. Arkansas, Mississippi, North Carolina, and the two Dakotas were the only states in 1950 in which the rural-farm population exceeded the urban.

Trends

From the time the first census was taken in 1790 there has been a strong and uninterrupted tendency for the population of the United States to concentrate in urban districts. (See Figure 8.) In the period

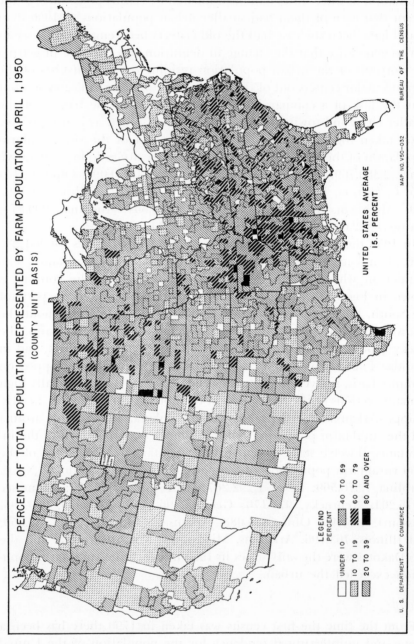

Figure 7. Relative importance of the farm population in the general population, by counties, 1950.

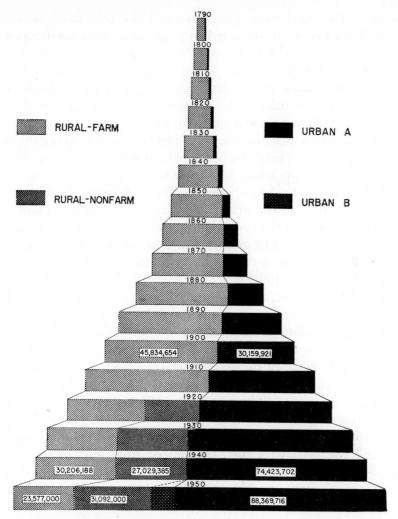

Figure 8. The growth of population in the United States, 1790 to 1950, by residence.

after 1840 this tendency was most pronounced in the decade ending in 1920, during which the rate of population increase in the urban centers was 9.06 times as high as that in the rural portions of the nation. It was least pronounced in the ten-year period that opened with the great economic depression, 1930 to 1940, when the urban population grew at a rate of only 1.23 times that of the rural. The years 1920 to 1930, when the rate of urban population increase was 6.2 times as high as that of the rural, most closely rivaled the preceding intercensal period in the extent to which urban population gains outstripped the rural; whereas the period ending in 1950, in which the urban population increased only 2.47 times as fast as the rural is the second lowest in this respect. These comparisons are, of course, on the basis of the "old" definition of urban, and it should not be forgotten that the period since 1930 was the one in which the tremendous concentrations of population took place in the areas just beyond the corporate limits of towns and cities. This phase of the urbanization process, the one that forced radical modifications in the census concept of urban, is not reflected in the ratios being presented here. Between 1840 and 1850 the rate of increase of the urban population was 3.16 times as high as that of the rural, and the corresponding figures for the other intercensal periods between 1840 and 1950 are as follows: 1850–1860, 2.65; 1860–1870, the period of the Civil War, 4.36; 1880–1890, 4.22; 1890–1900, 2.98; and 1890–1900, 4.37.

There are, of course, tremendous differences among the states with respect to the comparative rates of growth in the urban and rural segments of the population. In order to explore this aspect of the subject, a detailed study was made of the trends over the fifty years between 1900 and 1950. Some of the results deserve presentation here. In this half century, the urban population increased by 220 per cent, and the rural by 18 per cent. (The rural for 1950 includes the 7.5 million persons who were classified as urban on the basis of the "new" definition.) No state had a smaller urban population in 1950 than it had in 1900, and the percentage increases ranged from lows of 60 in New Hampshire, 64 in Massachusetts, 76 in Rhode Island, 81 in Vermont, 115 in Pennsylvania, and 119 in Iowa, to highs of 999 in California, 1,149 in New Mexico, 1,173 in Nevada, 1,595 in Florida, 2,034 in Arizona, and 2,425 in Idaho. On the other hand, eight states (Maine, Vermont, Indiana, Illinois, Iowa, Missouri, Nebraska, and Kansas) had smaller rural populations in 1950 than in 1900. These decreases ranged from 23.1 per cent in Missouri to 4.3 per cent in Maine.

In the nation as a whole, during the half century under consideration, the rate of growth of the urban population was exactly twelve times as high as that of the rural. Similar ratios may be calculated for the forty states that did not lose rural population during the period, and the list of these is topped by those for Georgia (432), Alabama (77), Arkansas (70), Texas (61), Mississippi (41), and Tennessee

(40). Of course all of these southern states had comparatively small urban populations in 1900, but even this should not entirely discount the significance of the rates at which they are urbanizing. Other states in which the differential rate of growth of urban population over the rural greatly outstripped the average for the nation, with the ratios showing the number of times the rate for the former exceeds that for the latter, are as follows: Oklahoma, 37; Kentucky, 26; South Carolina, 24; Virginia, 22; South Dakota, 21; Idaho, 20; Ohio, 18; New Hampshire, 18; Michigan, 17; Louisiana, 16; and New York, 16.

Because the rural population as of 1950 used in the above comparisons include such large numbers of those reclassified as urban in that year, it is well to consider the recent trends in the rural-farm population, a category that was influenced to no very significant extent either by the changes in definition of urban introduced in the 1950 census or by the surge of population into the areas surrounding the corporate limits of urban centers which made such changes essential.

In 1940 the rural-farm population of the United States numbered 30,216,188, men, women, and children, a total corresponding almost exactly to that, 30,157,513, enumerated in 1930. By 1950, however, the number of persons in this category had fallen to 23,076,539, a decrease of 7,139,649 or 23.6 per cent from the figure for 1940. On a relative basis, the rural-farm population fell from 24.6 per cent of the total in 1930 to 23.3 per cent in 1940 and to 15.3 per cent in 1950. Furthermore in every one of the forty-eight states there were fewer persons in the rural-farm category in 1950 than in 1940. One could hardly ask for more convincing data relative to the extent to which the nation is urbanizing from the Atlantic to the Pacific and from Canada to the Gulf of Mexico.

Before closing this chapter, reference should be made to the tremendous rate of population growth in the areas that were classified as rural-nonfarm territory on the basis of the "old" definition of urban. Between 1940 and 1950 this segment of the population increased by 43.2 per cent, in comparison with increases of 14.5 per cent in the total population and 19.5 per cent in the urban population. This tendency has continued since 1950 and the mushrooming of the suburbs surrounding urban centers of all sizes is by far the most important residential change going on as we move well along into the second half of the twentieth century. This makes imperative further drastic revisions in the definitions to be employed in the 1960 and subsequent censuses so that those living in the suburbs of the small cities and towns also will be included in the urban category.

SUGGESTED SUPPLEMENTARY READINGS

Anderson, Walfred A., *The Characteristics of New York State Population.* Cornell University Agricultural Experiment Station, Bulletin No. 925, Ithaca (1958), pp. 26–31.

Bogue, Donald J., *The Population of the United States.* Chicago: The Free Press, 1959, chapters 2–3.

Bogue, Donald J., "The Spread of Cities," *The Journal of the American Economic Association,* XLVI, No. 2 (1956), 284–292.

Landis, Paul H., and Paul K. Hatt, *Population Problems: A Cultural Interpretation* (Second Edition). New York: American Book Company, 1954, chapter 18.

National Resources Committee, *Our Cities: Their Role in the National Economy.* Washington: Government Printing Office, 1937, pp. 1–27.

Phelps, Harold A., and David Henderson, *Population in Its Human Aspects.* New York: Appleton-Century-Crofts, Inc., 1958, part II.

Smith, T. Lynn, "The Emergence of Cities," in Rupert B. Vance and Nicholas J. Demerath (Editors), *The Urban South.* Chapel Hill: University of North Carolina Press, 1954, chapter 2.

Smith, T. Lynn, and Homer L. Hitt, *The People of Louisiana.* Baton Rouge: Louisiana State University Press, 1952, chapter IV.

Schnore, Leo F., "The Growth of Metropolitan Suburbs," *American Sociological Review,* 22, No. 2 (1957), 165–173.

Statistical Office of the United Nations, *Data on Urban and Rural Population in Recent Censuses,* Population Studies, No. 8. Lake Success, New York, 1950.

Statistical Office of the United Nations, *Demographic Yearbook, 1956.* New York: United Nations, 1956, pp. 1–16.

Taeuber, Conrad, and Irene B. Taeuber, *The Changing Population of the United States.* New York: John Wiley & Sons, 1958, chapters 6 and 7.

Truesdell, Leon E., "The Development of the Urban-Rural Classification in the United States: 1874 to 1949," *Current Population Reports,* Series P-23, No. 1 (1949).

Chapter 5

Race, Color, Ethnic Stock,
and Nativity

OF ALL THE FEATURES that distinguish one population from another, or different segments of a given population from one another, the characteristics variously known as race, color, ethnic stock or affiliation, and nativity are among the most obvious. At most times and places throughout the historical period, they also have been the attributes to which people in general have attached the most significance. Perhaps at some future date the reservations which most of those working in the fields of anthropology, psychology, and sociology have with respect to the validity of reputed innate differences in the intelligence and capabilities of the various racial and ethnic subgroups of mankind may gain popular acceptance. If so, possibly many of the causes of tension and turmoil during the twentieth century will be removed; but as these lines are written, as we move well along into the atomic age and man-made satellites are circling the earth, the prospects do not appear bright for any such development in the decades immediately ahead.

Many modern censuses, including that of the United States, use a classification of the population by race (or color) and nativity as one of the primary subdivisions in their tabulations of the data. In the United States, as indicated in the previous chapter, only the rural-urban differentiation takes precedence over this fundamental breakdown. This is sound procedure, for so great are the differences between the cultural backgrounds and the economic status of the native-born and the foreign-born and of the white races and the colored races that considerable differentials in their birth rates, mortality rates, mobility, intelligence quotients, and other social indexes are generated. Usually it is a waste of time to attempt comparisons of any demographic phenomenon in one region with that in another, in rural and urban areas, or of the same population at two different points of time, unless the data are first subdivided according to race (or color) and nativity. This is especially true in countries such as Brazil, Colombia, Peru, and the United States where the various racial groups are unevenly distributed among the regions, where the rural populations contain higher proportions of the colored races than the cities, and where the racial composition of the population is undergoing considerable change. For example, in the United States there is very little value in the comparison of a southern state, such as South Carolina, with a northern one, such as Wisconsin, unless the comparisons are made separately for the white and Negro populations with each further subdivided according to rural or urban residence. To do otherwise is likely to demonstrate nothing more than that the former is the home of large numbers of rural Negroes, a fact that is well known and which may be demonstrated very simply.

Concepts and Classifications

The 1950 census of the United States employed the dichotomy of white and nonwhite as a basis for all further subdivisions having to do with race, color, ethnic stock, and nativity. Tables for the larger geographic divisions given in the summary reports use, chiefly, the four categories of native white, foreign-born white, Negro, and other races in these classifications, but in some of the tables the materials for other races are further subdivided into those for Indians, Japanese, Chinese, and all other, respectively. In the cross-tabulations of such data with those for residence, age, employment status, and other characteristics, however, the division almost invariably is merely according to color (white and nonwhite). Similarly in the reports for the various states, the color dichotomy is most generally employed in furnishing the detailed statistics for counties and other units, although some separate tables give information for Indians, Japanese, and Chinese in selected counties and cities. Special reports were issued to give more detail about the "Nativity and Parentage" and the "Nonwhite Population by Race." For earlier censuses the general reports contain a wealth of detail relating to the countries of birth of the foreign-born white population, but for 1950 materials on this subject one must go to a special report.[1]

[1] U. S. Bureau of the Census, *U. S. Census of Population: 1950*, Vol. IV, *Special Reports*, 3A, "Nativity and Parentage" (Washington: Government Printing Office, 1954).

As in the case of the rural and urban definitions, it is essential to emphasize that the racial classifications employed by the modern census do not correspond with those developed by the scientists most concerned with the subject. For example, many of the persons classified as Negro for census purposes possess few of the physiological features that would be used by the zoologist or the anthropologist to distinguish Negroids from the other principal racial divisions of mankind. Strictly speaking, social and legal criteria are the ones employed. In the words employed in the census reports themselves:

The concept of race as it has been used by the Bureau of the Census is derived from that which is commonly accepted by the general public as reflected in the action of legislative and judicial bodies of the country. It does not, therefore, reflect clear-cut definitions of biological stock, and several categories obviously refer to nationalities. Although it lacks scientific precision, it is doubtful whether efforts toward a more scientifically acceptable definition would be appreciably productive, given the conditions under which census enumerations are carried out.[1]

Relative to those placed in the Negro category, the report states:

In addition to full-blooded Negroes, this classification also includes persons of mixed white and Negro parentage and persons of mixed Indian and Negro parentage unless the Indian blood very definitely predominates or unless the individual is accepted in the community as an Indian.[2]

It should be stressed, however, that the more precise definitions of race, those based upon three or more physical characteristics such as color, height, and the cephalic index, hardly would be practicable for census purposes.

The division of the white population according to nativity into the native-born and the foreign-born categories is another of the threads that runs through a considerable part of the tabulations prepared in connection with the census of population in the United States. These concepts, though, are too self-evident to require definition. Similar classifications are employed in the census reports in many other countries. In several U. S. censuses, and particularly those for 1930 and earlier, the division of the native white population into persons of native

---

[1] U. S. Bureau of the Census, *U. S. Census of Population: 1950,* Vol. II, *Characteristics of the Population* (Washington: Government Printing Office, 1952), p. x.

[2] *Ibid.,* p. x.

parentage and those of foreign or mixed parentage occupied a prominent place, but as the foreign-born stocks have decreased in importance this feature since has been relegated to a position of minor importance.

Ethnic stocks or affiliations are terms applied to groups of mankind discriminated on the basis of common customs and characteristics. When one refers to an ethnic group all connotations of physiological uniformities are not necessarily ruled out, but certainly they occupy a position of secondary importance to those such zoological features have when the concept of race is employed. As will be indicated below, in some countries considerable use is made of ethnic classifications of the population. Yugoslavia is a case in point, with the population classified into categories such as Serbs, Croats, and Slovenes, in addition to those, such as Hungarians, Czechs, Poles, and so forth, which indicate cultural and nationality affiliations with other large groups not mainly resident within Yugoslavia itself. In the United States comparatively little has been done, in connection with the census, to secure demographic data separately for such important ethnic groups as the Pennsylvania Dutch, the Louisiana French, or the Spanish-American people of the Southwest. In 1940 and 1950, however, special reports did supply information about the languages spoken in the home and mother tongue which are of some value for one interested in ethnic stocks, and for 1950 a special report was published giving considerable detail about persons of Spanish surname.[1]

International Comparisons

Anything resembling a definitive classification of the world's population, country by country, according to race or ethnic affiliations is still to be done. Known in a general way is the fact that the bulk of the population in China, Japan, and some of the neighboring countries belong to the Mongoloid or yellow varieties of mankind, that Europe is peopled mainly by those of the Caucasoid or white races, that the population of India is the result of a blending over a long period of various white and colored races, that Africa and Australia originally were the homes of Negroid or black peoples, and that the Americas were occupied at the time of Columbus' discovery by various copper-colored

---

[1] U. S. Bureau of the Census, *U. S. Census of Population: 1950*, Vol. IV, *Special Reports*, C, "Persons of Spanish Surname" (Washington: Government Printing Office, 1953).

stocks whom he designated as Indians and who commonly are referred to as redmen. Known also is the fact that persons of European stocks supplanted the natives in many parts of the New World, including Canada, the United States, Costa Rica, Argentina, and Uruguay, and that they came to dominate politically and economically, if not numerically, most other sections of the Americas. Known, finally, is something of the extent to which the Europeans, in the dominant roles they occupied in world affairs from the sixteenth to the twentieth centuries, transplanted the Negroes from Africa to various parts of the New World, persons from India to South Africa and Trinidad, and workers of various colors and hues from many sections of the world to plantation areas in the West Indies, Hawaii, and elsewhere. But anything resembling a summary statement of the racial or ethnic composition of the world's population is still to be developed.

Not until the eighth issue of the *Demographic Yearbook* [1] did those responsible for the collection and collation of international demographic statistics turn their attention to racial and ethnic classifications employed in the various countries of the world; and the results they then were able to assemble reveal how much is still lacking in this respect. A brief summary of the types of data secured and published in this invaluable compendium should serve to establish the present status of attempts in this field.

Not surprising, perhaps, is the extent to which the censuses in various parts of Africa have supplied information relating to the racial and ethnic composition of the population. In Angola, Mozambique, and Portuguese Guinea, the Portuguese in 1950 employed a classification of the population into two principal categories, indigenous and non-indigenous. The former then was subdivided into two groups, Negro and mixed; and the latter into white, Negro, mixed, and other.

In the parts of Africa which were in colonial status under the British crown at the time of the latest censuses a variety of classifications was used. In the Gold Coast (1948), the groups distinguished were labeled as follows: African, British, Lebanese-Syrian, European, United States, and other. In Kenya (1948) and in Uganda (1948) the following categories were employed: African, Indian (East), European, Arab, Goan, coloured, and other. In Mauritius (1952) the ethnic or racial groupings employed are: Indo-Mauritian (Hindus, Mohammedan, Christian),

[1] New York: United Nations, 1957.

general (settlers of European descent and native-born of mixed origin), and Chinese. In the Federation of Rhodesia and Nyasaland (1950) and Southern Rhodesia (1948), the censuses distinguished the indigenous (Bantu) population from the nonindigenous, and then subdivided the latter into European, Asiatic, and coloured.

The census of the Union of South Africa (1951) classified the population as Bantu, white, coloured (persons not of pure European, Bantu, or Asiatic stocks), and Asiatic.

In addition to those just listed a classification of the population of the former Spanish Zone of Morocco (1950) also is available. In this the total was first divided into Semites and Aryans, and then the former was subdivided into Berbers, Arabs, and Jews, and the latter into Spaniards and others.

For America, too, those preparing the *Yearbook* were able to secure some kind of an ethnic or racial classification of the population for a number of the countries. In addition to the United States, where the fundamental division of the population into white and nonwhite categories, with the latter subdivided into Negro and other-races subgroups, has already been mentioned, some materials were secured for Canada, Costa Rica, Cuba, the Dominican Republic, Guatemala, Honduras, Trinidad and Tobago, Bolivia, and Brazil. In Canada (1951) the basic division is into thirty-four ethnic groups identified by the language spoken by the paternal ancestor on first arrival on the North American continent. Along with French, English, Scottish, Irish, German, Ukrainian, Netherlands, Polish, Jewish, American Indian, and Italian, and various others, groups designated as Negro and Eskimo appear in the list. The Costa Rican census of 1950 classified the population according to color as white, Negro, Indian, yellow, and others. That of the Dominican Republic (1950) used white, Negro, mulatto, and yellow as the designations for the four groups into which its population was divided; and that of Honduras (1945) divided the inhabitants into categories designated as white, black, Indian, mixed, and yellow. Guatemala census officials in 1950 used Indian and *Ladino* as the designations for the two racial or ethnic classes into which the population was separated. The *Ladino* group included all who, on the basis of socio-economic criteria, were not considered as Indians. In the British colonies of Trinidad and Tobago (1946) the population was classified as black, Indian, mixed (coloured), white, Chinese, Syrian, and unknown. The Bolivian census (1950) distinguished only two racial or ethnic components, namely, indigenous and nonindigenous; and that of Brazil (1950) classified the population on the basis of color as white, black, yellow, and *pardo* (brown, i. e., mixed). The latter includes substantial numbers of mulattoes and of mestizos.

For all of Asia the issue of the *Demographic Yearbook* referred to above includes racial or ethnic classifications for only seven major political entities, and three of these were British dependencies at the time the enumerations involved were made. In the Federation of Malaya (1947) the population was classified as Malayan, Chinese, Indian, Eurasian, European, and other; in Sarawak (1947) as Sea Dyak, Chinese, Malayan, Land Dyak, Melanau (indigenous), European, and other; and in Singapore (1947) as Chinese, Malayan, Indian, European, and Eurasian. Burma's census of 1953 distinguished the principal ethnic or racial groups in the country as Burmese, Indian, Chinese, Karen, Shan, Chin, Kachin, European, Kayak, and other; and that of Ceylon (1953) used the following categories: Low Country Shinalese, Kandyan, Indian, Ceylon Tamil, Ceylon Moor, Burgher, Malayan, Europeans, Pakistini, and others. The census of the Philippines (1948) classified the population as brown, yellow, mixed, black, white, or unknown; and that of Thailand (1947) used Thai, Chinese, Annamese, Indian, Malayan, Burmese, Javanese, Cambodian, British, American, French, and other as the designations for the ethnic or racial categories it distinguished.

Most European countries, of course, are inhabited almost exclusively by those who belong to the Caucasoid races, so it is not strange that few of their censuses include racial or ethnic classifications in the tabulations. Only the Vatican and Yugoslavia figure in the compilations under discussion in these paragraphs. The census of the Vatican (1948) classified the population as white or black, and that for Yugoslavia (1953) employed the following categories: Serb, Croat, Slovene, undetermined Yugoslav, Macedonian, Squiptar, Hungarian, Montenegrin, Turk, Slovak, Romany, German, Romanian, Bulgarian, Wallach, Czech, Italian, Ruthenian, Russian, Pole, Austrian, Jew, Greek, other, and unknown.

In Oceania only Australia and New Zealand figure in the list of countries included in the United Nations' compilation from which the information in these paragraphs was taken. In Australia (1947) the population was classified as European, half caste, full-blooded non-European, and aborigine; and in New Zealand (1951) the racial or ethnic categories used included European, Maori, European-Maori, Chinese, Polynesian, Indian, Cook Island Maori, Lebanese, Syrian, Melanesian, Negro, Burmese, West Indian, Arab, Micronesian, Japanese and nine others.

For all of the countries and groups or categories mentioned above, some recent statistical information is available. However, for many of the more thickly populated parts of the world the data are completely lacking; and there is little comparability in the approach, criteria, or classifications for the countries and territories that it was possible to include. Distinctions comparable to those made by some of the countries would be legion if they were attempted for such countries as China, India, or Russia; and even within small countries such as Belgium, Switzerland, or Czechosolvakia, several fairly distinct ethnic groups are to be found. It is to be hoped that those in charge of making the compilations for the *Demographic Yearbook* will continue their efforts to assemble and present comprehensive international statistics on race, nativity, and ethnic affiliations.

Color, Race, and Nativity of the Population of the United States

The tabulations of the United States Census are so planned that it is possible to determine in great detail the color or racial composition and the nativity of the population. The most recent count, that for 1950, showed a white population of 134,942,028 and a nonwhite population of 15,755,333; or 89.5 per cent of the inhabitants were classified as white and 10.5 per cent as nonwhite. In 1940 the corresponding percentages were 89.8 and 10.2, respectively. Of the whites in 1950, a total of 124,780,860 fell in the native-white category and 10,161,168 in the foreign-born group; and of the nonwhites, 15,042,286 were classified as Negroes and 713,047 as belonging to other races. The latter in turn were subdivided as follows: Indian, 343,410; Japanese, 141,768; Chinese, 117,629; and all other, 110,240. On the relative basis 82.8 per cent of the total population were classified as native white, 6.7 per cent as foreign-born white, 10.0 per cent as Negro; and 0.5 per cent as belonging to other races.

Data showing the country of birth of the foreign-born white population are available, and these have been assembled in Table V. Notable is the large number of countries that have sent sizeable contingents of immigrants to the United States, even though in 1950 those born in Italy alone made up almost one-seventh of the foreign-born population.

Of those born outside the United States, as indicated by this latest census, slightly over one-half came from five countries, or from Italy, Canada, Germany, the U.S.S.R., and Poland. Even greater were the numbers, proportions, and heterogeneity of the foreign-born population in 1930, the materials for which were selected for more intensive analysis below.

Rural-Urban Differences

It has long been known that the "foreign" elements in a given population tend to concentrate in the cities whereas the "native" elements constitute relatively high proportions of the people of the rural areas.[1] The validity of this principle is illustrated excellently with data from the most recent census of population in the United States, although the materials from each of the earlier enumerations likewise might be used for this purpose. In 1950 in the country as a whole only 2.5 per cent of the rural-farm and 3.6 per cent of the rural-nonfarm population were foreign-born whereas 8.7 per cent of the urban population had been born in another country. If each residential category had contained precisely the same proportion of the foreign born as it did of the general population, it might be said to have had exactly its pro rata share of those born outside the United States. As it was, however, the percentages just given indicate that in 1950 the rural-farm population contained only 36 per cent, the rural-nonfarm population 54 per cent, and the urban population 132 per cent of their pro rata shares of the nation's foreign-born inhabitants. On the other hand, the same year the native-white population made up 81.1 per cent of the urban, 87.7 per cent of the rural-nonfarm, and 87.7 per cent of the rural-farm population, and the indexes of the extent to which each of these residential categories contained more or less than its pro rata share of this nativity group are 98, 106, and 101, respectively. The differences between the rural-nonfarm and the rural-farm populations in this respect merely reflect the extent to which the other large group of the native-born, the Negroes, are concentrated on the farms. A regional difference also is involved since the farms on which the large numbers of Negroes are found are located in the South, whereas the rural-nonfarm areas

[1] Cf. Pitirim A. Sorokin and Carle C. Zimmerman, *Principles of Rural-Urban Sociology* (New York: Henry Holt & Company, Inc., 1929), pp. 23, 108–109; and T. Lynn Smith, *The Sociology of Rural Life* (Third Edition), (New York: Harper & Brothers, 1953), pp. 69–76.

Table V. Country of Birth of the Foreign-born White Population of the United States, 1950

Country of birth	Number	Per cent
All countries	10,161,168	100.0
Italy	1,427,145	14.0
Canada	994,562 [1]	9.7
Germany	984,331	9.7
U.S.S.R.	894,884	8.8
Poland	861,184	8.5
England and Wales	584,615	5.8
Ireland (Eire)	504,961	5.0
Mexico	450,562	4.4
Austria	408,785	4.0
Sweden	324,944	3.2
Czechoslovakia	278,268	2.7
Hungary	268,022	2.6
Scotland	244,200	2.4
Norway	202,294	2.0
Greece	169,083	1.7
Lithuania	147,765	1.5
Yugoslavia	143,956	1.4
France	107,924	1.1
Denmark	107,897	1.1
Netherlands	102,133	1.0
Finland	95,506	0.9
Romania	84,952	0.8
Switzerland	71,515	0.7
Portugal	54,337	0.5
Belgium	52,891	0.5
Spain	45,565	0.4
Northern Ireland	15,398	0.2
Other Europe	86,375	0.9
Other America	120,297	1.2
Asia	180,024	1.8
All other	69,568	0.7
Not reported	77,175	0.8

SOURCE OF DATA: U. S. Bureau of the Census, *U. S. Census of Population: 1950*, Vol. II, *Characteristics of the Population* (Washington: Government Printing Office, 1952), Table 49, p. 98.

[1] 238,409 classified as from "French Canada" and 756,153 from "Other Canada."

which contain high proportions of the native whites are spread throughout the entire nation.

The data for the Negro portion of the native-born population are especially interesting. To a far greater extent than is true of the native-white population, the Negroes are the descendants of persons who have been in the United States for more than a century and a half. Prior to the outbreak of the first world war they were largely concentrated in the rural sections of the nation's most rural region. As is indicated below, the labor shortage accompanying that war resulted in a mass transfer of Negro workers to northern cities, and the one produced by the second world war and its aftermath brought about their exodus in large numbers from the South to the cities of the Pacific Coast. For these reasons there is considerable validity in thinking of the Negro as a native element in the South and as a recent comer in other sections of the country. With this point in mind, it is not strange to find that the proportions of Negroes in the nation's urban, rural-nonfarm, and rural-farm populations are 9.7 per cent, 8.0 per cent, and 13.7 per cent, respectively. Since exactly 10.0 per cent of the nation's population in 1950 was classified as Negro, this is to say that the urban population contained 97 per cent, the rural-nonfarm population 80 per cent, and the rural-farm population 137 per cent of their pro rata shares of the members of this racial group. For the South, as defined by the Bureau of the Census, however, only 47.8 per cent of the Negroes were classified as urban, whereas for the remainder of the United States the corresponding percentage is 93.4. On the other hand, in the South 21.9 per cent of the Negroes fell in the rural-nonfarm and 30.1 per cent in the rural-farm category, in comparison with corresponding percentages of 5.3 and 1.3, respectively, in the rest of the nation. Expressed as the extent to which each of these residential groups contained more or less than its pro rata share of the area's Negro population, the indexes for the southern region are as follows: urban, 98; rural-nonfarm, 84; and rural-farm, 120. For all other sections of the country taken together the comparable indexes are: urban, 131; rural-nonfarm, 29; and rural-farm, 12.

The Geographic Distribution of the Race and Nativity Groups

The materials already presented make it evident that there are vast differences in the manner in which the various race and nativity groups are distributed throughout the United States, but the subject deserves a much more complete treatment. The data showing the proportions that the native whites, foreign-born whites, Negroes, and the members of other races constitute of the populations of the forty-eight states and the District of Columbia have been assembled in Table VI. A few other of the most pertinent facts are presented as called for in the discussion that follows.

Because the foreign-born are highly concentrated in urban areas, a

Table VI. Proportions of Native Whites, Foreign-born Whites, Negroes, and Other Races in Each State, 1950

| | Percentage of the population classified as: | | | |
Division and state	Native white	Foreign-born white	Negro	Other races
United States	82.8	6.7	10.0	0.5
New England				
Maine	91.5	8.1	0.1	0.2
New Hampshire	88.9	10.9	0.1	0.1
Vermont	92.2	7.6	0.1	. . .
Massachusetts	83.1	15.2	1.6	0.1
Rhode Island	83.8	14.3	1.8	0.1
Connecticut	82.4	14.8	2.6	0.1
Middle Atlantic				
New York	76.7	16.8	6.2	0.3
New Jersey	80.3	13.0	6.6	0.1
Pennsylvania	86.5	7.4	6.1	. . .
East North Central				
Ohio	87.9	5.6	6.5	. . .
Indiana	93.0	2.5	4.4	. . .
Illinois	83.4	9.0	7.4	0.2
Michigan	83.4	9.5	6.9	0.2
Wisconsin	92.4	6.4	0.8	0.4
West North Central				
Minnesota	92.0	7.0	0.5	0.5
Iowa	96.0	3.2	0.7	0.1
Missouri	90.1	2.3	7.5	. . .
North Dakota	90.3	7.9	. . .	1.8
South Dakota	91.6	4.7	0.1	3.6
Nebraska	93.9	4.3	1.4	0.4
Kansas	94.0	2.0	3.8	0.2

Table VI. Proportions of Native Whites, Foreign-born Whites, Negroes and Other Races in Each State (Continued)

| | Percentage of the population classified as: | | | |
Division and state	Native white	Foreign-born white	Negro	Other races
South Atlantic				
Delaware	81.7	4.4	13.7	0.2
Maryland	79.8	3.6	16.5	0.1
District of Columbia	59.6	4.9	35.0	0.4
Virginia	76.7	1.1	22.1	0.1
West Virginia	92.5	1.7	5.7	...
North Carolina	73.0	0.4	25.8	0.8
South Carolina	60.7	0.4	38.8	0.1
Georgia	68.6	0.5	30.9	...
Florida	73.7	4.4	21.7	0.1
East South Central				
Kentucky	92.6	0.5	6.9	...
Tennessee	83.4	0.5	16.1	...
Alabama	67.5	0.4	32.0	0.1
Mississippi	54.2	0.4	45.3	0.1
West South Central				
Arkansas	77.1	0.5	22.3	0.1
Louisiana	65.9	1.1	32.9	0.1
Oklahoma	90.2	0.8	6.5	2.5
Texas	83.6	3.6	12.7	0.1
Mountain				
Montana	89.5	7.3	0.2	3.0
Idaho	95.5	3.3	0.2	1.0
Wyoming	93.2	4.6	0.9	1.3
Colorado	93.4	4.5	1.5	0.6
New Mexico	90.0	2.5	1.2	6.3
Arizona	81.2	6.1	3.5	9.2
Utah	93.9	4.3	0.4	1.3
Nevada	87.0	6.6	2.7	3.7
Pacific				
Washington	89.3	8.0	1.3	1.3
Oregon	92.9	5.5	0.8	0.8
California	84.4	9.3	4.4	1.9

SOURCE OF DATA: U. S. Bureau of the Census, *U. S. Census of Population: 1950*, Vol. II, *Characteristics of the Population* (Washington: Government Printing Office, 1952), Table 59, p. 106.

. . . Less than 0.1 per cent.

few of the states containing the nation's major cities also contain the majority of the country's foreign-born population. To be specific, in 1950 the state of New York alone contained 2,500,429, or 24.6 per cent of the total foreign-born population of the United States. This aggregate was larger than that for the twenty-seven states and the District of Columbia which the Bureau of the Census places in the South and the West, even though one of them, California, counted almost 1 million of the foreign-born among its inhabitants. Taken together, New York, California (985,333), Illinois (783,277), and Pennsylvania (776,609) contained almost 50 per cent of the nation's foreign-born population, and if the total (713,699) for the fifth-ranking state, Massachusetts, is included, the proportion is swelled to 57 per cent. If, however, as may be noted from Table VI, the relative importance of the foreign-born in the population is considered, then the five ranking states, in the order named, are New York, Massachusetts, Connecticut, Rhode Island, and New Jersey. They have 251, 227, 221, 213, and 194 per cent, respectively, of their pro rata shares of the nation's foreign-born population. Comparable indexes for the ten largest cities are as follows: New York, 337; Chicago, 216; Philadelphia, 167; Los Angeles, 187; Detroit, 222; Baltimore, 81; Cleveland, 216; St. Louis, 73; Washington, 73; and Boston, 268.

Continuing this analysis, it is interesting to note some of the other significant variations in the distribution of the foreign-born population among the nation's major cities. As suggested by the low indexes for Washington, St. Louis, and Baltimore, the sources from which the various cities have recruited their populations differ radically from one part of the country to another. In general the cities in the South have grown by attracting migrants from the rural areas surrounding them, whereas the industrial centers and great ports in the Northeast have received many immigrants from European countries. On this point, the tabulations showing the proportions of the foreign-born in the 106 cities of 100,000 inhabitants or more deserve careful study. The general rule is for cities located in the census South to have lower proportions, and those outside the region to have higher proportions of the foreign-born than is true for the nation as a whole. As a matter of fact, in the entire South only Baltimore, El Paso, Miami, San Antonio, Tampa, Washington, and Wilmington contain proportions of the foreign-born that are above the national average of 6.7 per cent; and outside the South only Cincinnati, Columbus, Dayton, Denver, Des Moines, Evanston, Fort Wayne, Indianapolis, Kansas City (Kansas), Kansas City (Missouri), Long Beach, Peoria, Reading, St. Louis, and Toledo have proportions below the national mean. New York is most closely rivaled in proportion of foreign born in the population by New Bedford (21.8 per cent) and Hartford (18.3 per cent). The lowest proportion of all is that of 0.6 per cent in Knoxville; and Chattanooga, Evansville, Montgomery, and Nashville rank next, each with 0.8 per cent.

An examination of Table VI also makes apparent the tremendous variations found throughout the United States in the relative importance of Negroes in the population. In Mississippi over 45 per cent of the inhabitants are Negroes, in South Carolina almost 40 per cent, and in the District of Columbia 35 per cent. In Louisiana, Alabama, and Georgia approximately one out of every three persons is a Negro. On the other hand, in North Dakota less than 0.1 per cent of the population at the time of the 1950 census was classified as Negro, and in Maine, New Hampshire, Vermont, and South Dakota the proportion was only 0.1 per cent. In absolute numbers Georgia with 1,062,762 persons so classified had the largest Negro population, followed closely in this respect by North Carolina (1,047,353), Mississippi (986,494), Alabama (979,617), and Texas (977,458). Then follow New York (918,191), Louisiana (882,428), and South Carolina (822,077). Together these eight states had, in 1950, 51 per cent of the Negroes in the United States.

Within the states, too, the proportions of Negroes in the population vary tremendously from one county or minor civil division to another, and within a city the tendency is for the Negro population to be concentrated largely in a few well-defined areas. Both in rural and urban areas the practice is rather general of designating as a "black belt" the districts in which Negroes constitute the large majority of the population. Most noted of the urban sections inhabited almost exclusively by Negroes are a large portion of southside Chicago [1] and Harlem, a part of Manhattan borough in New York City. The great rural "black belts" are those portions of the "old South" in which early in the nineteenth century the most fertile lands were monopolized by large proprietors and the plantation system of agriculture was established to produce cotton, sugar cane, and rice. Slave labor was utilized almost exclusively in the monoculture of these large, highly commercialized estates, so that Negroes greatly outnumbered whites in the counties where the southern

[1] For a thoroughgoing study of this section, see, St. Clair Drake and Horace M. Cayton, *Black Metropolis* (New York: Harcourt, Brace & Company, 1945).

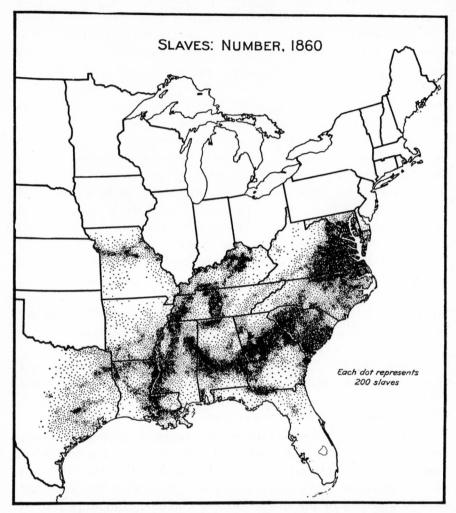

Figure 9. Distribution of slaves in the United States, 1860. (Illustration from the U. S. Bureau of Agricultural Economics)

gentry established their dominions. As evidenced by the distribution of slaves in 1860 (see Figure 9), on the eve of the Civil War, the three principal "black belts" in the United States were (1) that extending along both sides of the Mississippi River, in the rich deltas of the Mississippi and Yazoo valleys, from Tennessee to the "sugar bowl" in Louisiana; (2) a large crescent-shaped area extending from northeastern

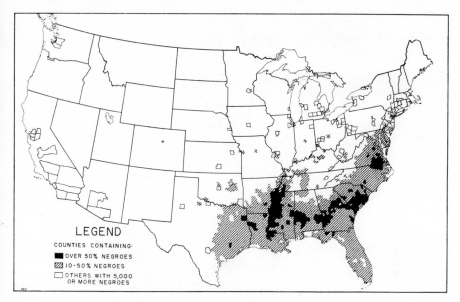

Figure 10. Relative importance of Negroes in the population, by counties, 1950.

Mississippi, through the central portions of Alabama and Georgia, and overspreading most of South Carolina; and (3) tidewater Virginia and the adjacent parts of North Carolina. In 1950, as delineated on the basis of the counties in which 50 per cent or more of the inhabitants were Negroes, the major "black belts" are the first two of the three just mentioned.

But even the county is a relatively large and heterogeneous area, and for many purposes even greater detail with respect to the distribution of the Negro population is desired. For example, the narrow flood plain of the Red River in Louisiana, famed as the setting for Harriet Beecher Stowe's *Uncle Tom's Cabin,* an area in which the close association between the best of the land, the plantation system, and a high proportion of Negroes in the population has persisted for more than 150 years, hardly is distinguishable in Figures 9 and 10, both of which were prepared on a county-unit basis. If, however, the smaller and more homogeneous minor civil divisions are employed in the delineations (see Figure 11), the association is immediately evident to all who are familiar with the state, its topography, and its principal type-of-farming areas. In sharp contrast, in 1940, as also was the case in 1840, the poor-

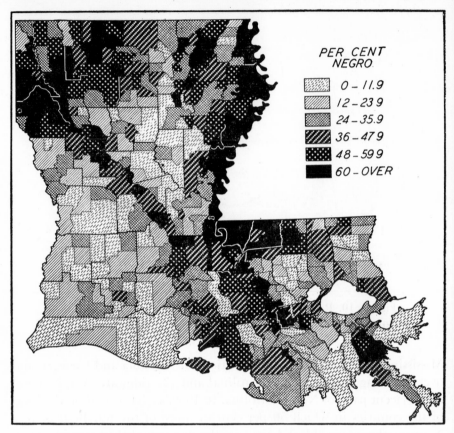

Figure 11. Relative importance of Negroes in the population of Louisiana, by wards, 1940. (Reproduced from J. Allan Beegle and T. Lynn Smith, "Differential Fertility in Louisiana," Louisiana Agricultural Experiment Station Bulletin No. 403, Baton Rouge, 1946, p. 13)

est, sandy, piney-woods sections of Louisiana were practically devoid of Negro inhabitants.[1]

More than 52 per cent of those classified in the other races category resided, at the time of the 1950 census, in the states of California, Ari-

[1] One interested in more of the details about the association between good land, the plantation system, and the Negro, will find them in T. Lynn Smith, *The Population of Louisiana: Its Composition and Changes*, Bulletin No. 293 (Baton Rouge: Louisiana Agricultural Experiment Station, 1937), pp. 8–14; and T. Lynn Smith and Homer L. Hitt, *The People of Louisana* (Baton Rouge: Louisiana State University Press, 1952), pp. 38–46.

zona, Oklahoma, and New York, almost 28 per cent of them in California alone. Of this heterogeneous group, the largest contingents of American Indians lived in the states of Arizona (65,761), Oklahoma (53,769), New Mexico (41,901), and South Dakota (23,344). The total of these numbers is equal to 54 per cent of all the Indians in the United States. Most of the Japanese (84,956 or 60 per cent) were in California, with Illinois (11,646) having the second largest number. California also had the largest number of Chinese (58,324), with New York second (20,171). Together these two states contained two-thirds of all persons so classified in the United States.

States in which the native-white population made up more than 90 per cent of the population are twenty in number, and include Maine and Vermont in New England, West Virginia from the South Atlantic group, Kentucky from the East South Central Division, Indiana and Wisconsin in the East North Central States, all of the West North Central States and Oklahoma which bounds them on the south, all of the Mountain States except Montana, Arizona and Nevada, and Oregon in the Pacific group. This subject is better explored, however, with data from the 1940 census in which the materials for the native-white population were divided into those for the native whites of native parentage and those for native whites of foreign or mixed parentage. To facilitate their study in relation to the geographical distribution of the various race and nativity groupings, Figure 12 was prepared. A study of this illustration serves to emphasize the extent to which the native whites of native parentage predominated in most of the states that have just been enumerated.

In order to show more clearly the portions of the United States in which the immigrants from the various countries and their descendants have made their greatest contributions to our civilization, a series of detailed maps showing the geographic distribution of the principal groups was constructed. The materials used in the preparation of this series are those from the 1930 census, since that was the census year in which the foreign-born population was at its maximum (13,983,405) and that was the census in which the relevant tabulations were prepared in the greatest detail. Comments on each of these maps are limited to the barest essentials.

The 1,790,429 persons born in Italy and enumerated in the 1930 census of the United States were highly concentrated in a few great urban industrial centers. (See Figure 13.) More than any of the other

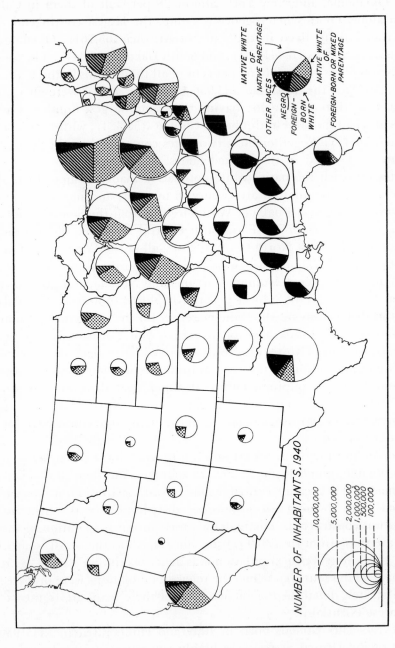

NUMBER OF INHABITANTS, 1940

NATIVE WHITE OF NATIVE PARENTAGE

OTHER RACES

NEGRO

FOREIGN-BORN WHITE

NATIVE WHITE OF FOREIGN-BORN OR MIXED PARENTAGE

10,000,000
5,000,000
2,000,000
1,000,000
500,000
100,000

Figure 12. Distribution of the population of the United States, by race and nativity, 1940.

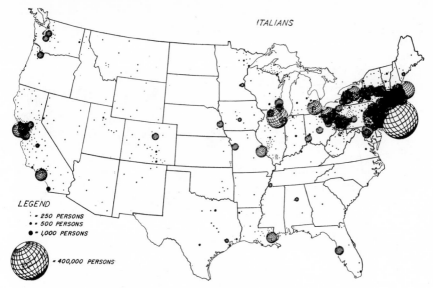

Figure 13. Distribution of immigrants from Italy, 1930.

of the nationality groups, they had settled in New York City and closely adjacent parts of the Northeast.

The 1,608,814 immigrants from Germany, on the other hand, ranked with those from England in the extent to which they were disseminated throughout the length and breadth of the land. (See Figure 14.) There was, to be sure, one very large aggregation in New York City and another in Chicago, but other major cities also had large contingents. In addition those born in Germany were widespread throughout the rural sections of the northern, midwestern, and northwestern states.

Of the large influx of persons who had been born across the border in Canada, the 370,852 classed as French-Canadians were found for the most part in the New England states, and the 915,537 others were widespread throughout the northern half of the national territory and on the Pacific Coast. (See Figures 15 and 16.)

In 1930 the number of persons enumerated as born in Poland totaled 1,268,583. (See Figure 17.) They were highly concentrated east of the Mississippi and north of the Ohio, and especially in New York City, Chicago, and Detroit.

New York City alone contained almost 40 per cent of the 1,153,628 persons born in Russia who figured in the 1930 census. (See Figure 18.)

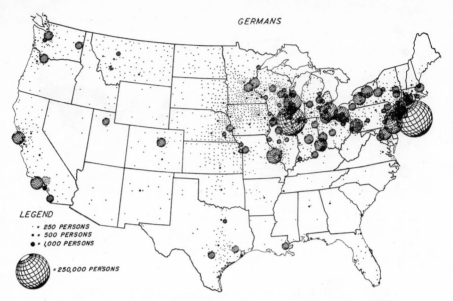

Figure 14. Distribution of immigrants from Germany, 1930.

Figure 15. Distribution of French-Canadian immigrants, 1930.

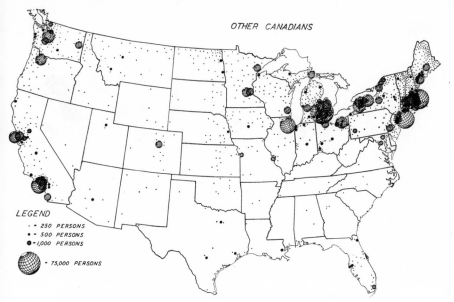

Figure 16. Distribution of other immigrants from Canada, 1930.

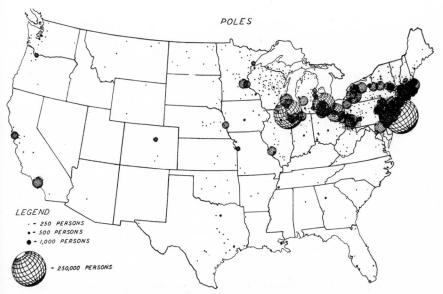

Figure 17. Distribution of immigrants from Poland, 1930.

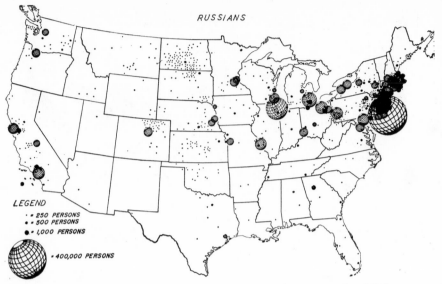

RUSSIANS

LEGEND
· ▪ 250 PERSONS
▪ ▪ 500 PERSONS
● ▪ 1,000 PERSONS

◉ ▪ 400,000 PERSONS

Figure 18. Distribution of immigrants from Russia, 1930.

Undoubtedly, large numbers of those of the Jewish faith are included in this total.

Persons born in the United Kingdom were 1,224,091 in number, according to the 1930 census, and of them 809,563 were reported as born in England, 354,323 in Scotland, and 60,205 in Wales. (See Figures 19, 20, and 21.) The English were widely spread throughout the United States, the Scots likewise, and the mining districts of Pennsylvania and Ohio seem to have attracted considerable portions of the Welsh who got beyond New York.

As shown by the 1930 inventory, the three Scandinavian countries had supplied 1,122,576 of the immigrants who were counted in the census of that year. Of these, 595,250 were reported as born in Sweden, 347,852 in Norway, and 179,474 in Denmark. (See Figures 22, 23, and 24.) The concentration of these groups in Minnesota and other northwestern states is proverbial, and this is largely borne out by the facts, especially with reference to the Swedes and the Norwegians. Persons born in all three of these countries early found their way in considerable numbers to the states on the Pacific Coast.

The survivors of the tremendous immigration of persons from Ireland that got underway about the middle of the nineteenth century totaled 923,642 at the time of the 1930 census, of whom 744,810 were

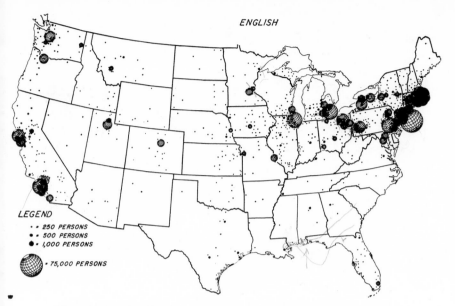

Figure 19. Distribution of immigrants from England, 1930.

Figure 20. Distribution of immigrants from Scotland, 1930.

Figure 21. Distribution of immigrants from Wales, 1930.

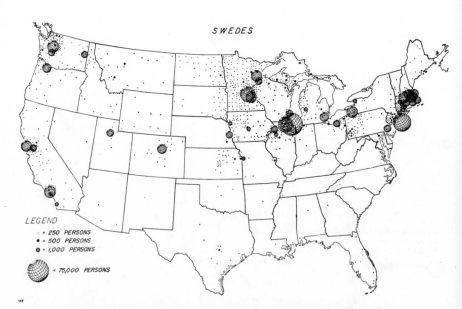

Figure 22. Distribution of immigrants from Sweden, 1930.

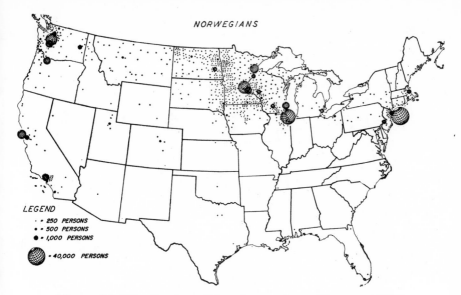

Figure 23. Distribution of immigrants from Norway, 1930.

from Eire. (See Figure 25.) The extent to which they remained in a few of the large cities is remarkable.

Persons born in Mexico numbered 641,462 in 1930, and they were largely concentrated in the border states from Texas to California. (See Figure 26.) Of all the groups included in this discussion, this is the one for which it would be more informative if the 1950 data were given with comparable detail. This is because the Mexican element in the population is holding its own or even increasing in importance.

The distribution in 1930 of the persons born in the other countries from which the largest contingents of immigrants had come was as follows: of the 491,638 persons born in Czechoslovakia, in Figure 27; of the 370,450 from Austria, in Figure 28; of the 274,450 from Hungary, in Figure 29; of the 211,416 from Yugoslavia, in Figure 30; of the 193,606 from Lithuania, in Figure 31; of the 174,526 from Greece, in Figure 32; of the 146,393 from Romania, in Figure 33; of the 142,478 from Finland, in Figure 34; and of the 135,492 from France, in Figure 35.

Trends

Since the United States began its life as an independent nation, two major trends stand out as the dominant ones among all the changes in the color or racial composition and the nativity of the population.

Figure 24. Distribution of immigrants from Denmark, 1930.

These are, first, the long-continued decrease in the relative importance of Negroes in the population, which was only reversed between 1930 and 1940; and, second, the sharp decline in the absolute numbers, as well as in the relative importance, of the foreign-born population taking place since Congress passed the Immigration Act of 1924.

To make readily available the principal statistical data on which these statements are based, Table VII has been prepared. It gives for each census from 1790 to 1950 the number and proportion of Negroes in the national population, and for each census from 1850 to 1950 comparable data for the foreign-born white population. Unless replenished by other immigrants, of course, the foreign-born population soon disappears. The number enumerated in 1950 was the lowest since 1890; and the proportion those born abroad constituted of the nation's inhabitants in 1950 was the lowest on record, the percentage being only about one-half of that prevailing through the period 1850 to 1920. The number of Negroes rose from about 0.75 million in 1790 to above 15 million in 1950. Since 1930 the proportion they constitute of the total population also has risen slightly. Nearly all of this growth is due to the natural increase of those who were in the United States in 1800, for the importation of slaves was prohibited and almost stopped in 1808, and there has been practically no immigration of Negroes. The breed-

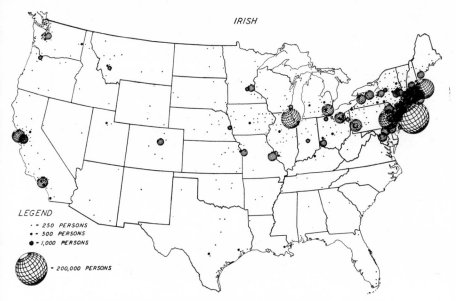

LEGEND
• = 250 PERSONS
• = 500 PERSONS
• = 1,000 PERSONS
= 200,000 PERSONS

Figure 25. Distribution of immigrants from Eire, 1930.

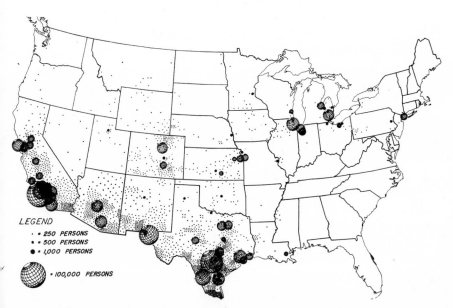

LEGEND
• = 250 PERSONS
• = 500 PERSONS
• = 1,000 PERSONS
= 100,000 PERSONS

Figure 26. Distribution of immigrants from Mexico, 1930.

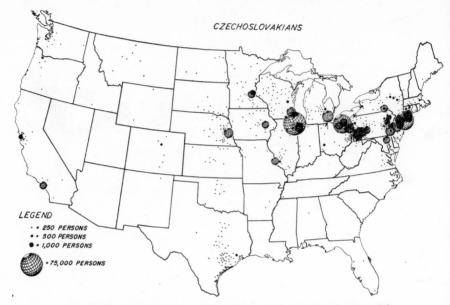

Figure 27. Distribution of immigrants from Czechoslovakia, 1930.

Figure 28. Distribution of immigrants from Austria, 1930.

Figure 29. Distribution of immigrants from Hungary, 1930.

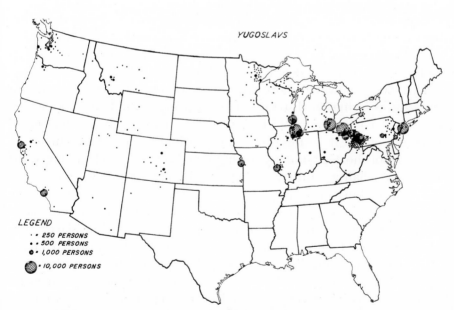

Figure 30. Distribution of immigrants from Yugoslavia, 1930.

Figure 31. Distribution of immigrants from Lithuania, 1930.

ing farms of the older slave states, particularly Virginia, were largely responsible for the increase of Negroes under slavery. From them, following the Louisiana Purchase, slaves were carried to the new plantations being opened in Mississippi, Arkansas, and Louisiana, and later on to the Black Waxy and other sections of Texas.

By 1860, as indicated above, the distribution of slaves, which is almost the same as saying the distribution of Negroes, in the United States was that depicted in Figure 9. This pattern remained almost unchanged until the outbreak of the first world war and the development of the severe labor shortage in northern industrial centers which accompanied it. For over half a century, while the white population was pushing to the west, making farms on the land that was to be had for the taking (from the Indians), the Negro population remained rooted in the same sections of the South in which it was located at the time slavery was abolished. (See Figures 36, 37, 38, and 39, which were constructed to be as comparable as possible with Figure 10.) Over the years there has been a tendency for the "black belt" to become gray, but the expansion of its limits has been very slow. Indeed during the last few decades its area has tended to contract.

The first big change came when World War I generated a large

Figure 32. Distribution of immigrants from Greece, 1930.

Figure 33. Distribution of immigrants from Romania, 1930.

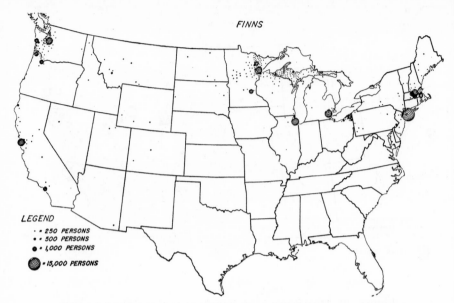

Figure 34. Distribution of immigrants from Finland, 1930.

Figure 35. Distribution of immigrants from France, 1930.

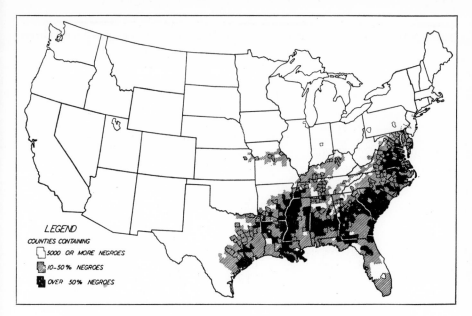

Figure 36. Relative importance of Negroes in the population, by counties, 1880.

exodus of Negroes from the rural South to Chicago and other northern industrial centers. For example, between 1910 and 1930 the Negro population of Chicago increased from 44,103 to 233,903, that of the Cleveland from 8,448 to 71,899, that of Detroit from 5,741 to 120,066, that of New York from 91,709 to 327,706, and that of Philadelphia from 84,459 to 219,599.

Next, with the onslaught of the great economic depression, in 1929, much of the migration of Negroes to the North was halted, but by this time the increased awareness on the part of the southern rural Negroes that there were alternatives to their customary mode of existence caused them to flock into southern towns and cities in unprecedented numbers. This trend was accentuated to a considerable degree by the existence of the federal relief program and the advantages enjoyed by those who were near the distribution points in the major cities and in county seats in general over those residing in the more remote areas.[1] As a result the Negro urban population of the South, as defined for census purposes, rose from 2,966,325 in 1930 to 3,616,218 in 1940, and

[1] On this point consult, T. Lynn Smith and Homer L. Hitt, "Population Redistribution in Louisiana," *Social Forces,* 20, No. 4 (1942), 443.

Table VII. Numbers and Proportions of Negroes and Foreign-born Whites in the Population of the United States, 1790 to 1950

Year	Number of Negroes	Percentage of Negroes in the total population	Number of foreign-born whites	Percentage of foreign-born whites in the total population
1790	757,208	19.3	. . . .	. . .
1800	1,002,037	18.9	. . . .	. . .
1810	1,337,808	19.0	. . . .	. . .
1820	1,771,656	18.4	. . . .	. . .
1830	2,328,642	18.1	. . . .	. . .
1840	2,873,648	16.8	. . . .	. . .
1850	3,638,808	15.7	2,240,535	9.7
1860	4,441,830	14.1	4,096,753	13.0
1870	4,880,009	12.7	5,493,712	14.2
1880	6,580,793	13.1	6,559,679	13.1
1890	7,488,676	11.9	9,121,867	14.5
1900	8,833,994	11.6	10,213,817	13.4
1910	9,827,763	10.7	13,345,545	14.5
1920	10,463,131	9.9	13,712,754	13.0
1930	11,891,143	9.7	13,983,405	11.4
1940	12,865,518	9.8	11,419,138	8.7
1950	15,042,286	10.0	10,161,168	6.7

SOURCES OF DATA: U. S. Bureau of the Census, *Negroes in the United States, 1920–1932* (Washington: Government Printing Office, 1935), p. 1; and U. S. Bureau of the Census, *U. S. Census of Population: 1950*, Vol. II, *Characteristics of the Population* (Washington: Government Printing Office, 1952), Table 36, p. 88.

the proportions of the Negro population of the region classified as urban rose from 31.6 per cent to 36.5 per cent during the same decade.

Finally, when World War II and the necessities connected with fighting a global war on two fronts produced a vast shortage of labor for all purposes, the Negroes at long last made their way in considerable numbers to the cities on the Pacific Coast. As a result the Negro population of the Pacific census division rose from 134,295 in 1940 to 504,392 in 1950, the change in California alone being from 124,306 to 462,172.

Since 1950, these three trends, accompanied by a strong tendency to mechanize agricultural processes throughout the southern region, have continued at an unabated pace. Negroes from the South are finding

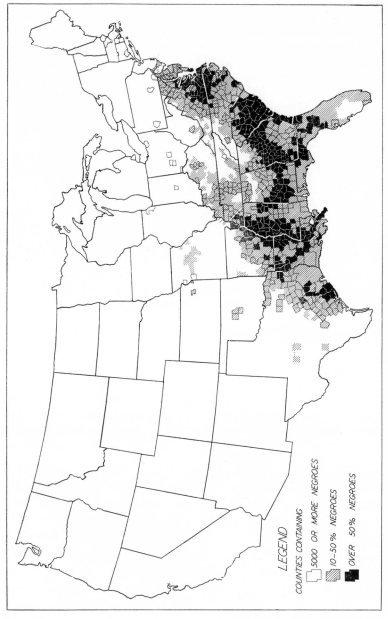

LEGEND

COUNTIES CONTAINING

5000 OR MORE NEGROES

10-50 % NEGROES

OVER 50% NEGROES

Figure 37. Relative importance of Negroes in the population, by counties, 1900.

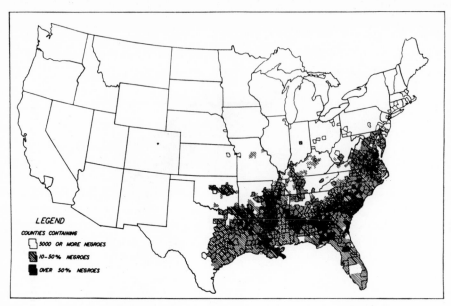

Figure 38. Relative importance of Negroes in the population, by counties, 1920.

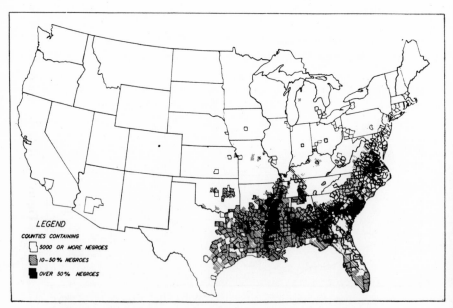

Figure 39. Relative importance of Negroes in the population, by counties, 1940.

their way in large numbers to the cities of the Northeast and those on the Pacific Coast, and Negroes from the farms of the region continue flocking into the towns and cities from Richmond, Savannah, and Jacksonville to those of which Texas is so proud.

SUGGESTED SUPPLEMENTARY READINGS

Anderson, Walfred A., *The Characteristics of New York State Population.* Cornell University Agricultural Experiment Station, Bulletin No. 925, Ithaca (1958), pp. 8–17.

Bogue, Donald J., *The Population of the United States.* Chicago: The Free Press, 1959, chapter 7.

Duncan, Otis Dudley, and Albert J. Reiss, Jr., *Social Characteristics of Urban and Rural Communities, 1950.* New York: John Wiley & Sons, Inc. (London: Chapman & Hall, Ltd.), 1956, chapter 4.

Landis, Paul H., and Paul K. Hatt, *Population Problems: A Cultural Interpretation* (Second Edition). New York: American Book Company, 1954, chapter 15.

Maclachlan, John M., "Health and the People in Florida," *Planning Florida's Health Leadership, No. 3.* Gainesville: University of Florida Press, 1954, chapter 4.

Maclachlan, John M., and Joe S. Floyd, *This Changing South.* Gainesville: University of Florida Press, 1956, chapter 3.

McMahan, C. A., *The People of Atlanta.* Athens: University of Georgia Press, 1950, chapter IV.

Phelps, Harold A., and David Henderson, *Population in Its Human Aspects.* New York: Appleton-Century-Crofts, Inc., 1958, part III.

Siegel, Jacob S., *The Population of Hungary.* U. S. Bureau of the Census International Population Statistics Reports, Series P-90, No. 9. Washington: Government Printing Office, 1958, chapter VI.

Smith, T. Lynn, *Brazil: People and Institutions* (Revised Edition). Baton Rouge: Louisiana State University, 1954, chapter VI.

Smith, T. Lynn, and Homer L. Hitt, *The People of Louisiana.* Baton Rouge: Louisiana State University Press, 1952, chapter IV.

Statistical Office of the United Nations, *Demographic Yearbook, 1956.* New York: The United Nations, 1956, pp. 29–34.

Taeuber, Conrad, and Irene B. Taeuber, *The Changing Population of the United States.* New York: John Wiley & Sons, 1958, chapter 4.

Thompson, Warren S., *Growth and Changes in California's Population.* Los Angeles: The Haynes Foundation, 1955, chapter VII.

Chapter 6

Age Composition

FOR THREE REASONS a knowledge of the age distribution is basic in nearly all population analyses. First, age is one of the most fundamental of one's own personal characteristics; what one is, thinks, does, and needs is closely related to the number of years since he was born. Second, as indicated more fully below, the absolute and relative importance of the various age groups are determinants of primary social and economic importance in any given society. Third, the qualified student of population must possess the technical skills needed to bring out the significant features of the age composition of a population with which he is concerned, and also those required to make the proper allowances or corrections for the age factor in all the comparisons he may attempt. This is because the age factor is so closely related to the birth rate, the mortality rate, marital status, the incidence of migration, and so on, that if it is not controlled adequately analyses and comparisons involving these phenomena are likely to be worse than useless.

Some of the most obvious of the uses of age data are those connected with the planning of military activities, educational facilities, and social welfare programs. But large employers, the entire life insurance business, and a host of other private and governmental organizations and agencies likewise rely in great measure upon comprehensive, current, and reliable information about the age distribution of the population. For the social scientist the age structure of the population is paramount in importance because in a multitude of ways, some of them extremely subtle, age conditions practically all social pheonomena.[1] This is especially true for the demographer, since, as indicated above, until the

[1] For a suggestive study of the relationship of age to the individual's likes, dislikes, and interests, see Edward K. Strong, Jr., *Change of Interests with Age* (Stanford, California: Stanford University Press, 1931.)

148

effects that should be attributed merely to differences in the age composition of two or more populations have been eliminated or corrected for, little significance may legitimately be attached to any seeming differences with respect to their mortality rates, birth rates, marriage rates, and so on.

Gauging the Reliability of Age Data

There are certain errors in the age data gathered in any census enumeration, and frequently these errors are of considerable magnitude. Most obvious of these is the tendency for many persons to report their ages as coming in the numbers ending with zero. (See Figure 40.) This is particularly true after the attainment of middle age, and usually produces a considerable concentration of persons in the ages forty, fifty, sixty, and so forth. Only slightly less pronounced is the tendency for the reported ages to concentrate on the numbers ending with five, and especially on forty-five, fifty-five, sixty-five, and seventy-five. In addition even numbers such as thirty-six and thirty-eight or forty-six and forty-eight also tend to be considerably more popular in various distributions showing the population by single years of age, than are the uneven numbers such as thirty-seven or forty-seven. The older the age group the greater is the percentage of error introduced by this practice of rounding off the numbers reported. For some strange reason there also is a tendency for the newest member of a family, the baby of less than one year of age, to be omitted when the mother or the father is supplying information to the census enumerator; or it may be that the census enumerators miss inordinately large proportions of families in which there is only one child, and it less than one year old. As a nation gains experience in the taking of censuses and as the educational status of the population improves, all of these types of errors decrease in importance, but they do not entirely disappear. For this reason indexes of the extent to which ages are reported correctly have considerable diagnostic value to the investigator who is concerned with the reliability of census materials in general. One scholar, Ellsworth Huntington, has even maintained that the extent to which there are discrepancies in reporting ages of those under twenty-five years of age is the best available indicator of "general intelligence" among a population.[1]

[1] See his contribution "Society and Its Physical Environment," in Jerome Davis and Harry Elmer Barnes (Editors), *An Introduction to Sociology* (Revised Edition), (Boston: D. C. Heath and Company, 1931), pp. 272–276.

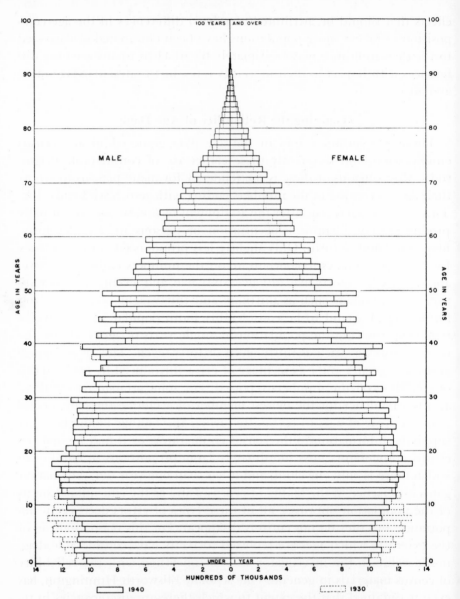

Figure 40. The population of the United States, by single years of age and sex, 1930 and 1940. (Illustration from the U. S. Bureau of the Census)

Some years ago while he was engaged in a series of population studies in the State of Louisiana the present writer devised a method for rating, grading, or scoring any given population with respect to the accuracy of age reporting in connection with census enumerations. Briefly the procedure is as follows. Take the distribution of ages by single years, from under one to ninety-nine, which most modern censuses publish, and ignore the very few who have passed their hundredth birthdays or whose ages are unreported. If all of the ages were known and reported correctly, almost exactly 10 per cent of the total should be in the first year of age and the others ending with 0, another 10 per cent in the other ages exactly divisible by five, 40 per cent in other even-number ages, and the remaining 40 per cent in the odd-numbers not divisible exactly by five. Thus all of the tendencies to concentrate mentioned above should reduce the percentages in the last of these four categories. Consequently, by comparing the total number of persons reported in the age groups one, three, seven, nine, eleven, thirteen, . . . ninety-three, ninety-seven, and ninety-nine, with the figure corresponding to 40 per cent of the total, one may secure an indicator of the reliability with which the ages have been reported. Perfect reporting would produce a score of 100, whereas any concentration on the ages ending in zero, five, or the other even numbers would produce an index of less than 100. The greater the error, the smaller the score. Such a system of scoring populations with respect to the accuracy of age reporting is far less complicated, logically and practically, than the task the university instructor in the course on population, or any other subject, must perform in evaluating student performance and assigning grades.

In the studies referred to above, these scores were computed for a considerable number of populations. For example the score for the total population of the United States in 1940 was 95.5, indicating a considerable amount of error in the data. By states the comparable indexes ranged from highs of 97.6 and 97.4, for Minnesota and North Dakota, respectively, to the low of 90.6 for Mississippi. The scores for the urban, rural-nonfarm, and rural farm populations, the same year, were 95.5, 96.2, and 95.0, respectively, and that for the white population was 96.1 as compared with 90.1 for the nonwhite population. Males scored slightly higher than females, or 96.0 in comparison with 95.5. Rural-farm nonwhites scored lowest of all, 88.5, although the index for urban

Table VIII. Scores Indicative of the Extent of Error in Reported Ages Along with the Percentages of Illiteracy in Various Countries Based on Data from the Most Recent Censuses

Country	Year	Score on age reporting	Percentage of illiteracy among those aged ten and over
Africa			
Egypt	1947	47.5	74.5
Union of South Africa	1946	79.3	70.9
North America			
Canada	1951	98.8	....
Costa Rica	1950	86.5	21.2
Dominican Republic	1950	81.0	56.8
El Salvador	1950	76.3	57.8
Guatemala	1950	77.2	70.3
Haiti	1950	70.1	89.4
Mexico	1950	77.6	....
Nicaragua	1950	73.6	....
Panama	1950	87.9	28.2
Puerto Rico	1950	85.2	25.6
United States	1950	97.2	....
South America			
Argentina	1947	98.5	13.3 [1]
Bolivia	1950	72.3	68.9
Brazil	1950	88.4	51.4
Chile	1952	91.0	....
Ecuador	1950	74.5	43.7
Venezuela	1950	80.9	51.1
Asia			
Ceylon	1946	77.1	36.2
Israel	1948	92.3	6.9
Japan	1950	99.9	....
Philippines	1950	81.1	37.8
Thailand	1947	96.6	46.3
Turkey	1950	69.8	65.4
Europe			
Austria	1951	101.6	....
Belgium	1947	99.1	3.1

Table VIII. Scores Indicative of the Extent of Error in Reported Ages Along with the Percentages of Illiteracy in Various Countries (Continued)

Country	Year	Score on age reporting	Percentage of illiteracy among those aged ten and over
Denmark	1950	97.7	. . . .
Finland	1950	99.4	. . . .
France	1946	99.7	3.3
Germany	1946	97.8	. . .
Western Germany	1950	99.1	. . .
Greece	1951	87.3	23.5
Iceland	1950	97.7	. . .
Ireland	1951	97.2	. . .
Luxembourg	1947	99.0	. . .
Netherlands	1947	96.6	. . .
Norway	1950	97.9	. . .
Portugal	1950	94.0	41.7
Sweden	1950	98.7	. . .
Switzerland	1950	98.8	. . .
United Kingdom			
England and Wales	1951	98.6	. . .
Northern Ireland	1951	97.6	. . .
Scotland	1951	98.7	. . .
Yugoslavia	1953	97.3	25.4
Oceania			
Australia	1947	97.8	. . .
New Zealand	1951	97.9	. . .

SOURCE OF DATA: The scores were computed from data given in the *Demographic Yearbook*, 1955 (New York: United Nations, 1955), Table 11; data on percentages of illiteracy are from Table 13.

[1] Among those aged fourteen and over.

nonwhites was only 91.3. Rural-farm whites, on the other hand, scored 96.3, slightly higher than the index, 95.9, for urban whites.[1]

[1] See T. Lynn Smith, *Population Analysis* (New York: McGraw-Hill Book Company, 1948), pp. 90–91; and T. Lynn Smith and Homer L. Hitt, *The People of Louisiana* (Baton Rouge: Louisiana State University Press, 1952), pp. 50–51.

The appearance of the 1955 edition of the *Demographic Yearbook*[1] made it possible to extend this type of analysis to many populations throughout the world. See Table VIII for the scores computed from the latest census data, along with information, for those cases for which it is available, showing the percentage of illiteracy among the population aged ten years and over. A study of these materials makes it evident that there is a close association between accuracy in reporting ages and the general educational level of the population; and it also suggests that long experience in census taking probably helps reduce the margin of error in this and other items included in the inventory of the population.

The score for Egypt is by far the lowest for any of the forty-seven countries included, with those for Turkey, Haiti, and Bolivia coming next in order. Japan, France, Finland, Belgium, Western Germany, and Luxembourg all have scores of 99 or better, indicating a high degree of accuracy in the age data collected by their respective censuses. In most other European countries and in Canada, Argentina, the United States, Australia, and New Zealand the indexes also are in the high 90's. In most of Latin America, however, the scores are comparatively low, and the same is true for Ceylon and the Philippines. In the case of Austria the index is above 100, a puzzling fact indeed. In the materials for this country concentrations in such ages as eleven, twenty-nine, forty-one, and forty-nine are very difficult to explain; and they play a big part in producing the index as included in Table VIII.

The Age-Sex Pyramid

In their raw state, of course, the millions or even hundreds of millions of observations relative to ages gathered by a modern nation in its periodic census of population would be absolutely useless. No mind could begin to grasp their significance nor use them for any meaningful purposes. They must all be classified and organized in various ways before they can contribute to understanding. The tabular organization is, quite naturally, the principal device used for such purposes, but a number of graphic forms also are employed to a considerable extent. Of these, the most widely used is the one known as the age and sex pyramid, often referred to as the "tree of ages." Various examples of such pyramids are presented in this chapter.

[1] New York: United Nations, 1955, Table 11. Those in charge of the preparation use another device, called "Whipple's Index" for grading the reliability of the age data. See *ibid.*, p. 21.

Construction of an age and sex pyramid is fairly simple. Age group-ings are placed in order on the vertical scale, with the youngest age group located at the bottom and the oldest age group at the top of the diagram. Thus for the age classes conventionally used, the group aged zero to four, inclusive, is placed at the base; immediately above it, the group five to nine; and so on, with the age group seventy-five and over at the top of the scale. On the horizontal axis are plotted the per-centages that each specified age group constitutes of the total, with the portion corresponding to the male segment placed to the left of the central dividing line and that representing the female part placed to the right of it. Building from bottom to top with bars representing the percentages of the total population constituted by males and females of the respective age groups gives rise to the age and sex pyramid. The pyramid itself represents the entire group or 100 per cent. If the dia-gram is not to be used for purposes of comparison, absolute numbers rather than percentages may be used in its construction.

The age and sex distribution of a given population is a record of nearly a century of societal experience. Just as the geologist may read much of the earth's history by examining the exposed strata near its surface, one familiar with the subject may see reflected in the profile of a given society's age and sex distribution many important events which have occurred over the century prior to the census involved. Wars, epi-demics, migrations to or from the area concerned, precipitous declines or sharp increases in the birth rate—all of these leave distinctive marks or scars upon the age-sex pyramid.

Factors Affecting the Age Distribution

The primary factors with which one must reckon in explaining the general configuration of any age-sex distribution, any specific features it may exhibit, and any changes it may undergo, are, of course, the same three that may be involved in any population change, namely, births, deaths, and migrations. However, for some purposes it is well to include some of the secondary factors, such as war and epidemics, mentioned above, which by exerting special influences upon mortality, fertility, or migration, leave very distinctive marks upon the age-sex pyramid.

The General Levels of the Birth Rate and the Mortality Rate

As is indicated in the following section, in various countries the pro-portions of those under fifteen, between fifteen and sixty-five, and those aged sixty-five and over, differ drastically from one country to another.

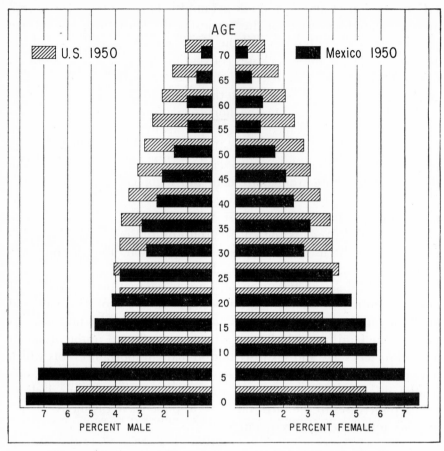

Figure 41. A comparison of the age-sex pyramids for Mexico
and the United States, 1950.

In Mexico (see Figure 41), for example, which is fairly representative
in this respect of most of the Latin American countries, in 1950, 41.9 per
cent of the population were less than fifteen years of age, 54.7 per cent
in the ages fifteen to sixty-four, inclusive, and only 3.4 per cent in the
more advanced ages of sixty-five and over. The same year in the United
States the corresponding percentages were, 26.8, 65.0, and 8.2. (See
Table IX for comparable data for other countries throughout the
world.) Leaving aside for the moment the details with respect to the
peculiarities of each of the pyramids, which are discussed to some extent
below, it is well to concentrate first upon why the proportions of the

young, those in the productive ages and those at or near the retirement ages, differ so greatly from one nation to another. Why do some age-sex pyramids, such as those for Canada, the United Kingdom, and the United States, have the elongated form, whereas others, such as those prevailing rather generally in Latin America, the Near East, and parts of the Far East, have such broad bases? Why are the latter so squat in form?

In any country in which the birth rate and the death rate both are very high, the age-sex pyramid will be a very squat one, that is, the proportions of children and of young adults will be high, and those of persons who have passed forty-five and those sixty-five and over will be low. On the other hand, where over a period of years a comparatively low birth rate has been accompanied by a low death rate, the age-sex pyramid will take on the elongated form, that is the proportions of children and young adults will be low, and those of persons above forty-five and especially those sixty-five and over will be relatively high. Immigration and emigration will modify this to some extent, but only in extreme cases, such as that of Israel since it became a state, does migration become the principal factor in determining the proportions of the various ages in the population.

War

Next consider briefly the ways in which the age-sex pyramids get some of their other distinctive features. Highly important among these is sculpturing brought about by a serious war in which the nation in question has been involved. The principal effects of such a struggle are two in number, first that produced by the deaths of combatants and second that brought about by the sharp decline in the birth rate due to such a war. Most of the combatants who lose their lives as a result of war are in the ages twenty to thirty. Therefore, deaths among members of this age group produce a huge scar or indentation on the male side of the pyramid (see, for example, Figure 42 representing the age distribution for Germany in 1934), and this scar is to be observed in the pyramids representing the age-sex distributions of the population for subsequent censuses, at progressively older ages, for some sixty years thereafter. It does not entirely disappear until all those who were coming to maturity at the outbreak of the war have passed up the age ladder and out of the group aged seventy-five and over. Of even greater duration is the other substantial scar, that produced by the

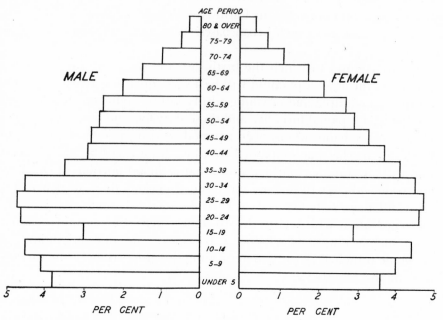

Figure 42. Age-sex pyramid for Germany, 1934.

lowered birth rate that goes with a serious war. Other things being equal (and, as indicated below, this was not the case in the United States between 1941 and 1945), in any serious and sustained war, within a year after general mobilization the birth rate begins to fall, and it continues to go down until the war is over and demobilization has enabled married men to return to their wives and unmarried soldiers to consummate the long postponed marriages. Then it rises sharply for a year or so to heights considerably above prewar levels, after which it falls again and resumes the prewar trend. As a result the small number of babies born during the war years stands out sharply as an age group, in comparison with the much larger numbers born in the years just before and just after the war. Thus in Germany in 1934 the smallness of the age group fifteen to nineteen was due to the low birth rate during the first world war. The most striking examples for the

United States were produced by the small number of babies born during the Civil War, especially in the South, where the struggle's ravages were felt most deeply. This was reflected at successive censuses in every age group through which those born between 1860 and 1865 passed, until in 1930 it was directly responsible for the relatively small numbers of persons aged sixty-five to sixty-nine.[1] An interesting study of the effects of the first world war upon the birth rates in the countries most seriously affected has been published in the *Statistical Bulletin* of the Metropolitan Life Insurance Company.[2] In this publication the minimum birth rate during the war for each of the countries was expressed as a percentage of the rate prevailing 1911 to 1913. These are as follows: Bulgaria, 41.7; Hungary, 47.5; Germany, 49.5; Belgium, 49.8; France, 50.5; Italy, 56.7; Austria, 57.1; and England and Wales, 73.1.

Sharp Changes in the Birth Rate

Precipitous declines in the birth rate and rapid upsurges in the rate of reproduction quickly produce some of the more pronounced changes in the configuration of the age and sex pyramid for a given country. Such rapid and pronounced changes have characterized the age distribution of the United States since 1920. Thus the decline in the birth rate of the United States, which had been going on for more than a century, became precipitous between 1920 and 1935. As a result, in the fifteenth census children aged zero to four were fewer in number than those aged five to nine, and in the sixteenth census there was a marked scarcity in the population of all persons less than fifteen years of age. Therefore, the age-sex pyramids for the United States in 1930 and 1940 were characterized by the truncated bases, so apparent in Figure 40, and so different from those representing the age distributions for 1920 and earlier years. Even so, however, the long continued downward trend of the birth rate was largely responsible for the steady decrease in the proportion of those of less than five years of age in the population, which was 15.4 per cent in 1860, 12.1 per cent in 1900, 10.9 per cent in 1920, and only 9.3 per cent in 1930. In the years between the two world wars, rapidly declining birth rates in many of the European countries

[1] See T. Lynn Smith, "The Demographic Basis of Old Age Assistance in the South," *Social Forces,* 17, No. 3 (March, 1939), 356–361.
[2] Volume 21 (March, 1940), 3–6.

were producing similar changes at the bases of the age-sex pyramids representing their populations. Observe again in this connection, Figure 42 for Germany in 1934.

Although checked to some extent by the second world war (see chapter 14), the sharp rise in the birth rate following 1936, and especially after 1945, produced each year from 1945 to 1949 almost 4 million babies to add to the base of the age distribution, in comparison with less than 2.5 millions per year from 1932 to 1939, so that by 1950 the age-sex pyramid for the United States took the form portrayed in Figure 41. As a result of these changes in the birth rate, since 1920 tremendous gyrations have taken place in the configuration of our own age-sex pyramid. Rarely in historical times has the age distribution of any nation experienced transformations equal to these. Because the birth rate has remained at its 1950 level, at the time of the 1960 census the pyramid will be characterized by a broad base, formed by the three bars representing the ages up to fifteen, and the severe pinched effect, corresponding in 1950 to the age groups ten to twenty-five, will then be exhibited by the bars for those aged twenty to thirty-five.

Migration

Great migrations constitute other significant forces which have a direct influence upon the configuration of age-sex pyramids, both those in the areas in which the migrants originate and in those to which they move. As will be indicated below (chapter 20), the nature of the migration and the distance spanned are the principal determinants of the extent to which males and females of various ages participate in the migrations. Thus most of those who emigrate from one country to establish new homes in another are young adults and predominantly of the male sex; whereas those who flock into a nation's cities from the rural districts immediately surrounding them, although mostly in the ages from seventeen to twenty-five, include many more females than males. Consequently, the country that is sending out large numbers of emigrants will have, other things being equal, an age-sex pyramid that is decidedly indented at the ages near the middle of the scale, and this will be much more so on the side representing the males than on the one representing females; and the pyramid for a rural district from which large numbers of persons are moving to nearby cities will exhibit the same general features, except that the scarcity of those from about twenty-five to forty-five years of age will be more pronounced for fe-

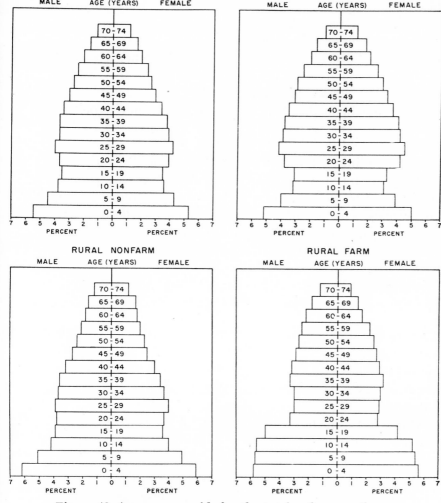

Figure 43. Age-sex pyramids for the total, urban, rural-non-farm and rural-farm populations of the United States, 1950. (Illustration from the U. S. Bureau of the Census)

males than for males. On the other hand, the pyramid for the country receiving the immigrants or for the city to which the farm-born migrants have moved will have the portions of their pyramids representing the ages involved considerably bulged by the newcomers. For example, the pyramid for the United States in 1930 (Figure 40) shows decidedly the influences of almost 15 million immigrants who were in the country at that time, whereas the age distribution of an urban population (see Figures 43 and 44) generally reflects clearly the fact that high proportions of young adults, preponderantly females, have moved from the rural districts to towns and cities. The other selective features of migration, discussed in chapter 20, each leaves its specific impress both upon the age-sex pyramid for the section in which the migrants originate and upon that for the one in which they settle.

Abrupt Changes in the Mortality Rate

A long-continued downward trend in the mortality rate has been an important factor in producing the elongated age-sex pyramids now characteristic of such countries as Australia, the Netherlands, and the United States. But one may be curious about the effects of recent precipitous declines of death rates throughout much of the world, including the twenty Latin American countries and most of Africa and Asia. These abrupt changes in the death rates have not produced transformations in the age-sex pyramids comparable to those brought about by the rapid drop in the birth rate in the United States, Germany, and other countries, which was discussed above. This is mainly because the reduction of deaths was spread over many age groups and not largely confined to a few of them. In addition, since in a given population the number of births usually exceeds the number of deaths, often by a considerable margin, mortality generally is of less importance than fertility in the explanation of population changes of any kind. It appears, however, that about one-fifth of the increase in the United States between 1940 and 1950 in the number of persons aged sixty-five and over was due to lowered mortality rates of those above the age of fifty-five. The so-called "wonder drugs" no doubt were responsible for this abrupt change in the expectation of life of those at or near the retirement ages.[1]

Some International Comparisons

Thanks to the work of the statistical bureaus in various countries and to the efforts of the Population Commission of the United Nations, it is now possible for the student of population to obtain fairly recent and comparable data relative to the age distributions in many countries.

---

[1] See T. Lynn Smith, "The Changing Number and Distribution of the Aged Population," *Journal of the American Geriatrics Society*, III, No. 1 (January, 1955), 2–4.

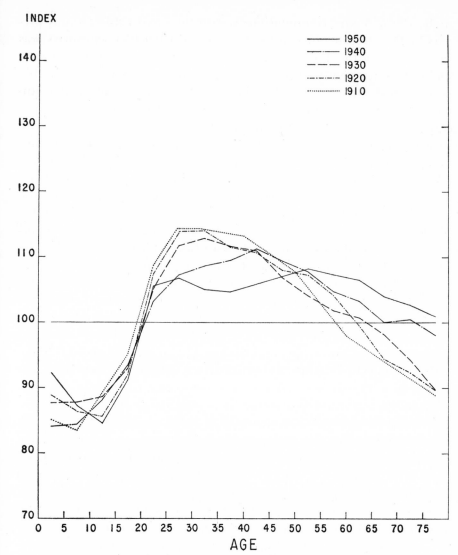

INDEX

Figure 44. Indexes showing the extent to which each age group in the urban population contained more or less than its pro rata share of those of corresponding age in the United States, 1920, 1930, 1940, and 1950.

For present purposes the materials indicating the proportions of the population falling into three large age groups (under fifteen, fifteen to sixty-four, and sixty-five and over) are most important; and, accordingly, the necessary computations were made and Table IX was prepared. The decision to employ these three particular categories was influenced by the following considerations: (1) certainly children should be separated from adults, and age fifteen is the most practicable point at which to draw the line between the two; (2) in many countries, including the United States, sixty-five is the age rather generally employed as the lower limit of eligibility for social welfare services, such as "old age assistance," that established for the beginning of voluntary or compulsory retirement, and that generally used for statistical purposes to separate the "aged" portion of the population from others; and (3) if these two criteria are employed, the persons in between the stated limits automatically constitute a third category. Included in Table IX are the results of the author's attempts to estimate the proportion of the inhabitants of the earth as a whole which fall in each of the three specified broad age groups. The computations carried out for this purpose indicated that at the middle of the twentieth century approximately 36 per cent of mankind were children of less than fifteen, 59.5 per cent in the ages fifteen to sixty-four, and 4.5 per cent in the ages sixty-five and over.

Most of the thirty-seven countries included in Table IX fall into a few rather sharply distinguished categories, if several definite criteria are employed as the basis for making such groupings. Guided by the percentages for the world as a whole, indicated above, the present writer used the following specifications to determine whether the population of each country was characterized by a *high, medium,* or *low* percentage of persons in each of the three broad age groups. If less than 30 per cent of the population were in the ages under fifteen, the proportion was considered as low, 30 to 39 per cent as medium, and 40 per cent or more as high. Similarly, if less than 57.5 per cent of the population were aged fifteen to sixty-four, the proportion was evaluated as low, 57.5 to 61.9 per cent as medium, and 62 per cent or more as high. Finally, less than 4 per cent in the ages sixty-five and over was designated as low, 4 to 7.9 per cent as medium, and 8 per cent or more as high. On the basis of these criteria, the largest group of nations consists of those in which a high expectation of life is the factor of prime importance in determining the general configuration of the age distribution. In all of those in this group the proportion of children is low, and the percentages of those in the productive ages and the most advanced ages both are high. Specifically, the United States, Austria, Belgium,

Table IX. Proportions of the Population in Three Broad Age Groups: Selected Countries

Country	Year of census	Per cent of the population aged		
		Under 15	15–64	65–over
Africa				
Egypt	1947	38.1	58.8	3.1
Union of South Africa	1946	37.7	58.2	4.1
North America				
Canada	1950	30.3	61.9	7.8
Costa Rica	1950	42.9	54.2	2.9
Cuba	1953	36.3	59.4	4.3
Dominican Republic	1950	44.5	52.6	2.9
El Salvador	1950	41.1	55.9	3.0
Mexico	1950	41.8	55.1	3.1
Panama	1950	41.7	55.1	3.2
United States	1950	26.9	65.0	8.1
South America				
Argentina	1947	30.9	65.2	3.9
Brazil	1950	41.9	55.7	2.4
Chile	1952	37.4	58.6	4.0
Colombia	1938	41.9	55.2	2.9
Ecuador	1950	42.5	53.7	3.8
Paraguay	1950	43.8	52.5	3.7
Venezuela	1950	41.9	55.4	2.7
Asia				
India	1951	37.4	59.0	3.6
Israel	1948	28.7	67.4	3.9
Japan	1950	35.4	59.7	4.9
Korea	1952	41.1	55.2	3.7
Turkey	1950	38.3	58.4	3.3
Europe				
Austria	1951	22.9	66.5	10.6
Belgium	1947	20.6	68.7	10.7
Denmark	1950	26.3	64.6	9.1
France	1954	23.3	64.6	12.1
West Germany	1950	23.6	67.1	9.3
Netherlands	1947	29.3	63.6	7.1
Norway	1950	24.4	66.0	9.6
Portugal	1950	29.5	63.5	7.0
Spain	1950	26.2	66.6	7.2
Sweden	1950	23.4	66.4	10.2

Table IX. Proportions of the Population in Three Broad Age Groups (Continued)

Country	Year of census	Per cent of the population aged		
		Under 15	15–64	65–over
Switzerland	1950	23.6	66.8	9.6
United Kingdom	1951	22.5	66.6	10.9
Oceania				
Australia	1947	25.2	66.8	8.0
New Zealand	1951	29.4	61.4	9.2
The world [1]	1947	36.0	59.5	4.5

SOURCE OF DATA: Compiled and computed from data in the *Demographic Yearbook, 1955* (New York: The United Nations, 1955), Table 10, except for the materials for Cuba, the Dominican Republic, El Salvador, Panama, Colombia, Ecuador, and Paraguay which were secured from the official census reports of the respective countries.
[1] Author's estimate based on data and estimates in the *Demographic Yearbook, 1949–50* (New York: United Nations, 1950), Table D and Table 4.

Denmark, France, West Germany, Norway, Sweden, Switzerland, the United Kingdom, Australia, and New Zealand make up this group. The other large category consists of those countries in which the high proportion of children is the dominating feature in the age distribution, so that both the proportions of those in the productive ages and those of sixty-five and over are low. This group includes Costa Rica, the Dominican Republic, El Salvador, Mexico, Panama, Brazil, Colombia, Ecuador, Paraguay, Venezuela, and Korea. A small group of four countries (Canada, Cuba, Chile, and Japan) rank as medium in all three respects, although Canada closely approximates the limits of the first of the groups mentioned above, and Cuba and Chile are not very different, in these respects, from the countries placed in the second group. Three of the nations, namely, the Netherlands, Portugal, and Spain, all rate as low in the proportion of children, high in the percentage of those in the productive ages, and medium with respect to the relative importance of aged persons. Three countries, Egypt, India, and Turkey, are medium with respect to the proportions of children and those in the productive ages, and low in percentages of those of sixty-five or over. Israel, due almost exclusively to the tremendous immigration it has received, ranked as low in proportion of children, high in percentage of those aged fifteen to sixty-four, and low in proportion of old people. Finally, Argentina's population includes medium proportions of the young, high proportions of those in the productive ages, and low proportions of those sixty-five and over.

Several of the specific percentages given in Table IX also call for mention, and this is especially true of the exceedingly high proportion of the aged (12.1 per cent) in France, and the extremely low percentage of children (20.6 per cent) in Belgium. Likewise it is evident from this table that the aging of the population has progressed greatly in the United Kingdom, Belgium, Austria, and Sweden; and that children make up very low proportions of the postwar populations of the United Kingdom, Austria, France, Sweden, West Germany, and Switzerland. Australia is the country in which the distribution of the population, as gauged by the proportions in the three age groups under consideration, is most similar to that of the United States.

The Age Distribution in the United States

Largely because of the extreme gyrations in the birth rate since 1920, the age distribution of the United States for 1950 exhibits some very distinctive features. Its form differs markedly from those of the 1930 and 1940 distributions, as these did from one another. Likewise it is radically different from the more conventional age-sex pyramids representing the data gathered in the 1920 and earlier censuses. Moreover, in 1960 and 1970 the age distributions of population in the United States is sure to take on additional rather unique or distinctive shapes. The cause of most of this is, of course, the small numbers of babies born in this country between 1925 and 1940. On the age-sex pyramid for 1950 these small baby crops are reflected in the shortness of the bars representing the age groups five to nine, ten to fourteen, and fifteen to nineteen, that is to say, for the "pinched" effect in the portion of the pyramid corresponding to these ages. This relative scarcity will pass on up the age scale, at successive censuses, and give a series of other distinctive shapes to the distribution corresponding to the years 1960, 1970, and 1980. Along with this, the birth annually since 1950 of more than 4 million babies is adding new broad bars at the base of the ever-changing age-sex pyramid.

The proportion of 8.1 per cent in the ages sixty-five and over also deserves comment. This is high, very high in comparison with anything hitherto prevailing in the United States, although smaller than the corresponding proportions in France, the United Kingdom, and a few other parts of western Europe. Moreover, the concentration in the upper half of the productive ages is a feature deserving specific mention. Thus in 1950, 26.9 per cent of the population were aged forty to sixty-four whereas in 1940 the corresponding proportion was 26.5 per cent, and in 1930 only 24.0 per cent.

The age distribution of the population varies widely from one state to another, from one city to another, between rural and urban areas, among the various racial and nativity groups, and so on. Some attention is given in turn to each of these.

State-to-State Variations

As is well known, there is considerable variation from state to state in the proportions of the young, those in the productive ages, and the old. In 1950 the relative importance of those of less than fifteen years of age in the population, for example, ranged from highs of 34.7 per cent in South Carolina, 34.0 per cent in Mississippi, and 33.4 per cent in Utah, to lows of 23.5 per cent in Rhode Island, 23.2 per cent in New Jersey, 22.6 per cent in New York, and 20.1 per cent in the District of Columbia. Much less pronounced were the state-to-state variations in the proportions of the population aged fifteen to sixty-four, but even so the extremes were 72.8 per cent in the District of Columbia, 68.9 per cent in New York, and 68.8 per cent in New Jersey, at one end of the scale, and 60.3 per cent in New Mexico, 60.2 per cent in Arkansas, 59.9 per cent in South Carolina, and 59.0 per cent in Mississippi, at the other. Most striking of all are the variations in the proportions of those aged sixty-five and over. The relative importance in the population of this group, the one considered as aged for statistical purposes, ranged from 10.8 per cent in New Hampshire, 10.5 per cent in Vermont, and 10.4 per cent in Iowa, to 5.5 per cent in North Carolina, 5.4 per cent in South Carolina, and 4.9 per cent in New Mexico.

The indexes presented in Table X enable one to note easily the nature and degree of the variations throughout the nation in the relative importance of the young, those in the productive ages, and the elderly. If each state had contained in 1950 exactly the same proportion of those in each age group that it did of the national population, all of the indexes would be 100. For example, in New Jersey 8.1 per cent of the population were aged sixty-five and over, the same proportion as that in the nation as a whole, so the corresponding index is 100. Massachusetts, on the other hand, contained 3.112 per cent of the national population and 3.818 per cent of those who had passed their sixty-fifth birthdays. Therefore, for it the index for the year is 123.

The factors immediately responsible for the variations in the relative importance of the different age groups are, of course, the same as those involved in all population changes, namely, births, deaths, and migrations. The high proportion of the young in New Mexico, for example, probably is largely due to the high birth rate in the state combined with a heavy influx of young married couples and their children. It may be that a relatively high death rate among parts of the Spanish American and Indian populations is also partly responsible. On the other hand, the low proportions of the young in the District of Columbia undoubtedly are due mainly to the low birth rate of a highly urban population along with the recent movement to the nation's capital of hundreds of thousands of young men and women seeking jobs in government service. Migrations, including those of persons from abroad, probably are primarily responsible for the varying percentages of those in the productive ages. Thus, on the one hand, the high proportions of persons fifteen to sixty-four in New York, New Jersey, and the District of Columbia undoubtedly reflect for the most part the very large numbers of migrants from other parts of the nation and from abroad who are numbered in their populations. The reverse of this, the low proportions of men and women in these ages in Mississippi, South Carolina, and Arkansas, on the other hand, is due largely to the heavy migration to other more urbanized and industrialized sections of the country of those born and reared in these states. In all cases, though, the patterns of causation involved are highly complex, and the situation prevailing in any state at a given time represents a balancing of many forces.

This proposition is illustrated best, perhaps, in connection with the very large variation from state to state in the relative importance of the aged portion of the population. If one merely considers the factor of migration, one state, for example, may have had a high proportion of those sixty-five and over in 1950 because a boom at the beginning of the century attracted to it tens of thousands of young men and women, who have gradually aged; whereas another may now have a high percentage of aged in its population largely because of immigrants who settled there immediately prior to the first world war. A state such as Montana may now be experiencing a rapid aging of its population primarily because the men and women who pioneered its development are now reaching the advanced ages, whereas another, such as Arkansas, should attribute the increasing proportions of the aged in its population largely to the fact that so many of its young men and women are migrating to other states. In Oklahoma both of these factors weighed heavily in producing the presently rather high proportion of old people in the state. Finally, California and Florida must attribute their slightly high proportions of the aged to the fact that so many of those at or near the retirement ages have moved to them from other parts of the nation. Were it not for the fact that many hundreds of thousands of those in the younger ages also were migrating to those states, by 1950 the aged parts of their populations would have reached startling proportions. These are only a few of the ways in which migration has entered into the causal pattern, and equally complex are the influences exerted by variations in the birth rate and the death rate.

Observation of the materials in Table X, though, suggests strongly that the degree to which a state is rural or urban may be the primary force in determining exactly how the factors of births, deaths, and migrations have combined to produce the variations in the proportions of the young, those in the productive ages, and those sixty-five and over currently prevailing. Accordingly, it is well to turn next to the analysis of ways in which the age distributions of the urban, the rural-farm, and the rural-nonfarm parts of the population differ from one another.

Rural-Urban Differences

The differences between the age distributions of rural and urban populations are best shown by means of charts such as those in Figures 44 and 45. These are designed to show the extent to which each of the three residential groups (urban, rural-nonfarm, and rural-farm) contained more or less than its pro rata share of those in each age group, zero to four to seventy-five and over. In order that any significant changes from one census to another may be noted, the diagram for the rural segments of the population portrays the data for all four of the censuses (1920 to 1950) for which information relating to the rural-farm and the rural-nonfarm categories are available; and that for the urban population includes data for the last five censuses.

The differences are striking; and most of them have persisted census after census. In general the urban population contains relatively few children and high proportions of those in the productive ages. This was true at every census from 1910 to 1950. In 1910, 1920, and 1930 it

Table X. Indexes Showing the Extent to Which Each State Had More or Less Than Its Pro Rata Share of the Population of Less Than 15 Years of Age, 15 to 64, and 65 and Over, 1950

State	Age group		
	Under 15	15–64	65–over
United States	100	100	100
New England			
Maine	103	96	126
New Hampshire	94	98	133
Vermont	108	95	130
Massachusetts	88	102	123
Rhode Island	87	104	110
Connecticut	88	104	109
Middle Atlantic			
New York	84	106	105
New Jersey	82	106	100
Pennsylvania	93	102	104
East North Central			
Ohio	96	100	110
Indiana	99	99	114
Illinois	90	103	107
Michigan	101	101	89
Wisconsin	97	100	111
West North Central			
Minnesota	103	98	111
Iowa	100	96	128
Missouri	93	100	127
North Dakota	116	94	96
South Dakota	109	96	105
Nebraska	98	98	121
Kansas	97	98	126
South Atlantic			
Delaware	96	102	103
Maryland	99	102	86
District of Columbia	75	112	88
Virginia	108	99	80
West Virginia	118	94	85
North Carolina	120	96	68
South Carolina	129	92	67
Georgia	117	95	79
Florida	97	100	106

Table X. Indexes Showing the Extent to Which Each State Had More or Less Than Its Pro Rata Share of the Population (Continued)

State	Age group		
	Under 15	15–64	65–over
East South Central			
Kentucky	114	94	99
Tennessee	112	97	88
Alabama	122	94	80
Mississippi	126	91	86
West South Central			
Arkansas	119	93	96
Louisiana	117	95	82
Oklahoma	107	96	107
Texas	106	100	83
Mountain			
Montana	107	96	106
Idaho	118	94	91
Wyoming	108	99	78
Colorado	102	98	107
New Mexico	129	93	61
Arizona	119	96	73
Utah	124	95	77
Nevada	96	104	85
Pacific			
Washington	98	100	110
Oregon	99	100	107
California	91	103	105

SOURCE: Computed from data in the *U. S. Census of Population: 1950*, Vol. II, *Characteristics of the Population* (Washington: Government Printing Office, 1952).

included far less than its pro rata share of the nation's old people. Such ceased to be the case by 1940, however, and in 1950 the towns and cities of the United States had slightly more than their fair quotas of those aged sixty-five and over. In 1950, due to the fact that in the years 1940 to 1950 the urban birth rate rose more rapidly than the rural, the scarcity of children under five in urban districts was less pronounced than in earlier years, but even so the urban population still contained less than its pro rata share of the youngest age group.

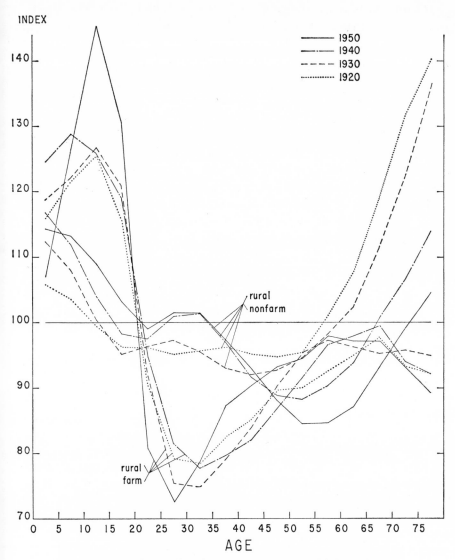

Figure 45. Indexes showing the extent to which each age group in the rural-nonfarm and rural-farm populations contained more or less than its pro rata share of those of corresponding age in the United States, 1920, 1930, 1940, and 1950.

High proportions of those less than twenty years of age and very low proportions of those in the most productive ages are the distinguishing features of the rural-farm population. In addition this category consistently has slightly less than its pro rata share of those over sixty-five. By 1950, due to the trends mentioned above, the proportion of children under five in the rural-farm population had fallen almost to the national level.

The catch-all category designated as rural-nonfarm long has had more than its pro rata share of children, but not to the extent of the rural-farm group. In 1920 and 1930, when the category consisted largely of villagers, it also contained excessively large proportions of the aged. This was in an epoch in which the village truly was America's "old folks' home" [1] and before the rise of retirement cities had progressed to any considerable extent in the United States.[2] By 1940, however, the relative importance of those sixty-five years of age and over in the rural-nonfarm population had fallen off greatly, and in 1950 only those seventy-five and over were overrepresented in this residential group and that only to a slight degree. In 1950 the most striking features of the age distribution in each of the principal residential groups were as follows: (1) the concentration of those aged twenty to seventy in the urban districts; (2) the scarcity of those aged forty to seventy in the rural-nonfarm areas; and (3) the high proportions of those from ten to twenty and the very low proportions of those twenty to thirty-five in the rural-farm districts.

In considerable part the distinctive features of the 1950 age distributions are the direct result of the operation of the following factors during the decade 1940 to 1950: a rise in the birth rate of the urban population which was considerably greater than the corresponding change for the rural population; an extremely heavy movement of young adults from the farms; and the mushrooming of the suburban parts of rural-nonfarm territory brought about by the location there of thousands of young couples who were just commencing their families. However,

[1] See Edmund deS. Brunner and John H. Kolb, *Rural Social Trends* (New York: McGraw-Hill Book Company, 1933), p. 23; T. Lynn Smith, "Some Aspects of Village Demography," *Social Forces*, 20, No. 1 (October, 1941), 15–25; and T. Lynn Smith, "The Role of the Village in American Rural Society," *Rural Sociology*, 7, No. 1 (March, 1941), 18–19.

[2] See T. Lynn Smith, "The Aging of the Population and the Rise of Retirement Towns and Cities in the United States," in *Proceedings of the World Population Conference, 1954* (New York: United Nations, 1955), III, pp. 753–764.

most of the distinguishing features of the three residential categories listed above, with the probable exception of the scarcity on the farms of those in the younger portion of the most productive span of years are unlikely to persist. Those living in the suburbs in 1950 are gradually aging, and as a result they are having fewer babies than was the case immediately prior to the latest census. At the time of the next census their presence in the rural-nonfarm population will offset to a considerable extent, the effects produced by the continuing movement of young couples to the suburbs. The urban population is coming to be such a major portion of the total population that the influx of young men and women from the farms, which leaves such a great void in the age structure of the rural-farm population, has relatively little effect upon that of the urban population. As a result of this, and of the increasing importance of the retirement function of many towns and cities, the age distribution of the urban population should gradually come to be more and more similar to that of the total population.

Differences Between the Age Distributions of the Foreign-born and the Native-born

Relatively little need be said concerning the ways in which the age distribution of the foreign-born population differs from that of the native-born. By definition babies and other young children are almost excluded from the foreign-born category. Therefore, the age-sex pyramid for this population looks as though it had been inverted, with the very narrow bars coming at the bottom rather than at the top of the diagram. Figure 46, showing the age distributions of the native white and foreign-born white populations of the United States in 1940, brings this out very clearly. In 1950 only 1.9 per cent of the foreign-born white population were less than fifteen years of age, and 26.7 per cent were sixty-five or over. In addition, of the 71.4 per cent in what here are considered as the productive ages, almost four-fifths were in the ages forty to sixty-four, inclusive. This is, of course, the inevitable result of the flocking of millions of young adults to the United States during the first quarter of the twentieth century, followed by the virtual elimination of immigration during the first world war, the drastic curtailment of it by legislation passed in 1922 and 1924, and by the effects of the great economic depression beginning about 1929 which for several years produced a net migration of persons from the United States. As a result in 1950 the median age of the foreign-born white population was 56.1, compared

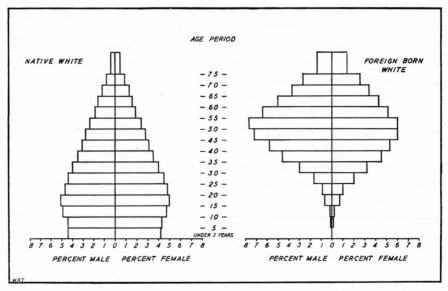

Figure 46. Age-sex pyramids for the native white and foreign-born white populations of the United States, 1940.

with 30.1 for the population as a whole, 28.6 for the native whites, and 26.1 for the Negroes.

Racial Differences

There are still important differences between the age distributions of whites and Negroes, as the data just given indicate, even though the great differentials prevailing in 1900 between the birth rates and the death rates of the two have largely been eliminated. In 1950 the proportions of native whites and Negroes, respectively, in each of the three large age groups being used in this discussion were as follows: under fifteen, 28.5 and 31.8 per cent; fifteen to sixty-four, 64.5 and 62.4 per cent; and sixty-five and over, 7.0 and 5.8 per cent. By 1960, because of the continued heavy movement of Negroes to urban districts and the extent to which this reduces the birth rate of those involved, and because of the continued rapid rise in the expectation of life of the Negro population, the differences between the age distributions of the white and Negro populations are likely to be even smaller than they were in 1950.

Trends

In addition to the current tendencies that have just been commented upon, two long-time trends deserve special attention. The first of these is the steady decline for almost a century in the proportions of children in the population, a trend that was only arrested and reversed to a slight extent by the rise in the birth rate since 1936. The second is the current "aging of the population" that has been so widely publicized during recent years. Each of these is discussed in turn.

A century ago the proportions of children in the population of the United States were comparable to those currently found in most Latin American countries and other "underdeveloped" portions of the world. At that time, in our own country, a high birth rate combined with a high death rate made for an extremely squat age-sex pyramid. As a result in 1850, 41.6 per cent of the population was less than fifteen years of age; and in 1860, on the eve of the Civil War, the corresponding percentage was 40.5. Even after the very short baby crop of the war years had exerted its influence, in 1870, the proportion of those in this age group in the total population was still 39.2 per cent. Thereafter the proportion continued to fall slowly and steadily, to 34.4 per cent in 1900, 32.1 per cent in 1910, 31.8 per cent in 1920, 29.4 per cent in 1930, and 25.0 per cent in 1940. Only between 1940 and 1950 were the effects of the upturn in the birth rate sufficient to halt the decline and to reverse the trend. By 1950, as indicated above, the proportion of those less than fifteen years old had risen to 26.9 per cent. This proportion is sure to be even greater in 1960, perhaps rising by then to about 30 per cent of the total population, since the annual number of births since 1950 has averaged well over 4 million.

The aging of the population—that is, the increase in the number and proportion of those sixty-five years old and over—is the second highly important trend in the age structure of the population of the United States during the middle decades of the twentieth century. Rather general awareness of the importance of this trend began to arise shortly after the 1940 census revealed a total of 9,019,314 persons (6.8 per cent of the population) in these older ages. This awareness received great impetus and led to considerable concern when the 1950 census revealed that the number of those in this age group had risen to 12,269,637, and the proportion to 8.1 per cent of the population. Merely by projecting this trend for a few decades, it was possible for some to create a widespread belief that very shortly the United States would become a nation of elderly people. Such predictions are extremely unreliable, as will be readily apparent to anyone who will make proper allowance in making the projections for the effects of the rise in the birth rate since 1936.

In 1900 in the United States persons aged sixty-five and over totaled 3,080,498 and they made up 4.1 per cent of the population. For the next thirty years the increase in those considered as aged for statistical purposes slightly more than kept pace with the growth of population in general; but even so in 1930 only 5.4 per cent of the population were aged sixty-five and over. Had it not been for the small numbers of births during the years of the Civil War, of course, a factor which sharply reduced the number of those aged sixty-five to sixty-nine in the 1930 enumeration, this proportion would have been significantly higher. As events transpired, however, it was not until after 1930 that the rise in the numbers and proportions of the aged became spectacular. Then, just before the outbreak of the second world war, the combined effects of the post-Civil War rise in the birth rate, the precipitous fall in the birth rate between 1900 and 1934, the gradual aging of the millions of immigrants who had flocked to the United States from Europe during the early years of the twentieth century, and a significant rise in the expectation of life at age sixty-five, led to the situation presently prevailing. The magnitude of the recent changes may be illustrated as follows. Between 1900 and 1950 the number of persons aged sixty-five and over increased by 297 per cent, whereas the population as a whole grew by only 98 per cent. At the opening of the century only one person out of every twenty-four was in the aged category, whereas at mid-century the corresponding ratio had risen to one in twelve.

In a study cited above, the present writer attempted to determine the relative influence of the three factors involved in the recent aging of the population.[1] For the changes taking place between 1940 and 1950, the decade in which the spectacular rise in the numbers and proportions of the aged occurred, this study showed the factors and their relative importance to be as follows: the increased size of the generation caused by the larger number of births in the decade 1875–1884 than in the decade 1865–1875—57 per cent; immigration (during the early

[1] See Smith, "The Changing Number and Distribution of the Aged Population," loc. cit., pp. 2–4.

years of the twentieth century, of course) —23 per cent; and lower mortality rates after 1940 of those aged fifty-five and over that year—20 per cent.

An analysis of the three factors involved gives every reason to expect a continued sharp rise in the number and proportion of aged persons in the immediate future. Specifically, the recent upward trend of the birth rate has neither been great enough nor sustained for enough time to offset fully the long period during the nineteenth century and the first one-third of the twentieth century in which the birth rate was falling rapidly. If the world experiences no tremendous castastrophe, such as would result from a war with atomic weapons, there should be in the United States in 1960 slightly more than 16 million persons aged sixty-five and over, and in 1970 about 19 million. If in the meanwhile there are other spectacular medical discoveries, such as the perfection of "wonder drugs" that aid greatly in controlling the causes of death among those who have passed their sixty-fifth birthdays, the numbers may be slightly larger than these. Unless there are such discoveries, however, the number of the aged should continue to increase until about 1990, after which the low birth rates of the years 1925 to 1934 should be reflected in an abrupt drop in the figure representing those aged sixty-five and over in the year 2000. Thereafter another rapid increase in the number of people of sixty-five and over should begin.

The relative importance of the aged in the general population also seems certain to increase in the decades immediately ahead. However, unless one is able to forecast future variations in the birth rate the extent of this cannot be predicted accurately. The most probable estimates seem to be that the proportion of those aged sixty-five and over will be about 9.3 per cent in 1960 and 9.8 in 1970. If the birth rate again drops rapidly before these dates, the proportions may be slightly higher; and if large reductions in infant mortality rates occur, the proportions may be a little lower.

SUGGESTED SUPPLEMENTARY READINGS

Anderson, Walfred A., *The Characteristics of New York State Population.* Cornell University Agricultural Experiment Station, Bulletin No. 925, Ithaca (1958), pp. 31–43.

Bogue, Donald J., *The Population of the United States.* Chicago: The Free Press, 1959, chapter 6.

Landis, Paul H., and Paul K. Hatt, *Population Problems: A Cultural Interpretation* (Second Edition). New York: American Book Company, 1954, chapter 5.

McMahan, C. A., *The People of Atlanta*. Athens: University of Georgia Press, 1950, chapter V.

Notestein, Frank W., "As the Nation Grows Younger," *Atlantic Monthly*, 200, No. 4 (1957), 131–136.

Phelps, Harold A. and David Henderson, *Population in Its Human Aspects*. New York: Appleton-Century-Crofts, Inc., 1958, chapter 10.

Sheldon, Henry D., *The Older Population of the United States*. New York: John Wiley & Sons, Inc., 1958, chapters 1–3.

Slade, E. H., *Census of Pakistan, 1951*, vol. I. Karachi: Manager of Publications, Government of Pakistan, n.d., chapter 3.

Smith, T. Lynn, and Homer L. Hitt, *The People of Louisiana*. Baton Rouge: Louisiana State University Press, 1952, chapter V.

Taeuber, Conrad, and Irene B. Taeuber, *The Changing Population of the United States*. New York: John Wiley & Sons, 1958, chapter 2.

Thompson, Warren S., *Growth and Changes in California's Population*, Los Angeles: The Haynes Foundation, 1955, chapter VI.

Chapter 7

Sex Composition

THE SEX COMPOSITION of the population is the fourth of the demographic characteristics to receive attention in this volume. But no particular significance should be attached to this order, since, as indicated in earlier chapters, the classification of the census data according to sex constitutes (along with those by age, rural or urban residence, and race and nativity) one of the principal threads in the pattern of modern census tabulations. Logically, this discussion of the proportions of the sexes in the population might just as well come before as after the three immediately preceding chapters.

Much the same reasons make for the importance of the sex characteristic in population study as those given in the preceding chapter to set forth the importance of the age factor. This is to say that: (1) whether one is male or female is a primary determinate of the person's needs, attitudes, activities, and social and economic roles throughout life; (2) the proportions of males and females in its population does much to shape the form and set the tempo of a given society; and (3) the population analyst must be able to control or correct for the influences arising from the sex composition of the population before he is in position to isolate and measure other demographic attributes or variables. There is no point, for example, to comparisons of the birth rates of two areas, such as that of Alaska or some other pioneer zone (where males greatly predominate) and that of the District of Columbia (where women greatly outnumber men), unless the necessary adjustments are made for the differences in the sex composition of the respective populations.

A little study and reflection will make it evident that the proportion of the sexes in a nation, state, county, or community has a direct bearing upon the marriage rate and the death rate, as well as upon the birth rate. Furthermore many of the more important social and economic relationships are largely dependent upon a balance between the sexes or the lack of it. Thus the comparative scarcity of women is probably mainly responsible for the reckless abandon that is so characteristic of life on the frontier, and the same demographic factor contributes to a high degree in shaping the distinguishing features of life in mining camps, in centers of heavy industry, in cities that are primarily seaports, and in many agricultural districts. The social activities in the Yukon and in the Amazon Basin, in Gary and Youngstown, in Butte and Kimberley, in Marseille and Hongkong, or in the farming districts of Alberta and Iowa would be far different if there were not so many more males than females in their populations. On the other hand the relative shortage of males (and especially of those eligible for marriage) is keenly felt in most textile centers and other towns and cities in which light industry prevails; in residential cities such as Washington, D. C.; in cities such as Atlanta, Georgia, and Recife, Brazil, which constitute the metropolises of large districts from which heavy currents of migration have been flowing to distant parts of their respective nations; and in tens of thousands of villages and small towns, spread throughout the agricultural sections of the world, where women, especially widows and elderly spinsters who have moved in from the surrounding farms, are principal elements in the population. In brief, to a high degree the tempo of life in any community is a function of the ratio of males to females in its population.

Data and Indexes

Every modern census ascertains the numbers and proportions of males and females in the population. In the United States even the first census taken in 1790 determined the sex composition of the white population; and beginning with 1820 the numbers of males and females in the other segments of the population also have figured prominently in tabulations of the data gathered in each census. Since the inquiry respecting sex is the simplest question on the census schedule, census officials probably are correct in concluding that the sex classification of the total population is the most reliable of all those included in the tabulations.[1] It is correctly indicated that there is no ambiguity about the

[1] Cf. U. S. Bureau of the Census, *Fifteenth Census of the United States, 1930, Population,* Vol. II, *General Report, Statistics by Subjects* (Washington: Government Printing Office, 1933), p. 93.

terms and rarely any motive for misrepresentation. In the United States imperfections do arise in connection with the tabulations of the data for the various racial, nativity, and residential groups, since there is a large floating male population, including many foreign-born. Of special significance in this connection is the substantial numbers of Mexican "wetbacks" and others who have entered the country illegally, for whom it is difficult or impossible to secure complete and accurate returns. No doubt a part of these, and more males than females, are incorrectly enumerated as native-born, thus giving rise to errors in the reported sex distributions. It is unlikely, though, that such discrepancies exert any considerable influence upon the reported numbers of males and females in the country.

There is, however, one striking and persistent inconsistency that undoubtedly indicates a significant amount of error in the sex classification. Census after census there is reported a larger number of females than of males among Negro children of less than one year of age. In 1950, for example, the numbers of nonwhite males and females of less than one year of age were reported as 203,595 and 206,260, respectively. This is not consistent with what is to be expected on the basis of the proportions of males and females among newly-born Negro babies and of the numbers of each sex dying during the first year of life. Nor is it consistent with the ratio between the sexes among all those of less than five years of age, in the ages five to nine and so on. Therefore there must be some persistent error in collecting the data, some mistake that recurs census after census. As a result of a study of this specific matter, the present writer has suggested that the data for many young Negroes may be secured from overseers on plantations and other persons who are not the parents of the children involved and who can report only in a general way. If so it is not unlikely that the error is introduced in this manner.[1] Even so it is still difficult to understand why at every census the mistakes total up to an excess of females, rather than occasionally indicating more males than females. Be this as it may, the fact remains that the incorrect reporting of the sex of young Negro children must be reckoned with by those who use the census materials.

The indexes commonly employed in the study of the sex composition of the population are few, simple, and easily understood. Logi-

[1] See T. Lynn Smith, "Errors in the Sex Classification of Negro Children in the United States Census," *Congrés international de la population* (Paris: Herman & Cie, 1938), Vol. V, pp. 97–106.

cally, any one of the four following relative numbers might very well serve the purpose: the percentage of males in the population; the percentage of females in the population; the ratio of males to females multiplied by some constant; and the ratio of females to males multiplied by a constant. One need not look far in the works of those who have written on population subjects until he will encounter examples of all four of these usages. However, the one most commonly employed by demographers is that known as the sex ratio. It is computed by dividing the number of males in the population by the number of females and then multiplying by 100. Therefore as used in this volume the terms sex ratio and number of males per hundred females are exactly synonymous. This is the index long relied upon by the U. S. Bureau of the Census. It also conforms to the most standard usage around the world during the last century by those most experienced in population study; and much confusion would be avoided if all those writing on population matters would employ this conventional device when discussing the proportions of the sexes.

The sex ratio would be more useful by itself and in meaningful correlations with other factors if it were possible to get reliable data showing how the proportions of males and females vary with age. However, the popular supposition that women are prone to understate their ages is amply substantiated by an analysis of the materials they furnish to census enumerators.[1] (See Figures 47 and 48 and Table XI.) These figures are based on data from the 1890, 1910, 1930, and 1940 censuses. By using them any possible complications resulting from the deaths of combatants during the second world war is obviated. However, the table contains data from the most recent enumeration made in the United States. The data are limited to those for native whites and Negroes, respectively, because they are the groups that are practically unaffected by either emigration or immigration. It is important to observe that for each of the census years which figure in the diagrams (except 1890 when the ages near fifty show the effects of the slaughter of males during the Civil War) the curve representing sex ratios by age among the native whites takes the form of a long, drawn-out S. It begins, as should be expected, at approximately 105, and declines steadily for the first fifteen years. This is exactly what the known sex ratio at birth

[1] A detailed study of this phenomenon will be found in T. Lynn Smith and Homer L. Hitt, "The Misstatement of Women's Ages and the Vital Indexes," Metron, XIII, No. 4 (Dec., 1939), 95–108.

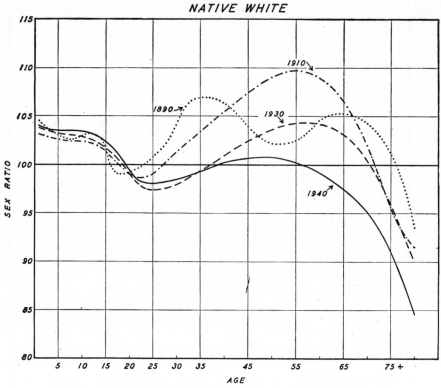

Figure 47. Sex ratios by age for the native white population
of the United States, 1890, 1910, 1930, and 1940.

and the higher mortality rates of males in comparison with females lead
one to expect. After age fifteen has been passed, however, the curve sags
greatly and reaches a low point at about age twenty-five, after which it
rises sharply to a high at about age fifty-five. Thereafter another decline
sets in which carries it down to very low levels among the group of
seventy-five and over. These variations are even more pronounced in
the curves representing the Negro population than they are in those
for whites.

It is important to note that the fluctuations in the curve for one year
closely parallel those for another. Neither the dips nor the peaks move
to the right from one census to another, as would be the case if they
represented an actual situation and not a constant error that is present
in enumeration after enumeration.

Theoretically the S-shape of the curve depicting sex ratios by age

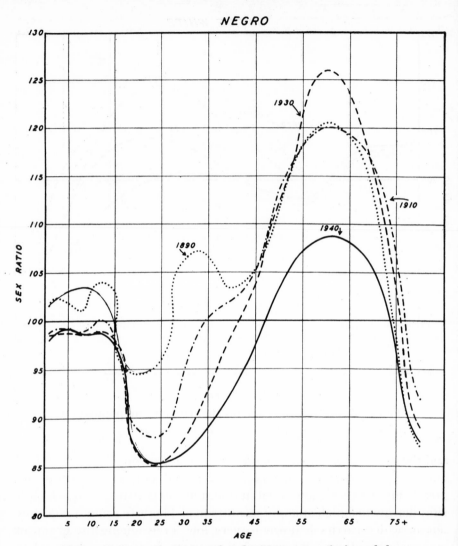

Figure 48. Sex ratios by age for the Negro population of the
United States, 1890, 1910, 1930, and 1940.

might arise in either of two ways: (1) if there were a tendency repeated
census after census for males in the ages of from fifteen to twenty-five to
overstate their ages, the result would be the dip in the curve followed by
the sharp rise such as appears in Figures 47 and 48; or (2) a similar result would occur if there were a tendency among women in the early
portion of adulthood to report themselves as somewhat younger than

Table XI. The Reported Number of Males and Females in Selected Age Groups in 1940 and 1950

1940		1950		Difference	
Age	Population	Age	Population	Number	Per cent

Native white
Males

5–9	4,733,600	15–19	4,653,840	−79,760	−1.7
10–14	5,231,893	20–24	4,873,460	−358,433	−6.9
15–19	5,433,529	25–29	5,135,855	−297,674	−5.5

Females

5–9	4,573,767	15–19	4,613,840	+40,073	+0.9
10–14	5,067,051	20–24	5,056,860	−10,191	−0.2
15–19	5,365,733	25–29	5,380,955	+15,222	+0.3

Negro
Males

5–9	643,781	15–19	591,550	−52,231	−8.1
10–14	661,351	20–24	563,730	−97,621	−14.8
15–19	630,079	25–29	579,880	−50,199	−8.0

Females

5–9	650,765	15–19	634,585	−16,180	−2.5
10–14	669,309	20–24	667,815	−1,494	−0.2
15–19	674,527	25–29	669,295	−5,232	−0.8

SOURCE OF DATA: Compiled and computed from data in U. S. Bureau of the Census, *U. S. Census of Population: 1950*, Vol. II, *Characteristics of the Population* (Washington: Government Printing Office, 1952).

their chronological ages. That the second alternative is responsible is amply demonstrated in a general way by the amount of the world's humor that hinges upon women's proverbial desire to pass as somewhat younger than their true ages, at least until late in life when exactly the opposite tendency may manifest itself. The statistics presented in Table XI also indicate that the understatement of women's ages is the factor producing the S-shape of the curve of sex ratios by age. Among the native white and Negro populations, the age groups five to nine, ten to fourteen, and fifteen to nineteen of one census should include the same persons as those fifteen to nineteen, twenty to twenty-four, and twenty-five to twenty-nine at the succeeding census, except for the reductions brought about by the death of some of the persons in the interim between the two decennial censuses. Among males, both native white and Negro, it will be observed that the decreases taking place as each of the age groups involved figured in the 1940 and the 1950 censuses were strictly in line with expectations. This is not so, however, in the case of females, where among both native whites and Negroes the age groups five to nine, ten to fourteen, and fifteen to nineteen in 1940 failed to decrease appreciably during the ten years required for them to figure as the age groups fifteen to nineteen, twenty to twenty-four, and twenty-five to twenty-nine in 1950. Such a buoying effect required the inclusion at the later date in the groups aged fifteen to nineteen, twenty to twenty-four, and twenty-five to twenty-nine of considerable numbers of women who actually belonged in higher age groupings. Indeed among native white women, the number actually increased as those aged five to nine and fifteen to nineteen in 1940 came to be those reported as fifteen to nineteen and twenty-five to twenty-nine ten years later!

It hardly needs to be said that these discrepancies destroy much of the usefulness of the data on the sex composition of the population. For those interested in the study of migration particularly, it is extremely unfortunate that the defective nature of the data on the proportions of the sexes by age precludes the employment of these materials in many of the analyses that otherwise would be simple.

Factors Directly Affecting the Sex Ratio

Most of the ways in which births, deaths, and migrations affect the proportions of the sexes in the population are simple and easily understood. One must merely keep in mind the following facts which are set forth more fully elsewhere in the appropriate places in this volume: (1) the sex ratio at birth is comparatively high, averaging probably about 105 in the United States and comparable magnitude in most other parts of the world; (2) in general the death rate of males, at all ages, is higher than that for females; (3) in migrations in which long distances are spanned, such as the overseas movements of population and most other types of immigration and emigration, males greatly outnumber females among the migrants; and (4) in migrations in which only short distances are covered, such as the exodus from the rural districts to nearby cities, females constitute disproportionately large numbers of those making the move.

In a population influenced by migration to a minor degree, the sex ratio among the general population depends almost entirely upon the magnitude of the birth rates and death rates. If both of these are high, so as to produce a heavy concentration of population in the younger years of life, the sex ratio will be comparatively high, perhaps about 100; if, on the other hand, both are very low, so as to make for relatively high proportions of persons aged forty or more, the sex ratio will be low, perhaps less than ninety-five. Other than this, the extent to which a country is losing by emigration or gaining by immigration is the major force determining the proportions of males and females in its population, with emigration tending to lower the sex ratio materially, or conversely, immigration exerting a buoying influence upon it.

As is to be noted in chapter 16, there may be some countries in the world, such as India, in which the death rates of females exceed those of males. In such cases, this differential mortality will cause the proportions of females, already high at birth, to rise steadily as age increases.

Some International Comparisons

As indicated above, the division of the population according to sex is probably the classification of census materials most generally employed throughout the world. Therefore, by using the data assembled in the *Demographic Yearbook* of the United Nations it is fairly easy to prepare and to keep up to date a table such as number XII. Furthermore, observation of such material serves to bring out the more important variations in the proportions of the sexes throughout the world, and it also serves to illustrate the manner in which the factors mentioned above have combined to produce the differences recorded. In making the comparisons it may be well to keep in mind as a norm the sex ratio of about ninety-six or ninety-seven which the present writer estimates as the probable current index for mankind as a whole.

Colonial areas, to which are attracted or carried large numbers of workers for highly commercialized plantation areas, are, of course, among the sections of the world in which males most greatly outnumber females in the population. Note the high sex ratios in Hawaii and the Federation of Malaya. Even greater is the scarcity of the numbers of women in Alaska and other frontier districts to which people have been attracted mainly by the hope of quick and rich rewards from prospecting and mining. Also some nations have attracted immigrants in sufficient numbers, within a period corresponding to man's life span, to

Table XII. Population Classified According to Sex and Sex Ratios for All Countries and for Territories of 1 Million or More Inhabitants for Which Data Are Available

Country	Year	Number of males	Number of females	Sex ratios Total	Sex ratios Ages 15–44
Africa					
Algeria (Moslem pop.)	1948	3,823,712	3,755,819	101.8	100.0
Egypt	1947	9,418,998	9,602,842	98.1	97.1
Libya	1954	566,617	525,213	107.9	.....
Union of South Africa	1951	6,432,085	6,235,674	103.1	100.9
Morocco (France)	1952	3,691,180	3,750,930	98.4	84.5
Tunisia (France)	1946	1,644,048	1,589,904	103.4	101.2
Angola (Portugal)	1950	2,033,568	2,111,698	96.3	.....
Mozambique (Portugal)	1950	2,755,927	2,976,390	92.6	.....
Morocco (Spain)	1950	499,771	510,346	97.9	.....
Gold Coast (United Kingdom)	1948	1,889,716	1,845,966	102.4	99.5
Kenya (United Kingdom)	1948	2,680,248	2,725,718	99.3	.....
Nigeria (United Kingdom)	1952–1953	14,529,264	15,186,895	95.7	88.3
Northern Rhodesia (United Kingdom)	1950	895,000	942,000	95.0	.....
Southern Rhodesia (United Kingdom)	1948	805,400	813,600	99.0	.....
Uganda (United Kingdom)	1948	2,481,394	2,477,126	100.2	95.7
Cameroons (British Adm.)	1952	715,753	724,117	98.8	92.8
Tanganyika (British Adm.)	1948	3,594,073	3,883,604	92.5	.....
North America					
Alaska (U. S.)	1950	79,472	49,171	161.6	183.7
Canada	1951	7,088,873	6,920,556	101.2	99.4
Costa Rica	1950	399,859	401,016	99.7	95.8

Cuba	1953	2,985,155	2,843,874	105.0	100.0
Dominican Republic	1950	1,070,742	1,065,130	100.5	95.9
El Salvador	1950	918,469	937,448	98.0	94.1
Guatemala	1950	1,410,775	1,380,093	102.2	98.4
Haiti	1950	1,504,736	1,592,484	94.5	89.4
Honduras	1950	685,935	682,670	99.5	98.7
Mexico	1950	12,696,935	13,094,028	97.0	91.8
Nicaragua	1950	520,448	536,575	97.1	91.4
Panama	1950	409,590	395,695	103.5	103.5
United States	1950	74,833,239	75,864,122	98.6	96.8
Jamaica (United Kingdom)	1943	598,267	638,796	93.7	.....
Puerto Rico (U. S.)	1950	1,110,946	1,099,757	101.0	97.5
South America					
Argentina	1947	8,145,175	7,748,652	105.1	103.6
Bolivia	1950	1,326,099	1,378,066	96.2	90.7
Brazil	1950	25,885,001	26,059,396	99.3	96.3
Chile	1952	2,912,558	3,020,437	96.4	94.1
Colombia	1951	5,742,067	5,806,105	98.9	.....
Ecuador	1950	1,594,803	1,607,954	99.2	96.0
Paraguay	1950	649,109	679,343	95.5	90.3
Peru	1940	3,067,868	3,140,099	97.7	96.2
Uruguay	1908	530,108	512,178	103.5	.....
Venezuela	1950	2,552,491	2,482,347	102.8	102.6
Asia					
Ceylon	1953	4,264,936	3,833,701	111.2	119.9
India	1951	183,333,874	173,545,520	105.6	106.3
Iraq	1947	2,127,345	2,438,840	87.2	85.9
Israel (Jewish pop.)	1948	370,273	346,405	106.9	106.3

Table XII. Population Classified According to Sex and Sex Ratios for All Countries (Continued)

Country	Year	Number of males	Number of females	Sex ratios Total	Sex ratios Ages 15–44
Japan	1950	40,913,711	42,504,974	96.3	92.8
South Korea	1949	10,188,238	9,978,518	102.1	104.2
Pakistan	1951	40,209,169	35,632,996	112.8	113.1
Philippines	1948	9,651,195	9,582,987	100.7	95.1
Syria	1947	8,722,155	8,720,534	100.0	......
Thailand	1947	8,722,155	8,720,534	100.0	99.0
Turkey	1950	10,527,085	10,420,103	101.0	102.6
Malaya, Federation of (U. K.)	1947	2,595,577	2,312,509	112.2	108.8
Europe					
Austria	1951	3,217,240	3,716,665	86.6	85.1
Belgium	1947	4,199,728	4,312,467	97.4	102.2
Bulgaria	1946	3,506,273	3,515,933	99.7	......
Czechoslovakia	1947	5,909,732	6,254,363	94.5	98.1
Denmark	1950	2,123,100	2,158,175	98.4	99.4
Finland	1950	1,926,161	2,103,642	91.6	93.8
France	1954	20,551,100	22,292,420	92.2	99.3
Germany	1946	28,527,837	35,929,652	79.4	67.9
Federal Republic	1950	22,350,692	25,344,980	88.2	84.7
Greece	1951	3,721,648	3,911,153	95.2	94.4
Hungary	1941	4,561,107	4,755,506	95.9	......
Iceland	1950	72,262	71,699	100.8	103.8
Ireland (Republic)	1951	1,506,597	1,453,996	103.6	105.5

	Year				
Italy	1951	22,905,000	24,127,000	94.9	.....
Luxembourg	1947	145,096	145,896	99.5	102.8
Netherlands	1947	4,791,443	4,834,056	99.1	98.6
Norway	1950	1,625,351	1,653,195	98.3	102.0
Poland	1931	15,618,975	16,488,277	94.7	.....
Portugal	1950	4,060,266	4,381,046	92.7	96.0
Romania	1948	7,671,569	8,201,055	93.5	91.5
Spain	1950	13,469,684	14,507,071	92.8	93.3
Sweden	1950	3,506,442	3,535,387	99.2	101.9
Switzerland	1950	2,272,025	2,442,967	93.0	95.3
United Kingdom	1951	24,117,810	26,107,414	92.4	96.0
England and Wales	1951	21,015,633	22,742,255	92.4	97.1
Northern Ireland	1951	667,819	703,102	95.0	80.0
Scotland	1951	2,434,358	2,662,057	91.4	93.2
Yugoslavia	1953	8,191,000	8,737,000	93.8	93.1
Oceania					
Australia	1954	4,546,113	4,440,415	103.2	104.4
New Zealand	1951	973,968	965,504	100.9	102.2
Hawaii (U. S.)	1950	273,895	225,899	121.2	125.4

SOURCE: Compiled and computed from the United Nations, *Demographic Yearbook, 1955*, New York, 1955, Tables 1 and 10.

increase materially the sex ratios among their populations. Israel is the most striking example of this; but Argentina, Cuba, Panama, Uruguay, Venezuela, and Australia also owe the considerable preponderance of males in their populations largely to immigration. In addition the Union of South Africa, Canada, the United States, Brazil, and New Zealand the sex ratios indicated by the latest censuses would have been considerably lower than those recorded had large contingents of immigrants not been included in their populations.

Migration, however, definitely is not the explanation of the very high sex ratios noted in Pakistan, Ceylon, and India, and probably it is not responsible for the high proportions of males in Libya and Tunisia. To a minor degree a tendency on the part of Moslems to be reticent about their women, to the extent that some of the females may have been omitted from the census enumerations, may be a factor in all of these countries except India. That it is not a major factor, however, seems to have been definitely demonstrated by those responsible for the latest census of Pakistan, so that some other explanation must be sought for the observed phenomenon.[1] The most likely possibility is that females in these parts of the world have higher mortality rates than males.

The lowest sex ratios in the world are found in those countries which long have been sending out considerable numbers of emigrants and in which World War II recently resulted in a decimation of the male population. Germany, Austria, Finland, and France are the most striking examples, but the group includes as well most other countries in southern and eastern Europe. In some of these, birth rates and mortality rates are comparatively high, so that their sex ratios are significantly above what would have been the case had young children constituted smaller proportions of their total populations.

In comparison with the situation in other parts of the world, most Latin American countries have fairly well-balanced proportions of the sexes in their population. On the whole the sex ratio for the countries taken collectively does not differ greatly from the figure of ninety-six or ninety-seven which, as stated above, probably is a fair approximation of the index for all mankind at the middle of the twentieth century. This means, of course, that few of the Latin American countries have experienced any large influx of persons from abroad such as those which are responsible for the high sex ratios in Hawaii, the Federation of Malaya,

---

[1] E. H. Slade, *Census of Pakistan, 1951* (Karachi: Manager of Publications, Government of Pakistan, 1955), I, 54–56.

Israel, Australia, and the Union of South Africa. Nevertheless, Argentina, to a considerable extent, and Brazil, Cuba, Panama, Uruguay, and Venezuela, to a lesser degree, have had the proportions of males in their populations significantly increased by immigration. In the second place, this also means that none of the Latin American countries has had the sex ratio of its population considerably reduced by a heavy emigration, as has been the case in countries such as Scotland, England and Wales, Portugal, Spain, Romania, Poland, and Italy; nor in spite of frequent so-called "revolutions" have any large proportions of their male populations been killed off in recent wars. However, the proportions of males in Haiti, El Salvador, Mexico, and Paraguay doubtless are considerably lower than would have been the case had not considerable numbers of their nationals been migrating to Cuba, Honduras, the United States, and Argentina, respectively. Finally, there is little indication in the data that any of the Latin American countries have had the sex ratios of their populations inflated by higher death rates among males than among females.

Additional comments may be made about the sex ratios in Jamaica and the Republic of Ireland. The former has contributed heavily of its young male population to the labor forces in Cuba, Panama, and other circum-Caribbean countries; and the latter, with a sex ratio of almost 104, may appear to be somewhat of an enigma for a country losing so heavily by emigration. Probably a large movement of young Irish women to Liverpool, London, and other large cities on the neighboring island, where they obtain positions as domestic servants, is the major factor in producing and maintaining the relative shortage of women in Ireland.

The Sex Composition of Population in the United States

The sex composition of the United States varies greatly from place to place, group to group, and time to time. It is well to examine all of these in considerable detail, for the ratio of 98.6 males per hundred females in the population as a whole, as shown by the census of 1950, represents merely the balancing of many varying and often contradictory influences.

Variations Among the Race and Nativity Groups

There are, to begin with, some very striking differences in the proportions of the sexes found among the various race and nativity groups which make up the population. As revealed by the 1950 census the numbers of males per hundred females among the major categories and subcategories in this classification were as follows: total white, 99.0; native white, 98.6; foreign-born white, 103.8; total non-white, 95.7; Negro, 94.3; other races—total, 131.7; Indian, 108.7; Japanese, 117.7; Chinese, 189.9; and all other, 194.8. Several of these call for comment, although it suffices to point out that the sex ratio among the principal component of the population, the native white category, is exactly the same as that among the total population; and that the high ratios among the Japanese, Chinese, and miscellaneous group of nonwhites are to be expected among those who have migrated in large part from other countries.

The comparatively low ratio among the foreign-born whites may appear strange, in view of what was said above about the preponderance of males among the immigrants. In this connection, though, it should be mentioned that the foreign-born population of the United States consists for the most part of persons who came to this country prior to the first world war. They now are heavily concentrated in the ages in which the greater longevity of the females has had time to reduce greatly the disproportions between the sexes that once existed. In 1910 the sex ratio among the foreign-born white population of the United States was 129.2, and in 1920 it was 121.7; and as late as 1940 it stood at 111.1.

The sex ratio of 108.7 among the American Indians demands attention, even though the population involved is relatively small. In 1900 the corresponding index was only 101.5, and in 1930 and 1940 it was 105.1 and 105.5, respectively. That conditions among the Indians are such as to favor the survival of the male in comparison with the female seems to be the only possible explanation.

The very low sex ratio among Negroes, the second largest component of the population, also deserves special comment. Since 1920, when there were 99.2 males per hundred females among the Negro population, the index has fallen steadily, being 97.0 in 1930, and 95.0 in 1940. In a large measure the low proportion of males in the Negro population stems from the low sex ratio at birth (approximately 103 as compared with 106 among the whites).[1]

[1] In turn this low sex ratio at birth probably is due to a considerable extent to the high proportion of stillbirths among births to Negro women. See T. Lynn Smith, "A Demographic Study of the American Negro," *Social Forces,* 23, No. 3 (March,

Immigration and emigration are of practically no consequence in determining the number of Negroes in the United States, since in 1950 there were only 113,842 foreign-born Negroes in the population, of whom 58,644 were male and 55,198 female; and since there is practically no emigration of Negroes from this country. Therefore migration has very little influence in determining the sex ratio among the American Negro population. The other significant factor that may have a bearing upon the sex ratio, namely the extent to which the population is concentrated in the younger ages of life (determined in turn by the levels of the birth rate and the death rate) makes for slightly higher sex ratios among Negroes than otherwise would be the case. This was demonstrated some years ago by the present writer by the use of the materials from the life tables for 1939–1941. At that time if there had been sex ratios at birth of 100 for both whites and Negroes, if the population of each race had been stationary, and if no factors other than the differences in expectation of life had influenced the sex ratios, there would have been only 93.7 males per hundred females among the whites as compared with 94.2 among the Negroes.[1] Therefore, the prevailing low sex ratios among Negroes in the United States would be even lower were it not for the fact that the average duration of their lives is still somewhat less than that of the whites. Because neither migration nor the average length of the life span helps account for the low sex ratio among the Negro population, the low sex ratio at birth, and the lower death rates among females than among males are the only factors to which the phenomenon may be attributed. Nevertheless, the recent marked increases in expectation of life at birth among Negroes, at a rate that is faster than the one for whites, helps explain why it is that the sex ratio among Negroes has fallen significantly during the last two decades.

Rural-Urban Differences

There also are sharp differences between the sex ratios of the populations in rural and urban areas. With few exceptions urban populations

1945), 382–383. This is because, for some unknown reason stillbirths run heavily to the masculine sex, the sex ratio probably being about 110 among all pregnancies and between 120 and 170 among stillbirths. See Sanford Winston, "The Influence of Social Factors upon the Sex Ratio at Birth," *American Journal of Sociology*, 37, No. 1 (July, 1931), 8–12.

[1] T. Lynn Smith, *Population Analysis* (New York: McGraw-Hill Book Company, 1948), p. 125.

Table XIII. Sex Ratios Among the Urban, Rural-Nonfarm, and Rural-Farm Populations of the United States, by Race and Nativity, 1950

	All Categories	Urban	Rural-nonfarm	Rural-farm
Race and nativity				
Total population	98.6	94.6	103.6	110.1
Native white	98.6	94.3	103.1	110.8
Foreign-born white	103.8	100.5	116.3	136.5
Negro	94.3	90.0	101.7	101.7

SOURCE OF DATA: Compiled from U. S. Bureau of the Census, *U. S. Census of Population: 1950*, Vol. II, *Characteristics of the Population* (Washington: Government Printing Office, 1952), p. 88.

are characterized by very low sex ratios, and farming populations by very high ones. See Table XIII which gives the most recent data for the United States. Much the same disproportions prevail among the various residential groups census after census. It also should be recalled that among persons who are married and among children the proportions of the sexes are approximately equal. Therefore, such a high sex ratio in the farming districts means that the farmer seeking a mate has the odds strongly against him, whereas the low sex ratio in urban areas determines that hundreds of thousands of young women in the cities are similarly disadvantaged. Undoubtedly both the marriage rate and the birth rate are below what they would be if the sexes were more equitably distributed in rural and urban areas.

State-to-State Variations

Most of the differences in the sex ratios of the various states are due to the differing proportions of the white and Negro, native-born and foreign-born, and rural and urban categories in their respective populations. Nevertheless, there are still other important variations from one state to another, such as that brought about by the rush of males to frontier and mining areas. Today the disproportions produced by such phenomena are of course much less than once was the case, but even so they are not to be entirely overlooked by one who would understand the reasons for observed differences in the sex ratios throughout the

United States. In order to make it possible to note the state-to-state variations in the proportions of the sexes in the two principal race and nativity groups, further subdivided into the three residential categories, and also in the population as a whole, the materials presented in Table XIV have been selected from the mass of information that is available. By means of such subsorting it is possible for one to study the manner in which the sex ratios differ from one part of the nation to another without running the risk of proving no more than that there are great differences from state to state in the extent to which the population resides in towns and cities, in the proportions of Negroes in the population, and in the relative importance of the foreign-born white population.

Because of the low sex ratios in urban areas and among Negroes, it is not surprising that the District of Columbia, entirely urban and with Negroes comprising more than a third of its inhabitants, has a sex ratio considerably below that for any of the states. It is most closely rivaled in this respect by two of the most highly urbanized states, New York and Massachusetts, with Georgia, Alabama, and Missouri following in the order named. At the other extreme, the highest sex ratios in the nation prevail in those portions of the country in which the frontier epoch is not long past, in which there are very few Negroes, and in which agricultural and mining activities predominate. Wyoming, with more than 114 males for each hundred females is the extreme in this respect, followed closely by Nevada, and then by Montana, North Dakota, South Dakota, Idaho, and Washington in the order named. North Carolina has a sex ratio exactly equal to that of the nation as a whole, and Maine, Vermont, and Illinois are almost in the same category.

Not only are the highest sex ratios in the nation to be found in the western states, but every state in the Mountain and Pacific divisions is characterized by a sex ratio that is above 100. California, in which the proportion of the sexes is almost exactly in balance, is the nearest to an exception to this uniformity, although males only slightly outnumber females in Colorado as well. In addition to the high proportions of males in both western geographic divisions, all of the states which border on any of the Mountain states, from Texas to North Dakota (with the exception of Oklahoma, which comes in this category only by grace of its long, narrow, and thinly populated panhandle) are ones in which males outnumber females. From the Dakotas this area of male pre-

Table XIV. Sex Ratios in the Various States by Race and Residence, 1950

State	Total population	Native white population			Negro population		
		Urban	Rural-nonfarm	Rural-farm	Urban	Rural-nonfarm	Rural-farm
United States	98.6	94.3	103.1	110.8	90.0	101.7	101.7
New England							
Maine	98.8	93.6	102.7	113.5	.....	.....	.....
New Hampshire	96.9	95.3	98.3	113.6	.....	.....	.....
Vermont	98.8	90.9	98.2	117.6	.....	.....	.....
Massachusetts	93.8	93.5	100.6	113.8	95.6	128.3	.....
Rhode Island	97.3	95.7	112.9	115.0	98.4	.....	.....
Connecticut	97.0	94.9	100.5	112.8	97.0	.....	.....
Middle Atlantic							
New York	95.4	93.3	100.5	112.6	84.5	137.0	.....
New Jersey	97.2	94.8	108.8	112.0	91.6	127.8	123.1
Pennsylvania	97.0	93.6	100.7	110.3	91.9	125.6	.....
East North Central							
Ohio	97.8	93.9	101.2	109.5	95.3	128.9	117.8
Indiana	99.1	95.0	100.3	109.3	95.5	149.9	.....
Illinois	98.3	94.7	104.0	111.0	91.6	160.0	.....
Michigan	101.7	97.7	103.5	113.1	98.6	98.7	.....
Wisconsin	101.1	93.9	100.6	117.8	106.7	.....	.....
West North Central							
Minnesota	101.3	91.9	101.1	118.8	106.8	.....	.....
Iowa	100.0	93.2	96.0	112.8	103.3	.....	.....
Missouri	96.4	91.1	96.8	110.8	90.7	106.0	109.3

North Dakota	108.8	95.3	102.2	121.5	.....	.....	.....
South Dakota	106.9	95.9	101.9	119.3	.....	.....	.....
Nebraska	101.4	93.0	98.7	116.1	98.2	.....	.....
Kansas	100.2	93.4	101.8	113.6	92.6	162.4	.....
South Atlantic							
Delaware	97.9	93.4	99.7	109.8	96.9	105.8	105.8
Maryland	99.2	94.7	108.0	110.2	94.8	111.9	112.0
District of Columbia	89.1	87.7	.....	.....	89.9	.....	.....
West Virginia	100.7	92.5	101.6	109.4	95.4	105.0	105.0
Virginia	101.9	98.2	106.4	106.8	91.3	107.5	107.8
North Carolina	98.6	91.7	102.9	105.5	86.1	98.7	101.9
South Carolina	96.7	93.4	101.0	106.3	85.0	90.1	100.3
Georgia	96.2	91.0	103.8	107.2	83.2	94.4	99.7
Florida	97.3	92.9	107.3	107.9	89.7	104.0	106.1
East South Central							
Kentucky	100.4	91.3	103.4	108.1	89.9	110.0	110.2
Tennessee	97.3	90.8	100.4	105.8	87.5	103.5	103.0
Alabama	96.4	92.8	98.6	107.1	86.0	94.2	98.7
Mississippi	97.7	94.7	97.9	106.4	84.7	90.4	99.7
West South Central							
Arkansas	99.3	92.6	98.5	109.2	86.4	91.9	101.8
Louisiana	96.7	93.9	102.1	107.9	87.0	95.7	102.3
Oklahoma	99.8	94.4	101.2	112.2	88.1	100.5	104.8
Texas	100.4	97.2	105.0	109.8	91.0	99.8	103.2
Mountain							
Montana	109.9	99.7	108.5	127.1	.....	.....	.....
Idaho	106.2	98.7	107.8	113.8	.....	.....	.....
Wyoming	114.1	101.0	123.1	125.8	.....	.....	.....

Table XIV. Sex Ratios in the Various States by Race and Residence (Continued)

State	Total population	Native white population			Negro population		
		Urban	Rural-nonfarm	Rural-farm	Urban	Rural-nonfarm	Rural-farm
Colorado	100.8	94.5	106.7	114.6	101.1	.....	.....
New Mexico	104.2	98.2	109.5	110.5	99.4	172.2	.....
Arizona	102.3	97.2	107.4	112.8	97.4	125.1	.....
Utah	101.9	98.8	103.7	113.4	.....	.....	.....
Nevada	113.3	102.2	121.3	134.1	.....	.....	.....
Pacific							
Washington	106.0	98.1	117.7	113.6	113.1	.....	.....
Oregon	103.2	95.5	107.8	115.8	103.6	.....	.....
California	100.1	95.1	113.8	109.6	95.1	156.3	121.9

SOURCE OF DATA: Compiled from the various state reports of U. S. Bureau of the Census, *U. S. Census of Population: 1950*, Vol. II, *Characteristics of the Population* (Washington: Government Printing Office, 1952). . . . . Class containing less than 5,000 persons.

dominance extends eastward along the northern tier of states to include Minnesota, Wisconsin, and Michigan. Otherwise only in Virginia, West Virginia, and Kentucky is the sex ratio above 100.

New England, the highly urbanized Middle Atlantic States, and the South, with its high proportions of Negroes, are the sections in which the females most greatly outnumber males in the population.

Because more than half (52 per cent) of the people in the United States are native whites residing in urban areas, it is well to give special attention to the data for them. These are given separately in Table XIV. Among this highly important segment of the population, only in the very small urban populations of Nevada and Wyoming do males outnumber females. In addition to the sex ratio of only 87.7 for native whites in the District of Columbia, which reveals the extent to which women from all over the nation have flocked to Washington to work in government jobs, indexes of less than 93 are characteristic of the towns and cities of such widely distributed states as Vermont, Minnesota, Missouri, West Virginia, North Carolina, Georgia, Florida, Kentucky, Tennessee, Alabama, and Arkansas. Among the urban native white population, sex ratios below the national average are found in one or more of the states in every census division except the Mountain and the Pacific, and even there those for Colorado, California, and Oregon are all less than 96.

Other than in the South, Negroes are almost entirely an urban population, and even so ten of the states have less than 5,000 urban Negroes each. In a few of the others, to which the bulk of the Negroes residing in their towns and cities had migrated during the interim between the 1940 and 1950 censuses, males considerably outnumber females among this group of recent arrivals from distant parts. Wisconsin, Minnesota, Iowa, Colorado, Washington, and Oregon are the states coming in this category. In the South, from whose rural districts the exodus of Negroes has been especially marked during recent decades, sex ratios among urban Negroes of less than 90 are the rule rather than the exception. Note especially the ratios of 83.2, 84.7, 85.0, and 86.0 in Georgia, Mississippi, South Carolina, and Alabama, respectively. These are the states in which the proportions of Negroes traditionally have been the highest in the nation, the ones which contain the bulk of the counties wherein the number of Negroes exceeds that of the whites. In the flight of the Negroes from the farms of these states, large numbers of the males have gone to the cities of the North and the West in search of jobs, whereas the females in very large numbers have resorted to nearby cities such as Atlanta, Jackson, Columbia, and Birmingham. As a result it is not surprising that in 1940 and 1950 the sex ratios among the Negroes in these cities, respectively, were as follows: Atlanta, 78.7 and 82.7; Jackson, 81.1 and 87.0; Columbia, 85.3 and 89.3; and Birmingham, 86.4 and 88.7. Such northern states as New York, Pennsylvania, and Illinois, whose principal cities attracted hundreds of thousands of Negroes early in the present century, also now have comparatively low sex ratios among the colored residents of their cities and towns, with the number of males per hundred females in New York being especially low.

The rural-farm population is, of course, the residential group in which the excess of males is most pronounced. Among the native whites, who constitute the major share of this residential category, males exceed females in number in every state, with the sex ratio of 105.5 in North Carolina being the lowest in the list. This is merely the extreme expression of the fact that male preponderance in the native white rural-farm population is least pronounced of all throughout the southern region. Thus every state in the South, as defined for census purposes, except Oklahoma has a sex ratio for this group that is below the national average of 110.8; and, on the other hand, outside the South, in no states except Pennsylvania, Ohio, Indiana, and California are the sex ratios for this group below the national norm. The highest ratios of all, among the native whites residing on the nation's farms, are those for Nevada, Montana, Wyoming, North Dakota, and South Dakota, in the order named. Among Negroes, too, the sex ratios in the rural-farm parts of the various states are considerably higher than those for the other residential groups.

For the most part, the sex ratios of the rural-nonfarm population, native white and Negro, are intermediate between the very low ones of the urban population and the very high ones of the rural-farm population. However, in states such as Iowa and Missouri, in which the village population, with its high proportions of widows and spinsters, makes up the bulk of the category, the sex ratio is comparatively low; whereas, in the states such as those in the Mountain division in which considerable groups of those engaged in mining, lumbering, and other extractive industries are included in the rural-nonfarm population, the corresponding sex ratios are high. In this connection, it should be repeated, of course, that the high sex ratios in this region, in all residential categories, are due in large measure to the large numbers of males who followed the frontier into these states in the closing years of the nine-teenth century and the opening ones of the twentieth.

Other Significant Variations

The economic base or bases upon which a city or other area rests also is a powerful force in determining the proportions of the sexes. This has already been made apparent by the data showing the very high pro-portions of males prevailing in the rural-farm areas and in the sections of the country in which mining, lumbering, and other extractive indus-tries are of considerable importance. But it seems well to note some of the extremes in the degree to which the sex ratio varies from city to city throughout the United States. In general, if other factors are equal, cities which function chiefly as naval bases or other great seaports, cen-ters of heavy industry, and mining centers tend to have high propor-tions of males, whereas those devoted largely to light industrial activi-ties (such as textile manufacturing), residential cities, and those based largely on distribution services run largely to females. With these points in mind it is interesting to note that in 1950 the cities of 100,000 or more inhabitants having the highest sex ratios were as follows: Norfolk, 124.7; Gary, 104.3; San Diego, 103.7; San Francisco, 101.1; and Detroit, 100.4. All of these were more than 5.5 points above the ratio of 94.6 prevailing among the urban population as a whole. At the other ex-treme, was Pasadena, with only 79.8 males per hundred females, followed by ten southern cities and the nation's capital, namely, Little Rock (84.5), Montgomery (85.1), Atlanta (86.3), Nashville (86.7), Rich-mond (87.1), Chattanooga (87.9), Shreveport (88.3), Charlotte (88.4), Savannah (88.4), Jacksonville (88.9), and Washington (89.1), all of which had sex ratios at least 5.5 points below that of the nation's urban population.

Trends in the Sex Ratio

Changes in the sex ratio in the United States result largely from the flow and ebb of the immigrant tide. As indicated above, those who migrate long distances include many more males than females. There-fore, the relative numbers of males and females in a nation is strongly influenced by the numbers and proportions of the foreign-born in its population. Prior to 1910, when the sex ratio in the United States was 106.0, an all-time high, the highest proportions of males in this country occurred in 1890 (105.0), and 1860 (104.7). These indexes are considerably above the ratios of 103.1 registered in 1830 and 102.2 in 1870. The latter, coming at a time shortly after hundreds of thousands of males had been slain in battle and after war had practically halted immigration to this country, is the lowest on record except for 1940, when the sex ratio was 100.7, and 1950, when it had fallen to 98.6. Due mostly to the practical cessation of immigration brought about by the first world war, maintained by the imposition of restrictions and the quota system (1922 and 1924), and shut off almost entirely by the great economic depression, the number of males per hundred females in this country fell from the all-time high registered in 1910 to 104.0 in 1920, 102.5 in 1930, 100.7 in 1940, and then, for the first time in history, to less than 100 by 1950. The large loss of men during the second world war and in the early stages of the Korean War contributed materially, along with the high mortality rates of the rapidly aging foreign-born population, in bringing the sex ratio to the low of 98.6 at the time of the latest census.

Among native whites the sex ratio was reported as 103.1 in 1850 and as 103.7 in 1860, on the eve of the great Civil War. After the termination of this conflict, the next census, that of 1870, reported only 100.6 males per hundred females in the native white population, a strong reflection of the carnage that took place during the four years of conflict. Thereafter, the sex ratio for this group rose to 102.1 in 1880 and to 102.9 in 1890. Then it began to fall steadily, reaching 101.1 in 1930, 100.1 in 1940, and affected preceptibly by the years of conflict during the ensuing decade, to 98.6 in 1950.

Only during the early years of the Republic, when the heavy importation of male slaves was a factor, has the Negro population included more males than females. In 1820, the first census to make available the necessary data, the sex ratio among Negroes in the United States was 103.4, but by 1830 it had fallen to 100.0. Ever since this time the index has been less than 100, with the lows coming at the end of the Civil War (96.2), in 1940 (95.0), and 1950 (94.3). Undoubtedly there is a considerable margin of error in these indexes, but even so the sex ratio among Negroes is low and getting lower. In addition to the effects of the wars, which reduce the sex ratios through the deaths of combatants, the factors treated in the preceding chapter which are producing the rapid aging of the population, white and Negro, are the principal causes of the falling sex ratios in the United States during the twentieth century. By increasing the numbers and proportions of the population in the ages above forty, in which the lower death rates of females than of males have brought the sex ratio to very low levels, such a trend has contributed greatly to the gradual fall of the sex ratios of both the native white and the Negro populations.

As one decade succeeds another, there is a tendency for the differences in the sex ratios of the rural and urban populations to become more pronounced. The two had drawn considerably apart by 1920 when there were only 100.4 males per hundred females in the urban population of the United States in comparison with indexes of 106.5 for the rural-nonfarm and 109.1 in the rural-farm portions of the nation. At this time the sex ratio of the native white, urban population was only 96.9, whereas in rural-nonfarm territory the corresponding figure was 102.7, and in rural-farm areas it was 109.5. Similarly among Negroes the sex ratios were 95.4, 103.7, and 100.3, in the urban, rural-nonfarm, and rural-farm residential groups, respectively. By 1950, however, the sex ratio for the urban population had fallen to 94.6, a decrease of 5.8 points, whereas that of the rural-nonfarm population was down only to 103.6, a decrease of 3.0 points, and that of the rural-farm category was 110.1, a rise of 1.0 points. The sex ratio of the rural-farm portion of the native white population in 1950 was 110.8, which is actually an increase of 1.3 points over the level at which it stood in 1920, whereas for rural-farm Negroes the 1950 index of 101.7 is 1.4 points above the one prevailing thirty years earlier. In sharp contrast, between 1920 and 1950 in the urban districts the sex ratio for native whites fell to 94.3, a decrease of 2.6 points, and that for Negroes fell to 90.0, a decline of 5.4 points. Thus the concentration of males on the nation's farms and of females in its cities became much greater during the thirty years for which the census materials enable us to make the comparisons.

As has been suggested above, the pushing forward of the frontier from the Atlantic to the Pacific brought about severe imbalances between the proportions of the sexes in the various geographic divisions of the United States. To the West, to the frontier, went the males, making the sex ratios in many western states extremely high, whereas in the East and the South, the migrations left disproportionately large numbers of females in their wake. With the passing of the frontier, however, each succeeding census has revealed a strong tendency for these state and regional differences in the proportions of males and females in the population to become smaller or for the sex ratios in the various parts of the nation to cluster more closely around the national mean. For example, in the Mountain states, the last frontier, as late as 1920 there were 115.7 males for every hundred females in the population. By 1930, however, this ratio had fallen to 111.3, by 1940 to 107.4, and by 1950 to only 104.4. Whereas at the close of the first world war the sex ratio in this geographic division was 11.7 points above the national average, at mid-century it was only 5.8 points above. Even more pronounced was the tendency in the Pacific states. In 1920 there were on the West Coast 113.9 males for every hundred females, but by 1950 the corresponding index was only 101.4. As a result, at the time of the 1950 census the Pacific geographic division had a sex ratio only 1.6 points above that for the nation as a whole, whereas thirty years earlier its index was 9.9 points above. Likewise in the East North Central, the West North Central, and the West South Central geographic divisions, where the sex ratios are above the national average, as one census after another is consulted one may observe the tendency for the sex ratios in the areas to approach the national average. Thus in the East North Central states the sex ratio declined from 1.7 points above that of the United States in 1920 to only 0.7 points above in 1950. In the West North Central states the corresponding change was from 2.1 points above to 1.5, and in the West South Central states it was from 1.8 points above to 0.9.

In sharp contrast with these changes were those in the geographic divisions in which the sex ratios consistently have been lower than that for the nation. In each of these, during the interim between 1920 and 1950, the difference between the sex ratio of the division and that of the United States became less pronounced by the end of the period than it had been at the beginning. Thus New England, which is the section of the country in which the sex ratio is the lowest, had an index in 1950 that was only 2.9 points below the national average, compared with one 5.5 points below in 1920. This was entirely due, however, to the fact that the sex ratio of the nation fell more rapidly than that in the region, and not because of any increase in the proportions of males in the extreme northeastern part of the country. In 1950 the Middle Atlantic states had a sex ratio 2.4 points below that for the United States; the East South Central states, one 0.9 under the national average; and the South Atlantic states, one 0.4 less than that of the nation as a whole. However, thirty years earlier the sex ratios in these geographic divisions were less than the one for the entire country by 2.6, 2.9, and 2.8 points, respectively. As in New England, the narrowing of the difference was due in each case to the lowering of the national index, and not because the number of males per hundred females rose in any of these sections of the country. The net effect of these various regional trends is readily apparent: now that all portions of the United States are well settled, with the passing of each decade the regional differentials are being reduced and the ratios between the sexes in all parts of the nation are approaching the national average.

The nature of the current trends is indicated by an examination of the changes in the sex ratios of the various states in the decade 1940 to 1950. During this period the fall in the sex ratio in the nation as a whole was accompanied by decreases in the indexes for all of the states except New Hampshire, Rhode Island, Virginia, and North Carolina. In New Hampshire the change was from a sex ratio of 96.9 in 1940, much below the norm for the nation, to one of 99.3 in 1950, only slightly above the national average; and in Rhode Island, the change was from an index of only 96.0 in 1940 to one of 97.3 in 1950, almost as high as that for the United States. As a result of the changes, in both of these states the proportions of the sexes became much more nearly comparable with the ratio for the nation as a whole. In North Carolina the sex ratio did not change between 1940 and 1950, with the interesting result that the index for the state, which was substantially below the national average at the beginning of the decade, was exactly equal to the one for the United States at the time of our most recent census. In Virginia, however, the change in the sex ratio during the period under consideration was directly opposite the national trend. In this state a slight rise in the sex ratio of from 101.5 in 1940 to 101.9 in 1950 was sufficient to bring its index from a position of only 0.8 points above the national average to one 2.3 points above in 1950.

Of the forty-four states characterized by falling sex ratios from 1940 to 1950, twelve comprised the group with indexes in 1940 that were lower than the national average. The District of Columbia also was in this category. During the decade under consideration the indexes for ten of them (Alabama, Connecticut, Florida, Georgia, Louisiana, Massachusetts, Mississippi, New Jersey, South Carolina, and Tennessee) fell less rapidly than that for the nation, so that in 1950 the relative importance of males and females in their populations was nearer the national mean than had been the case ten years earlier. However, in two of these states (Missouri and New York) and in the District of Columbia, the sex ratio fell off more rapidly, between 1940 and 1950, than it did in the United States, so that the femininity of their populations, in comparison with that of the nation, became even greater in the course of the ten years.

In thirty-three of the states in which the sex ratio fell between 1940 and 1950, the sex ratios in 1940 were above the national average. Among these the index for one state (Illinois) fell by 2.1 points, the same amount as that for the nation, during the decade. Since the 1940 bases for the state and the nation were almost the same, the ratio of change in the two may be considered as approximately equal. In twenty-one others (Arkansas, Arizona, California, Colorado, Delaware, Idaho, Indiana, Maine, Michigan, Minnesota, Montana, Nevada, Ohio, Oklahoma, Oregon, Pennsylvania, Vermont, Washington, West Virginia, Wisconsin, and Wyoming), the fall in the index during the period was more rapid than that in the nation, thus bringing the proportions of males and females in their populations closer to the national average. The most pronounced changes in this respect were the reductions of the sex ratios by 12.1, 5.2, 4.9, 4.8, and 4.1 points in the states of Nevada, Idaho, Montana, Arizona, and Vermont, respectively. In the remaining group of ten states (Iowa, Kansas, Kentucky, Maryland, Nebraska, New Mexico, North Dakota, South Dakota, Texas, and Utah), the fall in the index for the state was less rapid than that in the one for the United States. Therefore, the ten, along with Virginia, constitute the exceptions to the rule. Nevertheless in the country as a whole, the tendency is clear: between 1940 and 1950 the changes generally were such as to reduce the extent to which the sex ratios in the various regions and states differed from that in the United States as a whole.

SUGGESTED SUPPLEMENTARY READINGS

Anderson, Walfred A., *The Characteristics of New York State Population*. Cornell University Agricultural Experiment Station, Bulletin No. 925, Ithaca (1958), pp. 18–25.

Bogue, Donald J., *The Population of the United States*. Chicago: The Free Press, 1959, chapter 8.

Duncan, Otis Dudley, and Albert J. Reiss, Jr., *Social Characteristics of Urban and Rural Communities*. New York: John Wiley & Sons, Inc. (London: Chapman & Hall, Ltd.), 1956, chapter 3.

Knox, John Ballenger, *The People of Tennessee*. Knoxville: University of Tennessee Press, 1949, chapter 5.

Landis, Paul H., and Paul K. Hatt, *Population Problems: A Cultural Interpretation* (Second Edition). New York: American Book Company, 1954, chapter 4.

McMahan, C. A., *The People of Atlanta*. Athens: University of Georgia Press, 1950, chapter VI.

Smith, T. Lynn, and Homer L. Hitt, *The People of Louisiana*. Baton Rouge: Louisiana State University Press, 1952, chapter VI.

Thompson, Warren S., *Growth and Changes in California's Population*. Los Angeles: The Haynes Foundations, 1955, chapter V.

Chapter 8

Marital Condition

AN INDIVIDUAL'S PERSONAL HAPPINESS is probably more closely dependent upon his marital condition or status than upon any other factor.
Likewise the well-being of any society is influenced highly by the proportions of its population that are single, married and living with their
mates, separated, widowed, and divorced. For both of these reasons
the subject is of concern to students of population. In addition such
important demographic processes as the birth rate and the death rate
seem to be correlated to some significant degree with the marital condition of the population.

Data and Classifications

Every modern census includes items on the marital condition of the
population, and the tables presenting the information secured from
these questions figure prominently in the tabulations that are published. Indeed in many of the census reports, including those of the
United States, the amount of space given to such materials looms large
in the total. In the United States a query on marital status was used
for the first time in 1880, but the data for that year were never published. Beginning with the reports of the 1890 census, however, and
continuing through those for 1950, information on this important
characteristic fills many pages in the census volumes.

During the sixty years in which information on marital condition has
been supplied for the population of the United States, much has been
learned about the most effective and efficient manner of tabulating such
material. For example, the 1950 tables refer only to the population
fourteen years of age and over, a practice that also is widely used in reports issued in other countries. Excluding children of less than fourteen
is good procedure under the conditions prevailing in most countries at

212

the present time, since very few persons nowadays either contract matrimony or are given in marriage before they have passed through the stage of adolescence. Thus, in the United States in 1950 only 6,660 of the 1,090,020 boys aged fourteen were reported as married; and the corresponding figure for girls was only 6,980 in a total of 1,047,370. In countries in which child marriage still prevails to any considerable extent, there might be more reason, of course, for including the very young in the tabulations; but throughout most of the modern world the inclusion of the children in the tables merely introduces unnecessary complications in connection with the organization, manipulation, analysis, and interpretation of the data. It also is expensive and highly wasteful of space that might be much better used for other valuable tabulations.

There are, of course, four standard categories used for classifying the population according to marital status, namely, single, married, widowed, and divorced. Naturally, since the legal, religious, and moral sanctions governing unions between men and women vary so widely from time to time, from one society to another, and even within a given society at a stated time, those responsible for a census may experience considerable difficulty in deciding precisely whom to place in the married group. Much of the perplexity is related to the matter of proper handling of common-law or other fairly stable unions entered into without benefit either of clergy or of commissioned representatives of the state. Even the courts sometimes have trouble in determining whether or not one of these unions should be considered as a marriage. Therefore, it is not likely that the census taker will be able to classify all cases perfectly. Nevertheless, many countries do attempt to distinguish in their census tabulations between the persons who are legally married and those who are united only by some common-law contract.

In the United States the attempt is made to include in the married category those living under common-law arrangements and also those reported as separated. Those whose marriages have been annulled, on the other hand, are classed as single. The fact that in the United States the ordained representatives (priests, ministers, rabbis) of various religious bodies are authorized to act for the state in the performance of legal marriage ceremonies spares our census officials some of the difficulties encountered in some countries. In Brazil, for example, the couple wishing to marry legally and also according to the rites of the church must have two separate and distinct ceremonies performed, one by the commissioned officer of the state and the other by the priest, minister, or rabbi.[1] Otherwise, the union will lack either legal validity or religious sanction. Under these circumstances census takers must resolve the question as to what distinction, if any, shall be made between those who are legally married only, those united in a church union only, and those married both in accordance with the law and in accordance with the rules of the church.

There also are important differences among those who are married at any given time with respect to previous marriage of part of the married population and the ways in which any earlier marriage contracts were terminated. The married category includes, of course, many persons who remarried after one or more earlier unions had ended. Thus, those classified as married at the time of the census include those for whom the current union is the only one, widows and widowers who have remarried, divorcees who have remarried, and those who have had two or more previous wives or husbands. As yet, however, it has not proved practicable for a census to attempt detailed classifications of the married which would set forth precisely the facts about previous marital conditions of the persons involved.

In 1940 and 1950 the United States Census classified the population of fourteen years of age and over into the four broadly recognized groups (single, married, widowed, and divorced), with the married category subdivided into the cases in which the spouses were living together in the home and those in which they resided in different households.

Age and Marital Status

The average person's marital condition depends largely upon his age; and the proportions of the single, the married, and the widowed in a population is determined to a large extent by the nature of its age distribution. Therefore, the first step in all well-conceived attempts to analyze and compare the marital status of various populations must be the adoption or development of adequate methods for controlling the age factor. Some of the ways of doing this are employed in constructing Figures 49 through 52. These are relied upon heavily in the comparisons attempted in this chapter. First of all, though, it is well to examine in some detail the manner in which marital condition varies with age.

[1] See T. Lynn Smith, *Brazil: People and Institutions* (Revised Edition), (Baton Rouge: Louisiana State University Press, 1954), pp. 175, 530–532.

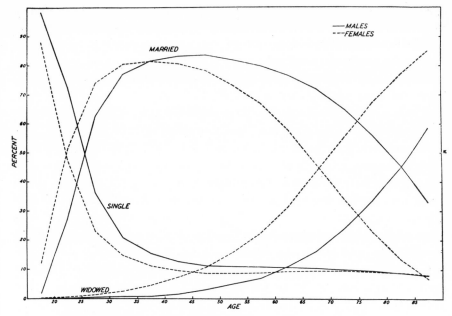

Figure 49. The relationship of age to marital status among the population of the United States, 1940.

In most modern societies child marriages are almost nonexistent. Therefore in a population such as that of Japan, France, Turkey, or the United States, the beginning of adolescence finds 100 per cent of the population in the single category. (See Figure 49 which compares the marital status of the male and female populations of the United States in 1940 and which is fairly representative of many western societies about the middle of the twentieth century.) A very small number of marriages involve those of about twelve years of age, but it is not until age fifteen has been reached that significant proportions enter into the marriage contract. Thereafter the curve showing the percentage single falls as age advances, precipitously at first, very slowly later on, until about the age of seventy-five. After this age has been attained, very few persons marry for the first time. As is evident from Figure 49, in the United States in 1940 about one out of twelve persons in the age group of eighty-five and over had never married at all, the exact proportions being 7.9 per cent for males and 8.0 per cent for females. In 1950 the corresponding proportions were 7.7 per cent and 9.7 per cent.

As indicated above, by the time age fifteen has been reached, significant numbers of people transfer from the category of single to that of married. Accordingly, the curve showing the proportion married rises rapidly, to accompany the fall in the one representing the single. Females marry at somewhat younger ages than males, so that the curve for the former rises somewhat earlier than for the latter. The data in Figure 49 indicate that before women had completed their twenty-second year of life, wives already outnumbered their unmarried sisters; but it was only while men were in their twenty-fifth year that the number of the married came to exceed that of the single. The curves for both sexes continue to rise with increasing age, since the number of new marriages is more than sufficient to offset the ones disrupted by death or divorce. That for females reaches its maximum height (at 81.7 per cent married) in the age group thirty-five to thirty-nine; and that for males, which rises more slowly, arrives at its zenith (at 83.3 per cent married) in the age group forty-five to forty-nine.

After these maximum proportions have been attained, the percentage married begins to fall off, rather rapidly among women and not so fast among men. As a result, by the time the ages above eighty-five had been reached, only 5.9 per cent of the women remained in the married category, in comparison with 32.2 per cent of the men. This differential is explained, of course, by the facts that women outlive men and that widowers are more likely than widows to remarry.

The proportions of the widowed in the population are insignificant during the years of late adolescence and early adulthood, but they rise steadily with increasing age. The curve representing the females rises more rapidly than that for the males, and the former also ascends to heights considerably above those attained by the latter. At about the age of forty-five the number of widows comes to exceed the number of single females in the population, whereas among males the curve for the widowers does not rise above that for the single until age sixty-two has been reached. At age seventy, one out of every five males was a widower and one out of every two females a widow.

Since the expectation of life at birth in the United States in 1950 was about seventy, it is interesting to note the marital condition of the population at that age. For the man who had attained his seventieth birthday, the chances were about one in twelve that he would have remained a bachelor, seven out of ten that he would be living with his first wife or a subsequent one, and only about one out of five that he would be a widower. For the women, however, the probabilities are very different.

The chances that she would have lived to age seventy without marrying at all were only one in eleven, that she would be living in the married condition only one out of two, and that she would be a widow were two in five.

Some International Comparisons

Although it is obvious that marriage patterns and the marital condition of the population vary widely from country to country, it is not easy to make valid international comparisons of marital status. This is largely because of the relationship between age and marital status just discussed, coupled with the fact that the age distributions of various populations are so different from one another. Unless the age factor is carefully controlled, therefore, it is nonsense to attempt comparisons of the marital condition of the population in such a country as Mexico or India, in which high proportions of the adult population are concentrated in the ages at which high proportions are married, and one, such as the United Kingdom or the United States, in which large proportions of the adult population are beyond the age of fifty.

In an attempt to make readily available to the student some of the more significant features of the marital condition of people throughout the world, Table XV was prepared. In it are presented, for a large share of the countries for which the data permit such comparisons, current information pertaining to the following "indicators" of marital status: the age group in which the curve showing the proportion of that population that is married reaches its maximum height; (2) the percentage of the persons in this age group who are classified as married; and (3) the proportion of those who have passed their seventy-fifth birthdays who are still single, and who, therefore in all probability will never marry. Each of these three indicators is given separately for both the male and the female portions of the population.

From the materials in Table XV a number of significant generalizations may be made relative to the marital condition of various populations throughout the world.

1. Without exception, the curve showing the percentage married reaches its maximum at an earlier age for females than for males.

2. In all countries except Panama, Ceylon, India, Thailand, Sweden, and Australia, the figure showing the maximum height of the curve representing the proportion of married in the population is higher for males than the one for females.

Table XV. Some Indicators of Marital Condition of the Population in Selected Countries

Country	Year	Age group in which the proportion married is maximum				Percentage of those 75 & over who are single	
		Males		Females		Males	Females
		Age group	Per cent married	Age group	Per cent married		
Africa							
Egypt	1947	45–49	93.6	30–34	87.6	1.2	0.6
Union of South Africa	1946	45–49	87.5	35–39	82.6	5.3	4.5
North America							
Canada	1951	40–44	85.2	35–39	84.8	10.9	11.2
Costa Rica [1]	1950	45–49	81.5	35–39	72.4	12.6	22.1
El Salvador [1]	1950	50–54	81.4	30–34	70.1	17.9	31.2
Panama [1]	1950	40–44	75.0	30–34	76.0	26.5	32.6
United States	1950	40–44	85.2	30–34	83.7	7.8	9.5
South America							
Ecuador [1]	1950	45–49	84.2	30–34	75.9	6.6	15.9
Paraguay [1]	1950	45–49	81.7	35–39	65.5	17.6	39.8
Venezuela [1]	1950	45–49	73.4	30–34	66.8	24.8	41.3
Asia							
Ceylon [1]	1946	45–49	85.9	30–34	87.0	6.5 [2]	3.4 [2]
India	1951	35–44	87.7	25–34	89.1	2.9	1.1
Japan	1950	40–44	95.0	30–34	83.3	2.0	1.4
Philippines	1948	40–44	88.1	35–39	79.8	2.5 [2]	5.9 [2]
Thailand	1947	35–39	88.9	30–34	86.1	6.6	4.1
Turkey	1945	45–49	92.8	30–34	91.3	6.1	4.3

Europe

Austria	1951	85.4	50–54	71.6	40–44	8.5	14.2
Belgium	1947	87.0	50–54	83.5	35–39	9.2	13.4
Denmark	1950	84.9	45–49	82.4	30–34	6.9	14.6
France	1954	84.0	55–59	82.7	30–34	6.2	10.3
West Germany	1950	90.4	50–54	75.5	40–44	5.6	10.4
The Netherlands	1947	87.7	45–49	80.0	35–39	8.6	12.8
Norway	1950	81.1	45–49	78.7	35–39	10.1	19.6
Portugal	1950	83.9	50–54	75.2	35–39	7.4	13.9
Sweden	1950	80.3	45–49	81.6	35–39	11.6	20.7
Switzerland	1950	82.9	45–49	76.4	35–39	10.5	17.3
United Kingdom	1951	87.1	45–49	82.4	35–39	8.4	17.2

Oceania

Australia	1947	82.4	40–44	83.3	35–39	13.3	13.7
New Zealand	1951	85.1	40–44	84.0	35–39	11.6	13.9

SOURCE: Compiled and computed from data in the United Nations, *Demographic Yearbook, 1955* (New York: United Nations, 1955), pp. 380–435.

[1] Includes those classified separately as consensually married.

[2] Ages sixty-five and over.

3. India and Thailand are the countries in which the tendency to marry at the earliest ages is most pronounced, and Austria, West Germany, and France the ones in which the tendency to postpone marriage until later in life is the strongest. In the case of France, however, women marry fairly young, whereas the curve showing the proportion of the married among the male population continues to rise until the age group fifty-five to fifty-nine is reached.

4. The curves showing the marital status of the population in Australia, New Zealand, Canada, and the United States are very similar.

5. The countries in which persons are most likely to marry during the course of their lifetimes are Egypt, Ceylon, India, and Japan.

6. Those in which they are least likely to contract formal marriage arrangements are the Latin American countries, including Costa Rica, El Salvador, Panama, Ecuador, Paraguay, and Venezuela.[1]

Differentials in Marital Status

In addition to the relationship between age and marital condition discussed above, it is possible to demonstrate the manner in which several other factors influence the marital condition of a population. These include sex, residence in rural or urban areas, and race or color. It is likely that there also are regional differences in marital condition, quite over and above those that may appear because the age, sex, racial, and residential composition of the population varies widely from one region to another, but much meticulous work, with all of the factors just enumerated carefully controlled, would be necessary in order to discover exactly what they are and to measure their magnitude. Unless this were done, any comparisons attempted would merely demonstrate that one region is more rural or urban, has higher proportions of whites or non-whites or has a different sex ratio than another. These facts are well known and susceptible of demonstration in much less cumbersome ways. As yet, however, there has been little effort to discover the extent to which such regional differences are present in the United States or any other country. Likewise any substantial efforts to determine the nature of the relationship, if any, between marital condition and such

[1] This is in accord with an earlier generalization to the effect that of all the people in the world "Latin Americans are in a class by themselves when it comes to shying away from legal matrimonial ties." T. Lynn Smith, *Population Analysis* (New York: McGraw-Hill Book Company, 1948), p. 137. See also, Smith, *Brazil*, p. 175.

INDEX

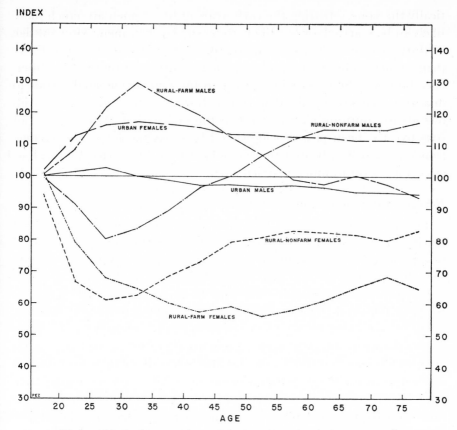

Figure 50. Index numbers showing the extent to which the white urban, rural-nonfarm, and rural-farm populations of the United States had more or less than their pro rata shares of single persons of each age group, by sex, 1950.

factors as religious affiliations, occupational status, educational status, and social status are still to be made.

In the discussions that follow, the data for the United States are used for purposes of illustration.

Sex and Marital Condition

The nature and extent of the differences between the marital status of males and females are readily apparent through an examination of Figure 49. (Conclusions based upon the 1950 census materials are practically the same.) During the early years of life women are much more likely to be married, or less likely to be single, than men. After the age of thirty-five or forty has been passed, however, men are more likely than women to be living in the married condition, although the difference between the sexes with respect to the percentage single tends to disappear. This is explained, of course, by the fact that at any time widows greatly outnumber widowers in the population. After the age of sixty-five has been passed, widowhood becomes the lot of the average woman, whereas only after the age of eighty has been passed do widowers come to outnumber married men.

Race or Color and Marital Status

The associations between race and marital status and residence and marital status are so interdependent that the two must be analyzed simultaneously. To handle these two relationships at the same time that the essential age and sex classifications also are included is an involved procedure. This has been done by the present writer, however, for both 1940 and 1950,[1] and the results may be presented in summary form.

The nonwhite (largely Negro) population of the United States mates at an earlier age than the white and also is less likely than the white to reach the advanced ages without marrying at all. After nonwhites have attained the age of twenty-five, however, males and females alike are much less likely to be living in the married state than are the whites. Largely because of the low sex ratio and the relatively high mortality rates of the Negro population, the proportions of the widowed among the nonwhite population is very high. The Negro man who lives in the South has abundant opportunities to secure another mate, if for any reason he loses his wife, and as a result is more likely to be classified as married than is the white man. In northern cities, on the other hand, the sex ratio does not operate in his favor, and after the age of about thirty-five he is less likely to be married and living with his wife than is the white man in the same city.[2]

The data for the nonwhite population are not sufficiently accurate to make it worthwhile to carry the analysis much beyond these points; and

---

[1] For the 1940 materials see Smith, *Population Analysis, loc. cit.*, pp. 140–143.

[2] For additional comparisons of the marital conditions of whites and Negroes, see T. Lynn Smith and Homer L. Hitt, *The People of Louisiana* (Baton Rouge: Louisiana State University Press, 1952), pp. 78–81.

for this reason, in the following section, the comparisons are based exclusively on the materials for the white portion of the population.

Residence and Marital Status

The association between residence and marital condition is a very close one. The central portions of a city, the suburbs, the town, the village, and the open country differ greatly in their power to attract and hold single, married, widowed, and divorced persons. Furthermore, the nature of the social and cultural environments in each of the residential categories has much to do with whether or not a person will marry and, for those who do, with whether or not the marriage will be terminated by death or divorce.

In order to bring out the more essential differences between the marital condition of the urban, rural-nonfarm, and rural-farm populations of the United States in 1950, Figures 50, 51, and 52 were prepared. These show the extent to which the white population in each of these three residential categories had more or less than its pro rata share of the nation's single, married, and widowed persons in each age group from fifteen to nineteen to seventy-five and over. Naturally, the indexes were computed separately for each of the sexes. A study of these charts brings out clearly the nature of the principal associations between residence and marital status.

Thus, they indicate that the most pronounced feature of the urban districts in this respect is the extent to which they attract and hold women who are single or widowed. On the other hand, they have slightly less than their pro rata share of the nation's single men, and barely their fair proportion of the widowers. In spite of the abundance in the urban districts of women who are eligible for marriage, the urban population does not quite contain its pro rata share of the country's married men. On the other hand, married women are substantially under-represented in it.

The rural-nonfarm areas, which it is well to remember are largely suburban, stand out because of their high proportions of married women, especially the young and the old. Their lack of young single men, coupled with their high proportions of bachelors over the age of fifty, and their relatively high numbers of young married men also deserve mention.

The rural-farm population contains far more than its pro rata share of the nation's married women, a fact that is closely linked to extreme

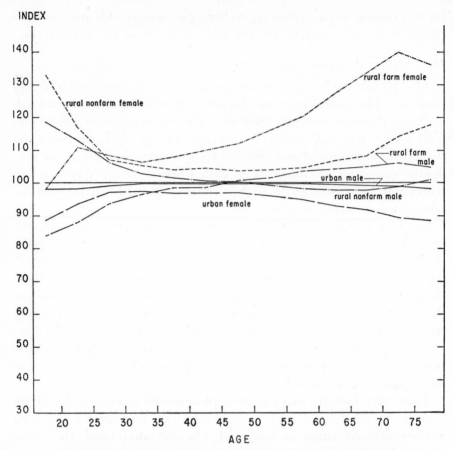

Figure 51. Index numbers showing the extent to which the
white urban, rural-nonfarm, and rural-farm populations of
the United States had more or less than their pro rata shares
of married persons of each age group, by sex, 1950.

scarcity of marriageable women, be they single, divorced, or widowed
in the farming districts. The proportion of young widowers is high in
the rural-farm population, although the numbers involved are not
large; but for the ages above fifty the indexes indicate that this residential group has considerably less than its pro rata share of this category.
In spite of the difficulties they encounter in finding a mate, due to the
exceedingly high sex ratio among the marriageable population of the
farming areas, the rural-farm males who have passed the age of forty-

INDEX

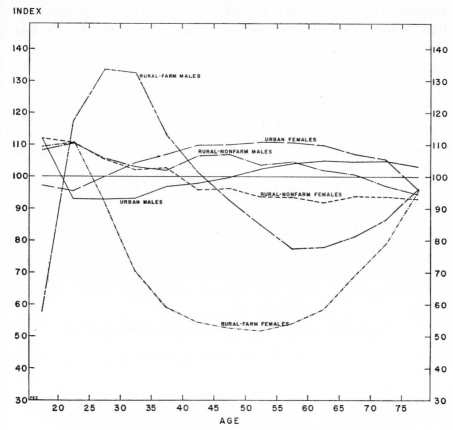

Figure 52. Index numbers showing the extent to which the white urban, rural-nonfarm, and rural-farm populations of the United States had more or less than their pro rata shares of widowed persons of each age group, by sex, 1950.

five are actually more likely to be living in the married condition than are their fellows in the urban and rural-nonfarm districts.

Trends

In the United States the proportion of married persons in the population increased substantially during the first half of the twentieth century, and the likelihood is strong that this trend will continue for several decades to come. (See Table XVI.) In 1950 the percentage of married persons in each age group was above the corresponding figure for

1900 in all cases, for women as well as for men, with the single exception of males aged sixty-five and over. Most striking of all is the fact that among men aged twenty to twenty-four the proportion classified as married in 1950 was eighty-five per cent higher than the index for 1900. Next most pronounced were increases of 41 per cent in the proportions of males aged twenty-five to twenty-nine and females aged twenty to twenty-four who were classified as married. But the percentages registered on the basis of the 1950 census were substantially above those evidenced by the 1900 enumeration in all cases, with the one exception mentioned above.

In large part this change is due to the fact that both men and women are marrying at ages considerably younger than was the case at the opening of the century. As a result, during the fifty years under consideration the proportions of the single among females of specified ages fell as follows: ages fifteen to nineteen, from 88.7 per cent to 82.9 per cent; ages twenty to twenty-four, from 51.6 per cent to 32.3 per cent; ages twenty-five to twenty-nine from 27.5 per cent to 13.3 per cent; and ages

Table XVI. Trends in the Marital Status of the Population of the United States, by Age and Sex, 1900 to 1950

| | Per cent married | | | |
| | Male | | Female | |
Age	1900	1950	1900	1950
14 years	0.1	0.6	0.5	0.7
15–19	1.0	3.1	10.9	16.7
20–24	21.6	39.9	46.5	65.6
25–29	52.6	74.2	68.9	83.3
30–34	69.8	84.3	78.0	86.2
35–44	78.8	87.0	79.5	84.2
45–54	82.2	85.6	73.9	77.3
55–64	79.7	81.1	60.5	64.7
65–over	67.1	65.7	34.2	35.7
Total	52.8	67.5	55.2	65.8

SOURCE: Compiled and computed from data in U. S. Bureau of the Census, *U. S. Census of Population: 1950*, Vol. II, *Characteristics of the Population*, Part 1, "United States Summary" (Washington: Government Printing Office, 1953), pp. 179–180.

thirty to thirty-four, from 16.6 per cent to 9.3 per cent. Likewise the comparable proportions of the single male population decreased as follows: ages fifteen to nineteen, from 98.8 per cent to 96.7 per cent; ages twenty to twenty-four, from 77.6 per cent to 59.1 per cent; ages twenty-five to twenty-nine, from 45.8 per cent to 23.8 per cent; and ages thirty to thirty-four, from 27.6 per cent to 13.2 per cent.

To a considerable extent, however, the increasing proportions of the married in the population result from the reduction that has taken place in the death rate which in turn has substantially lowered the percentages of widows and widowers. Thus between 1900 and 1950 the percentages of widowers in the male part of the population decreased as follows: ages thirty to thirty-four, from 2.0 per cent to 0.4 per cent; ages thirty-five to forty-four, from 3.6 per cent to 1.0 per cent; ages forty-five to fifty-four, from 6.8 per cent to 3.0 per cent; and ages fifty-five to sixty-four, from 11.9 per cent to 7.7 per cent. Similarly, during the same fifty year period the proportions of widows among the females fell off as follows: ages thirty to thirty-four, from 4.6 per cent to 1.6 per cent; ages thirty-five to forty-four, from 8.6 per cent to 3.9 per cent; ages forty-five to fifty-four, from 17.6 per cent to 11.3 per cent; and ages fifty-five to sixty-four, from 32.3 per cent to 25.2 per cent.

Were it not for the increasing proportions of the divorced in the population, of course, the percentages of the married would have mounted even more rapidly than has been the case. It would be easy, though, to attach too much importance to this factor. The following facts are useful in helping one to keep the proper perspective. Among males the maximum proportion of the divorced in any age category rose from 0.6 per cent among those forty-five to sixty-four in 1900 to 3.0 per cent among men aged fifty to fifty-four in 1950; and among females, the corresponding maximum from 0.7 per cent among women aged thirty to thirty-four in 1900 to 3.7 per cent among those aged forty to forty-four in 1950.

SUGGESTED SUPPLEMENTARY READINGS

Anderson, Walfred A., *The Characteristics of New York State Population.* Cornell University Agricultural Experiment Station, Bulletin No. 925, Ithaca (1958), pp. 43–50.

Bogue, Donald J., *The Population of the United States.* Chicago: The Free Press, 1959, chapter 10.

Burnight, Robert G., and Thea Field, *Characteristics of the Population, 1900–1950*. Storrs Agricultural Experiment Station Bulletin No. 326. Storrs, Connecticut: University of Connecticut, 1956, pp. 16–17.

Duncan, Otis Dudley, and Albert J. Reiss, Jr., *Social Characteristics of Urban and Rural Communities, 1950*. New York: John Wiley & Sons, Inc. (London: Chapmann & Hall, Ltd.), 1956, chapter 5.

Glick, Paul C., *American Families*. New York: John Wiley and Sons, Inc., 1957, chapter 8.

Groves, Ernest R., and William F. Ogburn, *American Marriage and Family Relationships*. New York: Henry Holt and Company, 1928.

Knox, John Ballenger, *The People of Tennessee*. Knoxville: University of Tennessee Press, 1949, chapters 11 and 12.

Locke, Harvey J., Georges Sabagh, and Mary Margaret Thomes, "Interfaith Marriages," *Social Problems*, IV, No. 4 (1957), 329–333.

McMahan, C. A., *The People of Atlanta*. Athens: University of Georgia Press, 1950, chapter VII.

Smith, T. Lynn, and Homer L. Hitt, "The Characteristics of the Populations of Southern Cities," in T. Lynn Smith and C. A. McMahan, *The Sociology of Urban Life*. New York: The Dryden Press, Inc., 1951, pp. 239–241.

Smith, T. Lynn, and Homer L. Hitt, *The People of Louisiana*. Baton Rouge: Louisiana State University Press, 1952, chapter VI.

Taeuber, Conrad, and Irene B. Taeuber, *The Changing Population of the United States*. New York: John Wiley & Sons, 1958, chapter 8.

Thompson, Warren S., *Growth and Changes in California's Population*, Los Angeles: The Haynes Foundation, 1955, chapter VIII.

Chapter 9

Occupational Status

THE OCCUPATIONAL STATUS of the population deserves careful study for several reasons. First, the data on occupations are the ones on which all indicators of employment and unemployment must be based. Second, occupational status is a major component in the establishment of general social and economic position or status. And, third, the classification of the employed workers by occupation and industry offers a sound basis for significant comparisons of the social and economic functions of cities, states, and other political entities.

Abundant materials on the occupations of the population and the industries in which the workers are engaged are collected regularly in connection with the censuses of population taken throughout the world. These data constitute very substantial portions of the demographic reports which are issued by most countries, including the United States; and their practical application in securing knowledge about such matters as employment and unemployment, the supply and distribution of various types of manpower, and so forth, is readily apparent to all. Nevertheless, it is fair to say that their analysis is still among the least developed parts of the entire field of population study. In many ways the voluminous reports issued census after census, along with substantial compilations of information gathered annually or as the result of special surveys, represent practically unexplored social and economic jungles. As yet neither the frame of reference nor the methodology that has been developed is adequate for the purpose of gaining from this multitude of facts the knowledge which is so badly needed. The study of occupations, which promises so much for the understanding of basic similarities and differences between two or more societies or the various parts of any given society, is still in its swaddling clothes.

229

Terminology and Classifications

Since 1930, and especially since the organization of the United Nations, much headway has been made in the development and refinement of meaningful terminology to be employed in the analysis of occupational statistics, and familiarity with some of the results of these accomplishments is essential for all students of population.

The Labor Force or the Economically Active Population

Especially important are the distinctions, developed largely since 1930, designed to exclude from the tabulations and classifications of occupational statistics all persons who are neither actively engaged in economically productive activities nor seeking such employment. "Labor Force" is the term used by the United States Bureau of the Census to designate the large category of persons for which an occupational classification is of primary importance, and the meaning of this term corresponds closely with the "Economically Active Population" as used in the *Demographic Yearbook* and other publications of the United Nations.

It is no easy matter to design a set of criteria that are entirely adequate for the purpose of distinguishing those in the labor force or in the economically active population from those who should be excluded from the category. This is illustrated by the procedures used in the 1950 census of the United States. In this fundamental compilation, three big groups of persons made up the labor force; namely, the employed, the unemployed, and members of the armed forces. The third of these included all persons on active duty with the United States Army, Air Force, Navy, Marine Corps, and Coast Guard, but the definition of the other two groups was considerably more difficult.

The *employed* class included all civilians aged fourteen and over who were either "at work," that is who during the week preceding the visit of the census enumerator "did any work for pay or profit, or worked without pay for fifteen hours or more on a family farm or in a family business," and also those "with a job but not at work." The latter was intended to include as employed persons and as members of the labor force those who had jobs or businesses from which they were absent temporarily "because of vacation, illness, industrial dispute, bad weather, or layoff with definite instructions to return for work within

30 days of layoff." It also included those with new jobs to which they were scheduled to report within thirty days.[1]

The *unemployed* subcategory included the persons of fourteen years of age and over who were looking for work or would have been doing so except that they (1) were temporarily ill, (2) expected to return to a job from which they had been laid off for an indefinite period, or (3) believed no work was available in their community.[2]

Persons classified as "not in the labor force," included all civilians of fourteen years and over who qualified for neither the employed nor the unemployed designations. It consisted largely of persons "primarily occupied with their own housework," those unable to work because of "long-term physical or mental illness or disability," inmates of institutions, and a miscellaneous group composed largely of students, retired persons, those too old to work, the voluntarily idle, "seasonal workers for whom the census week fell in an 'off' season," and those for whom employment status was unreported.[3]

In the compilations of data for various nations presented in several issues of the *Demographic Yearbook,* the technicians of the United Nations sought to define the "working" or "economically active population" as including "all persons of either sex engaged or seeking to be engaged in productive work in some branch of economic activity during a given period of time." The endeavor was made to include the following:

(1) Unpaid family workers, as well as employers, employees, and own-account workers

(2) civilians as well as members of the armed forces

(3) employed and unemployed persons, including those seeking work for the first time

(4) persons engaged even part-time in economic activities

(5) domestic servants.[4]

The "inactive" group, on the other hand, includes housewives, students,

[1] U. S. Bureau of the Census, *Census of Population: 1950,* Vol. II, *Characteristics of the Population,* Part 1, "United States Summary" (Washington: Government Printing Office, 1953) , p. 49.

[2] *Ibid.*

[3] *Ibid.*

[4] United Nations, *Demographic Yearbook, 1956* (New York: United Nations, 1956) , p. 35.

inmates of institutions, retired persons, children below the working ages, persons past the working ages, and so forth.

A glance at some of the materials presented in the fundamental compilations made by the United Nations makes apparent some of the difficulties involved in the attempt to get comparable data on the economically active populations of various nations and serves to emphasize the necessity of much caution on the part of those making international comparisons of the data that are assembled. In Egypt in the latest census (1947), 86.4 per cent of all persons aged five years and over were classified as "economically active," with the ratio reaching 99.0 for those aged fifteen to nineteen and 99.6 for those thirty to thirty-nine, inclusive. Even among persons of sixty-five and over the figure was 76.0 per cent. On the other hand in the United Kingdom (1951) only 59.6 per cent of the persons fifteen years of age and over were placed in the economically active category, and the index at its maximum in the sixteen to nineteen age group was only 85.9 per cent. Among those aged twenty to twenty-four the proportion was only 79.9 per cent, and thereafter it continued to decrease, with increasing age of population, until it was only a mere 10.2 per cent among those seventy years or more in age.

Still a different practice is evidenced in the data for Brazil in which 46.8 per cent of those ten years of age and over at the time of the 1950 census were placed in the economically active group. This index was only 19.8 per cent for the age group ten to fourteen, and then rose sharply to 50.9 for those fifteen to nineteen. This was near the maximum, however, for the figure rose only slowly to 54.7 among those aged forty to forty-nine, after which it fell, with increasing age, to 27.3 per cent among persons of seventy and above.

All three of these practices are considerably different from that used in the statistical compilations of such countries as the United States, Japan, and Israel. In the United States, for example, on the basis of the 1950 census, only 53.4 per cent of the population aged fourteen and over figured in the economically active class. At age fourteen the index was only 8.7 per cent. With increasing age the percentage rose to a maximum of 64.8, in the age-group forty to forty-four, and then fell off to 21.8 per cent of those seventy to seventy-four, and to 9.8 per cent of those beyond the seventy-fifth birthday.

Occupation and Industry

The classification of the experienced members of the labor force or the economically active population according to the major industries in which they are engaged and the major occupation groups or categories of workers is another fundamental procedure used in the preparation of modern census materials. The 1950 census of the United States made use of 148 categories of industries organized into the following thirteen major groups: (1) agriculture, forestry, and fisheries; (2) mining; (3) construction; (4) manufacturing; (5) transportation, communication, and other public utilities; (6) wholesale and retail trade; (7) finance, insurance, and real estate; (8) business and repair services; (9) personal services; (10) entertainment and recreation services; (11) professional and related services; (12) public administration; and (13) industry not reported. One who contemplates the use of any of these materials would do well to spend considerable time studying the specific components of each of these categories.[1]

Those in charge of assembling data on the economically active population for the publications of the United Nations use the set of nine major divisions from the International Standard Classification of All Economic Activities. These divisions are as follows: (1) agriculture, forestry, hunting, and fishing; (2) mining and quarrying; (3) manufacturing industries; (4) construction; (5) electricity, gas, water, and sanitary services; (6) commerce; (7) transport; (8) services; and (9) not classifiable elsewhere.[2]

The system used by the United States Bureau of the Census for the classification of occupations consists of twelve major groups which in turn are made up of 469 items, of which 270 are specific occupation categories and the remainder subgroupings, mainly on the basis of industry, of thirteen of the categories. The twelve major occupation groups are as follows: (1) professional, technical, and kindred workers; (2) farmers and farm managers; (3) managers, officials, and proprietors, except farm; (4) clerical and kindred workers; (5) sales workers; (6) craftsmen, foremen, and kindred workers; (7) operatives and kindred workers; (8) private household workers; (9) service workers except private household; (10) farm laborers, unpaid family workers; (11) farm laborers, except unpaid, and farm foremen; and (12) laborers, except farm and mine.[3]

As in the case of the classification of industries, this system used by the

[1] For the details of the classification see, U. S. Bureau of the Census, *op. cit.,* pp. 57–61, and U. S. Bureau of the Census, *1950 Census of Population, Classified Index of Occupations and Industries* (Washington: Government Printing Office, 1950).

[2] *Demographic Yearbook, 1956,* p. 38, and Table 12.

[3] U. S. Bureau of the Census, *Census of Population: 1950,* Vol. II, *Characteristics of the Population,* Part 1, "United States Summary," pp. 52–57.

United States Census Bureau is slightly more detailed than that employed in the *Demographic Yearbook* and other publications of the United Nations. The classification used by this international agency is as follows: (1) professional, technical, and related workers; (2) managerial, administrative, clerical, and related workers; (3) sales workers; (4) farmers, fishermen, hunters, lumbermen, and related workers; (5) workers in mine, quarry, and related occupations; (6) workers in operating transport occupations; (7) craftsmen, production process workers, and laborers not elsewhere classified; (8) service workers; (9) members of the armed forces; and (10) workers not classifiable elsewhere.[1]

Class of Worker or Status in the Profession

The modern census also attempts to classify the members of the active labor force according to what the U. S. Bureau of the Census designates as "class of worker" and the United Nations calls "status" in English and *selon la situation dans la profession* in French. Probably none of these is a very adequate expression of the basic idea involved, for, as is apparent from the categories employed, the basic objective seems to be to separate those who are employers from the employees with some further subdivision of each of these groups. The United States Census reports distinguish four categories, namely, private wage and salary workers, government workers, self-employed workers, and unpaid family workers; and the United Nations classifies the workers according to "status" as employers, workers on own account, salaried employees, and unpaid family workers.[2]

Some International Comparisons

Were it possible to determine accurately for various countries the extent to which the efforts of those who work are expended in the major lines of endeavor such as agriculture, manufacturing, trade and commerce, transportation, and personal services, some of the most enlightening comparative studies of various societies would be feasible. Casual observation, for example, would make it appear that some societies expend high proportions of the available manpower merely in adding

[1] *Demographic Yearbook, 1956*, pp. 39–40, and Table 13.
[2] *Ibid.*, pp. 40–41 and Table 14; and U. S. Bureau of the Census, *Census of Population: 1950*, Vol. II, *Characteristics of the Population*, Part 1, "United States Summary," pp. 61–62.

to the ostentation with which the members of a small elite class are privileged to live, whereas in others the number of domestic servants and other retainers has been reduced almost to the vanishing point. Again, in some societies the amount of human labor lavished on agriculture seems almost beyond belief to those from parts of the world in which each farmer combines large amounts of power and equipment with his own efforts in order to carry on various farm enterprises. Unfortunately, however, it is likely to be many years before the occupational data for various countries are sufficiently precise and comparable to justify their use in any except the most general studies of the situation in various nations.

This conclusion seems adequately supported by the data assembled in Table XVII which show the proportions of the male labor force of selected countries classified as engaged in agriculture, manufacturing, commerce, and the services, respectively. Probably the extent to which the economically active population is occupied in agriculture is reflected fairly accurately, and therefore of considerable use for comparative purposes. Certainly, the fact that nearly all the Latin American countries, along with such Asian countries as Ceylon, India, the Federation of Malaya, Pakistan, and the Philippines, have considerably more than one half of their gainfully male workers employed in agriculture seems in accord with general impressions and information obtained in other ways. It is more difficult, though, to account for the extent to which the proportions of those reported as occupied in manufacturing or in commerce vary from country to country; and the "services" category, which indicates that only 2 per cent of Bolivia's male labor force is so engaged, in comparison with 10 per cent of Brazil's or 19 per cent of Israel's, probably is entirely useless for comparative purposes.

In spite of the fact that inadequate data make significant international comparisons difficult or impossible, the materials for any given country are highly important for the study of the situation and trends within its borders. For obvious reasons, therefore, the discussion in the following pages of the various uses to which they may be put is illustrated with data for the United States.

Employment and Unemployment

In modern society the number of jobs that are filled at any given time, the ratio of this to the number of persons in the labor force, and

Table XVII. Proportions of the Male Economically Active Population of Selected Countries Who Are Engaged in Agriculture, Manufacturing, Commerce and the Services

Country	Year	Percentage engaged in			
		Agri-culture	Manu-facturing	Commerce	Services
Africa					
Egypt	1947	52	9	8	11
North America					
Canada	1951	24	26	14	14
Costa Rica	1950	63	10	8	6
Cuba	1953	47	16	12	13
Dominican Republic	1950	65	6	5	5
El Salvador	1950	73	9	3	6
Haiti	1950	87	4	1	4
Panama	1950	59	7	8	8
Puerto Rico	1950	47	11	12	13
United States	1950	15	28	17	17
South America					
Argentina	1947	30	20	15	15
Bolivia	1950	68	8	4	2
Brazil	1950	63	..	7	10
Chile	1952	37	17	10	12
Ecuador	1950	62	15	6	8
Paraguay	1950	63	12	6	10
Venezuela	1950	48	9	10	12
Asia					
Ceylon	1946	51	..	9	14
India	1951	69	10	6	11
Israel (Jewish population)	1948	11	26	12	19
Japan	1950	40	20	12	11
Malaya, Federation of	1947	61	7	11	13
Pakistan	1951	76	6	5	6
Philippines	1948	64	6	5	11
Europe					
Austria	1951	25	30	8	11
Belgium	1947	14	38	11	9
Czechoslovakia	1947	40	..	6	14
Denmark	1950	30	29	13	10

Table XVII. Proportions of the Male Economically Active Population of Selected Countries Who Are Engaged in Agriculture, Manufacturing, Commerce and the Services (Continued)

Country	Year	Percentage engaged in			
		Agri-culture	Manu-facturing	Commerce	Services
Finland	1950	46	21	6	6
France	1954	26	26	12	12
West Germany	1950	16	35	9	13
Greece	1951	50	14	9	12
Hungary	1949	52	21	4	8
Iceland	1951	46	14	10	11
Italy	1951	43	..	..	19
Netherlands	1947	20	27	13	19
Norway	1950	31	26	9	8
Portugal	1950	52	17	8	9
Spain	1950	53	16	7	9
Sweden	1950	25	34	10	8
Switzerland	1950	22	37	10	12
United Kingdom	1951	6	37	12	18
Oceania					
Australia	1947	19	26	13	12
New Zealand	1951	22	24	15	13

SOURCE: Computed from materials in the *Demographic Yearbook, 1956* (New York: United Nations, 1956), pp. 344–387.

the indexes of employment and unemployment are vitally important as gauges of social and economic well-being. Obviously fairly reliable and current information on the workers in all industries and in all occupations must be at hand for such purposes; and this information must come from well-done censuses taken periodically, supplemented by frequent surveys during the intercensual periods. Figure 53, showing trends in the United States in employment and unemployment from January, 1947 to July, 1958, illustrates two of the more important ways in which such materials may be arranged. For some purposes, of course, the relative numbers showing percentages of the employed or the unemployed among all those in the labor force are even more significant than the absolute figures.

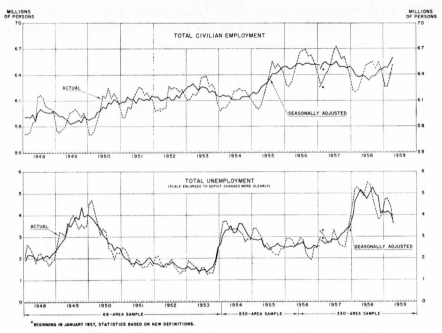

Figure 53. Trends in employment and unemployment in the United States, January, 1947, to July, 1958. (Illustrations from the U. S. Bureau of the Census)

Class of Worker

The manner in which the occupational data for the United States are classified and tabulated makes it possible to determine the numbers and proportions of those in the civilian labor force who earn wages or salaries by working for private employers, who work for government at one level or another, who are self-employed, and who are unpaid family workers. When such materials are further subdivided according to sex and rural or urban residence, several highly important facts and relationships stand out. (See Table XVIII.) As late as 1950, it should be stressed, over 70 per cent of the civilian labor force were employed by private companies or individuals and less than 10 per cent by government of all types. The self-employed, even including unpaid members of families, constituted less than one fifth of the total. Men are less likely than women to work for private employers or the government and more likely to be self-employed. Self employment continues to be the rule in the rural-farm areas, almost 60 per cent of the males coming in this category, which is indicative of the extent to which the family-sized system of farming retains its strength in many parts of the nation. Unpaid family labor has almost disappeared from the urban and rural-nonfarm areas, but because the family-sized farm continues as the basic unit in American agriculture, it still is important in the rural-farm areas.

Major Occupation Groups

The classification of occupations in the United States into major occupation groups also provides highly significant information pertaining to the manner in which the nation's workers gain their livelihoods. See Table XIX, in which the materials have been assembled to show the absolute and relative importance of each of the twelve major categories in providing employment for the male labor force. In order to enhance the value of this information, the data are further classified according to residence. Even such a simple procedure is ample to bring out several highly significant facts and relationships. Thus, the two categories which include the craftsmen and the operatives are composed of highly skilled workers, and the two together account for almost 40 per cent of the employed male workers in the nation. Domestic workers are conspicuous by their absence; and unskilled laborers, those who work on farms and all the others combined, make up less than 13 per cent of the males who were gainfully employed in 1950, a proportion only slightly larger than that of managers, officials, and proprietors exclusive of the farmers. Only a little more than 15 per cent of the nation's male labor force was employed in agriculture at the time of our latest enumeration, and even with numerous boys of less than twenty-one included considerably more than two-thirds of these were farm operators.

These data should also assist in making more untenable the position of many social scientists who are accustomed to using the data on residence as though they pertained to occupations. A specific error frequently encountered in social and economic literature is the practice of taking the ratio between the product produced on farms and dividing it by the number in the rural-farm population in order to determine the per capita production. However, it is evident from Table XIX that more than 8 per cent of the nation's male farm operators and one-third of its male farm laborers did not live on farms, whereas all the other

Table XVIII. The Civilian Labor Force of the United States According to Class of Worker, by Residence and Sex, 1950

Residence and sex	Total		Class of worker							
			Private wage and salary workers		Government workers		Self-employed workers		Unpaid family workers	
	Number	Per cent	Number	Per cent	Number	Per cent	Number	Per cent	Number	Per cent
Total	56,239,449	100	40,037,668	71.2	5,495,690	9.8	9,591,482	17.1	1,114,609	2.0
Male	40,519,462	100	27,793,416	68.6	3,466,249	8.6	8,624,154	21.3	635,643	1.6
Female	15,719,987	100	12,244,252	77.9	2,029,441	12.9	967,328	6.2	478,966	3.0
Urban	38,405,547	100	30,302,187	78.9	4,069,262	10.6	3,907,462	10.2	126,636	0.3
Male	26,188,118	100	20,304,656	77.5	2,573,953	9.8	3,282,109	12.5	27,400	0.1
Female	12,217,429	100	9,997,531	81.8	1,495,309	12.2	625,353	5.1	99,236	0.8
Rural nonfarm	9,859,856	100	7,136,212	72.4	1,103,067	11.2	1,503,419	15.2	117,158	1.2
Male	7,495,784	100	5,446,415	72.7	707,044	9.4	1,292,198	17.2	50,127	0.7
Female	2,364,072	100	1,689,797	71.5	396,023	16.8	211,221	8.9	67,031	2.8
Rural farm	7,974,046	100	2,599,269	32.6	323,361	4.1	4,180,601	52.4	870,815	10.9
Male	6,835,560	100	2,042,345	29.9	185,252	2.7	4,049,847	59.2	558,116	8.2
Female	1,138,486	100	556,924	48.9	138,109	12.1	130,754	11.5	312,699	27.5

SOURCE: Compiled from U. S. Bureau of the Census, *U. S. Census of Population: 1950*, Vol. II, *Characteristics of the Population*, Part 1, "United States Summary," (Washington: Government Printing Office, 1953), p. 101.

major occupational categories, including craftsmen, operatives, proprietors and officials of businesses other than farms, and even professional men were found in considerable numbers in the rural-farm population.

Major Industry Groups

The materials from the 1950 census make it evident that manufacturing is by far the most important source of employment for the nation's labor force, since 25.9 per cent of all employed workers were classified as engaged in manufacturing. Wholesale and retail trade, accounting for 18.8 per cent of the jobs, was second, and agriculture (including forestry and fisheries) with 12.5 per cent, third. Then came professional and related services, 8.3 per cent; transportation, communication, and other public utilities, 7.8 per cent; personal services, 6.2 per cent; construction, 6.1 per cent; public administration, 4.4 per cent; finance, insurance, and real estate, 3.4 per cent; business and repair services, 2.5 per cent; mining, 1.7 per cent; industry not reported, 1.5 per cent; and entertainment, 1.0 per cent.

Since a person's work is such a powerful determinant of what he is or what he becomes, it is interesting and important to note how the relative importance of several of the major industry groups varies from one state to another. For this purpose, the three major categories of manufacturing, wholesale and retail trade, and agriculture, which together in 1950 furnished employment for more than 57 per cent of the nation's workers, were selected. Data for them are assembled in Table XX. These materials fully support the widely-held belief that the northeastern sections of the country are the manufacturing areas *par excellence*. It is interesting to note, however, that both North Carolina and South Carolina, in addition to Delaware, also were states in which the proportions of the employed workers engaged in manufacturing exceeded the national average. At one end of the scale, North Dakota had less than 3 per cent of its workers employed in manufacturing, while at the other end 44 per cent of Rhode Island's workers were so engaged. Connecticut, Michigan, and New Hampshire are other states in which more than 40 per cent of the workers were employed in manufacturing; and South Dakota, Nevada, New Mexico, Wyoming, Montana, Arizona, Idaho, Nebraska, and Oklahoma are additional ones in which less than one worker in ten was in the manufacturing industry.

The noticeable feature of the data about wholesale and retail trade is the slight extent to which the proportion engaged in it varies from

Table XIX. Occupations of Employed Males 14 Years of Age and Over, by Residence, 1950

Major occupation group	Total		Urban		Rural nonfarm		Rural farm	
	Number	Per cent of total	Number	Per cent of group	Number	Per cent of group	Number	Per cent of group
Total	40,510,176	100.0	26,187,404	64.6	7,491,164	18.5	6,831,608	16.9
Professional, technical, and kindred workers	2,970,256	7.3	2,435,371	82.0	454,182	15.3	80,703	2.7
Farmers and farm managers	4,189,882	10.4	112,645	2.7	228,339	5.4	3,848,898	91.9
Managers, officials, and proprietors (except farm)	4,340,687	10.7	3,406,461	78.5	800,755	18.4	133,471	3.1
Clerical and kindred workers	2,602,610	6.4	2,206,717	84.8	324,181	12.5	71,712	2.8
Sales workers	2,596,786	6.4	2,137,477	82.3	383,723	14.8	75,586	2.9
Craftsmen, foremen, and kindred workers	7,537,016	18.6	5,544,071	73.6	1,619,303	21.5	373,642	5.0
Operatives and kindred workers	8,127,433	20.1	5,715,577	70.3	1,874,517	23.1	537,339	6.6
Private household workers	73,156	0.2	52,867	72.3	15,775	21.6	4,514	6.2
Service workers, except private household	2,373,410	5.9	1,997,509	84.2	324,584	13.7	51,317	2.2
Farm laborers and foremen	1,950,458	4.8	166,284	8.5	482,183	24.7	1,301,991	66.8
Laborers, except farm and mine	3,290,253	8.1	2,136,789	64.9	878,633	26.7	274,831	8.4
Occupation not reported	458,229	1.1	275,636	60.2	104,989	22.9	77,604	16.9

SOURCE: Compiled and computed from data in U. S. Bureau of the Census, *U. S. Census of Population: 1950*, Vol. II, *Characteristics of the Population*, Part 1, "United States Summary," (Washington: Government Printing Office, 1953), pp. 270–271.

Table XX. Relative Importance of Three Major Industry Groups in Providing Work for All Employed Persons in the United States, by Divisions and States, 1950

Division and states	Per cent employed in		
	Agriculture, forestry, and fisheries	Manufacturing	Wholesale and retail trade
United States	12.5	25.9	18.8
New England	4.0	38.5	18.1
Maine	11.1	34.2	16.8
New Hampshire	6.7	40.4	15.8
Vermont	18.6	24.6	15.6
Massachusetts	2.1	37.4	19.3
Rhode Island	1.7	44.0	17.9
Connecticut	3.0	42.6	16.8
Middle Atlantic	3.3	33.0	19.3
New York	3.0	29.8	20.9
New Jersey	2.6	37.7	17.9
Pennsylvania	4.2	35.5	17.5
East North Central	8.9	35.2	18.3
Ohio	7.0	36.6	18.2
Indiana	11.6	34.8	17.6
Illinois	7.1	32.0	19.5
Michigan	6.8	40.9	17.6
Wisconsin	18.8	30.6	17.3
West North Central	24.8	15.4	19.4
Minnesota	22.8	16.3	20.0
Iowa	28.5	15.2	19.2
Missouri	17.6	21.8	19.6
North Dakota	44.3	2.9	17.7
South Dakota	40.5	4.9	17.7
Nebraska	29.6	9.2	19.0
Kansas	23.0	12.6	19.4
South Atlantic	16.7	21.7	16.9
Delaware	9.0	32.4	16.1
Maryland	6.6	24.9	18.9
District of Columbia	0.2	7.3	17.6
Virginia	15.1	20.5	16.4
West Virginia	9.8	18.9	15.5
North Carolina	24.9	27.9	14.3
South Carolina	26.2	27.9	13.5

Table XX. Relative Importance of Three Major Industry Groups in Providing Work for All Employed Persons in the United States (Continued)

Division and states	Per cent employed in		
	Agriculture, forestry, and fisheries	Manufacturing	Wholesale and retail trade
Georgia	22.1	23.0	16.1
Florida	13.3	10.7	23.8
East South Central	27.4	18.4	15.4
Kentucky	25.8	15.8	15.5
Tennessee	21.9	21.1	17.0
Alabama	24.6	21.8	14.9
Mississippi	42.6	12.6	13.3
West South Central	19.6	13.3	20.1
Arkansas	35.3	13.8	15.8
Louisiana	18.3	15.1	19.4
Oklahoma	20.6	9.8	19.9
Texas	16.2	13.5	21.4
Mountain	18.1	9.5	20.1
Montana	25.2	8.5	19.1
Idaho	27.2	9.2	19.2
Wyoming	20.7	6.0	17.0
Colorado	15.2	12.2	21.1
New Mexico	18.6	5.9	19.0
Arizona	14.9	8.8	21.9
Utah	12.6	12.2	20.4
Nevada	10.7	5.1	19.9
Pacific	8.6	20.2	21.9
Washington	10.1	21.2	20.7
Oregon	12.7	22.7	20.5
California	7.6	19.6	22.4

SOURCE: Compiled from U. S. Bureau of the Census, *U. S. Census of Population: 1950*, Vol. II, *Characteristics of the Population*, Part 1, "United States Summary" (Washington: Government Printing Office, 1953), p. 135.

state to state. Thus the range is only from the low of 13.3 per cent in Mississippi to a high of 23.8 per cent in Florida. In this respect the former is most closely rivaled by South Carolina, and the latter by Cali-

fornia. This suggests that a major factor in such variations is the extent
to which tourism is a basic factor in a state's economy.

The variations in the extent to which the jobs in the various states
are directly in agriculture are of the same order as those in manufacturing. In this case, however, those states with higher proportions are
less regionalized, since very high percentages are found in the Dakotas
and some of their neighbors, and also in Mississippi and Arkansas. In
six states, namely, Rhode Island, Massachusetts, New Jersey, Connecticut, New York, and Pennsylvania, in 1950 less than 5 per cent of the
gainfully employed were engaged in agricultural pursuits.

The census data on major industry groups have proved particularly
useful to those geographers and sociologists who have been concerned
with the study of the functions of cities.[1] It is easy for one to determine, for example, the extent to which the gainfully employed in a
given city are engaged in manufacturing, trade and commerce, transportation, and each of the other major categories of industry groups;
and this information, in turn, forms a sound basis for inferences about
the functions in which each city specializes. An analysis of the pertinent
materials from the 1950 census does much to bring out the roles played
in the social and economic affairs of the United States by all its major
cities.

Manufacturing is, of course, the principal activity on which is based
the existence of most of the cities of the United States in their present
form. As a matter of fact, in 1950 over 33 per cent of the male workers
in forty-five of the nation's 106 cities of 100,000 or more inhabitants
were employed in manufacturing activities, and the proportion rose as
high as 63.4 per cent in Gary, Indiana, and 65.2 per cent in Flint, Michigan. There are, of course, cities in which manufacturing is practically
nonexistent, and of these, Austin, Miami, and Washington, D. C., are
the most striking examples. In none of them in 1950 were as many as
10 per cent of the workers engaged in manufacturing. Similar are the
extremes in the extent to which each of the other major groups of industries supplies the jobs from which are derived the livelihoods of the

---

[1] For a discussion of this subject and selected materials relating to it, see T. Lynn
Smith and C. A. McMahan, *The Sociology of Urban Life* (New York: The Dryden
Press, Inc., 1951), chapter 3; and T. Lynn Smith, *Current Social Trends and Problems in Latin America*, Latin American Monographs, No. 1 (Gainesville: University
of Florida Press, 1957), pp. 5–7.

families living in the various cities. A comprehensive analysis of all this is far beyond the scope of this chapter, but even so a glance at lists showing the cities which specialize to the greatest extent in each of the major industry categories is highly informative.

Flint, Michigan, as mentioned above, is the city with the highest proportion of its male workers engaged in manufacturing. The figure of 65.2 per cent for this city is 2.05 times as large as the corresponding one (31.9 per cent) for the urban population of the United States as a whole, so that Flint may be said to have 205 per cent of its pro rata share of the nation's male workers who are employed in manufacturing. In 1950 it was most closely rivaled in this respect by the following: Gary with an index of 199 per cent; South Bend, 184 per cent; Waterbury, 179 per cent; and Youngstown and Canton, each with an index of 175 per cent.

Phoenix, Arizona, was the city which in 1950 had the highest proportion of its male workers engaged in wholesale and retail trade, and the 29.6 per cent so occupied were equivalent to an index of 140 per cent of its pro rata share of the nation's urban males who were employed in such activities. Miami, Tampa, Charlotte, and Dallas, with indexes of 137, 134, 133, and 127, respectively, were next highest in the list.

Berkeley, California, which in 1950 had 17.4 per cent of its male workers employed in professional and related services, was in a class of its own in this respect. This was the equivalent of 300 per cent of its pro rata share of such workers in the urban portions of the United States. It was most closely followed by Austin, Cambridge, Pasadena, and Little Rock, with indexes of 253, 239, 189, and 150, respectively.

In 1950 Kansas City, Kansas, was the city specializing to the greatest extent in transportation, communication, and other public utilities. This category accounted for the employment of 22.1 per cent of its male workers, a proportion equal to 201 per cent of its pro rata share of those in the urban parts of the nation who were so engaged. Immediately below it in the list came Jersey City, with an index of 186, followed by El Paso (179), New Orleans (174), Duluth (171), and Omaha (171).

Personal services accounted for the employment of 9.3 per cent of all male workers in Miami in 1950, a proportion equal to an index of 259 per cent of its pro rata share of the urban men in this major industry category. Pasadena (210), Austin (176), Nashville (167), and Atlanta (163), were the other cities ranking highest in this list.

Corpus Christi, Texas, with 15.6 per cent (or 184 per cent of its pro rata share) of its male workers engaged in construction activities headed the list of this category. It was followed most closely by Austin, Miami, Baton Rouge, and Houston, with indexes of 179, 162, 161, and 159, respectively.

Public administration, which includes the civilian workers in national defense, is, of course, at its maximum in Washington, D. C. In the nation's capital 27.0 per cent of the male workers were so employed in 1950, a proportion equivalent to an index of 481 per cent of its pro rata share of such workers in the urban population of the nation. Because of their importance as centers of defense, Norfolk, San Antonio, and San Diego, with indexes of 333, 292, and 271, respectively, ranked second, fourth, and fifth in this list. A state capital, Sacramento, with an index of 326, was in third position.

The fact that Hartford, Connecticut, ranked first in 1950 with respect to the relative importance of finance, insurance, and real estate in providing employment for its male workers is not surprising. The actual percentage is 7.6, which was equivalent to an index of 204 per cent of its pro rata share of the nation's urban males who were so employed. New York, with its labor force of millions, ranked second (an index of 185), indicating the importance of this function in the nation's largest city, followed by Des Moines, San Francisco, and Pasadena, with indexes of 178, 170, and 170, respectively.

Finally, employment in business and repair activities category was at its maximum in Pasadena, California, where, in 1950, 5.1 per cent of the male workers were so engaged. This was the equivalent of 187 per cent of that city's pro rata share of the nation's urban workers of this category. The other cities highest in the list were Miami, Phoenix, Los Angeles, and Oklahoma City, with indexes of 186, 182, 174, and 167, respectively.

By considering simultaneously the data on the extent to which the various cities have specialized in the several categories, it is possible to classify them into a few distinct types. Manufacturing, wholesale and retail trade, and transportation and communication are, of course, the functions to keep principally in mind for this purpose, since they are the ones in which the large majority of the nation's urban workers are engaged. Even in the state capitals, and in the educational, recreational, cultural, and religious centers, they are the economic activities which furnish employment to the bulk of the workers. After considerable experimentation with the data from the 1940 census as well as those gathered in 1950, the figure of 17.0 per cent was taken as the basic criterion and each city was studied to determine which of the specified categories of industries were supplying employment to that proportion or more of the gainfully employed males in its population. Then the 106 cities of 100,000 or more inhabitants at the time of the 1950 census were classified into the following six categories or types:

1. *Manufacturing cities.* This group includes only those cities in which none of the general categories except manufacturing provided employment for as much as 17 per cent of the male workers. They are, of course, almost purely industrial cities, and they proved to be ten in number, namely: Akron, Cleveland, Dayton, Detroit, Elizabeth, Erie, Flint, Gary, South Bend, and Youngstown.

2. *Manufacturing and trading centers.* Cities which are highly specialized in the two functions of manufacturing and trade include the large majority of all the nation's major population centers. They in turn may be divided into two subgroups, namely, those in which manufacturing provides the jobs for more of the male workers than trade and commerce, and those in which the reverse is true. Of the seventy-one cities in the group as a whole, fifty-two were found to belong in the first of these subgroups, and only nineteen in the second. The cities in which manufacturing dominates are Allentown, Baltimore, Baton Rouge, Birmingham, Bridgeport, Buffalo, Cambridge, Camden, Canton, Chattanooga, Chicago, Cincinnati, Columbus, Evansville, Fall River, Fort Wayne, Fort Worth, Grand Rapids, Hartford, Houston, Indianapolis, Long Beach, Kansas City (Mo.), Los Angeles, Louisville, Milwaukee, Minneapolis, Nashville, Newark, New Bedford, New Haven, New York, Paterson, Peoria, Philadelphia, Pittsburgh, Providence, Reading, Rochester, St. Louis, Somerville, Springfield, Syracuse, Tacoma, Toledo, Trenton, Utica, Waterbury, Wichita, Wilmington, Worcester, and Yonkers. Those in which trade and commerce predominate are Atlanta, Boston, Charlotte, Dallas, Denver, Des Moines, Knoxville, Memphis, Oakland, Pasadena, Portland, Richmond, San Diego, San Francisco, Scranton, Seattle, Spokane, Tampa, and Tulsa.

3. *Trade centers.* There were in 1950 ten cities in which wholesale and retail trade was the only one of the large industry categories to provide employment to as many as 17 per cent of the male workers. They are Austin, Corpus Christi, Little Rock, Miami, Montgomery, Oklahoma City, Phoenix, Salt Lake City, San Antonio, and Shreveport (La.).

4. *Manufacturing, trade, and transportation centers.* For an additional eight of the nation's major cities the 1950 census data show that 17 per cent or more of the city's male workers were employed in each of three major industry categories, namely, manufacturing, trade, and transportation and communication. These cities are Albany, Duluth, Jersey City, Kansas City (Kan.), Mobile, Omaha, St. Paul, and Savannah.

5. *Transportation and trade centers.* Applying the criteria mentioned above, three cities fall into a group in which trade and transportation were the major industries supplying employment to the male workers. These are El Paso, Jacksonville, and New Orleans.

6. *Others.* Finally, four cities had, on the basis of the 1950 census data, principal functions in combinations that differed from those of any of the five types given above. In Norfolk, Sacramento, and Washington public administration and trade each accounted for the employment of 17 per cent or more of the male workers; and in Berkeley the category of professional and related services, as well as those of manufacturing and trade, more than met the minimum requirements for inclusion.

SUGGESTED SUPPLEMENTARY READINGS

Anderson, W. A. *The Characteristics of New York State Population.* Cornell University Agricultural Experiment Station, Bulletin No. 925, Ithaca (1958), pp. 60–66.

Bogue, Donald J., *The Population of the United States.* Chicago: The Free Press, 1959, chapters 16–19.

Davie, Maurice R., *Negroes in American Society.* New York: McGraw-Hill Book Company, 1949, chapter 5.

Landis, Paul H., and Paul K. Hatt, *Population Problems: A Cultural Interpretation* (Second Edition). New York: American Book Company, 1954, chapter 16.

Kaplan, David L., and M. Claire Casey, *Occupational Trends in the United States, 1900 to 1950,* Bureau of the Census Working Paper No. 5. Washington: U. S. Bureau of the Census, 1958.

McMahan, C. A., "Manpower and Labor Force Problems," chapter 3 in *Social Problems* by T. Lynn Smith *et al.* New York: Thomas Y. Crowell Company, 1955.

Maclachlan, John M., and Joe S. Floyd, *This Changing South.* Gainesville: University of Florida Press, 1956, chapter 5.

National Bureau of Economic Research, *The Measurement and Behavior of Unemployment*, Special Conference Series 8, Princeton, N. J.: Princeton University Press, 1957.

Phelps, Harold A., and David Henderson, *Population in Its Human Aspects.* New York: Appleton-Century-Crofts, Inc. 1958, chapter 15.

Smith, T. Lynn, and Homer L. Hitt, *The People of Louisiana.* Baton Rouge: Louisiana State University Press, 1952, chapter IX.

Taeuber, Conrad, and Irene B. Taeuber, *The Changing Population of the United States.* New York: John Wiley & Sons, 1958, chapter 11.

Thompson, Warren S., *Growth and Changes in California's Population.* Los Angeles: The Haynes Foundation, 1955, chapters X and XI.

U. S. Bureau of the Census, "Concepts and Methods Used in the Current Labor Force Statistics Prepared by the Bureau of the Census," *Current Population Reports,* Series P-23, No. 2 (1954).

Wynne, Jr., Waller, *The Population of Czechoslovakia.* U. S. Bureau of the Census International Population Statistics Reports, Series P-90, No. 3. Washington: Government Printing Office, 1953, chapter VI.

Chapter 10

Educational Status

AMONG ALL THE CRITERIA employed to describe or characterize the quality of a population, educational status probably is second only to health. Indeed, the two seem to be very closely associated, so that a people that ranks high on the health scale also makes a good showing with respect to educational accomplishments, and one that is low on the health scale is also low on the educational one. For this reason those who describe the attributes of populations in various parts of the world almost inevitably couple such adjectives as the following: illiterate and unhealthy, uneducated and disease-ridden, uninformed and short-lived, and healthy and well-educated. But whereas it usually is impossible to secure any comprehensive, reliable, and current data about the health scores of a given population and most of the conclusions on this subject must be based upon inferences from study of causes of death and mortality rates, information relating to educational status usually figures among the earliest substantial compilations of demographic data made for a given nation, state, or city.

Throughout the world during the second half of the twentieth century, it is almost taken for granted that the average person must have the ability to communicate orally, to read well, to write legibly, and to make and check a variety of arithmetical computations. This is true of persons in all walks of life, for those who live in the rural districts as well as those who inhabit the towns and cities. As a matter of fact, in the nuclear age the amount of schooling received by the oncoming generation is a direct reflection of the extent of the effort that the parents, the community, the state, and the nation are putting forth for the well-being of the society, and the number of years of formal schooling attained by the adult population is one of the best indicators of its quality.

251

Data and Indexes

Many modern censuses attempt to secure data that will enable the educational status of the population to be determined and that will permit comparisons of the educational attainments of the various segments into which the general population might be subdivided. Until quite recently it was deemed sufficient merely to ascertain whether or not those enumerated were able to read and write, so that judgments and comparisons could be made on the basis of the proportions of illiterates (or literates) in the total. A refinement early introduced in many countries was to eliminate from consideration those children too young to have acquired the skills involved in reading and writing and to give the information only for persons who had passed a given age, such as six years (as in Mexico), ten years (as in the United States), or fourteen years (as in Argentina). Prior to 1940, these data on the numbers and proportions of illiterates and literates were the only comprehensive materials on the educational status of the population that was assembled in the United States and in the other nations of the world. By 1930, however, the percentage of those in the United States and many other parts of the Western world who were unable to read and write had been reduced to such an extent that this index had lost most of the value it once had both for diagnostic and comparative purposes.

In the 1940 census schedule employed in the United States (and in those developed at approximately the same time in several other parts of the world) a query was included as to the number of years of formal schooling that had been completed. The data so obtained were assembled in cross-tabulation with those pertaining to age, sex, residence, race, and other characteristics. With these materials it is possible for the demographer to compute a number of simple but highly significant indexes, such as the percentage of those above a given age who lack formal schooling (a close approximation to the percentage of illiteracy), the median years of schooling completed, the percentage of high school graduates in the population, and the percentage of those above a given age who have completed four years of work in a college or university.

Some International Comparisons

Even in the second half of the twentieth century relatively few accurate generalizations may be made relative to the educational status of the population in many important parts of the world; and it is even more difficult if not impossible to rank the populations of the respective nations with respect to the educational level they have attained. It is true that the first issue of the *Demographic Yearbook* of the United Nations attempted to summarize the important data on this subject from around the world and that this endeavor has been continued with commendable vigor in connection with the preparation of subsequent compilations. But even if the fairly current information gathered by these coordinated efforts is supplemented by other data that are available, the gaps in our knowledge are still the most striking characteristics of such a summary as that presented in Table XXI. It is also true that much headway has been made since the close of the second world war, but even so much remains to be done before a comprehensive view of the world situation with respect to illiteracy or any other measure of the educational level of the population will be available to students of population.[1] Most discouraging of all is the fact that a great world organization has been unable to elicit data on the educational status of the population from most of the countries of Western Europe and from Australia and New Zealand, sections of the world in which undoubtedly the educational accomplishments of the population are fairly high.

Fragmentary though the data are, they still reveal the tremendous differences in educational status that prevail among populations in various parts of the earth. At one end of the scale are countries such as Canada, the United States, Belgium, and France in which all but a very small percentage of the adult population have acquired the skills involved in reading, writing, and elementary arithmetic. Were information available, many other European countries, along with Australia and New Zealand, also would be found in this group, since data for much earlier years showed the following proportions of illiteracy among those ten years of age and over: Czechoslovakia, 4.1 per cent in 1930; Finland, 0.9 per cent in 1930; Hungary, 6.0 per cent in 1941; Italy, 21.6 per cent in 1931; Poland, 23.1 per cent in 1931; and Sweden, 0.1 per cent in 1930.[2] Israel, Japan, and Algeria (French population) are other countries in which the benefits of an elementary education

---

[1] For a summary discussion of the situation prevailing prior to 1948, see T. Lynn Smith, *Population Analysis* (New York: McGraw-Hill Book Company, 1948), pp. 154–156.

[2] United Nations, *Demographic Yearbook, 1948* (Lake Success, New York: United Nations, 1949), pp. 7–9.

Table XXI. Variations in the Proportions of Illiteracy Among Persons Aged Ten Years and Over in Countries and Territories of More Than 1 Million Population for Which Data Are Available

Country	Year	Per cent illiterate
Africa		
Algeria (Moslem population)	1948	94.0
Algeria (European population)	1948	7.7
Egypt	1947	74.5
Union of South Africa (Bantu population)	1946	70.9
North America		
Canada	1951	1.9 [1]
Costa Rica	1950	21.2
Cuba	1953	22.4 [1]
Dominican Republic	1950	56.8
El Salvador	1950	57.8
Guatemala	1950	70.3
Haiti	1950	89.4
Honduras	1950	64.8 [2]
Mexico	1950	43.2 [2, 6]
Nicaragua	1950	65.2 [1]
Panama	1950	28.2
Puerto Rico	1950	25.6
United States	1951	2.1 [1]
South America		
Argentina	1947	13.3 [3]
Bolivia	1950	68.9 [4]
Brazil	1950	51.4
Chile	1952	20.2 [1]
Ecuador	1950	43.7
Paraguay	1950	31.8
Venezuela	1950	51.1 [5]
Asia		
Burma	1953	63.0 [1]
Ceylon	1946	36.2
India	1951	82.1
Israel (Jewish population)	1948	6.9
Japan	1950	7.7 [1, 6]
Malaya, Federation of	1947	61.7
Pakistan	1951	76.8 [2, 7]

Table XXI. Variations in the Proportions of Illiteracy Among Persons Aged Ten Years and Over (Continued)

Country	Year	Per cent illiterate
Philippines	1948	37.8
Thailand	1947	46.3
Turkey	1950	65.4
Europe		
Belgium	1947	3.1
France	1946	3.3
Greece	1951	23.5
Portugal	1950	48.7
Yugoslavia	1953	25.0

SOURCES: Compiled and computed from data in the 1955 and 1956 issues of the *Demographic Yearbook*, supplemented by materials from the official census reports of several countries.

[1] Less than one year of schooling.
[2] Data from official census reports.
[3] Population fourteen years of age and over.
[4] Population five years of age and over.
[5] Population seven years of age and over.
[6] Population six years of age and over.
[7] Population twelve years of age and over.

have been extended to the masses of the population. All of these are in the greatest contrast with many populous sections of the earth (India, Pakistan, Haiti, Egypt, and the Moslem population of Algeria) in which only the privileged few have ever studied in a schoolroom.

Between these two extremes fall the large majority of the countries for which materials are available. Among these, percentages of less than 30 in such parts of the earth as Costa Rica, Cuba, Panama, Puerto Rico, Argentina and Chile are indicative of the fact that illiteracy today is generally recognized as one of the major social problems confronting the respective societies and that strenuous efforts are being made to develop systems of universal education; [1] whereas indexes of more than 50 per cent in the Dominican Republic, Honduras, Nicaragua, Bolivia, Brazil, Venezuela, Burma, Malaya, and Turkey underscore the tremendous obstacles that these countries will have to over-

[1] Cf. T. Lynn Smith, *Current Social Trends and Problems in Latin America,* Latin American Monographs No. 1 (Gainesville: University of Florida Press, 1957), pp. 13–15, 24–25.

come before the masses of their populations weigh very heavily in the scales of international affairs.

Differentials in Educational Status

Even within a given nation or state there are highly significant differences in the educational status of the various segments or categories into which the population may be divided. Few societies give males and females equal amounts of formal education, the rural population almost never receives as much instruction as the urban population, racial or ethnic identification may be a powerful determinant in establishing whether or not a child may be privileged to attend school, occupation frequently is closely related to educational opportunities, and so forth. Fortunately, the data for the United States are adequate for the study of most of these associations, and frequently they may be supplemented with information for other parts of the earth in which one or more of these relationships is of particular significance. Consider first the materials in Table XXII which has been prepared in a manner that will enable one to determine the differences between the sexes, the residential groupings, and the white and nonwhite populations without running the risk of attributing to one of these factors any differences that may be merely a reflection of one of the others.

Sex Differentials

In the United States there is a significant and persistent tendency for girls to acquire more formal education than boys. This differential was evident from the materials gathered in the 1940 census which indicated that among native whites and Negroes alike in each one of the three residential categories, the median years of schooling completed by those who were aged twenty-five years or more was lower for men than for women. Furthermore, in every one of the forty-eight states and in the District of Columbia a similar differential was observed. Again in 1950, as is evident from an examination of Table XXII, this same consistent difference may be noted. In the nation as a whole and in the urban, rural-nonfarm, and rural-farm segments of which it is composed, and with the data for each further subdivided according to the color of the population, the indexes for women are above those for males. This is to say that urban women, white and nonwhite alike, complete more years of schooling than urban men and that comparable differences pre-

Table XXII. Median Years of Schooling of the Population Twenty-five Years of Age and Over in the United States, by Sex, Residence, and Color, 1950

Sex and color	Total	Residence		
		Urban	Rural-nonfarm	Rural-farm
Total population	9.3	10.2	8.8	8.4
Male	9.0	10.0	8.7	8.3
Female	9.6	10.2	9.0	8.6
White population	9.7	10.5	8.9	8.6
Male	9.3	10.3	8.8	8.4
Female	10.0	10.6	9.3	8.7
Nonwhite population	6.9	7.8	5.5	4.8
Male	6.4	7.5	5.1	4.3
Female	7.2	8.0	5.9	5.4

SOURCE: Compiled from data in U. S. Bureau of the Census, *Census of Population: 1950*, Vol. II, *Characteristics of the Population*, Part 1, "United States Summary" (Washington: Government Printing Office, 1953), pp. 96, 236–243.

vail among the two main categories into which the rural population is divided.

Since woman's role in passing on the cultural heritage from one generation to another is so much more important than man's, the sociologist may readily suggest that there is a sound basis for such a differential. But it should be emphasized that the tendency for girls to acquire more formal training than boys seems to be restricted largely to such countries as the United States and Canada. In the latter, as shown by the 1951 census data, 48.6 per cent of the females had completed nine years or more of formal schooling, whereas only 41.1 per cent of the males had attained a comparable level of training. Elsewhere in the world the general rule is for the efforts of the parents to be concentrated to a much greater extent upon the education of their male offspring than upon the schooling of their daughters. Representative differentials, as computed from the materials readily at hand in the 1955 issue of the *Demographic Yearbook,* are assembled in Table XXIII.

Several comments about these data seem to be in order. First, in general the lower the educational status of a population the greater the extent by which the index for the male part of the population exceeds

Table XXIII. Proportions of Illiteracy Among the Population Ten Years of Age and Over in Selected Countries, by Sex

Country	Year	Per cent illiterate	
		Male	Female
Africa			
Egypt	1947	64.4	84.3
North America			
Costa Rica	1950	21.0	21.5
Dominican Republic	1950	55.7	57.8
El Salvador	1950	54.7	60.6
Guatemala	1950	65.8	74.8
Haiti	1950	87.5	91.3
Honduras	1950	64.5	68.2
Panama	1950	27.6	28.8
Puerto Rico	1950	21.9	29.4
South America			
Argentina	1947 [1]	11.9	14.9
Bolivia	1950	60.4	77.0
Brazil	1950	47.2	55.6
Ecuador	1950	38.4	48.9
Paraguay	1950	23.6	39.4
Venezuela	1950 [2]	47.9	54.5
Asia			
Ceylon	1946	21.5	53.2
India	1951	70.4	90.6
Israel	1948 [3]	4.5	9.5
Philippines	1948	34.8	40.7
Thailand	1947	32.6	59.9
Turkey	1950	50.6	80.0
Europe			
Belgium	1947	3.0	3.2
France	1946	3.1	3.4
Greece	1951	11.0	35.1
Portugal	1950	33.3	49.3
Yugoslavia	1953	13.8	35.1

SOURCE: Computed from data in the *Demographic Yearbook, 1955* (New York: United Nations, 1955), pp. 436–471.

[1] Population aged fourteen and over.
[2] Population aged seven and over.
[3] Population aged five and over.

that for the female portion. Second, countries such as Costa Rica and Panama, in which remarkable progress in raising the educational status of the population has been achieved during the last quarter of century, along with Belgium and France, are the ones in which the sex differentials are most similar to those in the United States and Canada. Third, the Asiatic countries and Greece, and Yugoslavia are the ones in which the educational status of women compares most unfavorably with that of men.

Even in the United States, if the index used in making the comparisons is one indicative of the extent to which the higher and professional levels of training are achieved (such as the proportions of high school or university graduates in the population) it is evident that higher percentages of men than of women receive such instruction. Thus, in 1950, among the population aged twenty-five and over in the United States 6.0 per cent had completed four years or more of college or university work, but whereas this index was 7.1 per cent for the men it was only 5.0 per cent for the women; and in 1940 the comparable figures were 4.6 per cent, 5.4 per cent, and 3.7 per cent, for the total, male, and female populations, respectively. Furthermore, in both 1950 and 1940 these differences favorable to the male population prevailed in each of the residential and color categories into which the population may be classified. Therefore it is evident that in general in the United States, girls are more likely than boys to complete the eight years of elementary schooling, but that at the higher levels this situation is reversed and that men are more likely than women to complete professional and other university courses of study. The fact, though, that in 1950, 5,284,445 persons (6.0 per cent of those aged twenty-five and over, or whose schooling might be thought of as completed) had secured at least four years of college and university training is indicative of an exceptionally high general level of educational achievement among the population of the nation.

Rural-Urban Differentials

The relationship between residence and educational status is definite and substantial: the urban population ranks considerably above the rural-nonfarm population, and persons in the rural-nonfarm category in turn make a far better showing than those classified as rural-farm. This is evident if such an index as the median years of schooling is employed in the comparisons, and it stands out even more clearly when gauges such as the percentage completing four years of high school or four years of college or university training are relied upon. Note in Table XXII that among the total, the white, and the nonwhite segments and in each of these groups further subdivided by sex, the median is highest for the urban category, intermediate for the rural-nonfarm, and lowest for the rural-farm portion of the nation's inhabitants. If the percentage of the population completing four years of high school is used in making the comparisons, these differences between the educational status of the various residential groups are even more striking. Thus, in 1950, 33.4 per cent of the population of the United States aged twenty-five and over had completed the four years required for graduation from high school. Among the urban population, however, the proportion was 37.8 per cent, compared with 27.8 per cent for the rural-nonfarm and only 19.6 per cent for the rural-farm population. On the basis of the percentage completing at least four years of college or university training, the index is highest (7.2 per cent) for the urban, intermediate (4.6 per cent) for the rural-nonfarm, and lowest (only 2.2 per cent) for the rural-farm categories, respectively.

There can be little doubt but that similar rural-urban differentials prevail in other parts of the world. Indeed, the strong presumption is that in most countries the differences between the educational levels achieved by the residents of towns and cities and those of the rural districts are even more pronounced than those in the United States. The materials assembled to date by the United Nations and other international agencies do not permit a thoroughgoing study of this matter, but the extant data for the various Latin American countries deserve thoughtful consideration: In 1950 among the population aged ten years and over, the percentages of illiteracy among the rural and urban populations, respectively, of the countries for which the necessary data are available were as follows: Costa Rica, 28.5 and 8.1; Cuba (1953), 41.7 and 11.6; the Dominican Republic, 66.2 and 29.7; El Salvador, 73.2 and 32.5; Honduras, 74.7 and 43.6; Panama, 42.9 and 7.2; and Brazil, 67.7 and 21.4.

Color or Racial Differentials

The information in Table XXII indicates that the median number of years of schooling attained by the nonwhite (mostly Negro) population of the United States is substantially lower than that secured by the white population. This is true in the general population and in each of the residential categories. It also is the case when the data for each are further subdivided according to sex. Furthermore, the differentials are even more pronounced if the comparisons are based upon such indexes as the proportions of high school or college graduates in the population. Thus, the proportion of the persons twenty-five years of age and over who had completed four years of high school was only 13.2 per cent for the nonwhite population, whereas it was 35.4 per cent for the white; and the proportion completing four years or more of college or university work was only 2.2 per cent for the former in comparison with 6.4 per cent for the latter.

Such racial or color differentials in educational status are decidedly more extreme in the other countries for which comparative data (needed for the comparisons) are available. For example, in Brazil, a country wherein the numbers of Negroes and mulattoes closely approximate those in the United States, the materials gathered in the 1950 census may be analyzed in ways that make the differentials under consideration stand forth clearly. When this is done, it is evident that Negroes and persons of mixed ancestry compare much less favorably in educational status with their white fellows than is true in the United States. Thus, among the population ten years of age and over the proportion of those unable to read and write, which was only 34.2 per cent for the white population (and only 17.4 per cent for the yellow or Japanese population), rose to 68.9 per cent among the mixed (*pardo* or brown category) and to 73.3 per cent among the sizeable portion of the population that was classified as black. Likewise, if one studies the relevant materials it is found that of a total number of 36,537,990 people aged ten years and over, only 158,070 (0.4 per cent) possess degrees from institutions of higher learning. But this level of educational attainment had been achieved by 152,934 (or 0.7 per cent) of the whites, 3,568 (0.4 per cent) of the *pardos*, 924 (0.4 per cent) of the Japanese, and only 448 (0.01 per cent) of the blacks or Negroes.

Similar differences with respect to educational status exist between the white and Indian portions of the densely populated Andean sections of South America, a fact apparent to all who visit these portions of America. They are somewhat difficult to demonstrate statistically, however, since the racial or color classifications either are missing entirely from the censuses that have been taken or the racial materials are not cross-tabulated with those on educational status. For Bolivia, however, it is possible to secure the data which enable one to determine that 69.6 per cent of the population aged twenty and over was classified as illiterate, and that this index was 84.1 per cent for the adult Indian population and only 44.8 for the remainder of the inhabitants of the country.[1] Since those classified as Indian or "indigenous" constituted 63 per cent of the total, these figures make it readily apparent that the educational status of the white and mestizo part of the population is vastly superior to that of the Indian.

Since caste and class systems rooted in conquest and slavery prevail in most other parts of the world in which there are any considerable numbers of substantially different racial or ethnic stocks included in a given population, it is likely that the data as they become available will reveal differentials in educational status comparable to those demonstrated for the United States, Brazil, and Bolivia. In all cases it probably will be found that the groups once occupying a servile or semi-servile status have far to go before achieving a degree of schooling remotely approximating that of those who once were the masters, irrespective of whether the latter achieved their positions of dominance through conquest or by other means.

Regional and State-to-State Variations

In any given country the educational status of the population differs substantially from one part of its territory to another. In a considerable measure, of course, such regional or state variations are merely a reflection of the fact that the rural and urban portions of the population and the racial or ethnic groups of which it is composed are distributed quite unequally among the various sections of the nation under consideration. Even after such rural-urban and racial or color differentials are taken into account, however, frequently there remain substantial differentials which must be attributed to regional differences or still other factors. This is apparent to anyone who will study the data for the various states of the United States which are given in Table XXIV.

Generally speaking, there is a tendency for the median years of schooling attained by the adult population to vary directly with the relative importance of the urban and the white components in its make-up. This is to say that the more urban the state and the smaller

---

[1] The tabulations on which these computations are based are given in Asthenio Averange Mollineado, *Aspectos Generales de la Población Boliviana* (La Paz: Editorial Argote, 1956), p. 101; and Mario Arce Vargas, *Monografía Estadística Indigena de Bolivia* (La Paz: Editorial Fenix, 1954), p. 41.

the proportion of Negroes or other nonwhite elements among its inhabitants, the higher the index of educational status. Therefore it is not surprising that in the general population the median years of schooling is at its maximum (twelve years) in the District of Columbia, and lowest in the five southern states (South Carolina, Louisiana, Georgia, Alabama, and North Carolina) which have high proportions of Negroes and which are substantially more rural than the average for the nation. But neither the degree of urbanization nor the racial composition of the population is sufficient to explain why the score for the District of Columbia is matched by that for Utah, nor why California, Nevada, Washington, and Wyoming are the next four states in the list when these are ranked according to the educational status of the adult population. Therefore, it is important to study the materials in Table XXIV which show for each of the residential groups, further subdivided by color, the median years of schooling completed by the respective populations in each of the states.

If attention is centered upon the largest segment of the population of the nation, that portion of the white population that also is urban, some very interesting results are apparent. Among this part of the population (57.6 per cent of the total), the District of Columbia is the subdivision of the nation having the highest index in 1950 (a median of 12.4 years of schooling), followed by Utah, Nevada, and Mississippi (all with scores of 12.1 years), and then by Wyoming and California. The presence of Mississippi in this list of the leaders may surprise some people, although probably not to the extent that was the case when it was shown that the educational status of Mississippi's urban white population in 1940 was the highest in the nation.[1] Likewise, the fact that in 1950 Rhode Island and Kentucky were the states in which the educational status of the urban white population was lowest (medians of 9.3 years), closely rivaled for this dubious honor by New Hampshire, Connecticut, New Jersey, Pennsylvania, and Missouri (all with medians of 9.6 years), may not be in accord with previously held opinions on the matter.

Similarly the data given in Table XXIV, since they are tabulated separately for the color and residential groupings, make possible a wide variety of other significant state and regional comparisons of the edu-

[1] For the data, see T. Lynn Smith and Louise Kemp, *The Educational Status of Louisiana's Farm Population,* Louisiana Agricultural Experiment Station Bulletin No. 424, Baton Rouge, 1947, pp. 11–12.

Table XXIV. State-to-State Variations in the Median Years of Schooling Completed by the Population Twenty-five Years of Age and Over, by Color and Residence, 1950

Region and state	Total	Urban		Rural-nonfarm		Rural-farm	
		White	Nonwhite	White	Nonwhite	White	Nonwhite
United States	9.3	10.5	7.8	8.9	5.5	8.6	4.8
New England	10.4						
Maine	10.2	10.4	8.7	10.2	8.3	9.5	...
New Hampshire	9.8	9.6	...	10.3	...	9.8	...
Vermont	10.0	10.8	...	9.9	...	8.9	...
Massachusetts	10.9	10.9	9.2	11.2	8.3	10.1	...
Rhode Island	9.3	9.3	8.5	9.6	8.5	8.8	...
Connecticut	9.8	9.6	8.4	10.8	8.5	8.9	...
Middle Atlantic	9.3						
New York	9.6	9.8	8.6	9.9	8.0	8.9	7.7
New Jersey	9.3	9.6	8.2	9.5	7.3	8.7	6.4
Pennsylvania	9.0	9.6	8.2	8.8	8.0	8.6	7.7
East North Central	9.6						
Ohio	9.9	10.5	8.4	9.4	8.1	8.9	8.3
Indiana	9.6	10.3	8.4	9.2	8.2	8.8	8.1
Illinois	9.3	10.0	8.5	8.8	7.6	8.7	6.9
Michigan	9.9	10.5	8.5	9.6	7.9	8.7	8.2
Wisconsin	8.9	9.9	8.5	8.8	8.1	8.5	8.2
West North Central	9.0						
Minnesota	9.0	10.8	9.7	8.9	7.7	8.5	...
Iowa	9.8	11.0	8.7	9.0	7.6	8.9	...
Missouri	8.8	9.6	8.2	8.7	6.8	8.5	5.1

North Dakota	8.7	10.9	...	8.7	6.9	8.5	6.8
South Dakota	8.9	11.3	8.8	8.9	8.1	8.7	7.7
Nebraska	10.1	11.6	8.8	9.2	8.4	8.9	8.7
Kansas	10.2	11.5	8.7	9.4	8.4	8.9	8.4
South Atlantic	8.6						
Delaware	9.8	10.8	7.7	10.3	6.5	8.6	5.9
Maryland	8.9	10.0	7.2	8.9	6.4	8.2	5.5
District of Columbia	12.0	12.4	8.8	...	...	...	...
Virginia	8.5	11.5	6.9	8.2	5.5	7.4	5.0
West Virginia	8.5	9.9	8.3	8.3	7.0	8.1	6.4
North Carolina	7.9	10.4	6.7	8.5	5.8	7.4	5.3
South Carolina	7.6	10.3	5.7	8.4	4.4	7.9	4.4
Georgia	7.8	10.4	5.6	8.4	4.3	7.5	4.0
Florida	9.6	11.7	6.3	9.5	4.7	8.4	4.3
East South Central	8.3						
Kentucky	8.4	9.3	7.7	8.3	6.8	8.0	5.9
Tennessee	8.4	10.6	6.9	8.4	5.9	7.8	5.3
Alabama	7.9	10.8	6.2	8.4	4.7	7.5	4.4
Mississippi	8.1	12.1	6.1	10.1	5.1	8.6	4.7
West South Central	8.8						
Arkansas	8.3	11.0	6.5	8.6	5.3	8.1	4.9
Louisiana	7.6	10.2	5.6	7.8	3.6	7.0	3.4
Oklahoma	9.1	11.4	8.4	8.6	7.1	8.5	6.7
Texas	9.3	10.7	7.4	8.9	6.1	8.3	5.9
Mountain	10.7						
Montana	10.1	11.4	8.5	9.8	7.9	8.9	7.8
Idaho	10.6	11.7	8.8	9.8	7.4	9.7	8.7
Wyoming	11.1	12.0	8.7	10.4	8.6	9.7	8.1

Table XXIV. State-to-State Variations in the Median Years of Schooling (Continued)

Region and state	Total	Urban		Rural-nonfarm		Rural-farm	
		White	Nonwhite	White	Nonwhite	White	Nonwhite
Colorado	10.9	11.8	10.0	9.4	7.5	8.9	9.0
New Mexico	9.3	11.1	7.9	8.6	5.5	8.2	2.0
Arizona	10.0	10.8	7.8	10.5	4.9	8.9	2.0
Utah	12.0	12.1	11.0	11.1	4.6	11.0	7.6
Nevada	11.5	12.1	7.7	10.9	7.3	10.0	6.5
Pacific	11.5						
Washington	11.2	11.9	9.0	10.3	8.3	9.3	8.2
Oregon	10.9	11.8	9.0	10.2	8.5	9.3	8.7
California	11.6	12.0	9.2	10.2	8.2	9.2	8.1

SOURCE: Compiled from U. S. Bureau of the Census, *1950 Census of Population*, Vol. II, *Characteristics of the Population*, Parts 1–49 (Washington: Government Printing Office, 1953). (. . . Number too small for figure to be significant.)

cational status of the population. Among the rural population, both farm and nonfarm, and among whites as well as nonwhites, the southern states without exception rank far down in the list. In New England, the Middle Atlantic states, and in Utah, persons residing on farms have secured almost as much schooling as their fellows who live in the urban districts, and in the East North Central states the differences are of the order of about 1.5 years. But throughout the South the unfavorable situation of the farm population stands out. The relatively high educational status of its white urban population accompanied by the low educational status of its farm population, white and Negro, is one of the most striking features of the region. The differential between the amount of schooling achieved by the urban and rural-farm segments of the white population reaches its maximum (4.1 years) in Virginia, followed by Mississippi (3.5 years), Alabama and Florida (3.3 years) Louisiana (3.2 years), and North Carolina (3.0 years), in the order named, but it is considerable in all the southern states except Kentucky. It is important to note, however, that similar differentials, only slightly less pronounced, prevail in the West North Central states, in Colorado, New Mexico, and Montana, and in all three of the Pacific states.

Among all residential categories, the very low educational status of the nonwhite population in the various southern states is the most conspicuous regional difference exhibited by the data in Table XXIV. It is interesting to note, however, that the lowest indexes of all (medians of 2.0 years) are those for the nonwhite portions of the rural-farm populations of Arizona and New Mexico.

If one attempts to rank the various states, with due regard for the residential and racial differences in the make-up of their populations, Utah definitely belongs at the top of the list. In the urban, the rural-nonfarm, and the rural-farm categories the white population (only 1.7 per cent of its population is nonwhite) either stands alone at the top of the list or is tied for first place. Massachusetts probably is its closest rival. Louisiana, on the other hand, definitely makes the poorest showing, followed most closely by Georgia.

SUGGESTED SUPPLEMENTARY READINGS

Anderson, Walfred A., *The Characteristics of New York State Population.* Cornell University Agricultural Experiment Station, Bulletin No. 925, Ithaca (1958), pp. 55–60.

Bogue, Donald J., *The Population of the United States*. Chicago: The Free Press, 1959, chapter 13.

Davie, Maurice R., *Negroes in American Society*. New York: McGraw-Hill Book Company, 1949, chapter 6.

Glick, Paul C., and Hugh Carter, "Marriage Patterns and Educational Level," *American Sociological Review*, 23, No. 3 (1958), 294–300.

McMahan, C. A., *The People of Atlanta*. Athens: University of Georgia Press, 1950, chapter VIII.

Phelps, Harold A., and David Henderson, *Population in Its Human Aspects*. New York: Appleton-Century-Crofts, Inc., 1958, chapter 13.

Siegel, Jacob S., *The Population of Hungary*. U. S. Bureau of the Census International Population Statistics Reports, Series P-90, No. 9. Washington: Government Printing Office, 1958, chapter VII.

Smith, T. Lynn, and Homer L. Hitt, *The People of Louisiana*. Baton Rouge: Louisiana State University Press, 1952, chapter VIII.

Smith, T. Lynn, and Louise Kemp, *The Educational Status of Louisiana's Farm Population*. Louisiana Agricultural Experiment Station Bulletin No. 424. Baton Rouge, 1947.

Taeuber, Conrad, and Irene B. Taeuber, *The Changing Population of the United States*. New York: John Wiley & Sons, Inc., 1958, chapter 10.

Thompson, Warren S., *Growth and Changes in California's Population*. Los Angeles: The Haynes Foundation, 1955.

Wynne, Jr., Waller, *The Population of Manchuria*. U. S. Bureau of the Census International Population Statistics Reports, Series P-90, No. 7. Washington: Government Printing Office, 1958, chapter VI.

Part Four

THE VITAL PROCESSES

Chapter 11

Measuring the Rate of Reproduction

THE RATE AT WHICH the population is reproducing is the central feature of population study. Reproduction itself quite properly is designated as one of the two *vital processes,* mortality being the other. Since in most populations throughout human history births have substantially exceeded deaths in number, usually the rate of reproduction is considerably more important than the mortality rate in determining the number of inhabitants, their distribution, and the rate at which the population is changing. Only in rare cases is it rivaled in importance by the only other primary factor, namely migration, which may be involved in the changing number and distribution of the population.

A variety of terms may be used to denote the reproduction of the human species; and the student of population should be well acquainted with several of them. Those encountered most frequently are: birth rate, fertility, fecundity, and natality. Most demographers are now agreed that the term *fecundity* should be relied upon to designate the potential and the word *fertility* to specify the actual reproduction of the population. *Natality* as yet has received no specific connotations and is employed as synonymous with the reproduction of the population. The expression *birth rate* is used in popular terminology to refer to reproduction in general, although technically it refers to one specific way of measuring or gauging the fertility of the population.

Indexes for Measuring Fertility

Students of population long have been interested in objective methods for determining the level of reproduction in a given population at a stated time and for comparing the fertility of two or more populations. So far, two indexes, the birth rate and the fertility ratio, are in most general use, although a number of others sometimes are applicable and valuable for specific purposes.

Birth Rate

The measure known as the birth rate is by far the most commonly used index of the rate of reproduction. In its crudest and simplest form, the birth rate is merely the ratio of the number of births during a stated interval of time (one year) to the total number of persons in the population. Since the population is larger than the number of births, the decimal fraction resulting from this arithmetical operation generally is multiplied by a constant so that the index may be expressed as a simple number of two digits. Thus the birth rate for the United States in 1950 may be determined as follows:

$$\frac{\text{Number of births during 1950}}{\text{Population April 1, 1950}} \times 1{,}000 = \frac{3{,}554{,}149}{150{,}697{,}361} \times 1{,}000 = 23.6$$

Obviously this index would be slightly more accurate if the population as of July 1 were used instead of that given by the census enumeration for April 1. In this case such a refinement is not particularly difficult, and the necessary estimate of population is not likely to be greatly in error, since the number of births registered during 1950 exceeded the number of deaths recorded that year by 2,101,695 and it is known that the net immigration during the three-month period could not have been very great. Consider in this connection that the population of the United States as of July 1, 1950, as estimated by the U. S. Bureau of the Census, was 151,234,000, or almost exactly that which would be secured by adding to the April 1 count of 150,697,361 one-fourth of the natural increase for the year (one-fourth of 2,101,695 or 585,447) . Such a refinement would reduce the birth rate in question from 23.6 to 23.5. Even so, however, there is little point to making such a correction in the denominator, unless one also is prepared to evaluate and correct for even more significant errors in the numerator. Tests of the completeness of birth registration in the United States indicate that in 1950 only 97.9 per cent of the births were registered. If this is the case, then the actual number of births for the year was about 3,630,400, instead of the 3,554,149 used in the above calculation; and if this number and the estimated population for July 1 are used in the computations, the birth rate for 1950 is raised to 24.0. In most cases, however, so little is known about the extent of error in the reported number of births and in the estimated size of the population that such corrections are impossible; and even were this not the case, there is little point to such refinements in connection with the crude birth rate.

Whoever makes use of vital statistics should realize that the unrefined or crude birth rate is a most unreliable gauge of human fertility. Variations in the age and sex composition of populations are large, and these influence so greatly the magnitude of the crude birth rate that little valid comparison of the fertility of different groups may be made until these variations have been corrected for or allowances have been made for their effects. For example, in Chapters VI and VII it was shown that the rural population of the United States contains high proportions of males and of children less than fifteen years of age, whereas the urban population has high proportions of females and of those in the productive years of life. Obviously a population which includes high percentages of males and of those who are physically immature should not be expected to produce as many babies per thousand population as one in which women in the childbearing ages constitute a disproportionately large share of the total. On the frontier, in the Yukon or the Amazon, where males constitute the bulk of the population, the crude birth rate is certain to be low even though each woman bears her maximum number of children. Thus, until proper allowances are made for the age and sex composition, it is impossible to make valid assertions concerning the rate of reproduction of a given population or to compare the fertility of one group with that of another.

In *Population Analysis* [1] data for the white population of the United States are used to demonstrate the process of correcting or standardizing the birth rate for the rural and urban portions of our country. This material may be summarized as follows. The total population of the United States in 1940 was taken as the standard or base to which the urban white and rural white segments of the population were to be equated. Next the birth rate of each specific age group in the population was determined, namely, the birth rates for the age groups fifteen to nineteen, twenty to twenty-four, twenty-five to thirty, and so forth. Then in the urban population and in the rural population each of these age-specific birth rates was allowed the same weight or importance that it had in the base or standard population. This enabled a calculation to be made to show, on the basis of the observed age-spe-

[1] T. Lynn Smith (New York: McGraw-Hill Book Company, 1948), pp. 194–196.

Table XXV. Illustration of the Procedures Involved in the Standardization States, 1940

Age (1)	Number of females of stated ages		Number of births to women of stated ages		Age-specific birth rates	
	Urban (2)	Rural (3)	Urban (4)	Rural (5)	Urban (6)	Rural (7)
Under 10	4,477,944	4,634,505	. . . .	. . . . . .	. . . .	. . . .
10–14	2,629,977	2,463,711	421	706	0.2	0.3
15–19	3,028,611	2,419,516	108,134	121,476	35.7	50.2
20–24	3,246,296	1,980,211	358,700	288,108	110.5	145.5
25–29	3,158,974	1,853,283	348,560	237,310	110.3	128.0
30–34	2,927,168	1,705,994	210,925	153,101	72.1	89.7
35–39	2,699,471	1,562,821	91,889	86,651	34.0	55.4
40–44	2,520,514	1,420,379	23,899	30,104	9.5	21.2
45–49	2,341,743	1,348,400	1,673	2,923	0.7	2.2
50–54	2,028,243	1,200,347	54	68	0.0	0.1
55 and over	5,609,181	3,509,033	. . . .	. . . . . .	. . . .	. . . .
Total	34,668,122	24,098,200	1,144,255	920,447		

SOURCE: *Sixteenth Census of the United States, 1940, Population, Second Series, Characteristics of States,* Supplement, 1939–1940, Part III, Tables IV and V, pp. 28 and 40.

[1] The age and sex distribution of the total population of the United States as of 1940.

cific rates, how many births would have occurred in the rural and urban populations of the given sizes providing each had had an age and sex composition corresponding exactly to that of the total population of the nation. The birth rates derived from these data, known as the *standardized birth rates,* are the ones that would have prevailed among the rural and urban white populations of the nation, given the actual fertility of each group, had each of them had exactly the same age and sex composition. The arithmetic involved in the determination of such standardized birth rates is shown in Table XXV.

The age distributions of the urban females and rural females (columns two and three) and the numbers of births classified according to

of the Birth Rates for the Urban and Rural White Populations of the United

Women in the standard [1] population		Number of women there would be if standard [1] age-sex distribution prevailed		Number of births there would be if standard [1] age-sex distribution prevailed	
Number (8)	Per cent of the total population (9)	Urban (10)	Rural (11)	Urban (12)	Rural (13)
10,452,515	7.94	5,397,042	3,989,219		
5,793,606	4.40	2,990,804	2,210,650	598	663
6,153,370	4.67	3,174,331	2,346,304	113,324	117,784
5,895,443	4.48	3,045,182	2,250,844	336,493	327,498
5,645,976	4.29	2,916,034	2,155,384	321,639	275,889
5,172,076	3.93	2,671,332	1,974,512	192,603	117,114
4,799,718	3.65	2,481,008	1,833,835	84,354	101,594
4,368,708	3.32	2,256,698	1,668,036	21,439	35,362
4,045,956	3.07	2,086,766	1,542,431	1,461	3,393
3,504,096	2.66	1,808,077	1,336,438	. . . . . .	134
9,776,219	7.42	5,043,583	3,727,960	. . . . . .	. . . . . .
65,607,683	49.83	33,870,857	25,035,613	1,071,911	979,431

the Population, United States Summary, Table 7, pp. 16–20; and *Vital Statistics of the United*

the ages of the mothers (columns four and five) , makes the calculation of the age-specific birth rates for women (columns six and seven) very simple. The number of women in the standard population, and the proportion those of each stated age make up of the total population is shown in columns eight and nine. Applying the percentages in column nine to the total urban and the total rural populations produces the figures (columns ten and eleven) showing the number of women of each stated age there would be in each of these populations if it had the same age and sex distribution as the standard. Then from the age-specific birth rates (columns six and seven) it is easy to determine how many children would have been borne by each age group of women (columns twelve and thirteen) if the age and sex distribution had corresponded to the standard. These hypothetical totals of births are then used in the usual way along with the total urban and rural populations in the computation of the birth rates.

The objective of these computations and the effect of the adjustments so made is to correct for, to "iron out," or to eliminate the differences in the birth rates that are due solely to the variations in the age-sex distributions of the populations under study. The necessity of making such refinements before using the birth rate as the index upon which to base comparisons of fertility in rural and urban areas, or between any populations that have substantially different age and sex distributions, is emphasized by the results of the procedures illustrated in Table XXV. Thus in 1940 the reported crude birth rate of the white urban population was 16.8 compared with one of only 18.3 for the white rural population. Correcting in the manner described for the differences in the age and sex distributions of the two populations lowers the urban rate to 15.8 and raises the rural rate to 19.5. Because in 1940 the data on births in the United States were faulty, with more frequent failure to record the babies born in rural than in urban areas, even these standardized birth rates were not truly indicative of the rural-urban differentials in the fertility of the population. Nor would such be the case if 1950 materials were used in the computations. Indeed, before one engages in the lengthy arithmetical calculations involved in the standardization of birth rates, he should make as certain as possible that the data he is using are sufficiently accurate to justify such time-consuming endeavors. For most purposes this still is not the case for the United States and probably is even less so for most other parts of the world. In this, as in so many other portions of demography, and of the social sciences in general, improved observation, more reliable recording of the facts, and more useful classifications of the data, rather than the elaboration of highly refined mathematical procedures, seem to be the way in which our knowledge of the field will be most greatly advanced.

The use of the birth rate as a measure of fertility has several distinct advantages, but it also has a few serious shortcomings. Among its advantages are the following: (1) it is simple to calculate and easy to understand; (2) where a registration system has been established, it can be secured annually; and (3) it is the index with which most people are familiar, and the only one with which many persons, including the scholars in many fields, are acquainted.

Among the most serious disadvantages of the birth rate as a gauge of human fertility are the following: (1) the crude birth rate when used by those with relatively little experience in population study is likely to be highly misleading, while the computation of standardized rates is involved and laborious; (2) rarely are birth statistics reasonably complete, so that most of the data presented and interpretations offered relating to levels, differentials, and trends in birth rates are vitiated by the faulty nature of the basic facts; and (3) births usually are not reported for small areas, so that at the community level only rarely can the birth rate be used to measure the rapidity with which the population is reproducing.

The Fertility Ratio

The second index in somewhat general use for gauging the fertility of the population is known as the *fertility ratio*. It differs from the birth rate, or any other measure based upon a count of the births, in that the data needed for its computation are not secured through the registration system. Instead, all of the materials needed for calculating this important index are secured by a census of the population, or even by such an enumeration as generally is made in connection with most community surveys. This makes it especially useful for gauging the fertility of population in many parts of the world in which systems for registering births are either entirely lacking or are very faulty, as well as for determining the rate of reproduction in hundreds of small communities which wish to take stock of their human resources.

The fertility ratio is computed by taking the ratio between the number of young children and the number of women in the childbearing ages, and multiplying this ratio by a constant in order to transform the result into a simple and easily manipulated number. Naturally, the specific age groupings used in the tabulation of census materials may produce variations in the age limits employed by various people for different countries, but insofar as it is feasible the present writer prefers to use children under five and women aged fifteen to forty-four. Those in charge of preparing the *Demographic Yearbook* of the United Nations, on the other hand, use children under five and women aged fifteen to forty-nine; and in many of the studies made between 1930 and 1940, when this index was gaining acceptance among population students, women aged twenty to forty-four figured in the computations. It has become conventional to use 1,000 as the constant in the formula for the fertility ratio, but this results in a figure containing three or even four digits, of which no more than the first two can be considered as mathematically sound. Therefore, the present writer breaks with general practice and employs 100 rather than 1,000 in the computation of the index. To illustrate, the computation of the fertility ratio for Argentina in 1947 is as follows:

$$\frac{\text{Number of children under five}}{\text{Number of women fifteen to forty-four}} \times 100 = \frac{1,781,409}{3,810,191} \times 100 = 46.8$$

For most purposes this index is sufficiently refined as it stands. By its use in the comparison of fertility levels, differentials, and trends any sex differences in the composition of the population are automatically eliminated, as are the effects of varying proportions of those too young to bear children and those who have passed the childbearing ages.

As compared with the birth rate, the fertility ratio has some rather obvious merits or advantages, and it also suffers from several disadvantages. Of primary importance is the fact that data secured by the registration of births, materials that usually are highly defective, are not essential for its computation. Because it automatically is rather highly standardized for the age and sex composition of the population, it is far less likely than the birth rate to lead the nonspecialist astray. It also is easily calculated from the materials gathered in the census or even from those secured in the ordinary community survey. On the other hand, the usefulness of the fertility ratio may be impaired if there are significant differences between the populations being compared in the proportions of women in the younger one-half of the childbearing span, a matter for which it is difficult or impossible to standardize. Likewise, even for large areas such as states or nations, it may not be computed annually, but only for the five-year period immediately preceding a census. In the United States this means that the use of this index is limited mostly to such periods as April 1, 1945 through March 31, 1950, April 1, 1935 through March 31, 1940, and so forth. Since several years are required in order to prepare the details of a given census for publication, this signifies, in turn, that the fertility ratios for the period 1945–1949 will be the most recent ones available until about 1963 or 1964 when the age-sex distributions from the eighteenth census should be generally available. For many purposes such a lag is a serious disadvantage. Finally, the fertility ratio may not be used to measure the rate of reproduction of any group, such as the foreign-born, in which mothers come in one category and their native-born children in another. Such is the present state of birth statistics throughout the world, however, that the fertility ratio is much to be preferred over the birth rate for studies of levels and differentials in fertility; and so defective are birth statistics for past years that if one would avoid deceiving himself and others with respect to historical and present trends in the rate of reproduction, he is almost forced to use the fertility ratio rather than the birth rate as the index on which to base his comparisons.

Other Indexes of the Rate of Reproduction

Demographers use a variety of other measures in their studies of human reproduction, of which it suffices here to mention two, namely, the *gross reproduction rate* and the *net reproduction rate*. Since the number of births, registered or estimated, enters into the computation of all of these, the cautions already indicated in connection with the defects in birth statistics should be kept in mind when using any of these.

The gross reproduction rate is an arithmetical fiction designed to determine how many female babies would be borne in the course of their lifetimes by 1,000 females all born at the same time, providing both of the following assumptions were true: (1) all of the 1,000 female babies lived through the childbearing period; and (2) all of them produced female children as they passed from age group to age group at the specific rates determined by an analysis of the birth statistics at the date on which they were born.[1]

The net reproduction rate is the number of female children that would be borne in the course of their lifetimes by 1,000 women assumed to have been born at the same time, providing the age specific death rates and birth rates prevailing at the time of their births were to continue until all of them had passed through the childbearing period. As described by the U. S. Bureau of the Census in a study of net reproduction rates in the United States:

The net reproduction rates . . . show the number of daughters a group of 1,000 newly-born female infants would bear during the course of their lifetime if this group were subject at each year of age to a particular set of birth

[1] For details on computating the gross reproduction rate, see Margaret Jarman Hagood, *Statistics for Sociologists* (New York: Reynal and Hitchcock, Inc., 1941), pp. 890–891.

rates and death rates, or, in this instance, to the respective fertility rates prevailing in the periods April 1945 to 1950 and April 1935 to 1940 and to life tables for the years 1945 to 1950 and for the decade 1930 to 1939. For exact replacement in the next generation, the group should produce 1,000 daughters. Only net reproduction rates based on the lifetime experience of an actual cohort of women born in the same period provide an accurate measurement of replacement, however.[1]

Data on the Fertility of the Population

Casual observation of standard sources is likely to make it appear that a plethora of material is readily available to anyone interested in studying the fertility of the population in various parts of the world. Data compiled from the registers of births occupy an important place in the *Statistical Yearbook* published each year by many countries. Reports on the numbers of births and computation of the birth rates for most of the independent countries, and for many colonies and possessions as well, figure prominently in the numerous issues of the *Statistical Yearbook* of the League of Nations, and they have been reproduced for the years 1905 to 1930 in the 1951 edition of the *Demographic Yearbook* of the United Nations. Other editions of the latter contain the materials from 1930 almost to date, and the various issues of the *Statistical Bulletin* supply the latest official data very shortly after they are received from the member governments. In addition various other statistical compendia contain substantial compilations of birth statistics for specific parts of the world, of which particular mention should be made of the *Summary of Biostatistics* for each of the Latin American countries prepared and published by the U. S. Bureau of the Census in cooperation with the Office of the Coordinator of Inter-American Affairs. These important volumes, which appeared during the early 1940's, contain substantial tabular and graphic materials on births and birth rates going back to 1900 in most cases. These are only a few of the sources, but a casual examination of them is sure to give the impression that all of the materials needed for thoroughgoing study of the birth rate in most parts of the earth are readily at hand.

Closer scrutiny of the data, however, is likely to dispel much of one's initial enthusiasm, and many students when attempting to use much of

---

[1] U. S. Bureau of the Census, "Estimated Net Reproduction Rates for the White Population, by Counties, April 1945 to 1950 and 1935 to 1940," *Current Population Reports*, Series P-23, No. 4, July 29, 1957.

the data for comprehensive analysis or detailed comparisons are likely to become exasperated. For country after country, one is likely to find it difficult to establish any internal consistency among the data presented; and if he turns to some of the more general compilations, such cautions as the following are encountered:

The data presented in this summary are selected from a much larger bulk of available statistical information. It should be emphasized that the figures presented are taken directly from these official sources, and although they have been converted into a series of fairly uniform tables for presentation, no attempt has been made to modify or correct the figures on the basis of any arbitrary hypothesis regarding their accuracy.

Demographic and vital statistics for the American republics are admittedly deficient in many respects. In some countries censuses are taken only at infrequent or irregular intervals and technical methods are inadequate. Another important factor is the irregularity and incompleteness of birth and death registration with resulting errors in population estimates. . . . Attention should also be called to the fact that frequently two distinct figures are published by different official agencies for the same area and year, and it is difficult to judge which is more accurate.[1]

The warning is very much to the point, but, of course, except as a restraint on what may be a too general tendency to accept official statistics at their face value, it does little to assist one in determining the fundamental matters pertaining to the actual rate of reproduction in the country involved.

If one turns to the demographic publications of the United Nations, one will see that a slight beginning has been made in the evaluation of birth statistics throughout the world. Elementary details are given for the various countries relative to the extent to which the data are presented on the year-of-occurrence rather than the year-of-registration basis, whether or not stillbirths are included in the totals, and the way in which multiple births are counted. In addition those responsible for the United Nations' demographic publications queried the national agency in each country responsible for the collection and tabulation of the birth statistics relative to the completeness of the coverage and the reliability of the data; and on the basis of these reports the nations,

[1] U. S. Bureau of the Census in cooperation with the Office of the Coordinator of Inter-American Affairs, *Cuba: Summary of Biostatistics* (Washington, D. C., 1945), p. 4. The same statement appears in each of the nineteen companion reports.

colonies, and possessions were classified into three large categories: (1) those in which there was "a complete, or virtually complete coverage of the events occurring each year"; (2) those having only an incomplete coverage or "subject to considerable irregularity"; and (3) those for which no comprehensive data are available.[1] For the most part the nations falling in the third category do not figure in the tabulations of birth statistics presented in the various issues of the *Demographic Yearbook*.

In order to simplify the examination of these materials, attention was restricted to those countries, territories, or possessions in which 25,000 or more births were reported for some year subsequent to 1945. Prior to the issue of the 1955 edition of the *Demographic Yearbook* those in charge of the demographic work of the United Nations had succeeded in securing from seventy-three of these countries and other areas materials deemed worthy of publication. Of these areas forty were classified as reporting that their birth statistics were complete or virtually complete, twenty-six as falling in the second category, and seven as those for which no comprehensive data were available. Such important and populous parts of the earth as China, the U.S.S.R., Brazil, and Indonesia do not figure in the list at all, nor do a number of other independent countries, such as Haiti, Ethiopia, and Uruguay.

Almost all the European countries (Austria, Belgium, Bulgaria, Czechoslovakia, Denmark, Finland, France, Western Germany, Berlin, Hungary, Ireland, Italy, the Netherlands, Norway, Poland, Portugal, Spain, Sweden, Switzerland, the United Kingdom, and Yugoslavia) were placed in the first group, of which they constitute the large majority. Greece, however, was placed in the second category, and Romania in the third. No data are given on any tests of the completeness of the coverage in birth registration for any of these European countries. Other countries, territories, and possessions classified as having complete or virtually complete coverage in birth registration are as follows: the Union of South Africa (European population only), Canada, Honduras, Jamaica, Mexico, Trinidad and Tobago, the United States, Argentina, Chile, Venezuela, Ceylon, China (Taiwan only), Israel (Jewish population only), Japan, Federation of Malaya, the Rykuku Islands, Singapore, Australia, and New Zealand (European population only). Relative to these the following information con-

[1] United Nations, *Demographic Yearbook, 1951* (New York: United Nations, 1951), p. 30.

cerning tests of the completeness of birth registration is given: Canada, 98 per cent complete in 1941; Honduras, 1940–1949 figures have been adjusted for 2 per cent underregistration and 1950 data for 1.5 per cent underregistration; United States, 92.5 per cent complete in 1940 and 97.9 per cent complete in 1950; Argentina, estimated to be 97 per cent complete; Chile, 1951 data have been adjusted for 8.8 per cent underregistration and those for 1952–1953 for 5 per cent underregistration; and Ceylon, 89 per cent complete in 1953. Furthermore, fourteen of the entities in the category of those with the complete or virtually complete birth statistics are those in which the data are known to be by year of registration rather than by year of occurrence. They are as follows: Honduras, Mexico, Trinidad and Tobago, Argentina, Chile, Venezuela, Ceylon, Taiwan, Israel, Singapore, Ireland, Northern Ireland and Scotland in the United Kingdom, Australia, and New Zealand.

The twenty-six countries, territories, or possessions in the second group, those in which the coverage of birth registration is admittedly far from complete, are as follows: Algeria, Angola, Madagascar, Mozambique, Tunisia, Costa Rica, Cuba, the Dominican Republic, El Salvador, Nicaragua, Panama, Puerto Rico, Bolivia, Colombia, Ecuador, Paraguay, Peru, India, Iran, Iraq, Jordan, Lebanon, Pakistan, the Philippines, Syria, and Greece. In addition, some materials are presented for the following, although they are coded neither as C nor as U: Egypt, Guatemala, Hong Kong, South Korea, Thailand, Romania, and Eastern Germany.

From the materials that have just been given, two things should be apparent to every student of population: (1) only the barest beginning has been made in the evaluation of the official birth statistics for most parts of the world; and (2) one should exercise a reasonable amount of skepticism before he accepts at face value the data and conclusions, which are so liberally spread throughout the writings by sociologists, economists, geographers, and others who include population data in their presentations, relating to the magnitudes and trends in the birth rate in various parts of the world. Before concluding the discussion of this topic, however, it is necessary to indicate that the faulty nature of the birth statistics are not responsible for all of the large and puzzling discrepancies one finds in data for the same area and period published in two or more of the official sources, or in various editions of the *Demographic Yearbook*. There frequently are difficulties with the denominator as well as the numerator of the formula for the birth rate. For example, so great was the overestimation of the population of Guatemala prior to the 1950 census that the birth rates for that country as published in the 1948 edition of the *Demographic Yearbook* were 33.8, 33.7, and 36.8 for the years 1945, 1946, and 1947, respectively. More recent issues of this important sourcebook give the same numbers of births for each of these years as those in the volume mentioned. Following the collection of more reliable population data by the 1950 census, however, the later editions of the *Yearbook* carry birth rates of 48.7, 48.2, and 52.2, respectively, for the three years specified.

Fertility Data for the United States

The United States lagged badly, in comparison with many European countries, in the collection of basic data on the fertility of the population. The gathering and organization of birth statistics was one of the functions of government that long was left strictly to the states. Some of them, and some municipalities as well, developed fairly adequate systems for registering births, but such was not the case throughout large parts of the nation. When the Bureau of the Census was established by the Permanent Census Act, approved on March 6, 1902, the collection of birth statistics was one of the functions specifically assigned by the act to the new agency. It was not until 1915, however, that the organization was established to begin this work, and then it was a cooperative venture between the Bureau and the states. Prior to this time federal attempts to gather and disseminate data on the fertility of the population had been limited to the highly unsatisfactory technique of trying to determine the number of births from the answers to questions that were included on the schedules used in the decennial census.

Apparently the first of these endeavors was made in connection with the 1850 census, and it consisted of an attempt to estimate the number of births during twelve months preceding the census date from the number of children under one year of age reported in the enumeration. The resulting figure was corrected by adding the estimated number of babies born during the year who died before it was over, and the figure of 28.2 was published as the birth rate for the year. This was absurdly low, of course, and the table showing the rates for the various states was admitted to have little value.[1] It does represent, however,

[1] Cf. Walter F. Willcox, *Introduction to the Vital Statistics of the United States, 1900 to 1930* (Washington: Government Printing Office, 1933), p. 55.

the first compilation of fertility data for each state in the union. Nothing more was done in the eighth census, but in 1870 another rather fruitless attempt was made to determine the birth rate by analyzing the data on the number of children under one year of age.

In 1880 and again in 1890 Dr. J. S. Billings, a highly competent man, was in charge of the division of vital statistics in the Census Office. In the reports of the census of 1880 Billings stated that the data on children under one, corrected for infants both born and dying during the preceding year, indicated a birth rate of 31.4. This he thought too low, and he estimated that the true birth rate was about 36.[1] Following the census of 1890, in connection with which he again prepared the reports on vital statistics, Billings severed his connection with the Census Office and published in a popular review his startling conclusion that "the birth rate has really diminished in the United States." [2] One's curiosity with respect to what happened in the Office is whetted by the fact that this conclusion, subsequently demonstrated to be fully valid, is greatly at variance with the one published in the *Report on Vital and Social Statistics in the United States at the Eleventh Census, 1890,*[3] which carries his name as the one responsible for the report.

As indicated above, the Permanent Census Act authorizing the Bureau of the Census to collect birth statistics was approved in 1902, but it was not until 1915 that a birth registration area was established. At its inception this area included only ten states (Connecticut, Maine, Massachusetts, Michigan, Minnesota, New Hampshire, New York, Pennsylvania, Rhode Island, and Vermont) and the District of Columbia. Together these embraced at that time about 30 per cent of the nation's population. Gradually other states were added, beginning with Maryland in 1916, until, with the admission of Texas to the birth registration area in 1933, birth data became available for the entire United States and each of its major subdivisions. As a result one using the birth statistics for the period 1915 to 1932, inclusive, must be pre-

[1] *Report on the Mortality and Vital Statistics of the United States as Returned at the Tenth Census,* Part II (Washington: Government Printing Office, 1886), p. cxl.

[2] J. S. Billings, "The Diminishing Birth Rate in the United States," *The Forum,* 15 (June, 1893), pp. 467–477.

[3] Part I, "Analysis and Rate Tables" (Washington: Government Printing Office, 1896), p. 481. In order to avoid the conclusion that the nation's birth rate was falling, those finally responsible for the text of this report accepted an estimate that the enumeration of children was 25 per cent incomplete in 1890 and only 5 per cent incomplete in 1880!

pared to deal with two separate and distinct series: (1) the data for the original birth registration area and (2) the data for the expanding birth registration area. From 1933 on, of course, the data for the United States are those for the nation as a whole. Even so, however, studies made about 1930 [1] showed the data to be seriously incomplete, and two more decades were to elapse before fairly complete and reliable materials on births would be available for use by students in the United States.

By 1950 the coverage of birth registration had become sufficiently complete so that for many purposes the birth statistics could be used for fairly reliable comparisons of fertility. Even then, however, only 97.9 per cent of the births throughout the nation were registered, and the coverage was still quite inadequate for births to Negro parents and those occurring in the remote sections of the country in which significant proportions of the deliveries took place outside hospitals. (See Figure 54.) This makes the use of the birth rate difficult in racial and rural-urban comparisons of fertility, even for large areas such as regions or states; and it practically destroys the possibility of using this measure for fair comparisons of the rate of reproduction at the county or community levels, which are the ones that are of greatest significance for most theoretical and applied purposes.

The major bodies of data on the fertility of the population of the United States currently available for use by population students may be listed in summary manner as follows: (1) The birth statistics collected annually, first by the U. S. Bureau of the Census, and more recently by the National Office of Vital Statistics. Although this series goes back to 1915, all of the states in the nation were not included until 1933, and even as late as 1950 tests showed the coverage to be only 97.9 per cent complete. It is very difficult to match exactly various components of the population, such as the residential and racial or color categories, with the birth data so as to get birth rates for such important groupings. These difficulties, added to those arising from the incompleteness of the coverage in birth registration make the computation of reliable birth rates for counties and other small areas extremely diffi-

---

[1] See P. K. Whelpton, "The Completeness of Birth Registration in the United States," *Journal of the American Statistical Association*, XXIX, No. 186 (1934), 125–136; and T. Lynn Smith, "Rural-Urban Differences in the Completeness of Birth Registration," *Social Forces*, XIV, No. 3 (1936) 368–372.

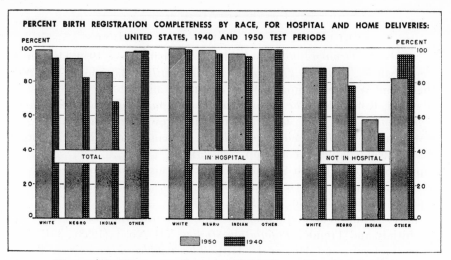

Figure 54. The completeness of birth registration in the
United States, 1940 and 1950, by race and place of delivery.
(Illustration from the National Office of Vital Statistics)

cult and time consuming if not impossible. (2) The age and sex distributions secured in the various decennial censuses of the United
States since 1800. These materials may be used to compute the fairly
well standardized measure of the rate of reproduction known as the
fertility ratio. They are of fundamental importance for the study of
fertility trends and differentials. From 1930 on, the availability of rather
detailed age and sex distributions for the various residential and race
or color categories for units as small as the counties makes these data of
primary importance to all those interested in levels, differentials, and
trends in fertility in specific parts of the United States. (3) Data from
three inquiries on the number of children ever born and the number
of own children under five in the household conducted in connection
with the 1910, 1940, and 1950 censuses of population. The 1910 and
1940 materials are available in a special report of the 1940 census [1] and
those for 1950 in a special report of the 1950 census.[2]

[1] U. S. Bureau of the Census, *Sixteenth Census of the United States: 1940, Special
Reports*, "Differential Fertility, 1940 and 1910" (Washington: Government Printing
Office, 1947).

[2] U. S. Bureau of the Census, *U. S. Census of Population: 1950*. Vol. IV, *Special
Reports*. *"Fertility"* (Washington: Government Printing Office, 1955), Part 5,
chapter C.

SUGGESTED SUPPLEMENTARY READINGS

Cox, Peter R., *Demography.* Cambridge: University Press, 1950, chapter 8.

Kiser, Clyde V., *Group Differences in Urban Fertility.* Baltimore: The Williams and Wilkins Company, 1942, chapters 1 and 2.

Kuczynski, Robert R., *The Measurement of Population Growth: Methods and Results.* New York: Oxford University Press, 1936, chapters I–IV.

McMahan, C. A., *The People of Atlanta.* Athens: University of Georgia Press, 1950, chapter XI and pp. 226–231.

Shapiro, Sam, and Joseph Schachter, "Birth Registration Completeness in the United States and Geographic Areas, 1950," part I, *Vital Statistics— Special Reports,* 39, No. 2 (1954), 39–52.

Smith, T. Lynn, "The Reproduction Rate in Latin America: Levels, Differentials, and Trends," *Population Studies,* XII, No. 1 (1958), 3–17.

Smith, T. Lynn, and Homer L. Hitt, *The People of Louisiana.* Baton Rouge: Louisiana State University Press, 1952, pp. 137–141.

Statistical Office of the United Nations, *Demographic Yearbook, 1954.* New York: The United Nations, 1954.

U. S. National Committee on Vital and Health Statistics, "Statistics Needed Concerning Fertility," *Vital Statistics—Special Reports,* 33, No. 11 (1952), 193–202, pp. 16–27.

Whelpton, Pascal K., *Cohort Fertility: Native White Women in the United States.* Princeton; N. J.: Princeton University Press, 1954, chapters 1–3.

Willcox, Walter F., *Introduction to the Vital Statistics of the United States, 1900 to 1930.* Washington: Government Printing Office, 1933, pp. 55–81.

Willcox, Walter F., *Studies in American Demography.* Ithaca: Cornell University Press, 1940, chapter 17.

Chapter 12

Fertility Levels

THE RATE OF REPRODUCTION varies greatly in time and space. Within the course of history, for example, the birth rate of a given people fluctuates widely; and at any one time there are likely to be vast differences between the birth rates of the various residential, racial, ethnic, religious, and socio-economic groups of which a population is composed. Thus in colonial times women in North America bore about as many children as physiology permitted, whereas in the 1930's the fertility of the population was so low that the question as to whether or not the women of the United States were bearing enough children to offset the then very low mortality rates was a matter of considerable concern. Nowadays, as will be indicated below, the birth rate of those who live on farms is much higher than that of city people, Negroes have higher rates of reproduction than whites, and certain ethnic and religious groups have greater fertility than others.

Differences in the fertility of various peoples, races, classes, residential groups, and so on are of tremendous social, economic, and political significance. To be specific, it is very likely that changes between 1870 and 1914 in the relative importance and strength of France and Germany as world powers were due in large measure to the higher birth rate and consequently more rapid growth of population in the former. During the years under consideration millions of Germans emigrated to other parts of the world, while relatively few Frenchmen sought new homes in other lands. Nevertheless, the population of Germany rose from slightly less than 36 million in 1870 to around 60 million in 1914, whereas that of France increased merely from 38 million to 40 million during the interval. Generations of future historians will be required to evaluate adequately the results of the momentous shift in relative importance and power that accompanied these changes. Largely responsible for this world-shaking change, however, were the differences reflected in the following birth rates of these two great powers: 1866–1870, France 26 and Germany 38; 1905–1909, France 20 and Germany 32; and 1911–1913, France 18 and Germany 27. The significance of these differences was not lost on such despots as Hitler and Mussolini who later sought determinedly to increase the might of Germany and Italy by measures designed to bring about an increase of the birth rates in these countries.

Rates of Reproduction Throughout the World

A seemingly elementary task for students of population is the determination of the level of the rate of reproduction throughout the various parts of the world. One who attempts to get fairly complete and reliable birth statistics for the different nations and their possessions, however, discovers that this elementary task is by no means an easy one to perform. Nor is the difficulty entirely overcome if one resorts instead to the data needed for the computation of fertility ratios. The present state of world affairs in this respect will become evident to anyone who examines Table XXVI with care and attention. It contains the most recent crude birth rates and fertility ratios for all countries and for all territories of 1 million or more inhabitants for which data are available. In addition it also presents the present writer's estimates of the actual birth rates for those countries in which the birth data are admittedly or obviously incomplete. These estimates, in turn, were made in the following manner.

According to the materials supplied in the more recent issues of the *Demographic Yearbook* of the United Nations, thirty-six of the countries in which fairly recent censuses have been taken also figure as those in which birth registration is complete or fairly complete. Therefore for these thirty-six areas one is enabled to determine the correlation between the two measures of the rate of reproduction, namely the fertility ratio and the birth rate. (See Figure 55.) When this is done, the value of the Pearsonian coefficient of correlation (r) is found to be +0.903, indicating that about 81 per cent of the variation in the magnitude of the crude birth rate is accounted for by differences in the size of the fertility ratio. As is readily observed in Figure 55, the straight line is an adequate description of the relationship between the two variables; and when such a line is fitted by the method of least squares, the resulting regression equation is $Y = -2.49 + 0.65 X$, with X des-

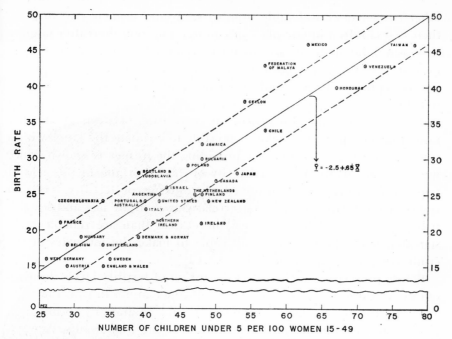

Figure 55. Correlation between the fertility ratio and the crude birth rate based on thirty-six countries for which fairly recent and complete data are available.

ignating the fertility ratio and Y the crude birth rate. This indicates that on the average an increase of 1.0 point in the fertility ratio is accompanied by an increase of 0.65 in the birth rate. This formula, in turn, can be applied to determine the most reasonable values for the birth rates in those countries or territories listed in Table XXVI for which adequate birth statistics are lacking but for which fairly recent age and sex distributions of the population are available.

In interpreting the ratio between the birth rate and the fertility ratio in any given country, there are, of course, a number of factors that may make for a relatively high score in the one in comparison with that registered for the other. Thus if infant and child mortality rates are high, the birth rate tends to be relatively large in comparison with the fertility ratio. In such cases an estimate of the birth rate from the regression equation given above is likely to be somewhat too low. This may help explain in part the positions (Figure 55) of the points representing Mexico, the Federation of Malaya, and Ceylon. On the other hand if a considerable number of young women give birth to their first children in one place or country and soon thereafter migrate to another, the birth rate will be inflated in the former and the fertility ratio in the latter. It is possible that the positions in Figure 55 of the points representing Scotland, England, and Wales are due in part to this factor. Irrespective of the reasons for the situation of any given country, however, the closeness of the correlation between the fertility ratio and the birth rate makes it possible to estimate the latter with a considerable degree of accuracy providing the former is known. Since most persons, including the majority of those working in the field of population study, are accustomed to thinking of fertility levels in terms of the birth rate, and since relatively accurate age and sex distributions are available for many more areas than are reliable birth statistics, it has been deemed advisable to make the estimates of the crude birth rates given in Table XXVI.

Before proceeding with a brief discussion of fertility levels throughout the world, it is well to consider briefly the manner in which fertility and the two other factors (mortality and migration) bear upon changes in the number and distribution of the inhabitants. At most times and places, the number of births is the major factor in such changes, with deaths in second position and migrations in third. Births also may be regarded as the primary moving forces in population changes, since obviously men and women must be born before they can move about or die. Therefore, the significance of any level of reproduction rests largely upon its relationship to the mortality rate, and, generally to a lesser degree, upon the extent to which the population is increased or decreased by migration to or from the area under consideration. If, for example, the death rate is above 30, as it probably has been at most times among the various peoples who have inhabited the earth, a birth rate of 40 or above is required to produce an increase of population of 1 per cent per annum; whereas, if the death rate is only 10, a level attained by many contemporary peoples, and one that soon may prevail over additional large sections of the earth, a birth rate of 35 is sufficient, assuming no migration, to make the population mount at 2.5 per cent per annum. During the second half of the twentieth century there is much alarm in some circles, with talk of a "population explosion" or a "population bomb," because of the recent rapidly mounting number of people on the earth. This has developed largely because the high death rates which prevailed until recently in large and densely

Table XXVI. Fertility Ratios and Crude Birth Rates for Countries, and for the Territories with 1 Million or More Inhabitants, for Which Data Are Available

Country or territory	Year	Number of children under 5 per 100 women 15–49	Crude birth rate (reported)	Crude birth rate (estimated)
Africa				
Algeria (France)	1948	63	22	39
Angola (Portugal)	1940	54	9	33
Egypt	1947	55	44	34
Kenya (United Kingdom)	1948	68	. .	42
Morroco (France)	1951 [1]	51	27	31
Mozambique (Portugal)	1940 [1]	78	31	48
Northern Rhodesia (U. K.)	1951 [2]	53	32	32
Southern Rhodesia (U. K.)	1951 [2]	50	29	30
Tanganyika (U. K.)	1948	70	. .	43
Tunisia (France)	1946	. .	40	. .
Moslem population	1946	62	. .	38
European population	1946	37	. .	22
Uganda (U. K.)	1948	88	30 [3]	52
Union of South Africa				
European population	1946	44	27	26
Non-European population	1946	59	. .	36
North America				
Canada	1951	50	27	†
Costa Rica	1950	69	47	43
Cuba	1953	50	28 [4]	30
Dominican Republic	1950	75	37	46
El Salvador	1950	62	49	38
Guatemala	1950	69	51	43
Haiti	1950	45	. .	27
Honduras	1950	67	40	†
Jamaica (United Kingdom)	1943	48	32	†
Mexico	1950	63	46	†
Nicaragua	1950	65	41	40
Panama	1950	70	33	43
Puerto Rico (U. S.)	1950	73	39	44
United States	1950	42	24	†

Table XXVI. Fertility Ratios and Crude Birth Rates for Countries, and for the Territories with 1 Million or More Inhabitants (Continued)

Country or territory	Year	Number of children under 5 per 100 women 15–49	Crude birth rate (reported)	Crude birth rate (estimated)
South America				
Argentina	1947	42	25	†
Bolivia	1950	65	40	40
Brazil	1950	65	36 [5]	40
Chile	1952	57	34	†
Colombia	1938	68	36	42
Ecuador	1950	71	47	44
Paraguay	1950	69	22 [6]	43
Peru	1940	66	27	40
Uruguay	1908	65	21 [7]	40
Venezuela	1950	71	43	†
Asia				
Burma	1931	56	28 [8]	34
Ceylon	1946	54	38	†
China (Formosa only)	1935	78	46 [8]	†
India	1951	55	25	34
Israel (Jewish population)	1948	43	26	†
Japan	1950	53	28	†
South Korea	1952	53	19 [9]	32
Malaya, Federation of (U. K.)	1947	57	43	†
Pakistan		..	18 [5]	..
Philippines	1948	65	32	40
Thailand	1947	63	24	39
Turkey	1950	61	..	37
Europe				
Austria	1951	29	15	†
Belgium	1947	29	18	†
Bulgaria	1934	48	30 [8]	†
Czechoslovakia	1947	34	24	†
Denmark	1950	39	19	†
Finland	1950	48	25	†
France	1946	28	21	†
Germany	1933	23	16 [8]	13
Eastern Germany	1946	24	..	14
Western Germany	1950	26	16	†

Table XXVI. Fertility Ratios and Crude Birth Rates for Countries, and for the Territories with 1 Million or More Inhabitants (Continued)

Country or territory	Year	Number of children under 5 per 100 women 15–49	Crude birth rate (reported)	Crude birth rate (estimated)
Greece	1940	42	25	25
Hungary	1941	31	19	†
Iceland	1950	53	29	32
Ireland (Republic)	1951	47	21	†
Italy	1936	40	23 [10]	†
Luxemburg	1947	24	15	13
Netherlands	1947	47	25	†
Norway	1950	39	19	†
Poland	1931	46	29 [8]	†
Portugal	1950	40	24	†
Romania	1930	52	34 [8]	32
Spain	1940	32	25	19
Sweden	1950	35	16	†
Switzerland	1950	34	18	†
United Kingdom				
England and Wales	1951	34	15	†
Northern Ireland	1951	41	21	†
Scotland	1951	36	18	†
Yugoslavia	1948	39	28	†
Oceania				
Australia	1947	40	24	†
New Zealand				
European population	1951	49	24	†
Maori population	1951	84	45	†
U.S.S.R.	1926	58	..	35

SOURCE: Compiled and computed from data given in various issues of the *Demographic Yearbook*. († Estimate not given for countries in which birth data are considered by the United Nations as complete or virtually complete.)

[1] Non-indigenous population.
[2] European population.
[3] Birth rate is for 1947.
[4] Birth rate is for 1949.
[5] Data are for 1948.
[6] Data are for 1949.
[7] Data are for 1944.
[8] Data are for 1930–1934.
[9] Data are for 1948.
[10] Data are for 1935–1939.

populated sections of the world have been cut sharply, whereas as yet there has been little or no corresponding fall in the birth rates. Therefore the birth rates of 35 or above presently prevailing in many parts of the world are making for tremendous change, and this is giving rise to considerable alarm at home and abroad. A few decades ago such levels of reproduction were offset by high mortality rates and occasioned little thought in the countries involved or elsewhere.

With these facts in mind, it is well to observe with some care the data given in Table XXVI. Possibly it will facilitate comparisons if birth rates of various levels are designated as follows: 40 or above, *very high;* 30 to 39, *high;* 20 to 29, *medium;* and less than 20, *low.* On this basis, the Latin American area, generally speaking, is the section of the world in which very high rates of reproduction prevail to the greatest extent, although a few parts of Africa (Kenya, Mozambique, Tanganyika, and Uganda), the Island of Formosa, the Federation of Malaya, the Philippines, and the Maori population of New Zealand also are characterized by very high birth rates. Of the twenty Latin American countries, only Argentina, Chile, Cuba, and Haiti definitely do not belong in the category with the highest birth rates, although Uruguay, because of the antiquity of the available information, also probably should be grouped with them. One of the immediate effects of these very high reproduction levels may be mentioned. Because the birth rates have remained high throughout Latin America, while drastic reductions in the death rates were being accomplished, the proportion of Latin Americans in the world population has moved up from about 2.7 per cent in 1900 to approximately 6.5 per cent in 1957. One also should note in this connection that the parts of Latin America with the very highest rates of reproduction constitute a significant portion of what nowadays frequently are designated as the underdeveloped parts of the world.

Likewise other underdeveloped areas are the ones in which, for the most part, the birth rates designated as high are found to prevail. Thus in most of Africa and in the sections of Asia for which information is available the birth rates range between 30 and 39. Iceland also falls in this category. The completely outdated information available also would place the U.S.S.R. and Romania in this category, but it is unlikely that present birth rates in either of these countries are above 30.

Birth rates designated here as medium currently prevail throughout most of Europe, the United States and Canada, Argentina, Japan, Australia, and New Zealand. Low birth rates, on the other hand, are limited exclusively to western Europe, with those in England and Wales, Austria, Germany, and Sweden commanding particular attention. Mortality rates in much of Europe are so low, of course, that even these low birth rates make for a considerable increase in population, except in those countries in which they are offset to some extent by emigration.

In concluding this section on the rate of reproduction throughout the world, it is well to fill as much as possible the most obvious gap in the data presented in Table XXVI, namely, the lack of data for China. Fortunately France's leading demographer, Alfred Sauvy, has presented the results of two comprehensive attempts to determine the rate of reproduction in the world's most populous nation. One of these, based on materials secured in 1953 from 30 million persons indicated a birth rate of 30; and the other, a study of sixteen districts, with a total population of over 1.8 million made in the years 1951–1954, indicated a birth rate of 42.[1]

Fertility Levels in the United States

All through the twentieth century the rate of reproduction in the United States has proved to be highly variable, in time, in space, and from group to group. Since 1900 the sharp reversals in the trend of the birth rate have scarcely been equalled in any other major nation; the state and regional differences in fertility hardly can be matched in other parts of the world; and the rural-urban and other differentials have been of a magnitude that should command attention by every student of population. All of this makes the study of fertility levels, differentials, and trends in the United States particularly significant, but there are other reasons as well why a comprehensive study of these matters in this country is of unusual importance for the demographer.

First, census taking and registration procedures are now at a level of perfection that is surpassed in few parts of the world. This means that fairly accurate and reliable data may be used for various comparisons, with less need for various makeshifts and improvisations than is the case if one is studying rates of reproduction in many other parts of the world. Second, the extensive and highly diverse territory of the nation is divided into fifty states and the District of Columbia, for each of which every effort is made to collect, tabulate, and publish exactly

[1] Alfred Sauvy, "La Population de la Chine," *Population,* 12 année, no. 4 (1957), 697–698.

comparable data, information that is as comprehensive in all essential respects as is that for the country as a whole. This applies alike to the materials obtained through the registration of births and those secured in the decennial census. Much of the detail is also made available separately for the thousands of counties into which the states are subdivided, and for other thousands of cities, towns, and villages found throughout the nation. Indeed, large portions of the information may be had for the minor civil divisions of which the counties are composed and for small segments of the various cities. Third, despite the nation's political solidarity, it is composed of highly diverse elements (ethnic, racial, cultural, religious, agricultural, industrial, occupational, and so forth), all of which are distributed very unequally throughout the various states. Thus a summary of existing knowledge relative to fertility levels, differentials, and trends in the United States is especially important to the student of population; and the materials available for study offer unusual opportunities for gaining additional understanding of the reproduction rate and the factors responsible for its variations.

As indicated above, since about 1950 the level of fertility in the United States as a whole has stood at about 25, as measured by the birth rate, or 50, as gauged by the fertility ratio. This level corresponds to that prevailing in this country about 1915, and it is much above that registered during the 1930's and slightly below that for the years immediately following the second world war.

The rate of reproduction for the United States represents, of course, a net product which comes from including the widely divergent birth rates or fertility ratios prevailing in the various subdivisions of the nation. The actual rate in each of these, in turn, is influenced by the extent to which its people are rural or urban, white or colored, native-born or foreign-born, of one religious persuasion or another, or composed of other ethnic, social, or economic groupings which affect in one way or another the reproductive behavior of mankind. Therefore, it is highly important to observe how fertility levels vary throughout the United States.

To enable the reader to make a careful examination of the extent to which the rate of reproduction varies from one part of the United States to another, Tables XXVII and XXVIII and Figure 56 have been prepared. The first of these presents fertility ratios computed by the present writer from the materials gathered in the 1950 census (i.e. fertility data for the period April 1945 to 1950), and crude birth rates

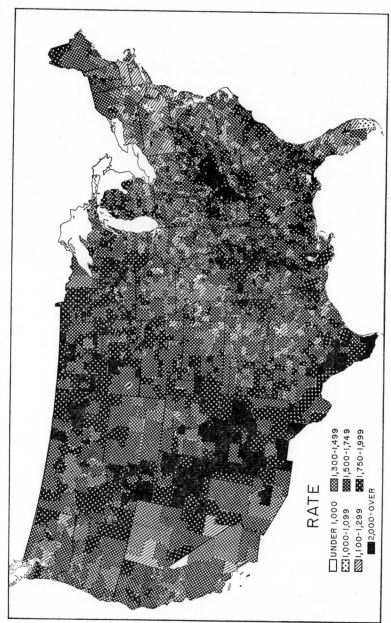

RATE

☐ UNDER 1,000 ▨ 1,300-1,499
▨ 1,000-1,099 ▨ 1,500-1,749
▨ 1,100-1,299 ▨ 1,750-1,999
■ 2,000-OVER

Figure 56. Variations in the net reproduction rate of the white population of the United States, by counties, 1945–1950.

Table XXVII. The Forty-eight States and the District of Columbia Ranked According to the Fertility Levels of Their Populations, and Proportions of the Population Classified as Rural

State	Fertility ratios, 1950 [1]		Birth rate, 1949–1951 [2]		Rural Population, 1950 [3]	
	Index	Rank	Index	Rank	Per cent of total	Rank
United States	47.9	..	24.6	..	36.0	..
New Mexico	62.0	1	35.1	1	49.8	19
Utah	61.4	2	31.9	2	34.7	36
Mississippi	59.1	3	30.9	4	72.1	2
North Dakota	59.0	4	27.7	12	73.4	1
Idaho	58.1	5	27.8	11	57.1	10
South Dakota	57.3	6	27.6	13	66.8	4
South Carolina	56.9	7	31.1	3	63.3	8
Montana	55.8	8	26.5	19	56.3	11
Arkansas	55.5	9	27.1	14	67.0	3
Wyoming	54.9	10	26.9	17	50.2	18
Arizona	54.6	11	30.9	4	44.5	26
Kentucky	54.4	12	27.1	14	63.2	9
Louisiana	54.2	13	30.1	6	45.2	25
Alabama	53.7	14	28.5	8	56.2	12
West Virginia	53.1	15	27.0	16	65.4	6
Vermont	53.1	15	24.2	33	65.4	6

Minnesota	52.7	17	25.7	23	45.5	24
Georgia	52.5	18	28.7	7	54.7	14
North Carolina	52.3	19	27.2	10	66.3	5
Maine	51.5	20	23.7	39	48.3	21
Washington	51.4	21	24.0	36	36.8	35
Iowa	51.4	21	24.4	30	52.3	17
Wisconsin	50.7	23	24.7	26	42.1	29
Texas	50.6	24	28.2	9	37.3	33
Colorado	50.4	25	26.6	18	37.3	33
Nebraska	50.1	26	24.5	27	53.1	15
Tennessee	50.0	27	26.1	20	55.9	13
Oregon	49.6	28	24.1	34	46.1	23
Virginia	49.4	29	26.1	20	53.0	16
Kansas	49.2	30	23.8	38	47.9	22
Oklahoma	49.1	31	23.4	40	49.0	20
Indiana	48.6	32	24.7	25	40.1	30
Michigan	48.6	32	26.0	22	29.3	41
New Hampshire	48.0	34	22.2	43	42.5	28
Ohio	47.1	35	24.4	30	29.8	39
Maryland	46.7	36	24.1	34	31.0	38
Nevada	46.6	37	24.3	32	42.8	27
California	45.6	38	23.9	37	19.3	44

Table XXVII. The Forty-eight States and the District of Columbia Ranked According to the Fertility Levels of Their Populations, and Proportions of the Population Classified as Rural (Continued)

State	Fertility ratios, 1950 [1]		Birth rate, 1949–1951 [2]		Rural population, 1950 [3]	
	Index	Rank	Index	Rank	Per cent of total	Rank
Florida	45.3	39	24.4	30	34.5	37
Delaware	45.1	40	24.5	27	37.4	32
Missouri	44.2	41	22.5	41	38.5	31
Massachusetts	42.5	43	20.8	46	15.6	46
Illinois	42.5	43	22.4	42	22.4	42
Rhode Island	42.5	43	20.9	45	15.7	45
Pennsylvania	42.0	45	21.8	44	29.5	40
Connecticut	41.9	46	20.7	48	22.4	42
New Jersey	40.5	47	20.8	46	13.4	48
New York	39.1	48	20.7	48	14.5	47
District of Columbia	32.8	49	25.3	24	0	49

SOURCES: Birth rates are from *Vital Statistics—Special Reports*, 38, No. 8 (June, 1954), 149. They are according to residence of the mothers, and the data were adjusted for underregistration of births. The fertility ratios were computed from data in *U. S. Census of Population, 1950*, Vol. II, *Characteristics of the Population* (Washington: Government Printing Office, 1952).

[1] Number of children under five per hundred women fifteen to forty-four

[2] Rates have been adjusted for underregistration of births.

[3] Based on the new definitions of rural and urban employed in the 1950 census.

for the years 1949–1951. Since one of the most obvious reasons for variations in the rate of reproduction is the degree to which the populations of the various states are rural or urban, information is also included showing the percentage of the total population of each state in 1950 that was classified as rural. Birth rates centered on the year 1950 are given, rather than those for a later period, for the reason that 1950 is the most recent year for which accurate data are available, or will be available prior to about 1961, on the number of inhabitants in each of the states. This is because even for the nation as a whole computations of birth rates for the years subsequent to 1950 are subject to considerable error, solely because estimates of the population must be used in their calculation; and those for the various states are likely, for the same reason, to be seriously wrong. The averages for the three years, 1949–1951, are used instead of the rates for 1950 in order to reduce the effects of random variations that may be present in the indexes for a given year. In comparing the standings of a given state on the basis of the two indexes used, it should be remembered that the fertility ratios are fairly well standardized for age and sex differences in the respective populations, whereas the crude birth rates are not. As a result a highly urbanized state, such as Delaware or Missouri or the District of Columbia (to whose cities large numbers of young women have been attracted) ranks much higher in the list when the birth rate is employed as a basis for the ratings than it does when the fertility ratio is used in making the comparisons. On the other hand, the most rural state, North Dakota, from which large numbers of young women have migrated to towns and cities in other parts of the nation, ranks much higher when the fertility ratio is used than it does if the birth rate is employed in making the rankings. Still other states such as Arizona and Florida, which received such large contingents of migrants from other states, including thousands of women in the childbearing ages, during the decade 1940 to 1950, rank much higher on the basis of the birth rate than they do according to the fertility ratio.

Table XXVIII presents net reproduction rates for the white populations of the various states, ranked according to the magnitude of their respective indexes. Comparable rates for the nonwhite population are not given by the Bureau of the Census, in the report from which these materials were assembled. The data are given as they appear in the source from which they were taken, with 1,000 women used as the base for the indexes, even though there is slight likelihood that any of the

Table XXVIII. Net Reproduction Rates for the White Population of the United States, April 1945 to 1950, by States

State	Net repro-duction rate	Rank
New Mexico	1853	1
Utah	1745	2
North Dakota	1722	3
Idaho	1718	4
Kentucky	1698	5
South Dakota	1647	6
Arkansas	1630	7
Montana	1615	8
Mississippi	1602	9
Vermont	1587	10
West Virginia	1586	11
Wyoming	1566	12
Arizona	1547	13
Alabama	1527	14
Texas	1522	15
Minnesota	1516	16
Maine	1515	17
Nebraska	1512	18
South Carolina	1486	19
Georgia	1481	20
Louisiana	1479	21
Colorado	1474	22
Texas	1464	23
Wisconsin	1463	24
Iowa	1447	25
Kansas	1445	26
Oklahoma	1436	27
Washington	1433	28
North Carolina	1424	29
Oregon	1420	30
New Hampshire	1407	31
Indiana	1398	32
Michigan	1390	33
Virginia	1355	34
Ohio	1339	35
Nevada	1311	36

Table XXVIII. Net Reproduction Rates for the White Population of the United States (Continued)

State	Net reproduction rate	Rank
California	1304	37
Missouri	1293	38
Maryland	1259	39
Florida	1254	40
Illinois	1235	41
Delaware	1209	42
Pennsylvania	1196	43
Massachusetts	1187	44
Connecticut	1171	45
Rhode Island	1170	46
New Jersey	1144	47
New York	1129	48
District of Columbia	833	49

SOURCE: U. S. Bureau of the Census, "Estimated Net Reproduction Rates for the White Population by Counties, April 1945 to 1950 and 1935 to 1940," *Current Population Reports,* Series P-23, No. 4, July 29, 1957.

numbers are accurate to more than two places. Data for the white population, comparable to those in Table XXVIII, but for the various counties throughout the United States were used in the preparation of the map shown as Figure 56. Although the indexes for specific counties on which it is based undoubtedly include many that are seriously in error, this map does reveal to a large extent the extreme degree to which the reproduction rate of the white population varies throughout the United States.

If one centers his attention upon the state-to-state variations it will be noted that the two states with the highest rates of reproduction, New Mexico and Utah, head the list irrespective of the index used as a basis for the rankings. He will note further that the eight states with the lowest rates of reproduction for the total population are the same (New York, New Jersey, Connecticut, Pennsylvania, Rhode Island, Illinois, Massachusetts, and Missouri) when either the fertility ratio or the birth rate is used in making the comparisons. On the other hand, the District of Columbia, for which the fertility ratio (and also the net reproduction rate of the white population) is lower than that for any of the forty-eight states, has a birth rate that ranks twenty-fourth in the nation. Two factors probably account for most of this difference. First, thousands of young women have flocked to the national capital, so that women of childbearing age constitute an excessively large percentage of the residents of the District. Even though comparatively small proportions of them marry and give birth to children while they are in Washington, enough of them do so to make the ratio of births to population fairly large. When this abnormal age-sex distribution is adjusted for, however, either through the use of the fertility ratio or the net reproduction rate, the resulting index is very low. Second, there is a possibility that the attempt to allocate the births actually taking place in the hospitals of the nation's capital to the states in which the mothers reside, a complicated problem at best, is not entirely successful.

It is obvious from the data in Tables XXVII and XXVIII, and especially so from Figure 56, that the sections of the country with the lowest rates of reproduction are highly urban and that there is a strong tendency for the rate to increase as the degree of urbanization decreases. However, neither New Mexico nor Utah, for which all of the indexes are highest, is to be classed as among the more rural states of the Union. This suggests that other factors are largely responsible for the high birth rates in those states, and one immediately thinks of the Spanish-American heritage of the former and the influence of the Mormon religion in the latter as probably responsible for their high rates of reproduction. Somewhat comparable to the Spanish-Americans, in that it is an ethnic group that has held tenaciously to its distinctive social and cultural patterns, is the French-speaking population of south Louisiana. Therefore, it is interesting to note that Louisiana also ranks far higher on the various scales than would be predicted solely on the basis of the degree to which its population resides in urban areas. Likewise the large Mormon populations of Idaho and Arizona may account in part for the relatively high rates of reproduction in those states.

The varying importance of Negroes, whose birth rate almost universally is assumed to be very high, also may be a factor in accounting for the relative rankings of the various states. In this connection it may be noted that Mississippi, which ranks third from the top among the states on the basis of the fertility ratio and fourth on the basis of the birth rate, is only ninth in rank with respect to the net reproduction rate among the white population. Similarly the other states with very high proportions of Negroes in their populations (South Carolina, Louisiana, Georgia, and Alabama) rank somewhat higher in terms of the two indexes for the total population than they do on the basis of the one for the white population only. But it is hardly profitable to pursue such analysis further, since a study of differential fertility is the better way to determine the nature and significance of such variations.

SUGGESTED SUPPLEMENTARY READINGS

Dinkel, Robert M., "Peopling the City: Fertility," in Rupert B. Vance and Nicholas J. Demerath (Editors), *The Urban South*. Chapel Hill: University of North Carolina Press, 1954, chapter 5.

Grabill, Wilson H., Clyde V. Kiser, and Pascal K. Whelpton, *The Fertility of American Women*. New York: John Wiley & Sons, Inc., 1958, chapters 1–3.

Landis, Paul H., and Paul K. Hatt, *Population Problems: A Cultural Interpretation* (Second Edition). New York: American Book Company, 1954, chapter 11.

Lorimer, Frank, and Associates, *Culture and Human Fertility*, pp. 22–57. Paris: UNESCO, 1954.

National Resources Committee, *The Problems of a Changing Population*, pp. 119–148. Washington: Government Printing Office, 1938.

Smith, T. Lynn, *Brazil: People and Institutions* (Revised Edition). Baton Rouge: Louisiana State University Press, 1954, chapter VIII.

Vance, Rupert B., and Nadia Danilesky, *All These People: The Nation's Human Resources in the South*. Chapel Hill: University of North Carolina Press, 1945, chapters 7 and 8.

Whelpton, P. K., "Births and Birth Rates in the Entire United States, 1909–1948," *Vital Satistics—Special Reports*, 33, No. 8 (1950), 137–162.

Whelpton, P. K., and Ronald Freeman, "A Study of the Growth of American Families," *American Journal of Sociology*, LXI, No. 6 (1956), 595–601.

Chapter 13

Differential Fertility

THERE IS MUCH INTEREST in and importance attached to the facts with respect to the differences in the rate of reproduction of white and Negro, rural and urban segments of a population. Even greater significance may be attached by some to any differentials, much more difficult to establish, that may be found between the fertility of those who pertain to the lower social and economic classes and those who are in the middle and upper classes of their respective societies. Likewise there is considerable interest in knowing what differences if any exist between the birth rates of different religious groups, occupational groups, and those who live in various regions of a country. There is good reason for having an interest in and attaching importance to any differential fertility of these types.

Within a given nation differences in the birth rate, and especially in the net reproduction rate, of various ethnic, color, residential, and other categories can quickly bring about fundamental changes in the biological make-up of its population. The following illustration should serve to demonstrate the rapidity with which such a change can occur. In 1940 Illinois had a white population of 7,504,202 persons, a figure only slightly below that for the four East South Central states (Kentucky, Tennessee, Alabama, and Mississippi) which annually send such large contingents of migrants to Chicago and other parts of the state. Suppose for illustrative purposes that the total were exactly 15 million persons, of whom one-half were in Illinois and the other half in the East South Central states. Net reproduction rates for the white population in 1940 were as follows: Illinois, 82; and the East South Central states, 121. Differences in the mortality rates, if any, were very slight, so that the differentials were almost entirely due to the higher birth rate in the four southern states. If there were no changes in the age-specific birth rates and death rates, such a generation of Illinoisans would leave only 6,150,000 descendants, who in turn would produce 5,043,000 offspring, who in their turn would give rise to a generation of 4,135,260 persons. In the East South Central states, the numbers in the corresponding generations would be 9,075,000, 10,980,750, and 13,286,708, respectively. Since the duration of a generation in the United States is only slightly more than twenty-five years, these calculations indicate that net reproduction rates employed would increase the total size of the generation from 15 million assumed for the first to 17,421,968 for the fourth. However, assuming no intermixture after 1940 only 23.7 per cent of the latter would be the descendants of the 7.5 million Illinoisans (50 per cent of the total) and 76.3 per cent would be the descendants of the 7.5 million white southerners. This demonstrates fairly well the rapidity with which differential birth rates such as those presently prevailing in the United States and many other parts of the world may change the basic ethnic components of a given population. Similar differences, if continued over several generations, could result in greatly varying numbers of descendants of persons presently in the lower, middle, and upper classes of a given society; in the proportions of whites and Negroes in countries such as the United States, Brazil, and Cuba; and in the numbers contributed to future national populations by those presently living on the farms and in the cities of various countries.

Rural-Urban Differentials

Its magnitude, the extent to which it persists from decade to decade, and its general social significance all make the rural-urban differential in fertility of prime importance. Whenever one takes a bird's-eye view of the rates of reproduction in a given country, as is possible for the United States by observation of Figures 56, 57, and 58, it is at once evident that the more urban an area the lower the fertility of the population and the more rural an area the higher the rate of reproduction. In our own country the highest birth rates prevail in the southern Appalachians, in other of the most rural portions of the southern region, and in the remote sections of the Rocky Mountains. On the other hand, the rate of reproduction is very low in all the great cities, which even seem to exert a depressing effect upon the birth rates of the population in the rural districts surrounding them.

In order to determine whether or not there are significant rural and

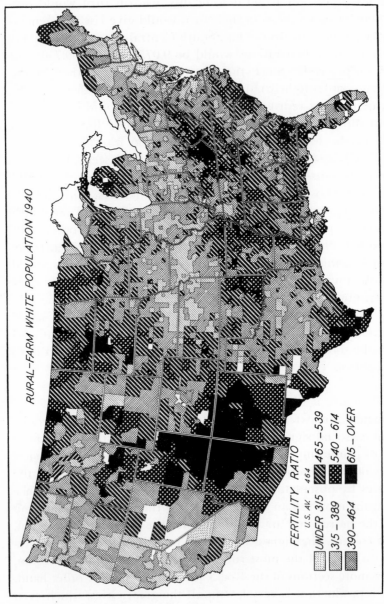

RURAL–FARM WHITE POPULATION 1940

FERTILITY RATIO

U.S. AV. – 464

UNDER 315
315 – 389
390 – 464
465 – 539
540 – 614
615 – OVER

Figure 57. Fertility ratios of the white rural-farm population of the United States, by counties, 1940. (Counties having less than a hundred white rural-farm women aged fifteen to forty-four are left blank. Reproduced from Beegle and Smith, "Differential Fertility in Louisiana," loc. cit.)

urban, residential, and state or regional differentials in fertility, it is necessary to have the data subsorted as they are in Tables XXIX and XXX. Otherwise when the various racial groups are so unequally represented in the different residential categories and each of these in the several regions, as is the case in the United States, one is likely to conclude that a given differential exists when in reality it is merely a reflection of another. In other words, one who goes to the trouble to compare the rates of reproduction in the Northeast and the South wants to demonstrate something more than that the latter is more rural or that it contains higher proportions of Negroes than the former. These facts are already well known and susceptible to simple and easy demonstration and proof. When the appropriate comparisons are made of the data in Table XXIX, it is observed that the fertility ratio of the urban population is substantially lower than that of either the rural-nonfarm or the rural-farm populations in the United States as a whole, and that this is the case for each one of the four major regional divisions of the nation. Furthermore this differential prevails not only for the population as whole, but also for both the white and the Negro populations taken separately. Except for the white populations of the South and the West, the ratios for the rural-farm population also are above those for the rural-nonfarm group.

If one makes even more refined comparisons using the data for states given in Table XXX, the strong and consistent tendency of the rural population to multiply more rapidly than the urban is even more convincingly demonstrated. Among the white population in every one of the forty-eight states, for the period between April, 1945, and 1950, the fertility ratio of the urban population is substantially lower than those for the rural-nonfarm and the rural-farm categories; and except in New York, Indiana, and Michigan, in which the numbers of rural persons involved is very small, the same is true among the Negro population. The tendency of the birth rate of the rural population of the United States to exceed that of the urban has been known, of course, for some time,[1] as has something about the factors responsible for the differential. Nevertheless, it is important to see the degree to which it persists throughout the length and breadth of the country, even after

[1] See the data and literature cited in T. Lynn Smith, *Population Analysis* (New York: McGraw-Hill Book Company, 1948), 209–211; and T. Lynn Smith, *The Sociology of Rural Life* (Third Edition), (New York: Harper & Brothers, 1953), pp. 128–145.

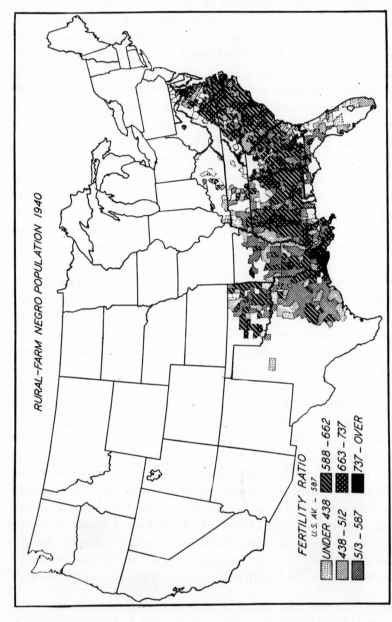

RURAL–FARM NEGRO POPULATION 1940

FERTILITY RATIO

U.S. AV - 587

UNDER 438
438 – 512
513 – 587
588 – 662
663 – 737
737 – OVER

Figure 58. Fertility ratios of the Negro rural-farm population of the United States, by counties, 1940. (Counties having less than a hundred Negro rural-farm women aged fifteen to forty-four. Reproduced from Beegle and Smith, "Differential Fertility in Louisiana," loc. cit.)

Table XXIX. Residential, Racial, and Regional Differentials in Fertility in the United States, April 1945 to 1950

Residential and racial categories	Number of children under 5 per 100 women 15–44				
	United States	North-east	North Central	South	West
Total Population	47.9	41.1	47.6	51.3	49.2
White	46.7	41.4	47.9	49.6	49.0
Negro	51.3	37.2	42.2	57.3	44.2
Urban population	42.2	38.8	43.3	43.7	45.4
White	42.2	38.9	43.4	43.3	45.4
Negro	42.4	36.8	41.7	44.9	43.3
Rural-nonfarm population	56.7	50.8	56.1	59.0	59.7
White	55.9	50.9	56.1	57.6	59.1
Negro	63.8	44.8	47.2	65.4	56.2
Rural-farm population	59.4	53.6	57.9	61.4	57.9
White	56.4	53.6	57.8	55.6	56.9
Negro	77.2	51.6	66.9	70.6	60.2

SOURCE: Computed from the data given in U. S. Bureau of the Census, *U. S. Census of Population: 1950*, Vol. II, *Characteristics of the Population* (Washington: Government Printing Office, 1952); and *U. S. Census of Population: 1950*, Vol. IV, *Special Reports*, Part 3, Chapter B "Nonwhite Population by Race" (Washington: Government Printing Office, 1953).

the upsurge in the urban birth rate since 1935 and after the elimination of so much of the difference between the rural and urban ways of life that has accompanied the perfection of modern means of communication and transportation.

Such rural-urban differentials in fertility are by no means limited to the United States. Indeed, that the birth rates of rural people have greatly exceeded those of city residents in various European countries and in other parts of the world for which even partially reliable data have been available, long has been known.[1] More recently it has become possible to compare the fertility of rural and urban populations

[1] The most comprehensive summaries of the facts and indications of the relevant literature on the subject are contained in P. A. Sorokin and Carle C. Zimmerman, *Principles of Rural-Urban Sociology* (New York: Henry Holt and Company, 1929), pp. 205–220; and P. A. Sorokin, Carle C. Zimmerman, and Charles J. Galpin, *A Systematic Source Book in Rural Sociology* (Minneapolis: University of Minnesota Press, 1932), III, 135–225.

Table XXX. Residential and Racial Differentials in Fertility April 1, 1945 to 1950, by States

| State | Number of children under 5 per 100 women aged 15–44 | | | | | |
| | Urban population | | Rural-nonfarm population | | Rural-farm population | |
	White	Negro	White	Negro	White	Negro
New England						
Maine	47	..	58	..	57	..
New Hampshire	46	..	54	..	51	..
Vermont	43	..	58	..	63	..
Massachusetts	41	43	51	55	47	..
Rhode Island	41	51	56	..	43	..
Connecticut	40	46	49	..	46	..
Middle Atlantic						
New York	38	33	52	28	57	..
New Jersey	40	40	48	51	47	55
Pennsylvania	39	41	50	42	52	..
East North Central						
Ohio	45	43	57	47	55	56
Indiana	45	45	56	40	52	..
Illinois	40	40	53	50	53	..
Michigan	46	43	60	41	56	..
Wisconsin	45	47	58	..	63	..
West North Central						
Minnesota	46	49	60	..	65	..
Iowa	45	51	54	..	61	..
Missouri	40	40	53	52	52	74
North Dakota	47	..	59	..	67	..

South Dakota	51	..	54	..	63	..
Nebraska	45	46	51	..	58	..
Kansas	46	47	52	49	55	..
South Atlantic						
Delaware	40	41	51	50	56	..
Maryland	44	44	53	59	53	67
District of Columbia	..	..	..	..	..	..
Virginia	43	44	56	63	52	69
West Virginia	40	40	62	58	58	..
North Carolina	40	43	56	66	54	76
South Carolina	44	49	56	72	56	80
Georgia	44	45	56	68	57	80
Florida	39	42	58	59	54	73
East South Central						
Kentucky	44	42	65	50	59	57
Tennessee	42	43	58	54	53	72
Alabama	43	50	57	68	55	76
Mississippi	43	50	52	65	56	81
West South Central						
Arkansas	43	51	57	65	61	78
Louisiana	45	52	60	71	57	82
Oklahoma	45	49	54	61	54	70
Texas	48	43	58	63	53	69

Table XXX. Residential and Racial Differentials in Fertility (Continued)

State	Number of children under 5 per 100 women aged 15–44					
	Urban population		Rural-nonfarm population		Rural-farm population	
	White	Negro	White	Negro	White	Negro
Mountain						
Montana	48	28	61	..	64	..
Idaho	54	54	60	..	64	..
Wyoming	50	48	63	..	63	..
Colorado	46	41	60	..	60	..
New Mexico	57	48	71	..	67	..
Arizona	49	45	58	60	61	..
Utah	58	46	69	..	63	..
Nevada	43	39	57	..	47	..
Pacific						
Washington	49	54	57	..	55	..
Oregon	43	51	58	..	51	..
California	44	42	58	49	52	49

SOURCE: Computed from data in U. S. Bureau of the Census, *U. S. Census of Population: 1950*, Vol. II, *Characteristics of the Population* (Washington: Government Printing Office, 1952 and 1953). (. . No ratios given for categories containing less than 1,000 women aged 15–44.)

in most of the Latin American countries. (See Table XXXI.) This is especially significant because the twenty Latin American countries taken together occupy a very substantial part of the earth's surface; the world division they constitute is the one in which current rates of population increase are the highest; [1] these nations make up a highly important part of the so-called "underdeveloped" areas of the world; and the various improvisations necessary in order to make the comparisons illustrate the types of difficulties encountered by those who undertake to study the populations of the areas containing the vast majority of the earth's people.

Even on the basis of these highly imperfect materials, it is readily evident that throughout Latin America the fertility ratio of the rural population is much higher than, frequently almost double, that of the urban population.

Study of the data in Table XXXI also leads one to the following conclusion: (the lower the general rate of reproduction in a country, the greater the rural-urban differential in fertility.) Therefore, since the factors presently in operation lead one to expect the continued urbanization and industrialization of the Latin American countries, the prevailing rural-urban differential in the birth rate is likely to be maintained for some decades to come. It may even become more pronounced in most parts of Mexico, Central America, the island republics, and South America. Eventually, of course, the point should be reached at which this tendency will produce a falling birth rate throughout the length and breadth of the area, for as the urban population becomes a more significant proportion of the total population, many national birth rates are certain to fall, perhaps sharply.

A special set of tabulations prepared as a part of the 1950 census of the United States which gives the characteristics of the inhabitants according to the size of the places in which they lived, enables one to explore two other significant aspects of the relationship between urbanization and the rate of reproduction. These are (1) the ways in which the fertility ratio varies as one passes from the greatest metropolitan cities, to cities of fewer inhabitants, to towns and villages, to the open country and (2) the differentials between the rates of reproduction of people living in the central cities of the urbanized areas and those living in the densely populated districts immediately adja-

[1] See T. Lynn Smith, "Current Population Trends in Latin America," *American Journal of Sociology*, LXII, No. 4 (1948) , 399–406.

Table XXXI. Rural-Urban Differences in the Fertility Ratios of the Latin American Countries, 1950

Country	Number of children under 5 per 100 women aged 15–44		
	Urban areas	Rural districts	The nation
Costa Rica	54.3	86.8	73.9
Cuba [1]	41.5	79.2	55.3
Dominican Republic	54.2	90.9	79.8
El Salvador	53.7	76.7	67.4
Guatemala	. . . .	. . . .	75.2
Haiti	36.7	52.0	49.7
Honduras	. . . .	. . . .	72.7
Mexico [2]	53.9	70.7	68.4
Nicaragua	58.5	78.1	70.2
Panama	54.8	92.3	75.4
Argentina [3]	24.8	52.9	46.8
Bolivia	. . . .	. . . .	68.5
Brazil [4]	49.4	77.8	70.5
Chile	. . . .	. . . .	56.7
Colombia [5]	46.6	72.1	67.6
Ecuador	66.8	77.6	75.6
Paraguay [6]	42.5	82.8	75.2
Peru [7]	53.5	74.6	71.5
Uruguay	. . . .	. . . .	. . . .
Venezuela [2]	60.3	79.7	76.7

[1] Data are for 1953.
[2] The Federal District is considered as urban, the remainder of the country as rural for the purposes of this comparison.
[3] The Federal Capital is considered as urban, the remainder of Argentina as rural for purposes of these comparisons. The data are for 1947.
[4] The urban category includes the suburban one as well.
[5] The municipio of Bogotá is considered as urban, the remainder of Colombia as rural. Data are for 1938.
[6] Asunción is considered as urban, the remainder of the nation as rural.
[7] The province of Lima is considered as urban, the remainder of Peru as rural for purposes of this comparison. The data are for 1940.

cent to such incorporated cities. To facilitate such comparisons, Table XXXII was prepared. Observation of the data it contains makes it readily apparent that among both the white and the nonwhite segments of the population, the fertility ratio increases steadily as the size

Table XXXII. Fertility Ratios in the United States According to Size of Place and Color of the Population, April 1945 to 1950

Size of place (urbanized areas)	Number of children under 5 per 100 women aged 15–44		
	Total population	White population	Nonwhite population
3,000,000 or more, total	43.3	43.6	40.8
Central cities	40.4	40.5	39.6
Fringes	49.1	49.5	48.2
1,000,000–2,999,999, total	47.8	47.8	47.8
Central cities	44.4	44.1	45.9
Fringes	53.1	52.7	60.1
250,000–999,999, total	50.3	50.2	50.8
Central cities	48.0	47.8	49.4
Fringes	56.9	56.7	61.3
Less than 250,000, total	51.1	50.7	53.6
Central cities	49.0	48.6	51.8
Fringes	58.6	58.0	69.4
25,000 or more	52.4	52.1	54.7
10,000–24,999	52.5	52.2	55.9
2,500–9,999	57.0	56.3	64.5
1,000–2,499	61.0	60.4	68.4
Less than 1,000	62.9	62.1	75.1
Other rural	74.0	71.1	97.2

SOURCE: Computed from data in U. S. Bureau of the Census, *U. S. Census of Population: 1950*, Vol. IV, *Special Reports*, Part V, Chapter A, "Characteristics by Size of Place" (Washington: Government Printing Office, 1953).

of community decreases. In fact, by comparing the two extremes it is noted that the index for the open-country districts is almost double that for the central cities of the greatest urban agglomerations. Furthermore, among the nonwhite population the index for the former is more than twice as large as the one for the latter. Also, without exception, for whites as well as nonwhites, and in urbanized areas of all sizes, the fertility ratios are substantially lower for those living in the central cities than for those living in the fringes. This is, of course, strictly in line with the general belief that many young couples establish residences in the suburbs in order to have a more advantageous environment in which to rear their families.

Finally, before leaving the subject of rural-urban differentials in fertility it is well to return once more to the matter of the variations within the open country districts themselves, and especially the manner in which the fertility of the population changes as the distance from centers of manufacturing, trade, and transportation increases. That the farther from such large urban centers, the higher the birth rate, seems apparent from Figure 56, to which reference was made above. This generalization is supported even more adequately by the fertility data for the rural-farm population, white and Negro, from the 1940 census. (See Figures 57 and 58.) As yet no one has done the immense number of arithmetical computations needed for the preparation of comparable maps on the basis of the 1950 census materials.

Racial Differentials

There is a widespread belief that the Negro and other colored elements of the population are multiplying much more rapidly than the white population in the United States and other parts of the Western Hemisphere. Coupled with this is the belief that the populations of the parts of the world inhabited chiefly by various colored races are growing more rapidly than those of Europe, the white populations of the American continents, and the descendants of Europeans in other parts of the world such as Australia, New Zealand, and South Africa. Indeed thousands, if not millions of well-educated persons in the United States have a haunting fear that very shortly the white population of this country will be completely drowned, at home and abroad, in the surging masses of Negro and other colored peoples. Even though such a phobia is absent, the differences, if any, between the rates of reproduction of whites, Negroes, and other races, in the United States, of whites, Negroes, and Indians in the Latin American countries, and so on are of considerable interest. This may be illustrated by a short quotation of a generalization by Frank Tannenbaum, noted historian and long-time student of the Negro in the Americas. After pointing out that the Negro has physical occupancy or possession of a large part of the two American continents, aptly described as the area within a huge half circle extending from Washington, D. C., to Rio de Janeiro, Brazil, this authority succinctly states:

And the density as well as the extent of this empire is increasing because Negro fertility is relatively high in comparison to the white. The only place where this biological expansion is being challenged is in Trinidad by the East Indians.[1]

Thus it is important for the student of population to establish what differentials, if any, exist between the rates of reproduction of the various racial groups in such countries as the United States, Brazil, Cuba, and South Africa, in which the population is composed of large groups of persons of highly diverse racial stocks.

In the United States, as was shown in Table VII, the proportion of Negroes in the population fell steadily from the time of the first census in 1790 until 1930. Thus, throughout most of our history, although the birth rate of the Negro population may have been above that of the white, the results of the differential were more than offset by the higher mortality rate of the Negroes, or by the immigration of whites, or a combination of these two factors. Reliable birth rates are, of course, not available for any part of this historical period, but fertility ratios for whites and Negroes separately may be computed from the materials gathered in each census from 1890 to date. These (the number of children under five per hundred women fifteen to forty-four) are as follows, with the index for the white population being given first in each case: 1890, 52 and 62; 1900, 51 and 59; 1910, 48 and 52; 1920, 47 and 44; 1930, 39 and 43; 1940, 32 and 37; and 1950, 47 and 51. Thus it appears that for the most part, from 1885 on, the Negro population actually had a slightly higher birth rate than the white population. Between 1915 and 1920, however, this seemingly was not the case. But be this all as it may, prior to 1935 the effective fertility of the Negro population was not sufficient to offset the other two factors (mortality and immigration) related to population change, and the proportion of Negroes in the population declined.

By 1930 it was possible to make fairly satisfactory comparisons of the rates of reproduction of whites and Negroes in the various residential categories. Then, and also in 1940, it was apparent that the fertility of the Negro population equalled or exceeded that of the white population only because the former lived in rural-farm areas in considerably greater proportions than the latter.[2] With this background in mind, the data in Tables XXIX, XXX, and XXXII should be analyzed to

[1] "Discussion," in Vera Rubin (editor), *Caribbean Studies: A Symposium* (Jamaica, B.W.I.: Institute of Social and Economic Research, 1957), p. 62.

[2] See Smith, *Population Analysis*, pp. 212–216.

determine what, if any, differentials prevailed between 1945 and 1950 in the rates of reproduction of whites and Negroes in the United States. (Among the total population, as is evident from Table XXIX, the fertility ratio of the Negroes is slightly above that for the whites. However, on a regional basis this is true only in the South; in the other three regional subdivisions, the ratios for the white population are above those for Negroes.) This immediately suggests that outside the South the Negroes live in urban centers in much greater proportions than the whites, so that the residential factor must be controlled before fair comparisons may be made. When this is done, as the detailed information given in the same table makes possible, it is seen that there probably are no significant differences between the rates of reproduction of the white and Negro residents of urban centers, and that outside the South the same is true for the rural-nonfarm population as well. Furthermore, other than in the South, there seems to be no significant differential in the rates of reproduction of the white and Negro rural-farm populations, since the white is the higher of the two in one of the three regional divisions, and the numbers involved in all are comparatively small. In the South, however, the region for which this comparison has real significance, there was between 1945 and 1950 a substantially higher birth rate among the Negroes residing on farms than among the whites of the same residential category. This is the region, of course, which contains nearly all of the Negro farm population, the one in which Negroes are still living on the land in much higher proportions than whites, and in which, generally speaking, Negroes probably tend to be concentrated in the most highly rural and agricultural portions of the open country. Thus because Negroes are still residents of the most rural region of the country and probably because they tend to live in the most rural sectors of that region, their rate of reproduction is slightly higher than that of the whites. Such a conclusion receives further support from a study of the detailed information for the forty-eight states given in Table XXX, and it is in line also with the indexes for the white and nonwhite populations, respectively, presented in Table XXXII.

In Latin America and many other parts of the world it is more difficult to determine what, if any, racial differentials in fertility prevail than it is to establish the rural-urban differentials presented above. A few countries, it is true, classify births according to color or race, and many of them include some kind of racial or ethnic classification of the population in the censuses that are made. Almost never, however, is it possible to match the births so classified with the necessary population data in order to compute reliable birth rates for various racial or color categories; and even if one could, there still would be many questions relative to the completeness or lack of it in the registration of the births. Even more disheartening to the population student is the fact that the age and sex distributions of the various racial groups, the data needed for the computation of the fertility ratios, generally are lacking. One who attempts to determine the extent of racial differentials in fertility throughout Latin America and most other parts of the world must be prepared to make even more improvisations than those generally called for in population analyses made in the United States and the European countries.

Some significant comparisons, though, are possible. For example, a number of students of population have for some time been convinced that differential fertility was producing a rapid "bleaching" or whitening of the Brazilian population. Since almost 6 million persons were classified as black or Negro by Brazil's 1950 census, since the number of mulattoes must be fully as large if not larger, and since the total population of Brazil was about 52 million at the time, the racial differentials in fertility in that great country have much to do with determining the nature of and direction of the changes in the racial composition of the population of the Americas. Fortunately the improved classifications used in the 1950 Brazilian census make it easy to compute the indexes needed for comparisons of the rates of reproduction of Brazil's white, black, yellow, and mixed-blood populations. (See Table XXXIII.)

A study of these materials makes it readily apparent that whites are multiplying more rapidly than Negroes and by a considerable margin. Throughout Brazil the fertility ratios for the Negro population are consistently lower than those for the white population. The ratios for the mixed category are inflated, of course, by any racial mixing in which either the whites or the Negroes are involved, but despite this fact, the indexes for the white population compare very favorably with those for the mixed group. The difficulties the Negro woman has in securing a mate, and the relative freedom of access which the upper class (white or whitish) man has to the (colored) women in the lower

Table XXXIII. Number of Children Under Five per Hundred Women Aged Fifteen to Forty-nine for Each Brazilian State and Territory, by Color, 1950

Region and state or territory	Total	White	Negro	Yellow	Pardo (mixed)
Brazil	65.3	65.3	55.6	79.6	69.2
North					
Guaporé †	73.0	70.7	51.9	....	76.9
Acre †	90.0	90.1	58.7	....	92.1
Amazonas	73.7	74.5	50.5	119.1	74.4
Rio Branco †	83.6	82.1	62.0	....	86.0
Pará	67.2	67.0	47.2	91.5	69.0
Amapá †	73.5	77.9	43.2	....	75.7
Northeast					
Maranhão	64.9	69.4	52.2	....	65.7
Piauí	75.6	78.5	60.5	....	77.6
Ceará	77.0	78.2	68.3	....	80.9
Rio Grande do Norte	73.1	74.5	61.1	....	73.9
Paraíba	70.0	72.3	60.0	....	69.1
Pernambuco	65.2	67.3	52.0	....	66.0
Alagôas	68.6	71.3	51.0	....	69.2
Fernando de Noronha †	65.2	....	....	....	....
East					
Sergipe	69.2	75.0	55.6	....	66.7
Bahia	65.4	66.9	54.1	....	68.9
Minas Gerais	67.5	69.7	56.2	82.1	69.3
Espírito Santo	74.5	76.5	63.0	....	75.7
Rio de Janeiro	66.9	65.5	65.4	78.6	71.2
Distrito Federal	36.8	36.2	34.0	56.7	41.3
South					
São Paulo	57.4	56.6	55.4	78.3	65.7
Paraná	72.9	73.4	64.5	89.4	70.1
Santa Catarina	80.5	81.2	71.5	....	73.0
Rio Grande do Sul	66.0	66.6	57.9	52.3	64.0
West Central					
Mato Grosso	76.7	77.9	63.9	81.5	78.4
Goiás	72.0	76.7	53.0	94.1	69.5

SOURCE: Computations based on data from the *VI Recenseamento Geral do Brasil*.

† Territory.

.. Rates not given for a category in which there were less than 100 women aged fifteen to forty-nine.

social classes probably are two of the more important factors explaining the observed differentials.[1]

A few data for some of the other countries also are available. Thus for Cuba in 1953 the fertility ratios for the four racial or color categories are as follows: white, 52.4; Negro, 57.2; yellow, 57.8; and mixed 68.8. For Costa Rica, in which the numbers and proportions of Negroes are very small, the fertility ratios for 1950 are 74.3 for whites and mestizos combined and 54.6 for Negroes; and in Panama, a veritable "melting pot," the fertility ratios for the various racial or color groupings used in the 1940 census are as follows: whites, 40.5; Negroes, 34.2; mestizo (largely mulatto), 68.9; and others, 55.2. All told these fragments of data do not fully support the hypothesis, based on Brazilian materials, that the white elements in the Latin American population are reproducing more rapidly than the colored ones, but neither do they fortify the belief so widely held that exactly the opposite is true.

Regional Differentials

When the data are assembled in the forms used in Tables XXIX and XXX and Figures 56 and 57, the nature of the regional differences is rather readily apparent. There are great variations, but most of them seem due to the fact that the northeastern states are highly urban and industrial whereas the South and the Rocky Mountain states are more rural. The heavy representation of Negroes in some of the more rural sections also seems to be a factor in making the birth rate for the area in general substantially higher than that for the nation, but in urban areas, and especially in those of the North and the West, the increasingly large Negro populations do not multiply more rapidly than their white fellows. Two western states, Utah and New Mexico, have the highest fertility ratios of any of the states; and when the data are subsorted for residence and race, they also are the states in which the indexes for the urban and the rural-nonfarm populations are the highest. Even among the white rural-farm population the fertility ratio for New Mexico is second only to that for North Dakota, and Utah stands

[1] See T. Lynn Smith, *Brazil: People and Institutions* (Revised Edition), (Baton Rouge: Louisiana State University Press, 1954), pp. 160–161; John Van Dyke Saunders, *Differential Fertility in Brazil* (Gainesville: University of Florida Press, 1958), pp. 58–62; and Giorgio Mortara, "The Brazilian Birth Rate: Its Economic and Social Factors," in Frank Lorimer, *et al.*, *Culture and Human Fertility* (Paris: UNESCO, 1954), p. 497, *passim*.

sixth highest. These facts hardly should be interpreted, however, as indicating that the rate of reproduction tends to be high in the region as such; rather they suggest that above and beyond the rural-urban differentials there are factors associated with the Spanish-American [1] and the Mormon social and cultural heritages that make for high birth rates in the communities in which these groups reside.

The most satisfactory generalization with respect to regional differences may be formulated as follows: every refinement introduced into the analysis of the rate of reproduction in the United States tends to emphasize the importance of the rural-urban differential in fertility and to minimize the importance of racial and regional differences in the birth rate. When the residential differentials have been fully isolated, there is little if anything left to attribute to these two factors.

Class Differentials

The determination of differentials in the fertility of the various social classes in a society is extremely difficult, and there has been little comprehensive study of the subject. This is particularly true with respect to the United States. Nevertheless through the use of occupational data it has been possible to determine to some extent the relationship between socio-economic standing and the rate of reproduction.

Interestingly enough, the fundamental relationship revealed by these studies is exactly opposite the one assumed to be the case by many, apparently largely through deduction based upon the principles formulated by Thomas R. Malthus near the close of the eighteenth century. In the United States and Europe, rarely is it found that the higher the social and economic status, the more rapid the rate of reproduction. Rather the old refrain to the effect that

> The rich get rich, and
> The poor get . . . children!

seems to be a much more accurate piece of demographic generalization. In other words, in Europe and the United States, there appears

[1] In an M.A. thesis submitted at the University of Florida in 1955, William W. Winnie, Jr., demonstrated that the rate of reproduction of the Spanish-American population of New Mexico was approximately 50 per cent higher than that of the other residents of the state.

to be an inverse relationship between economic status and fertility: as social and economic status increases, the birth rate decreases.

Consider a few of the data. On the whole, those presented in Figure 59 are still among the most comprehensive and satisfactory available. They show rather conclusively that the people with the higher (more desired, better paid, and more difficult to enter) occupations or professions have lower rates of reproduction than those lower in the occupational scale; and they also show a marked decrease in the fertility of rural people as one passes up the agricultural ladder from the farm laborers at the bottom to the farm owners on the upper rung.

Thompson's study of differential fertility in Butler County, Ohio, is among the most competently done examinations of this subject ever made in this country. With the cooperation of the Bureau of the Census, data from the census schedules were tabulated and analyzed in ways that contribute much to the understanding of differentials in fertility. By subsorting he controlled the residential factor and also differences in birth place of the women involved ("north born" and "south born"). A concise statement of the results is as follows:

> The findings of this study on the relation of economic status, as measured by family rentals, to average number of children can be summed up very briefly by saying that there was a very close and consistent inverse relation between them—the higher the economic status, the lower the average number of children.[1]

Clyde V. Kiser, working with data from the National Health Survey, which was attempted in 1935 and 1936, also demonstrated a close relationship between occupation or social class and the rate of reproduction. Specifically he computed standardized birth rates for women age fifteen to forty-four, married to native white men, and living in Oakland, Newark, Grand Rapids, St. Paul, and Fall River at the time of the survey. In these cities the number of live births per thousand women varied according to the occupational category of the head of the family as follows: professional, 101; proprietors, 85; clerks-salesmen, 96; skilled workers, 101; semiskilled workers not in manufacturing, 110; semiskilled workers in manufacturing, 122; and unskilled

---

[1] Warren S. Thompson, *Average Number of Children per Woman in Butler County, Ohio, 1930—A Study in Differential Fertility* (Washington: U. S. Bureau of the Census, 1941) , p. 9.

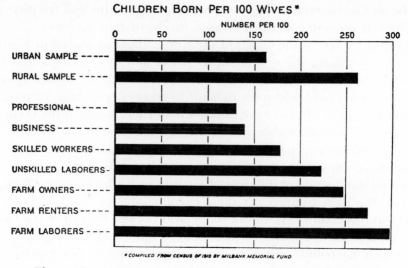

CHILDREN BORN PER 100 WIVES*

Figure 59. Occupational and tenure status in relation to the rate of reproduction in the United States, 1910. (Illustration from the Bureau of Agricultural Economics, U. S. Department of Agriculture)

workers, 137.[1] Similar is the conclusion to be drawn from the results of the study of fertility in Indianapolis, probably the most intensive investigation of the subject ever undertaken. The inquiry was limited to couples in which both man and wife were native white, but even so 41,498 married pairs were covered in the survey. Economic status was measured by the amount of rent paid per month, or its equivalent. This study indicated that fertility was at its maximum, 260 children born per hundred wives fifteen to forty-four years of age, among those paying less than ten dollars per month rent, and that this index fell steadily, as rent increased, until among those paying from fifty to fifty-nine dollars in rent there were ninety-three children per hundred wives. Thereafter the fertility index rose to 106 for the couples paying between sixty and seventy dollars in rent and to 138 for those paying eighty dollars or more.[2] These and other studies in the United States all confirm the conclusions reached by Frank W. Notestein in a study

[1] Clyde V. Kiser, "Variations in Birth Rates According to Occupational Status," *Milbank Memorial Fund Quarterly,* 16 (1938), 46.

[2] P. K. Whelpton and Clyde V. Kiser, "Social and Psychological Factors Affecting Fertility; I. Differential Fertility Among 41,498 Native-White Couples in Indianapolis," *Milbank Memorial Fund Quarterly,* 21 (1943), 238.

published in 1933. This thorough analysis of the 1910 census data indicated that in all types of urban areas and in rural areas as well, persons in the lower social and economic classes were reproducing more rapidly than those in the upper ones. Notestein also indicated that, in all probability, such differentials had prevailed as early as the closing decades of the nineteenth century.[1]

Similar are the results of the studies in Europe, of which some of those made in England are among the most satisfactory. In 1931 the number of births per thousand married men grouped, according to occupational classes were as follows: Class I (professional men, managers, officials and independents in certain finance and insurance businesses), 98; Class II (employers and managers), 102; Class IIIA (clerical workers), 111; Class III (skilled workers), 140; Class IV (semi-skilled workers), 162; and Class V (unskilled workers), 174.[2]

It is important to keep in mind, however, that most of the studies that show an inverse relationship between socio-economic status and the birth rate have been made in the most highly urbanized and industrialized areas of the Western world. It does not follow necessarily that the same is true in those areas in which agricultural and pastoral ways of life dominate the scene and in which hoary paternalistic patterns of family organization continue to function. As a matter of fact, and with much reason, Sorokin and Zimmerman, in explaining why vertical social mobility is so much greater in urban society than in rural, listed as one of the principal reasons differences in the differential fertility of the upper and lower classes in the two residential groups. On the basis of a considerable amount of evidence they concluded that among city populations "the differential fertility of the upper and lower classes is far greater than in rural populations."[3]

Although the quantitative data of the kind he would like to have are lacking, the present writer has become thoroughly convinced, through some twenty-five years of personal observation and study, that in Brazil, Colombia, and most other Latin American countries the fertility of the upper classes is fully as great as that of the lower social and economic strata. In fact he has come to believe that the very high rates

---

[1] "The Differential Rate of Increase Among the Social Classes of the American Population," *Social Forces,* 12, No. 1 (1933), pp. 17–33.

[2] J. W. Innes, "Class Birth Rates in England and Wales, 1921–1931," *Milbank Memorial Fund Quarterly,* 19 (1941), 75.

[3] *Op. cit.,* p. 43, *passim.* Cf. P. A. Sorokin, *Social Mobility* (New York: Harper and Brothers, 1927), *passim.*

of reproduction of the upper classes in Latin America have had much to do with shaping and maintaining some of the more distinctive psycho-social traits of the populations in these parts of the world.[1] Similarly, a rather comprehensive study made in Poland shows rather definitely that the size of the farm family is positively correlated with the size of the farm and this factor is then used to help explain the rapidity with which inheritance is decreasing the size of the agricultural holdings.[2]

Other Differentials

Undoubtedly, there are many other differentials in fertility between various groups of mankind, such as those between ethnic groups and religious groups that were mentioned above. Unfortunately, very few studies have been made, with residential and other variables sufficiently controlled, that would enable one to judge the nature and magnitude of such differences. Unfortunately, too, the complete lack of comprehensive data on the religious affiliations of the population of the United States makes practically impossible what otherwise would be the fairly easy task of disentangling possible differences in the rates of reproduction of the various religious elements in the population from those more properly attributed to rural-urban, racial, or other influences. It is rather generally supposed, however, that Jews have the lowest birth rates of any of the major religious groups, Protestants next lowest, and Roman Catholics and Latter-day Saints (or Mormons) the highest; and the few studies done with sufficient care and skill to be significant seem to indicate that such actually is the case.

The Indianapolis study mentioned above indicated that, with economic status held constant, the couples in which both the man and the wife were Roman Catholics definitely produced more children than those in which both were Protestants, and those in which one of the mates was Catholic and the other Protestant had the lowest birth rates of all.[3] An earlier study of 40,766 Wisconsin couples by Samuel A. Stouffer[4] and the study by Notestein quoted above[5] also showed that

[1] See T. Lynn Smith, "Values Held by People in Latin America which Affect Technical Cooperation," *Rural Sociology,* 21, No. 1 (1956), 72–74.

[2] W. Stys, "The Influence of Economic Conditions on the Fertility of Peasant Women" *Population Studies: A Journal of Demography,* XI, No. 2 (1957), 136–148.

[3] Whelpton and Kiser, *op. cit.,* p. 238.

[4] "Trends in the Fertility of Catholics and Non-Catholics," *American Journal of Sociology,* XLI, No. 2 (1935), 145–166.

[5] *Op. cit.,* pp. 32–33.

the married couples in which both mates were Roman Catholics had substantially higher rates of reproduction than those in which both were Protestants. Likewise a detailed study of the rate of reproduction in Louisiana showed very clearly that "the residents of the French, Catholic portion of Louisiana are characterized by much higher rates of reproduction than those of the Anglo-Saxon, Protestant portion. This is true for both racial groups in all of the residential classifications."[1] Finally, the data for the various states presented above seem to indicate rather definitely that the birth rate of the Mormons is comparatively high, possibly even higher than that among the Catholics, when due allowance is made for the rural-urban residential factor. The point to stress, however, is the extent to which we lack adequate studies of the differences between the birth rates of the principal religious segments of the population.

[1] J. Allan Beegle and T. Lynn Smith, *Differential Fertility in Louisiana,* Louisiana Agricultural Experiment Station Bulletin No. 403 (Baton Rouge: Louisiana State University, 1946), p. 27.

SUGGESTED SUPPLEMENTARY READINGS

Beegle, J. Allan, and T. Lynn Smith, *Differential Fertility in Louisiana.* Louisiana Agricultural Experiment Station Bulletin No. 403. Baton Rouge, 1946.

Grabill, Wilson H., Clyde V. Kiser, and Pascal K. Whelpton, *The Fertility of American Women.* New York: John Wiley & Sons, Inc., 1958, chapters 4–7.

Kiser, Clyde V., and P. K. Whelpton, "Social and Psychological Factors Affecting Fertility, XXXIII, Summary of Chief Findings and Implications for Future Studies," *Milbank Memorial Fund Quarterly,* XXXVI, No. 3 (1958), 1325–1372.

Landis, Paul H., and Paul K. Hatt, *Population Problems: A Cultural Interpretation* (Second Edition). New York: American Book Company, 1954, chapters 12–14.

Lorimer, Frank, and Associates, *Culture and Human Fertility.* Paris: UNESCO, 1954, parts 1 and 5.

McMahan, C. A., *The People of Atlanta.* Athens: University of Georgia Press, 1950, chapter XI.

Phelps, Harold A., and David Henderson, *Population in Its Human Aspects.* New York: Appleton-Century-Crofts, Inc., 1958, pp. 236–245.

Saunders, John V. D., *Differential Fertility in Brazil.* Gainesville: University of Florida Press, 1958.

Smith, T. Lynn, and Homer L. Hitt, *The People of Louisiana.* Baton Rouge: Louisiana State University Press, 1952, pp. 142–161.

Westoff, Charles F., "Social and Psychological Factors Affecting Fertility," in Morris Fishbein and Ruby Jo Reeves Kennedy, *Modern Marriage and Family Living.* New York: Oxford University Press, 1957, pp. 74–86.

Westoff, Charles F., Elliot G. Mishler, and E. Lowell Kelly, "Preference in Size of Family and Eventual Fertility Twenty Years After," *The American Journal of Sociology,* LXII, No. 5 (1957), 491–497.

Chapter 14

Fertility Trends

THREE SPECIFIC FERTILITY TRENDS weigh heavily in the thinking of most contemporary students of population. The first of these is the rapid and sustained fall in the birth rate that took place in many Western countries during the century which started about 1830 and ended during the great world economic depression. The second is really not a trend at all, but rather the absence of one. This is the tendency observed in recent decades throughout much of the world, and especially in the more densely populated parts of it, for the birth rate to remain at a high level, at the same time that the death rate was falling sharply. The third is the fairly substantial increase that took place in the birth rate of the United States and Canada during the period 1935 to 1955. As demographic knowledge increases, other equally significant trends in the birth rate may be observed and described; but for the present a discussion of these three will suffice.

The Long-Continued Fall in the Birth Rate in Selected Countries

Throughout most of the nineteenth century and the first three decades of the twentieth century, the falling birth rate throughout large parts of Western civilization was among the most important social and economic determinants in world affairs. France frequently is credited with being the original center from which the phenomenon of the falling birth rate spread to other countries. This may or may not actually be the case. There can be no doubt, however, that France was the first to develop a set of birth statistics that was sufficiently accurate for analysis to reveal what was going on in this important part of Europe during the opening half of the nineteenth century. (See Figure 60.) Either the data for other European countries were not sufficiently accurate or the fall in the birth rate was later in getting under way in

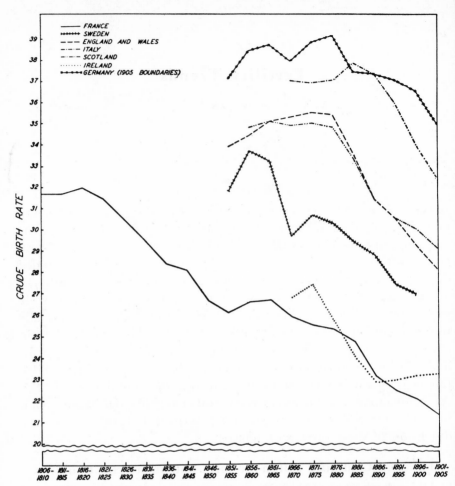

Figure 60. The trend of the crude birth rate in selected European countries during the nineteenth century. (Based on data in "Statistique Internationale du Mouvement de la Population," Paris: Imprimerie Nationale, 1907)

them, for, with the exception of Sweden, the curves for the other countries included in this chart did not start to fall until after 1870. In interpreting these materials one should make liberal allowance for improvements in the registration of births. This means that probably the declines in the various countries actually began earlier and were more rapid than would appear from this chart. Although they are extremely fragmentary, these materials do indicate that the decline in the birth

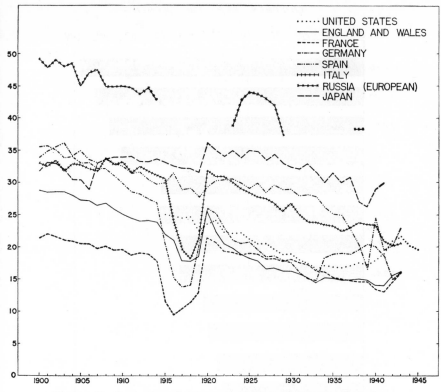

Figure 61. Variations in the reported crude birth rates of selected countries during the first part of the twentieth century.

rate got well underway in many of the Western countries before the end of the nineteenth century.

For the present century the data are, of course, much more abundant and far more reliable. Nevertheless the materials for the years prior to 1945, and especially those for the period 1900 to 1930, leave a great deal to be desired. From the information presented in Figure 61, however, one may gain a fair idea of the trends in the birth rate in selected important countries, for which the statistics are most reliable, between 1900 and 1940. It is important to note that the first one-third of the twentieth century certainly was characterized by a precipitous decline in the rate of reproduction in all of the larger European countries, in the United States, and in Japan; and also that this particular trend ended and the birth rate began to rise in most of the countries

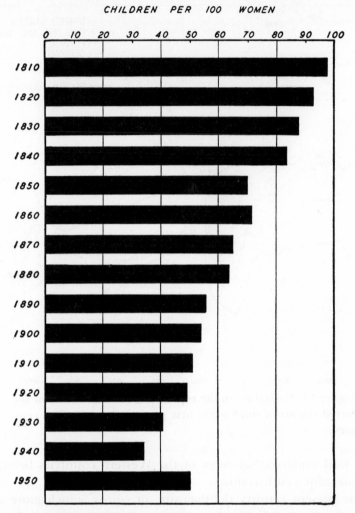

CHILDREN PER 100 WOMEN

Figure 62. Trends in the number of children under five per
hundred women aged sixteen to forty-four in the United
States, 1810–1950.

between 1930 and 1940. The effects upon the birth rate of the first
world war and the Spanish Civil War are so clearly revealed by Figure
61, however, that it should be studied in that connection as well.

Since comprehensive birth statistics for the United States go back
only to 1915, our own country is not among those for which materials

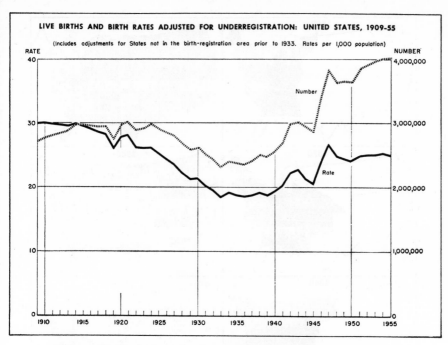

LIVE BIRTHS AND BIRTH RATES ADJUSTED FOR UNDERREGISTRATION: UNITED STATES, 1909-55

(Includes adjustments for States not in the birth-registration area prior to 1933. Rates per 1,000 population)

Figure 63. Variations in the crude birth rate in the United
States, 1909–1955. (Illustration from the National Office of
Vital Statistics)

are presented in Figure 60; and it also is represented for only a part of
the period included in Figure 61. By means of the fertility ratio, however, it is possible to demonstrate that the rate of reproduction in the
United States fell rapidly throughout the entire nineteenth century
(see Figure 62) ; and from the curve showing the birth rate adjusted
for underregistration of births (Figure 63) one may obtain a fairly accurate idea of the extent of the decrease in the fertility of the population between 1909 and 1936.[1] The materials on fertility ratios presented in Figure 62 and the birth data charted in Figure 63 indicate
that the birth rate in the United States during the opening decade of
the nineteenth century probably was above 50, from which it fell

[1] The report from which this chart is taken "Natality: United States and Each
State, and Alaska, Hawaii, Puerto Rico, and the Virgin Islands (U. S.), 1955," *Vital
Statistics—Special Reports*, 46, No. 15 (1957), does not indicate the manner in
which the data for the years 1909 to 1914 were derived.

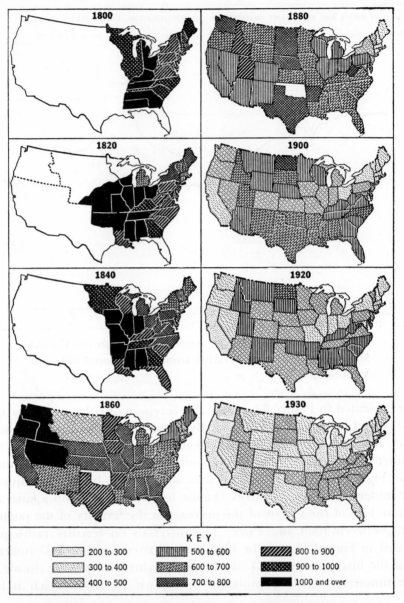

Figure 64. The number of children under five per thousand women aged fifteen to forty-nine in the United States from 1800 to 1930. (After O. E. Baker, "The Effect of Recent Public Policies on the Future Population Prospect," in "Rural Sociology," II (1937), 124)

steadily and persistently, except for a sharp dip during and an abrupt rise immediately after the Civil War [1] and a slighter gyration following the first world war, to the low of 18.4 recorded for 1933 and also for 1936.

Much insight relative to the factors responsible for the long-continued fall in the birth rate that took place in the United States throughout the nineteenth century and during the first one-third of the twentieth may be gained from a careful study of the materials mapped in Figure 64. It would seem that in the first few decades of the existence of the United States as an independent nation fertility was rather uniformly high throughout all parts of the new country. Apparently, though, it was somewhat higher on the frontier than in the older settlements. By 1840 the fertility of the population in Massachusetts and Connecticut had declined considerably and that in some of the other original states perceptibly. Obviously the declining birth rate began in the most urbanized parts of the nation, and just as obviously the spread of this phenomenon closely paralleled the industrialization and urbanization of the various states and regions. Successively in the decades after 1840, the tendency of the rate of reproduction to fall spread over the nation. By 1930 only the most rural sections of the nation (in the Rocky Mountain area, in the southern region, and in the Dakotas) retained any semblance of their earlier very high fertility ratios. By 1940, as is evident from Figure 57, the few areas in which the rate of reproduction remained at a high level stood out like the scattered peaks on an old peneplain. On this map the high rates of reproduction in rural settlements of the Mormons in the Rocky Mountains command attention, as do those of the Spanish-Americans spread along the Rio Grande Valley from the Gulf of Mexico to southern Colorado. Other scattered localities in which the birth rate had not fallen to any great extent by 1940 are found in Montana, the Dakotas, and northern Michigan. More important, because of the much larger populations involved, are the high fertility ratios that still prevailed in the Southern Appalachians, portions of the Ozarks, the hills of southeastern Oklahoma, in some areas along the South Atlantic Coast, and among the French-speaking people of south Louisiana. The only factor common to all the sections with high fertility ratios in 1940 is their geographical and cultural isolation. It therefore is evident that the falling

[1] On this point see T. Lynn Smith, "The Demographic Basis of Old Age Assistance in the South," *Social Forces*, 17, no. 3 (1939), 356–361.

birth rate in the United States was first a function of the developing urban and industrial way of life, that as these aspects of our civilization gained in size and momentum they exerted a depressing effect upon the rate of reproduction throughout the nation, and that by 1940 only in areas most removed from such urban influences had the fertility ratio maintained its previously high level. Following 1936, however, as will be indicated below, the tendency for increasing urbanization and decreasing fertility of the population to accompany one another came to an end. The former proceeded at a pace rarely equalled in the United States or any other part of the world, and the latter ceased its downward course and moved sharply upward. Furthermore, the increase in the birth rate was more rapid in the urban areas than it was in the rural.

The Persistence of High Birth Rates in Underdeveloped Countries

The fact that no substantial fall in the birth rate in many parts of the world has accompanied the rapid reduction in mortality that has been accomplished since the close of the first world war, is one of primary importance to all those concerned with population phenomena. This is the factor responsible for the currently rapidly mounting numbers of people on the earth's surface. It is a matter so important that it is even causing some of those in the fields of preventive medicine and sanitation to question the advisability of promoting measures for saving lives unless something can be done simultaneously to reduce the rate of reproduction of the population in the areas involved. Strictly speaking, of course, the persistence of the high fertility levels is not a trend at all, but rather the absence of one. Nevertheless, this is the place in which it seems most appropriate to include discussion of the phenomenon.

In comparison with most other analysis in these pages, any reasoning about the trend in the birth rate in most of the underdeveloped areas of the world must rest upon fragmentary and highly unreliable data. Probably the soundest procedure of all is to note in Table XXVI the high rates of reproduction that currently prevail in most parts of Asia for which data are available, in Africa, and in the Latin American countries; and then to reason that these levels are still so high that no substantial reductions could have taken place during the preceding twenty-five years.

For two extensive parts of the so-called underdeveloped portion of the world, however, enough data have been assembled and enough critical study of the rates of reproduction has been made to permit a direct approach to the matter under consideration. One of these is that dealt with by Kingsley Davis in his fundamental demographic analysis of the "teeming millions" of India and Pakistan.[1] Unlike most of those who have used the data on fertility for various parts of the world, Davis was not content to pass along official statistics at their face value. Instead he set about the task of determining as nearly as possible the actual rate of reproduction in the subcontinent once called India and now divided into the two large and densely populated independent nations of India and Pakistan. In this work he had as precedent the substantial work of Mr. G. F. Hardy, an actuary who was employed by the Indian Census to make life tables for the period 1891–1911. Hardy had made estimates of the birth rates of the various provinces for the decades 1881–1891, 1891–1901, and 1901–1911, and these estimates were all very much above the reported birth rates for the last of these decades. Hardy's computations gave no basis whatsoever for concluding that the birth rate in India was declining, but rather indicated that it continued at a level of about 50 throughout the thirty years studied.[2] Davis himself calculated the numbers of births during each decade from data on the numbers of children under ten reported at each census and the appropriate values from the life tables. For the four decades 1901 to 1941 his estimates of the actual birth rates, followed in each case by the officially reported rate, are as follows: 1901–1911, 48 and 37; 1911–1921, 49 and 37; 1921–1931, 46 and 33; and 1931–1941, 45 and 34. As a result of his studies Davis concluded that since 1921 the crude birth rate in India had fallen slightly; but he summarized the general situation as one of continued high fertility, "somewhat lowered mortality, and a growing rate of natural increase which is adding huge increments to India's population."[3]

The other comprehensive study of the levels and trends of fertility in the so-called underdeveloped areas is the present author's work on the rate of reproduction in Latin America. Working first with Brazilian data, he attempted to go beyond the published rates and to deter-

[1] *The Population of India and Pakistan* (Princeton, N. J.: Princeton University Press, 1951) .

[2] See the materials in *ibid.,* p. 68, which follows Gyan Chand, *India's Teeming Millions* (London: Allen & Unwin, 1939) , pp. 97–98.

[3] *Ibid.,* p. 69.

mine the extent to which the official statistics reflected the birth rates actually prevailing. By analyzing materials on baptisms by the Roman Catholic church and other fragments of data, he concluded that the birth rate in Brazil at the time of the second world war was about 38, and not 12, as reported in the official publications.[1] In the meantime efforts were extended to include the other Latin American countries, beginning with El Salvador, where he found that the birth rate must be about 45;[2] and in 1953 he published the preliminary results of his attempts to determine the levels of the rate of reproduction throughout Latin America.[3] More recently he has determined the changes in the fertility ratios in the various countries which have taken two or more censuses, thus making possible a study of the changes taking place in the rate of reproduction. These data are presented in Table XXXIV.

A study of these materials, along with those for some of the other countries for which data on current levels are available (see Table XXXI) makes it evident that the rate of reproduction remains high throughout most of Latin America. In 1950 in most of the countries the birth rate was still at levels comparable to those prevailing in the United States and Canada at the beginning of the nineteenth century. Only in Argentina and Cuba are there rather definite indications that the fertility of the population is decreasing. In and of themselves the indexes for most of the countries are high enough to indicate that little or no decrease could have taken place during recent decades. Furthermore, for ten of the thirteen countries for which successive censuses make possible a determination of trends, the fertility ratio for the most recent year is higher than the one at the time of the preceding census. One should hardly assert on the basis of this evidence that the birth rate is rising in these countries (improvement in census procedures

---

[1] T. Lynn Smith, *Brazil: People and Institutions* (Baton Rouge: Louisiana State University Press, 1946), pp. 231–234. Shortly after the publication of this book, Giorgio Mortara, with age and sex data from the 1940 Brazilian census at hand, concluded that the true rate was somewhere between 39.5 and 47.8, with 42.3 being a reasonable estimate of its magnitude. See his *Estimativas da Taxa de Natalidade paro o Brasil, as Unidades da Federação e as Principais Capitais*, Estudos de Estatística Teórica e Aplicada, Estatística Demográfica, No. 4 (Rio de Janeiro: Instituto Brasileiro de Geografia e Estatística, 1949).

[2] T. Lynn Smith, "Notes on Population and Rural Social Organization in El Salvador," *Rural Sociology*, 10, No. 4 (1945), 366–367.

[3] T. Lynn Smith, "The Reproduction Rate in Latin America," *Eugenical News Quarterly*, XXXVIII, No. 3 (1953), 64–70.

Table XXXIV. Number of Children under Five per Hundred Women Aged Fifteen to Forty-four in the Latin American Countries at Recent Census Dates

Country	Date	Fertility ratio
Costa Rica	1892	68.3
	1927	68.8
	1950	73.9
Cuba	1931	62.2
	1943	57.4
	1953	55.3
Dominican Republic	1935	78.2
	1950	79.8
El Salvador	1930	66.8
	1950	67.4
Guatemala	1940	72.2
	1950	75.2
Haiti	1950	49.7
Honduras	1935	56.6
	1945	71.2
	1950	72.7
Mexico	1930	62.1
	1940	63.0
	1950	68.4
Nicaragua	1940	71.9
	1950	70.2
Panama	1940	64.4
	1950	75.4
Argentina	1914	67.2
	1947	46.8
Bolivia	1950	68.5
Brazil	1920 [1]	66.8
	1940	68.9
	1950	70.5
Chile	1940	52.3
	1952	56.7
Colombia	1938	67.6
Ecuador	1950	76.5
Paraguay	1950	75.2
Peru	1940	71.5

Table XXXIV. Number of Children under Five per Hundred Women Aged Fifteen to Forty-four in the Latin American Countries (Continued)

Country	Date	Fertility ratio
Uruguay	. . . .	
Venezuela	1936	58.3
	1941	64.1
	1950	76.7

SOURCES: Computed from data given in the censuses of the respective countries.
[1] 54.5 per cent women aged forty to forty-nine considered as being forty to forty-four.

is probably the more likely cause of the observed changes), but it does lend strong support to the proposition that it is not falling significantly. Furthermore, there is little reason for supposing that the present high levels will not continue in most parts of Latin America for several decades to come. In the meantime, as is indicated in Chapter XVII, since 1900 the death rate in most of these countries has been reduced substantially. Therefore it is not surprising that currently the Latin American area is the major division of the earth's surface in which the growth of population is most rapid. (Between 1900 and 1957, according to the computations of the present writer, the proportion of the world's population made up of the inhabitants of the twenty independent Latin American republics rose from 2.7 per cent to 6.5 per cent.)

Although the results in terms of population increase of the continued high level of fertility combined with sharply reduced mortality in India and Pakistan, on the one hand, and the Latin American countries, on the other, are similar, the implications of such changes in these two important parts of the world are considerably different. India and Pakistan are already among the most densely populated parts of the earth's surface. They are areas in which the man-land ratio already is at or beyond the point at which mankind's present knowledge of resources and command over the ways of utilizing them permit a satisfactory level of production per person. In sharp contrast, throughout Latin America there are still immense areas which are devoid of inhabitants, sections capable of furnishing an abundant livelihood to many additional millions of persons providing large-scale organized human effort is devoted to the conquest of these important sections of the earth's surface. There is little reason for supposing that a continued high rate of reproduction in Brazil, Colombia, Venezuela, Peru, and many of the other Latin American countries poses any threat to the well-being of mankind in general. Instead the big problem in each case is the national one of devising ways and means for securing a better distribution of the population. This, of course, goes far beyond the scope of demographic studies and measures.

The Recent Rise in the Birth Rate in the United States and Canada

The upward movement of the rate of reproduction in the United States and Canada which took place between 1935 and 1948, and the maintenance subsequently of the 1948 level is one of the most significant demographic happenings on record. In many ways it also is one of the most puzzling. Considerably more study will be needed to identify and evaluate fully the various factors which were responsible for the revolutionary change in the reproductive pattern of the populations of the two countries. The actual changes in the birth rate of the United States since 1935 are clearly portrayed in Figure 63. In 1936, it will be noted, the birth rate once more equalled the all-time low recorded in 1933. Then a recovery commenced, haltingly at first, but soon becoming more rapid. As was to be expected, the all-out mobilization for the second world war and the dispatching of millions of men overseas halted the upswing and produced the dip, for the years 1944 and 1945, typical of a country in the midst of a serious struggle. With the end of the war and demobilization, the birth rate shot up to a peak in 1947, after which it dropped slightly and stabilized at a level of about twenty-five births per thousand population. In 1955 the rate was the same as it had been in 1925.

The changes in the birth rate in Canada, over the comparable period, were rather closely similar, although the general level at which they occurred was somewhat higher. (See Figure 65.) The rise in Canada after 1935, however, was somewhat less abrupt, and the dip occasioned by the war was somewhat less pronounced, than the comparable changes in the United States. These probably reflect the fact that Canada's all-out war effort was spread over a longer period than was that of her neighbor.

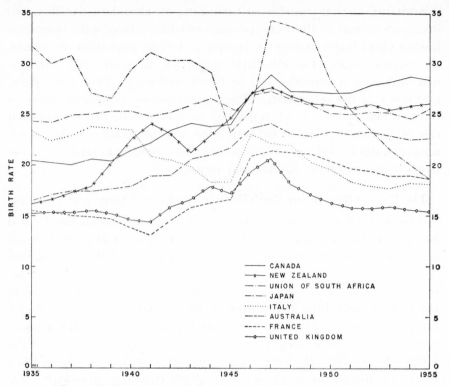

Figure 65. Recent trends in the crude birth rates in Canada and other selected countries.

In order to facilitate comparison of recent trends in the United States and Canada with those of other selected countries, the curves for the United Kingdom, the white population of the Union of South Africa, France, Italy, Australia, New Zealand, and Japan also are shown in Figure 65. This list embraces most of the larger nations of the so-called Western world for which the birth statistics are believed to be fairly complete and for which changes in territory and boundaries do not almost preclude the possibility of fairly accurate comparisons. It also includes Japan, the one large Asiatic power for which the records cover enough years and are sufficiently complete to justify their use.

Observation of this figure makes it evident that New Zealand is the nation in which the trends in the birth rate, following 1935, most closely paralleled those in the United States and Canada. France and

Australia, however, are countries in which the birth rate stabilized following the close of the war at a considerably higher level than that prevailing before the outbreak of the conflict. In the United Kingdom, on the other hand, the entire upswing in the birth rate, from the low level at which it stood in 1935, took place during the war years and the ones immediately following. Then the index dropped back down and stabilized at a level only barely above that which prevailed throughout the 1930's. As a result, after 1945 the United Kingdom replaced France as the large Western nation with the lowest rate of reproduction. The lack of any major trends in the birth rate is the most striking feature of the line representing the white population of the Union of South Africa. Throughout the entire period under consideration, one marked by recovery from deep economic depression, world military conflict on an unparalleled scale, and the tensions of the post-war years, the birth rate in this important part of Africa fluctuated only slightly above and below the level of twenty-five births per thousand population. In Italy the general trend in the birth rate was downward, with the extent of the dip during the war years, the relatively low postwar peak, and the comparatively low level at which the curve appears to have stabilized being other significant features. By 1955 the birth rate in Italy was only slightly higher than that in the United Kingdom and actually was lower than that in France. Finally, the trend of the birth rate in Japan since 1935 should command particular interest. Three of its features are especially striking, namely, the pronounced dip during the war, the rapid upsurge following the cessation of hostilities, and the precipitous drop since 1949. Who could have believed, as late as 1950, that only five years later, the birth rate in Japan would have fallen to the same level as that in France!

The general conclusion to be derived from these comparisons is that by no means should the recent trends in the birth rate in the United States and Canada be thought of as representative of those going on in other parts of the Western world, or in other countries, such as Japan, on which Western standards have had such a tremendous impact. Somewhat similar trends did take place in New Zealand; and there are some resemblances of the changes in France and Australia to those in the United States. In general, though, the trends in the birth rate in other parts of the world have been quite different from those taking place in the United States and Canada.

As indicated above, the factors responsible for the changes in the

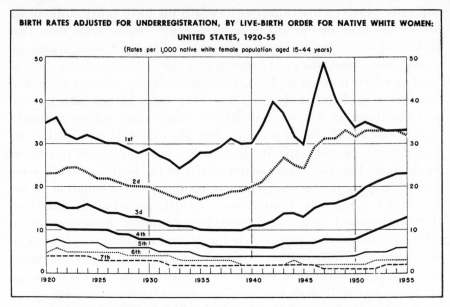

Figure 66. The changing pattern of fertility in the United
States. (Illustration from the National Office of Vital Statistics)

birth rate in the United States since 1935 have not been fully identified and evaluated. It is clear, however, that there has been a change
in the pattern of fertility within the typical family. Indeed, in the
years since 1950 the number of mothers giving birth to a second child,
the number bearing a third child, and the number having a fourth
child, out of each thousand native, white women of childbearing age,
has been about double what it was at the the lowest point during the
1930's. (See Figure 66.) As is evident from this chart, the number of first
births per thousand women aged fifteen to forty-four since 1950 is
only slightly above that for 1938 and 1939, whereas the corresponding
numbers of second, third, and fourth births have moved up to levels
very much above those for these years.

It will be observed that there are some interesting variations in the
time at which the curves representing the births of different orders
began to move upward. The one representing first births definitely
began to rise during 1934, that for second births in 1936, that for third
births in 1940, and that for fourth births in 1943. This suggests that
the same generation of women was responsible for the reversal of trend

in all four cases, just as a study of trends in the age-specific birth rates of women in the United States over the period 1920 to 1945 indicated that "the particular women who entered the childbearing period just after the close of the first world war are more responsible than the others for the low point to which fertility fell."[1] If this be the case, then cyclical variations in the attitudes and general behavior patterns of successive generations of young women may be the key to an understanding of the fundamental changes in the rate of reproduction.

Irrespective of the factors responsible for the upswing in the birth rate in the United States, however, the fact of the increase is among the most significant demographic phenomena of the twentieth century. It meant, to begin with, that the population of the United States could pass the 170 million mark in 1957, and could continue thereafter to increase by more than 2.5 million per year. In contrast, had the birth rate continued at its 1936 level, population increase would hardly have exceeded 1 million per year, and it probably would have been 1958 before the United States contained 150 million inhabitants. In addition to this, to the rise in the birth rate that began in 1937 should be attributed rather directly a wide variety of other important social, economic, and military facts. The following are a few of these: (1) the overcrowding of the schools that became so acute immediately after the second world war; (2) the housing shortage and the housing boom which have figured so largely in national affairs since 1946; (3) the mushrooming of suburban areas since 1950; (4) the shortage of facilities for higher education which became acute in the late 1950's; (5) an extremely large number and high proportion of men coming of military age during the 1960's; and (6) such a large generation to enter the childbearing ages about 1968, that other things being at all equal, another rapid upswing in the birth rate shortly thereafter appears certain.

[1] T. Lynn Smith, *Population Analysis* (New York: McGraw-Hill Book Company, 1948), p. 228.

SUGGESTED SUPPLEMENTARY READINGS

Davis, Kingsley, *The Population of India and Pakistan*. Princeton, N. J.: Princeton University Press, 1951, part III.

Grabill, Wilson H., "The Fertility of the United States Population," in Donald J. Bogue, *The Population of the United States*. Chicago: The Free Press, 1959, chapter 12.

Grabill, Wilson H., Clyde V. Kiser, and Pascal K. Whelpton, *The Fertility of American Women*. New York: John Wiley & Sons, 1958, chapters 2–3.

Kiser, Clyde V., "Fertility Trends and Differentials among Nonwhites in the United States," *The Milbank Memorial Fund Quarterly*, XXXVI, No. 2 (1958), 148–197.

Maclachlan, John M., *Health and the People in Florida*. Planning Florida's Health Leadership, No. 3. Gainesville: University of Florida Press, 1954, pp. 95–106.

Maclachlan, John M., and Joe S. Floyd, *This Changing South*. Gainesville: University of Florida Press, 1956, pp. 122–133.

Marshall, Douglas G., "The Decline in Farm Family Fertility and Its Relationship to Nationality and Religious Background," *Rural Sociology*, 15, No. 1 (1950), 42–49.

Phelps, Harold A., and David Henderson, *Population in Its Human Aspects*. New York: Appleton-Century-Crofts, Inc., 1958, pp. 229–236.

Siegel, Jacob S., *The Population of Hungary*, U. S. Bureau of the Census International Population Statistics Reports, Series P-90, No. 9. Washington: Government Printing Office, 1958, pp. 118–125.

Taeuber, Conrad, and Irene B. Taeuber, *The Changing Population of the United States*. New York: John Wiley & Sons, 1958, chapter 13.

Taeuber, Irene B., *The Population of Japan*. Princeton, N. J.: Princeton University Press, 1958, chapters XII–XIII.

Westoff, Charles F., "Differential Fertility in the United States: 1900 to 1952," *American Sociological Review*, 19, No. 5 (1954), 549–561.

Chapter 15

The Measurement of Mortality

MORTALITY IS THE SECOND of the vital processes and also the second of the three primary factors affecting the number and distribution of the population to receive attention in this volume. Ordinarily it is considerably less important than the other of the two vital processes (fertility) as a primary factor in population change, although now and then throughout human history years of plague and famine have contributed striking exceptions to this rule. Ordinarily, too, for any large group, it is far more important than the third of the primary factors (migration) in producing changes in the size and distribution of any large population, although frequently an exodus of people or an influx of those from elsewhere may be the principal factor in the gain or loss of inhabitants of a given village, town, city, or county and over a short period of time. In times of great upheaval, migration may even take the lead among the factors in producing increases or decreases of population at the national or regional levels; and sustained mass movements of population, such as those taking place in the United States since 1940, may make migration more important than mortality or even fertility in accounting for the increase of population in some states such as Arizona, Florida, and California. For the most part, though, mortality is the second most important factor in population change. For this reason the student of population must be well acquainted with the ways and means of measuring the mortality of a population.

It would be a mistake, however, to assume that the significance of the study of mortality is limited to the role this factor plays in population change. Longevity as such is one of the important criteria of the quality of a population. Moreover, from analysis of the data on mortality comes the most useful information on such matters of universal interest as the control of tuberculosis and other transmissible diseases; the progress if any in the fight against cancer, diseases of the heart, cirrhosis of the liver, and other causes of death that result from the deterioration of the body's vital organs; the "score" with respect to fatalities from automobile accidents, suicides, homicides, and other violent causes of death; and the situation with respect to the hazards of infancy. Indeed, because comprehensive data on morbidity are almost entirely lacking, mortality data have come to be the most commonly accepted means of measuring the health of a population; and society is almost entirely dependent upon indexes of mortality and longevity for accurate information concerning the effectiveness and efficiency of medical and sanitary sciences in the improvement of the welfare of mankind. In fact, one of the specific mortality indexes, the infant mortality rate, is often regarded as "the most sensitive index of social welfare and of sanitary improvements which we possess." [1] Finally, mention should be made of the fact that the mortality indexes, arranged in the form of life tables, constitute the scientific basis for one of the largest and most important financial institutions of modern times, namely, the life insurance business.

Mortality Data

In nearly every modern nation the keeping of mortality records has come to be an essential function of government. The value these data have in connection with the control and prevention of transmissible diseases alone more than justifies the organization and expense necessary to secure them. Fortunately the problems inherent in the registration of deaths are considerably less difficult than those involved in the registration of births, so that the coverage of the former usually is far more complete than that of the latter. But even so, to secure the registration of every death in a county, state, or nation, along with a record of the essential characteristics of the deceased (age, sex, race or color, rural or urban residence, marital condition, occupation, and so on), and an accurate diagnosis of the cause of death is no simple matter. In this connection it is important to have in mind that the information from the registers of vital statistics must be matched with those secured in the census enumeration before indexes can be computed for the various

[1] George C. Whipple, *Vital Statistics* (New York: John Wiley & Sons, Inc., 1923), p. 393.

segments of the population. Back of every valid statement with respect to how mortality varies with age, or with respect to differences in the death rates of males and females, whites and Negroes, farmers and industrial workers, or city people and country people, is a painstaking effort on the part of thousands of efficient public servants.

In every country the evolution of the registers of vital statistics is a long and involved story. The experience of the United States, however, serves to illustrate many of the problems that had to be faced and overcome. Prior to 1900 the responsibility for registration of vital statistics rested upon the states. A few of them maintained fairly adequate organizations for recording deaths, but in the majority of them little or no reliance could be placed upon the completeness and accuracy of the data. During the last half of the nineteenth century repeated efforts were made to secure comprehensive and reliable mortality statistics for the nation by means of queries included in the decennial censuses of population. The numerous bulky volumes of mortality statistics published in connection with every census from that of 1850 to that of 1900 supplied little or no trustworthy information on the subject. This was recognized by the ingenious mind of J. D. B. DeBow, who stated in connection with the statistics resulting from the first attempt that the data "can be said to have little value," and then elucidated as follows:

Upon the subject of the Deaths no one can be deceived by the figures of the Census, since any attempt to reason from them would demonstrate a degree of vitality and healthfulness in the United States unparalleled in the annals of mankind. . . . The truth is, but a part of the deaths have been recorded.[1]

It also was well known to Dr. J. S. Billings, who worked with the compilations made in connection with the censuses of 1870 and 1880. Some of his most telling comments are as follows:

The fact that it is impossible, in any large community, to collect complete and reliable data with regard to births and deaths by means of any inquiry made only at the end of the year for which the data are desired, is well known to all who are practically familiar with the subject of vital statistics; and the experience of the United States census furnishes no exception to this rule. The results of each of the four censuses in which an attempt has

[1] *The Seventh Census of the United States, 1850* (Washington: Robert Armstrong, Public Printer, 1853), pp. xxxix–xl.

been made to ascertain the number of persons who died in the United States during the preceding year, have shown that the enumerators did not obtain and record more than 60 to 70 per cent of the actual number of deaths.[1]

In spite of these evaluations by those in charge of the work, however, the attempts to secure mortality data in connection with census enumerations continued in 1890 and 1900.

When the Bureau of the Census was established on a permanent basis, by action of Congress in 1902, the collection of vital statistics for the nation was one of the functions specifically assigned to it. The organization the Bureau established for the registration of deaths rested entirely upon voluntary co-operation between the states and the federal government, and it remains so today. Willcox has given an excellent summary of the major features of the co-operative venture:

1. It recommends a State law and is not satisfied with a municipal ordinance.

2. The model law prohibits disposing of a corpse by burial, cremation, transportation, or otherwise until a burial or transportation permit has been secured.

3. To secure this permit a certificate of death properly made out on the standard form and including a statistical description of the deceased and a professional statement of the cause of death must be filed with the office issuing the permit.

4. The duty of preparing this certificate of death rests upon the undertaker, aided by a relative or friend of the deceased and by the attending physician, the coroner or other qualified person.

5. A standard nomenclature and classification of the causes of death, excluding vague and unsatisfactory ones like fever or old age, has been prepared and periodically revised.

6. Physicians, registrars, and other officers having to do with registration, are given detailed instructions about the nomenclature.

7. The local registrar is the only person authorized to issue a burial or transit permit and he only in exchange for a certificate of death.

8. The local registrar files with the State registrar each month the certificates of death which he has received.

9. The State registrar examines them and corresponds with the local registrars who are dilatory or send in defective returns.

10. At this point the Federal Government intervenes, for the first time, by purchasing copies of the certificates of death filed in a state or city office,

[1] *Report on the Mortality and Vital Statistics of the United States,* Part I (Washington: Government Printing Office, 1885), p. xi.

but only if it is convinced that the returns are complete enough to have statistical value.

11. From these copies the Bureau of the Census prepares uniform tables for the registration states and their main divisions.[1]

The first report on national mortality statistics issued under provisions of the 1902 law appeared in 1906 and contained data for the years 1900 to 1904, inclusive. The statistics presented were those for the states of Connecticut, Indiana, Maine, Massachusetts, Michigan, New Hampshire, New Jersey, New York, Rhode Island, and Vermont, along with the District of Columbia. These have since been known as the Original Registration States. Materials for 153 cities scattered throughout the remaining states also were given in the initial report. Following 1904, additional states gradually adopted the required standards and were admitted to the registration area until with the admission of Texas in 1933 the coverage included the entire continental United States. Because of the manner in which registration of vital statistics evolved, one who uses historical series relating to mortality in the United States must be prepared to deal with some tabulations for the "original registration area" and with others pertaining to the "expanding registration area."

A large share of the space devoted to mortality statistics in the official reports of most countries is given over to presentation of data concerning the causes of death. This is as it should be, for one must go further than a study of the gross rates if he would learn many of the most significant facts and relationships in the field of mortality.

The causes of death are, of course, lacking in precise scientific definition and standardization. Indeed, they may not always be recorded as accurately as the knowledge possessed would make possible. For example, it frequently is said that attending physicians refrain from reporting syphilis as the cause of death of prominent and well-to-do members of a community, even though it is evident to them that it was the principal factor in the complex involved. They may not hesitate to do so, however, in comparable cases involving less-esteemed residents in the locality. Nevertheless, much progress has been made in securing comparability in the reported causes of death throughout the world, due in large part to the use and perfection of the *International List of Causes of Death*.

[1] Walter F. Willcox, *Introduction to the Vital Statistics of the United States, 1900 to 1930* (Washington: Government Printing Office, 1933), p. 14.

This list had its inception in 1853, when the First Statistical Congress (convened at Brussels) appointed Dr. William Farr and Dr. Marc d'Espine to develop a system of classifying deaths that would be suitable for international use. After working upon the project for two years, these men submitted to the congress two separate lists, and the one finally adopted by it in 1855 was a compromise. It received little acceptance on the part of the various nations involved. Nevertheless this served as a basis for more work, and in 1893 a greatly revised system, prepared by Dr. Jaques Bertillon, was presented to and immediately adopted by the congress. Several countries began at once to use it in their official compilations, and from 1900, when the mortality statistics for the United States began, to the present time, it has been employed in this country. Since 1893, the list has been revised four times, so that the latest revision, that of 1948, is known as the *Sixth Revision*. The latter is intended for general use until the next revision, which should be put into effect in 1960, is ready.[1]

The Sixth Revision, whose use is specified for member nations by the World Health Organization, was employed for the first time in the United States for classification of the 1949 data. It consists of sixteen large categories of diseases and morbid conditions and one large category of injuries or external causes of death.[2] A total of 612 specific categories of disease or morbid conditions make up the subdivisions of the former, and 153 classes of external causes and 189 ways of characterizing the injuries are used in connection with the latter. The detailed list is prescribed for classification purposes, but condensed and abbreviated lists are provided for use in tabulating and publishing the materials.

Indexes of Mortality

Four principal measures are employed in the study of mortality. The *death rate* is one of these, and the rather special indexes called the *infant mortality rate* and the *maternal mortality rate* are others. The fourth, and in many ways the most important, is the set of *arithmetic*

[1] See the United Nations, *Demographic Yearbook, 1951* (New York: United Nations, 1951), pp. 18–19.

[2] These seventeen categories are as follows: infectious and parasitic, cancers and other tumors, rheumatic diseases, diseases of blood, chronic poisonings, nervous diseases, circulatory diseases, respiratory diseases, digestive diseases, genitourinary diseases, diseases of pregnancy, diseases of skin, diseases of bones, congenital malformations, diseases of early infancy, senility, and violent and accidental causes.

averages included in the life table, or the values commonly known as the *expectation of life*.

The Death Rate

The computation of the death rate is very similar to that of the birth rate. That for the total population of the United States in 1950 may be secured as follows:

$$\frac{\text{Number of deaths during 1950}}{\text{Population (April 1, 1950)}} \times 1,000 = \frac{1,452,454}{150,697,361} \times 1,000 = 9.6$$

Strictly speaking the population as of June 30 should be used rather than that of the census date, but such corrections are hardly worth while in the computation of crude death rates. Likewise there would be little point in using the average number of deaths per year for the years 1949, 1950, and 1951, rather than that for 1950 alone, in connection with the crude measure, whereas such a procedure is to be highly recommended if the death rate is to be adjusted or refined in any way.

Those who use either the data or the conclusions relative to mortality should realize that for most purposes the crude death rate is a highly unsatisfactory index. This is because the mortality rates of males and females are so different and especially because mortality is so closely related to age. (See the second column in Table XXXV.) Observe that the death rate is high for the very young, extremely low for those between one and fifty, and very high for those aged sixty-five and over. Therefore, since the age distribution differs so greatly from one population to another, from time to time in the same population, and between the various residential and racial groups in a given population, the crude death rate is a very unsatisfactory measure to use for comparative purposes.

If one is to make any pretense of accuracy, the specific rates for particular age and sex groups must be employed. The arithmetical procedures for making the calculations of such are exactly the same as those for determining the rate for the general population, except that the data used pertain to a specific age and sex segment of the population. For example, one could compute the death rate for males of twenty-six years of age, or that for females aged thirty-one. If these age-specific death rates are then combined so that the one for each age and sex segment is given the same weight that it would have in a normal or

Table XXXV. Life Table for the Total Population of the United States, 1949–1951

(1)	(2)	(3)	(4)	(5)	(6)	(7)
Year of age	Mortality rate	Of 100,000 born alive		Stationary population		Average remaining lifetime
Period of life between two exact ages stated x to $x+1$	Number dying per 1,000 alive at beginning of year of age q_x	Number living at beginning of year of age l_x	Number dying during year of age d_x	In year of age L_x	In this year of age and all subsequent years T_x	Average number of years of life remaining at beginning of year of age e_x
0–1	29.76	100,000	2,976	97,429	6,807,222	68.07
1–2	2.30	97,024	223	96,913	6,709,793	69.16
2–3	1.39	96,801	134	96,734	6,612,880	68.31
3–4	1.05	96,667	102	96,616	6,516,146	67.41
4–5	0.86	96,565	83	96,523	6,419,530	66.48
5–6	0.76	96,482	74	96,445	6,323,007	65.54
6–7	0.68	96,408	66	96,375	6,226,562	64.59
7–8	0.61	96,342	59	96,313	6,130,187	63.63
8–9	0.56	96,283	54	96,256	6,033,874	62.67
9–10	0.54	96,229	52	96,203	5,937,618	61.70
10–11	0.53	96,177	50	96,152	5,841,415	60.74
11–12	0.54	96,127	52	96,100	5,745,263	59.77
12–13	0.58	96,075	56	96,047	5,649,163	58.80
13–14	0.65	96,019	62	95,989	5,553,116	57.83

14–15	0.75	95,957	72	95,921	5,457,127	56.87
15–16	0.87	95,885	84	95,843	5,361,206	55.91
16–17	1.00	95,801	95	95,754	5,265,363	54.96
17–18	1.10	95,706	105	95,653	5,169,609	54.02
18–19	1.19	95,601	114	95,544	5,073,956	53.07
19–20	1.27	95,487	121	95,427	4,978,412	52.14
20–21	1.35	95,366	128	95,302	4,882,985	51.20
21–22	1.41	95,238	135	95,170	4,787,683	50.27
22–23	1.47	95,103	140	95,033	4,692,513	49.34
23–24	1.50	94,963	143	94,892	4,597,480	48.41
24–25	1.52	94,820	144	94,748	4,502,588	47.49
25–26	1.53	94,676	145	94,603	4,407,840	46.56
26–27	1.55	94,531	147	94,458	4,313,237	45.63
27–28	1.59	94,384	150	94,309	4,218,779	44.70
28–29	1.64	94,234	155	94,157	4,124,470	43.77
29–30	1.71	94,079	160	93,999	4,030,313	42.84
30–31	1.79	93,919	168	93,835	3,936,314	41.91
31–32	1.88	93,751	177	93,662	3,842,479	40.99
32–33	2.00	93,574	187	93,480	3,748,817	40.06
33–34	2.13	93,387	199	93,288	3,655,337	39.14
34–35	2.27	93,188	212	93,082	3,562,049	38.22
35–36	2.43	92,976	226	92,863	3,468,967	37.31
36–37	2.62	92,750	243	92,629	3,376,104	36.40
37–38	2.84	92,507	263	92,375	3,283,475	35.49
38–39	3.09	92,244	286	92,101	3,191,100	34.59
39–40	3.37	91,958	310	91,803	3,098,999	33.70
40–41	3.68	91,648	337	91,480	3,007,196	32.31
41–42	4.02	91,311	367	91,128	2,915,716	31.93

Table XXXV. Life Table for the Total Population of the United States (Continued)

(1)	(2)	(3)	(4)	(5)	(6)	(7)
42–43	4.40	90,944	400	90,744	2,824,588	31.06
43–44	4.81	90,544	436	90,326	2,733,844	30.19
44–45	5.27	90,108	474	89,871	2,643,518	29.34
45–46	5.75	89,634	516	89,377	2,553,647	28.49
46–47	6.28	89,118	559	88,838	2,464,270	27.65
47–48	6.85	88,559	607	88,255	2,375,432	26.82
48–49	7.45	87,952	656	87,624	2,287,177	26.00
49–50	8.08	87,296	705	86,944	2,199,553	25.20
50–51	8.76	86,591	759	86,212	2,112,609	24.40
51–52	9.50	85,832	815	85,424	2,026,397	23.61
52–53	10.33	85,017	878	84,578	1,940,973	22.83
53–54	11.24	84,139	946	83,666	1,856,395	22.06
54–55	12.22	83,193	1,017	82,684	1,772,729	21.31
55–56	13.27	82,176	1,090	81,631	1,690,045	20.57
56–57	14.41	81,086	1,168	80,502	1,608,414	19.84
57–58	15.63	79,918	1,249	79,293	1,527,912	19.12
58–59	16.93	78,669	1,332	78,003	1,448,619	18.41
59–60	18.30	77,337	1,416	76,629	1,370,616	17.72
60–61	19.77	75,921	1,500	75,171	1,293,987	17.04
61–62	21.33	74,421	1,588	73,627	1,218,816	16.38
62–63	23.02	72,833	1,676	71,995	1,145,189	15.72
63–64	24.75	71,157	1,761	70,276	1,073,194	15.08
64–65	26.52	69,396	1,841	68,476	1,002,918	14.45
65–66	28.43	67,555	1,921	66,595	934,442	13.83
66–67	30.60	65,634	2,008	64,630	867,847	13.22

67–68	33.13	63,626	2,108	62,572	803,217	12.62
68–69	35.98	61,518	2,213	60,411	740,645	12.04
69–70	39.08	59,305	2,318	58,146	680,234	11.47
70–71	42.49	56,987	2,422	55,777	622,088	10.92
71–72	46.26	54,565	2.524	53,303	566,311	10.38
72–73	50.44	52,041	2,625	50,729	513,008	9.86
73–74	54.99	49,416	2,717	48,057	462,279	9.35
74–75	59.88	46,699	2,796	45,301	414,222	8.87
75–76	65.16	43,903	2,861	42,472	368,921	8.40
76–77	70.89	41,042	2,909	39,588	326,449	7.95
77–78	77.13	38,133	2,942	36,661	286,861	7.52
78–79	83.80	35,191	2,949	33,717	250,200	7.11
79–80	90.85	32,242	2,929	30,778	216,483	6.71
80–81	98.41	29,313	2,884	27,871	185,705	6.34
81–82	106.61	26,429	2,818	25,020	157,834	5.97
82–83	115.58	23,611	2,729	22,246	132,814	5.63
83–84	125.33	20,882	2,617	19,574	110,568	5.29
84–85	135.76	18,265	2,480	17,025	90,994	4.98
85–86	146.88	15,785	2,318	14,626	73,969	4.69
86–87	158.67	13,467	2,137	12,398	59,343	4.41
87–88	171.12	11,330	1,939	10,361	46,945	4.14
88–89	184.24	9,391	1,730	8,526	36,584	3.90
89–90	198.03	7,661	1,517	6,902	28,058	3.66
90–91	212.49	6,144	1,306	5,491	21,156	3.44
91–92	227.62	4,838	1,101	4,288	15,665	3.24
92–93	243.43	3,737	910	3,282	11,377	3.04
93–94	260.12	2,827	735	2,459	8,095	2.86
94–95	277.68	2,092	581	1,802	5,636	2.69

Table XXXV. Life Table for the Total Population of the United States (Continued)

(1)	(2)	(3)	(4)	(5)	(6)	(7)
95–96	295.82	1,511	447	1,287	3,834	2.54
96–97	314.23	1,064	334	897	2,547	2.39
97–98	332.60	730	243	608	1,650	2.26
98–99	351.15	487	171	402	1,042	2.14
99–100	370.06	316	117	257	640	2.03
100–101	389.04	199	77	161	383	1.92
101–102	407.79	122	50	97	222	1.83
102–103	426.00	72	31	56	125	1.74
103–104	443.54	41	18	32	69	1.66
104–105	460.60	23	11	18	37	1.59
105–106	477.40	12	6	10	19	1.53
106–107	494.13	6	3	4	9	1.46
107–108	511.00	3	1	3	5	1.40
108–109	528.10	2	1	1	2	1.34
109–110	545.29	1	1	1	1	1.29

Data, with a few slight alterations, from "United States Life Tables, 1949–51," *Vital Statistics—Special Reports*, 41, No. 1 (1954), 8–9.

standard population, the results are compressed into what is called the *standardized death rate*. The procedures used in doing this are closely comparable to those employed in the standardization of the birth rate (see chapter 11). Usually, however, there is little point to such computations because, for most purposes, the construction of a *life table* is the procedure generally employed for adjusting the mortality rates of various populations for differences in their age and sex distributions. It should not be forgotten, of course, that the actual number of deaths occurring and the crude death rate are the materials that must be used in computing population changes or determining the amount and rate of natural increase.

The Arithmetic Averages Commonly Called Expectation of Life

A life table is made up of the results of a series of arithmetical computations designed to show the average number of years that would be lived by a number of persons born at the same time, or for those of any given age who are alive at the same time if the age-specific death rates prevailing during the year for which the table is constructed were to remain unchanged until all of the persons involved had died. Table XXXV, for the total population of the United States, 1949–1951, is an example of such a life table. The figures in this table that are most commonly used for applied purposes are the arithmetical averages shown in the last column. The first of these values, or 68.07, is the average amount of time that would be lived by 100,000 persons born at the same time in the United States were the age-specific death rates in this country to remain for another 110 years at the levels which prevailed during the years 1949 to 1951. Providing these mortality levels were to remain unchanged until the year 2060, this is the same average as that which would be obtained were a group of Methuselahs to amuse themselves for a little more than a century by observing the length of life of people in the United States. Suppose that such a group of "demographers" were to start stop watches at the birth of 100,000 babies born during 1950, so as to measure and record accurately the amount of time lived by each. Then, when the last one of these babies had passed away in 2060, if they added the figures to secure the total amount of time lived by the group as a whole, and then divided by 100,000, the resulting arithmetic average should be 68.07 years. This particular average refers, of course, to the time measured from the moment of birth. Similarly, the second figure in the last column, or 69.16, is the average measured from the beginning of the second year of life; the third figure, or 68.31, that secured if the beginning of the third year of life is taken as the point of departure; and so on. When other knowledge is lacking, the best guess with respect to the value of any one item in a frequency distribution is the arithmetic average of all the items in the distribution; hence the average length of life of the group measured from birth commonly is called the *expectation of life* at birth. Likewise it is customary to speak of expectation of life at age ten, at age twenty-one, age sixty-five, and so on. In each case such an expression denotes what the average duration of life would be for persons of the stated age who are alive at the beginning of the year for which the table is constructed if the age-specific death rates shown in the table were to remain unchanged until all the persons involved had died. Any specific characteristics possessed by a particular person in the group, which makes him likely to die earlier or live longer than the others, makes it less likely that the average is a fair approximation to the number of years he personally may expect to live.

The precise methods used by actuaries in the construction of life tables are too involved to be of general interest or significance. They suffer from many of the defects that arise when highly refined mathematical techniques are applied to observations or measurements which themselves are grossly lacking in precision. Nevertheless, the general outlines of life-table construction are fairly simple. To begin with one must have a distribution of the population by single years of age and also a distribution of deaths (for the year corresponding to the census of population, or preferably the three-year period centered on the census year) by age. With these in hand the computation of the death rate for each age group is a simple matter, and these in turn can readily be transformed into the conventional life table. One of the principal technical difficulties is the determination of the population of less than one year of age and another is the calculation of the average age at death of those who die before attaining the age of one year. In other words, the lack of precision in enumerating children of less than one year of age, the deficiencies of birth registration, and the rapid flow of vital events during the first year of life introduce some technical difficulties into the determination of the population and the specific death rate of those under one year of age. Another obstacle arises because of the obvious errors in the reporting of age, and this is true both with respect to the living and those who die. Therefore, in the construction of life tables the calculated age-specific death rates are subjected to a rather elaborate mathematical smoothing process in order to remove the fluctuations that are due merely to random events or pure chance. As Raymond Pearl once wrote, a highly esoteric cult has grown up around this particular phase of life-table construction.[1]

Notwithstanding the difficulties inherent in determining the death rate of persons of less than one year of age and the correction of the other age-specific death rates,[2] the understanding of the life table is not difficult. The steps involved in the computation and the values derived may be noted through a careful examination of Table XXXV. Column 1 gives the age classification by single years; column 2 contains the age-specific mortality rates; column 3 shows the number alive at the beginning of each year of life, starting with the hypothetical number of 100,-000; column 4 indicates how many persons of each age would die in the course of a year, calculated by applying the age-specific death rates given in column 2 to the respective numbers of persons alive at the beginning of the year given in column 2; column 5 indicates the total number of years lived by the survivors during each year of age; column 6 rearranges in cumulative form the data from column 5, with the cumulating process starting from the bottom of the table; and column 7 presents the series of computations showing the averages which are secured when the figures in column 6 are divided by the figures in the corresponding rows as given in column 2. This last operation is, of course, the actual computation of the arithmetic averages, and in each case the number of persons alive at the beginning of a given year of age is divided into the total number of years of life remaining to the group as a whole.

The materials in this table indicate that during the period 1949 to 1951, 2,976 out of each 100,000 babies born in the United States had died before attaining the age of one. (This, of course, corresponds closely to an infant mortality rate of 29.76.) Accordingly, of the theo-

[1] *Introduction to Medical Biometry and Statistics* (Philadelphia: W. B. Saunders Company, 1923) , p. 196.

[2] The interested student will find practical and relatively nontechnical discussions of these difficulties, along with tables to assist in the making of precise corrections, in Lowell J. Reed and Margaret Merrell, "A Short Method for Constructing an Abridged Life Table," *Vital Statistics—Special Reports,* 9, No. 54 (1940) , 681–712.

retical population of 100,000 born at the same time, only 97,024 would be alive to start the second year of life. If these died at the rate of 2.30 per thousand (column 2) , 223 of them would pass away in the course of the year, leaving 96,801 children alive to commence the third year of life. In this way, by applying the specific death rates to each succeeding number of survivors until all are accounted for, all of the values in column 4 may be determined.

The calculation of the values entered in column 5 presents some difficulties. The 97,429 entered for the age group zero to one represents 97,024 years contributed by the contingent who were still alive at the beginning of the second year of life, plus 405 years credited to the account by the 2,976 babies who died in the course of the first year of life. Thus by the procedures employed, it has been estimated that 0.136 was the average length of life of those who died before reaching the age of one. Similar are the procedures for the other age groups. For most ages the value to be entered in column 5 may be determined merely by adding to the figure representing the number of survivors at the end of the year an allowance of one-half of a year for each of those who died in the course of that twelve-month period. For example, the 95,-302 entry in column 5 corresponding to the age group twenty to twenty-one represents the 95,238 contributed by those who were alive at the beginning of the year and also at the end of it plus sixty-four years, or one-half of a year allowed for each of the 128 persons who died during the twentieth year of life.

Next, begin at the bottom of the table and observe that of the original 100,000, given the specific death rates prevailing from 1949 to 1951, 199 persons would celebrate their one hundreth birthdays. All told, these 199 persons would have a total of 383 years still to live, the data for each year being given in column 5. By cumulating from the bottom to the top, in column 6, the values entered in column 5, one secures the total number of years still be be lived by the persons in any given age group. Accordingly, at age zero, or birth, the entire group of 100,000 persons has a total of 6,807,222 years ahead of them, or an average of 68.07 year per person. After the risks of infancy have been passed, however, the 6,709,793 remaining years of lifetime divided by the 97,-024 persons who were alive at the beginning of the second year of life produces an average of 69.16 years. Similarly, the average remaining lifetime for each of the other age groups may be computed and entered in column 7.

Infant Mortality and Maternal Mortality Rates

As a simple device for gauging the general welfare of a population, the infant mortality rate has few serious rivals. As has been repeatedly indicated by those best informed on the subject, people who lack either the knowledge or the desire to care properly for their own helpless off-spring are unlikely to have the knowledge or the will to care for them-selves.

The infant mortality rate is computed by dividing the number of in-fant deaths taking place during the course of one year by the number of live births registered during the year and then multiplying by a con-stant so as to secure an index of two digits. Thus, for the United States in 1955, the infant mortality rate may be computed as follows:

$$\frac{\text{Number of infants (children under one) dying, 1955}}{\text{Number of live births, 1955}} \times 1,000 = \frac{106,903}{4,047,295} \times 1,000 = 26.4$$

It is important to note that the infant mortality rate is not the age-specific death rate of children of less than one year of age, although the values of the two are approximately equal. Note that the year used in this illustration is 1955, and that any other year might just as well have been chosen. The death rate of children under one, though, can be com-puted with accuracy only for years in which a census is taken, such as 1940 or 1950 in the United States. Even then, between three and four years elapse before the amount of work required to complete the age tabulations can be done and the data made available. The fact that the information on both infant deaths and live births are secured annually adds much to the usefulness of the infant mortality rate.

The maternal mortality rate also has many uses in gauging the well-being of various populations. Its computation may be illustrated with the following materials for the United States in 1955:

$$\frac{\text{Number of women dying from causes arising from deliveries and complications of pregnancy, childbirth, and the puerperium, 1955}}{\text{Number of live births, 1955}} \times 10,000 = \frac{1901}{4,047,295} \times 10,000 = 4.7$$

As is the case with the infant mortality rate, the usefulness of the ma-ternal mortality rate is greatly enhanced by the fact that it may be se-cured annually.

SUGGESTED SUPPLEMENTARY READINGS

Burrus, John N., *Life Opportunities,* Sociological Study Series, No. 3. Oxford: Bureau of Public Administration, University of Mississippi, 1951, chapter I.

Cox, Peter R., *Demography.* Cambridge: University Press, 1950, chapters 6 and 7.

Dublin, Louis I., and Alfred J. Lotka, *Length of Life: A Study of the Life Table.* New York: The Ronald Press Company, 1936, chapters 1 and 2.

Kuczynski, Robert R., *The Measurement of Population Growth: Methods and Results.* New York: Oxford University Press, 1936, chapter V.

Linder, Forrest E., and Robert D. Grove, *Vital Statistics Rates in the United States, 1900–1940.* Washington: Government Printing Office, 1943, pp. 1–50, and 60–90.

Smith, T. Lynn, *Brazil: People and Institutions* (Revised Edition). Baton Rouge: Louisiana State University Press, 1954, chapter IX.

Willcox, Walter F., *Introduction to the Vital Statistics of the United States, 1900 to 1930.* Washington: Government Printing Office, 1933, pp. 13–54.

Willcox, Walter F., *Studies in American Demography.* Ithaca: Cornell University Press, 1940, chapter 14.

Chapter 16

Mortality Levels,
Differentials, and Causes

THE MORTALITY RATE DIFFERS from the fertility rate in at least three fundamental ways. First, in modern times at least and in most large nations the level of mortality is much lower than the level of fertility— deaths are considerably fewer than births. In the United States, for example, even when the birth rate was at its lowest level in 1936 there were about 2,350,000 births in this country and less than 1,480,000 deaths, so that the natural increase of population was about 870,000 persons; and when the rate of reproduction was at the postwar peak, in 1947, there were about 3,820,000 births and only 1,450,000 deaths, with natural increase alone producing an increase of 2,370,000 in the population. Because the rate of reproduction generally is above the mortality rate, populations usually tend to increase—the fact that has given Malthusian principles their tremendous appeal. Second, the fluctuations in the death rate usually are far less pronounced, seemingly less capricious, than those in the birth rate. Again using the United States as an example, only in 1918, the year of the great influenza epidemic, was the number of deaths and the death rate in a given year strikingly above or below those for the preceding or the succeeding year. This means that ordinarily the number of deaths in a given population for the years immediately ahead may be predicted with a far greater degree of reliability than can the number of births. This, in turn, is a fact of much importance to those who need reliable bases for estimating populations for the years that have elapsed since a census or to those who need quick, simple, and fairly reliable ways of testing the accuracy of the estimates that others may make. For example, by the procedure illustrated in chapter 21, the official in Arizona or Alabama who needs to know the population of his state for a year such as 1959, almost a decade after the last census was taken, and almost a year before the results of the next one will be available to him, may use the death rates for earlier years and the number of deaths registered in 1959, as bases for making a simple and reliable estimate. Third, and closely related to the preceding difference, changes in the death rate generally take place more evenly and gradually than do those in the birth rate. This is to say that the curve representing the secular trend in the former moves up or down more slowly and steadily than does that depicting the long-time changes in the former. In turn, the gradual manner in which the trend in the death rate usually proceeds adds greatly to the value that may be derived from knowledge about the mortality of a population for purposes of estimating current changes in its number and distribution.

Some International Comparisons

Some of the most significant and reliable information relating to the levels of mortality throughout the world has been selected for presentation in Tables XXXVI and XXXVII. The first of these gives, for all countries or territories with one million or more inhabitants for which the data are available, the recent information on the crude death rate and the infant mortality rate. As much as possible, these materials are given for the latest census year, so as to minimize any variations in the crude death rates that might be due merely to overestimates or underestimates of the population. The second of these tables presents, for all countries for which life tables have been constructed in fairly recent years, the expectation of life at selected ages as shown in the latest available compilations. The ages selected are zero (or birth), twenty, forty-five, and sixty-five. Wherever possible the information is given separately for males and females.

Mortality Levels

A lengthy treatise would be required to explain fully the nature of and reasons for all the differences these various indexes reveal. Most striking of all is the great contrast between the relatively low death rates, the low infant mortality rates, and the high expectation of life at birth in northwestern Europe, the United States, Canada, Israel, Australia, and New Zealand and the high death rates, high infant mortality rates, and low life expectancy in Belgian Congo, Egypt, India, and among the colored population of the Union of South Africa. Whereas

Table XXXVI. Reported Crude Death Rates and Infant Mortality Rates for Countries, and for Territories of 1 Million or More Inhabitants, for Which Data Are Available

Country or territory	Year	Crude death rate	Infant mortality rate
Africa			
Algeria (France)			
Moslem population	1954	13.7	86
European population	1954	8.8	48
Egypt	1947	21.3	127
Uganda (United Kingdom)	1948	11.3 [1]	78 [1]
Union of South Africa			
White population	1951	8.8	33 [2]
Colored population	1951	19.4	129 [2]
Asiatic population	1951	9.7	64 [2]
North America			
Canada	1951	9.0	38
Costa Rica	1950	12.2	112
Cuba	1953	6.5 [2]	. . .
Dominican Republic	1950	10.0	88
El Salvador	1950	14.7	81
Guatemala	1950	21.8	107
Honduras	1950	12.0	86
Mexico	1950	16.2	96
Nicaragua	1950	10.8	82
Panama	1950	9.6	68
Puerto Rico (U. S.)	1950	9.9	68
United States	1950	9.6	29
White population	1950	9.5	27
Nonwhite population	1950	11.2	45
South America			
Argentina	1947	9.9	78
Bolivia	1950	15.0	107
Chile	1952	13.0	129
Colombia	1951	14.3	120
Ecuador	1950	17.7	110
Paraguay	1950	6.5 [3]	102
Peru	1940	13.2	128
Venezuela	1950	10.9	81

Table XXXVI. Reported Crude Death Rates and Infant Mortality Rates for Countries, and for Territories of 1 Million or More Inhabitants (Continued)

Country or territory	Year	Crude death rate	Infant mortality rate
Asia			
Burma	1953	21.6	224
Ceylon	1953	10.9	71
China (Formosa only)	1940	19.7	30 [4]
India	1951	14.4	124
Iraq	1947	4.1	44 [4]
Israel (Jewish population)	1948	6.8 [1]	36
Japan	1950	10.9	60
South Korea	1948	9.4	71
Malaya, Federation of (U. K.)	1947	19.4	102
Pakistan	1951	11.9	110
Philippines	1948	12.7	114
Thailand	1947	13.4	80
Europe			
Austria	1951	12.7	61
Belgium	1947	13.3	69
Bulgaria	1946	13.7	86 [4]
Czechoslovakia	1950	11.5	78
Denmark	1950	9.2	31
Finland	1950	10.1	44
France	1954	12.1	41
Germany			
East Germany	1950	11.9	72
West Germany	1950	10.3	56
Greece	1951	7.5	44
Hungary	1949	11.4	71 [5]
Iceland	1950	7.9	22
Ireland (Republic)	1951	14.3	46
Italy	1951	10.3	67
Netherlands	1947	8.1	22 [5]
Norway	1950	9.1	28
Poland	1950	11.6	108
Portugal	1950	12.2	94
Romania	1953	11.5	96
Spain	1950	10.9	70
Sweden	1950	10.0	21

Table XXXVI. Reported Crude Death Rates and Infant Mortality Rates for Countries, and for Territories of 1 Million or More Inhabitants (Continued)

Country or territory	Year	Crude death rate	Infant mortality rate
Switzerland	1950	10.1	31
United Kingdom	1951	12.6	31
England and Wales	1951	12.5	30
Northern Ireland	1951	12.8	41
Scotland	1951	12.9	37
Yugoslavia	1953	12.4	116
Oceania			
Australia	1954	9.1	23
New Zealand	1951	9.7	23

SOURCE: United Nations, *Demographic Yearbook, 1956* (New York: United Nations, 1956).

[1] Data are for 1949.
[2] Data are for 1952.
[3] Data known to be incomplete.
[4] Data are for 1954.
[5] Data are for 1953.

at birth children in the first group of countries have an average of almost seventy years of life ahead of them, in the latter the corresponding figure is less than forty. The countries of southern and eastern Europe, most portions of Latin America, and the few other Asiatic nations for which data are available rank substantially below the first group mentioned above. The population of Japan, however, has an expectation of life at birth which is much nearer that of the peoples of northwestern Europe, the United States and Canada, and other countries listed in the first category, than to that of the inhabitants of other parts of Asia.

Nonwhites (mostly Negroes) in the United States make a poor showing in comparison with their white countrymen, but even so they have an expectation of life at birth that compares favorably with that in southern and eastern Europe, and is considerably above that in any Latin American country or in the parts of Asia, other than Japan and Israel, for which it has been possible to prepare life tables. Similarly, in the Union of South Africa the expectation of life of the Negro (col-

Table XXXVII. Expectation of Life at Selected Ages by Sex for Those Countries for Which Life Tables Are Available

Country	Years	Sex	Age 0	20	45	65
Africa						
Belgian Congo	1950–1952	M	37	34	18	9
		F	40	36	20	10
Egypt	1936–1938	M	36	40	23	10
		F	41	46	27	13
Union of South Africa	1945–1947					
White population		M	64	48	26	12
		F	68	52	30	15
Colored population		M	42	37	21	11
		F	44	39	24	12
Asiatic population		M	51	40	21	10
		F	50	39	21	10
North America						
Canada	1950–1952	M	66	51	28	13
		F	71	54	31	15
Costa Rica	1949–1951	M & F	56	47	26	12
El Salvador	1949–1951	M	50	44	27	14
		F	52	47	28	15
Guatemala	1949–1951	M	44	41	24	12
		F	44	40	24	12
Mexico	1940	M	38	38	22	11
		F	40	40	23	11
United States	1949–1951					
White population		M	66	50	27	13
		F	72	55	31	15
Nonwhite population		M	59	44	24	13
		F	63	47	26	15
South America						
Argentina	1947	M	57	46	24	11
		F	61	50	28	13
Brazil (Federal District)	1949–1951	M	50	41	22	10
		F	56	47	27	13
Chile	1952	M	50	43	24	11
		F	54	47	27	13
Asia						
Ceylon	1952	M	58	50	28	13
		F	56	47	27	11

Table XXXVII. Expectation of Life at Selected Ages by Sex (Continued)

Country	Years	Sex	Age 0	20	45	65
India	1941–1950	M	32	33	18	8
		F	32	33	19	9
Israel (Jewish population)	1955	M	69	53	30	14
		F	72	55	32	15
Japan	1955	M	64	49	27	12
		F	68	53	31	15
Korea	1938	M	47	42	23	10
		F	51	45	26	12
Thailand	1947–1948	M	49	40	22	10
		F	52	43	25	11
Europe						
Austria	1949–1951	M	62	49	27	12
		F	67	53	30	14
Belgium	1946–1949	M	62	48	26	12
		F	67	52	30	14
Bulgaria	1925–1928	M	46	46	27	13
		F	47	45	28	14
Czechoslovakia	1929–1932	M	52	45	25	11
		F	55	47	27	12
Denmark	1946–1950	M	68	52	29	14
		F	70	54	30	14
Finland	1951–1953	M	63	47	25	11
		F	69	52	29	13
France	1950–1951	M	64	48	26	12
		F	69	53	31	14
East Germany	1952–1953	M	65	51	28	13
		F	69	54	30	14
West Germany	1949–1951	M	65	50	28	13
		F	68	53	30	14
Greece	1926–1930	M	49	44	26	13
		F	51	46	29	14
Hungary	1955	M	65	51	28	13
		F	69	54	30	14
Iceland	1931–1940	M	61	47	28	13
		F	66	51	31	16
Ireland	1945–1947	M	60	48	26	12
		F	62	49	28	13
Italy	1935–1937	F	57	49	28	13

Table XXXVII. Expectation of Life at Selected Ages by Sex (Continued)

Country	Years	Sex	Age 0	20	45	65
Luxembourg	1946–1948	M	62	48	26	12
		F	66	52	29	13
Netherlands	1950–1952	M	71	54	30	14
		F	73	55	32	15
Norway	1946–1950	M	69	53	31	15
		F	73	56	32	16
Poland	1948	M	56	47	26	12
		F	63	52	30	14
Portugal	1949–1952	M	56	47	26	12
		F	61	52	30	14
Spain	1940	M	47	40	22	10
		F	53	47	27	12
Sweden	1946–1950	M	69	52	29	14
		F	72	54	31	14
Switzerland	1948–1953	M	66	50	27	12
		F	71	54	30	14
United Kingdom						
England and Wales	1954	M	68	50	30	12
		F	73	55	32	15
Northern Ireland	1950–1952	M	65	50	27	12
		F	69	52	29	14
Scotland	1955	M	66	49	26	12
		F	71	53	30	14
Oceania						
Australia	1946–1948	M	66	50	27	12
		F	71	53	30	14
New Zealand	1950–1952					
European population		M	68	51	28	13
		F	72	55	31	15
Maori population		M	54	42	23	10
		F	56	43	23	12

SOURCE: United Nations, *Demographic Yearbook, 1956* (New York: United Nations, 1956).

ored) population and that of the Asiatic population both are substantially lower than that of the white population; and in New Zealand the index for the Maoris is substantially below that for the European or white population of the island.

As age increases, the differentials just noted are greatly decreased.

Thus, at birth the extreme range, among the countries represented in Table XXXVII, is from seventy-three for females in Norway, the Netherlands, and England and Wales to thirty-two for both males and females in India, whereas at age twenty the greatest disparity is that between the index of fifty-six years for females in Norway and the one of thirty-three for males and females alike in India. At age forty-five the differences are even more sharply reduced, with the upper extreme being the average of thirty-two years of future lifetime left to women in Israel, the Netherlands, Norway, and England and Wales and the lower that of eighteen years for males in the Belgian Congo and in India. At age sixty-five the highest of the calculations is that (sixteen) for the women in Iceland and Norway; the lowest, that (eight) for males in India. This means, of course, that much of the difference noted throughout the world in life expectation at birth is due to the varying levels of infant and child mortality.

Additional light is shed on the observation just stated by comparing, in various countries, the age at which the expectation of life again is reduced to an average equal to that at birth. (Since the very slight contributions made to the total years lived by the group by infants dying during the first year of life must be included in calculating the average, the expectation of life at age one always is significantly higher than that at birth; and if high child mortality rates prevail, the same may be the case at various ages beyond one.) Such comparisons are permitted, to a considerable extent, by the values from the life tables for various countries which have been assembled in the 1956 edition of the *Demographic Yearbook* of the United Nations. A careful scrutiny of these materials indicates that eight of the countries in the list are those in which by the beginning of the third year of life the expectation of life is again approximately equal to that at birth. These, of course, are the ones in which deaths during the first and second years of life have been reduced to the lowest levels, and in which the average length of life has been lengthened to the greatest extent by the saving of infant and child lives. They are as follows: the United States (white population), the Netherlands, Norway, Sweden, England and Wales, Scotland, Australia, and New Zealand (European population). These eight countries are most closely rivaled in this respect by the following ones, in which at approximately the beginning of the fourth year of life, the amount of future average lifetime is again equal to that at birth: the Union of South Africa (white population), Canada, Israel, Denmark, Finland, Switzerland, and Northern Ireland. Next comes a group of nations in which infant and child mortality rates have been reduced to such an extent that expectation of life at birth and at the beginning of the fifth year of life are approximately equal, and the countries in this category are as follows: the United States (nonwhite population), Japan, East Germany, West Germany, and Iceland.

At the other extreme are Egypt, in which only at age twenty-five is life expectation again approximately equal to what it was at birth; India, in which the corresponding age is twenty-two; Mexico and Bulgaria, in which it is about twenty; Guatemala, in which it is approximately sixteen; and the Belgian Congo, the Union of South Africa (colored population), El Salvador, and Formosa, where average future lifetime at birth and at age fifteen are approximately the same. Finally, the approximate age at which expectation of life is equal to that at birth in various other countries may be summarized as follows: age six, Austria, Belgium, and Hungary; age seven, Ireland and New Zealand (Maori population); age eight, Union of South Africa (Asiatic population) and Argentina; age nine, Thailand; age ten, Panama, Brazil (Federal District, only), Italy, and Poland; age eleven, Costa Rica, Ceylon, Portugal, and Spain; age twelve, Chile and Korea; age thirteen, Czechoslovakia; and age fourteen, Ecuador and Greece.

In passing, it should also be pointed out that these data offer little support for the thesis, which has enjoyed such wide popularity, that high infant and child mortality rates eliminate the weaklings, leaving alive only the strong and virile. Such a thesis would be supported if the countries in which expectation of life at birth is high were the ones in which expectation of life at age sixty-five is low, and if those in which the average calculated from birth is low were those in which the index for persons aged sixty-five is high. Definitely such is not the case. Generally speaking, the nations with high expectation of life at birth maintain their superiority at all ages throughout the life span.

The almost universal tendency for the female, at all ages, to enjoy a longer expectation of life than males also deserves comment. Ceylon is the only exception to this rule among the countries listed in Table XXXVII, although in India and West Germany at some ages the values for men and women are equal. In this connection it is interesting to note that at an earlier period in India, the calculations also indicated a higher expectancy of life among males than females.[1]

[1] See T. Lynn Smith, *Population Analysis* (New York: McGraw-Hill Book Company, 1948), p. 251–252.

Causes of Death

The tabulations prepared for the *Demographic Yearbook* of the United Nations now make it possible to explore, with comparative ease, the extent to which the various causes of death are assigned by those who prepare the death certificates in different parts of the world. Although one may be certain that uniformity in procedures is still far from being attained, for certain broad purposes this information probably is sufficiently reliable to make worthwhile comparisons possible. In general one may be quite sure that the extent to which deaths are attributed to "senility without mention of psychosis, ill-defined and unknown causes" and to "all other diseases" (categories B 44 and B 45 in the abbreviated list of the Sixth Revision of the International List of Causes of Death) is somewhat indicative of the need for substantial improvement in recording and reporting mortality statistics. Thus one might safely conclude that the rates given for various important causes of death, such as heart ailments or cancer, are more trustworthy for Denmark, in which only 1.2 per cent of the deaths are classified as being due to senility and 9.2 to the residual set of all other causes, than they are for France, in which the corresponding percentages are 17.5 and 11.4, respectively. Even so in France the death rate from senility in 1955 of 211 per 100,000 population is exceeded by those in Ceylon (218), Colombia (247), Guatemala (312), and Egypt (314); and the residual class of all other diseases is assigned frequently enough to account for rates of 203 per 100,000 population in Colombia, 214 in Belgium, 242 in Jamaica, and 253 in Ceylon. In view of this, great care is needed in comparing the absolute and relative importance of the different causes of death in the various nations.

Where modern methods of preventive medicine and sanitation, based on the germ theory of disease, have been applied on a large scale, what may be designated as the deteriorative ailments (heart disease, cancer, cirrhosis of the liver, vascular lesions or "stroke," and so on) stand at the top of the list of the causes of death; whereas where such applications of modern science have not been made, the germ-transmitted diseases continue to rank high in the list of killers. For this reason, even with all the limitations of the data indicated in the preceding paragraph, it is interesting to identify the three most important causes of death as reported for various nations throughout the world. Unfortunately, many of the most populous countries have not supplied the necessary information, but even so the compilations presented in Table XXXVIII deserve careful study. (The residual category of all other diseases was omitted from consideration in making this tabulation.)

Two patterns are evident in these materials. Where much has been done to control the ravages of preventable diseases (as is especially true in northwestern Europe, the United States and Canada, Australia, and New Zealand), heart disease, cancer, and vascular lesions are the leading causes of death; and collectively the three account for the large majority of all fatalities. In many other countries senility, gastritis, and one of the transmissible ailments make up the three most important categories. The fact that malaria, infective and parasitic diseases, tuberculosis, and pneumonia now figure among the top three causes of death in so few countries reflects the high degree to which the control of disease throughout the world has become an international concern. Nowadays the presence of yellow fever in a Latin American port, a violent scourge of malaria in some part of Africa, or an outbreak of cholera in Egypt is considered and dealt with as a menace to peoples in many lands.

Infant Mortality

The deaths of children of less than one year of age constitute such a large proportion of all deaths that infant mortality deserves special analysis. As indicated above the rates for all the principal portions of the globe, for which data are available, are presented in Table XXXVI. A fair approximation of the situation around the world at the opening of the second half of the twentieth century may be secured through a study of these materials.

The fact that by 1950 the infant mortality rate in Sweden had been reduced to 21 is a remarkable achievement, as are the other rates of less than 30 achieved in the Netherlands, Iceland, Australia, New Zealand, Norway, and the United States and those that are almost as low in England and Wales, Formosa, Denmark, and Switzerland. It seems reasonable to expect, therefore, that within a few more decades, a rate somewhat approaching the minimum possible may be registered by one or more of these countries. At the other end of the scale, though, are parts of the world in which very high proportions of all the children born fail to live through the first year of life. Burma, in which the reported rate would indicate that almost one child in every four dies before attaining the age of one year, is in a class by itself in this respect; but rates of 120 or above also are listed for the colored popula-

Table XXXVIII. The Three Leading Causes of Death in Selected Countries

Country	Year	Three leading causes of death	
		Name	Rate †
Africa			
Egypt	1954	1. Gastritis, etc. (B 36)	794
		2. Senility (B 45)	314
		3. Bronchitis (B 32)	191
Union of South Africa	1953		
White population		1. Heart disease (B 26)	188
		2. Cancer (B 18)	127
		3. Vascular lesions (B 22)	87
Colored population		1. Gastritis, etc. (B 36)	351
		2. Pneumonia (B 31)	282
		3. Tuberculosis (B 1)	209
Asiatic population		1. Pneumonia (B 31)	162
		2. Gastritis, etc. (B 36)	88
		3. Heart disease (B 26)	79
North America			
Canada	1955	1. Heart disease (B 26)	228
		2. Cancer (B 18)	130
		3. Vascular lesions (B 22)	91
Costa Rica	1955	1. Gastritis, etc. (B 36)	152
		2. Senility (B 45)	147
		3. Cancer (B 18)	76
Dominican Republic	1954	1. Senility (B 45)	153
		2. Gastritis, etc. (B 36)	93
		3. Infective and parasitic (B 17)	81
Guatemala	1955	1. Senility (B 45)	312
		2. Gastritis, etc. (B 36)	270
		3. Malaria (B 16)	210
Mexico	1954	1. Gastritis, etc. (B 36)	205
		2. Pneumonia (B 31)	172
		3. Senility (B 45)	136
Nicaragua	1950	1. Malaria (B 16)	280
		2. Senility (B 45)	109
		3. Infective and parasitic (B 17)	87
Puerto Rico	1954	1. Senility (B 45)	103
		2. Gastritis, etc. (B 36)	76
		3. Heart disease (B 26)	69
United States	1954	1. Heart disease (B 26)	277
		2. Cancer (B 18)	146
		3. Vascular lesions (B 22)	104

Table XXXVIII. The Three Leading Causes of Death (Continued)

Country	Year	Three leading causes of death Name	Rate †
South America			
Brazil (Federal District)	1954	1. Heart disease (B 26)	275
		2. Hypertension with heart disease (B 28)	163
		3. Cancer (B 18)	129
Chile	1954	1. Pneumonia (B 31)	229
		2. Senility (B 45)	160
		3. Other diseases of infants (B 44)	143
Colombia	1955	1. Senility (B 45)	247
		2. Gastritis, etc. (B 36)	106
		3. Pneumonia (B 31)	76
Uruguay	1953	1. Cancer (B 18)	141
		2. Heart disease (B 26)	91
		3. Vascular lesions (B 22)	83
Asia			
Ceylon	1955	1. Senility (B 45)	218
		2. Other diseases of infants (B 44)	117
		3. Pneumonia (B 31)	74
China (Formosa)	1955	1. Gastritis, etc. (B 36)	115
		2. Pneumonia (B 31)	111
		3. Senility (B 45)	65
Israel (Jewish population)	1955	1. Heart disease (B 26)	120
		2. Cancer (B 18)	90
		3. Vascular lesions (B 22)	61
Japan	1955	1. Vascular lesions (B 22)	136
		2. Senility (B 45)	88
		3. Cancer (B 18)	87
Europe			
Austria	1955	1. Cancer (B 18)	234
		2. Heart disease (B 26)	212
		3. Vascular lesions (B 22)	151
Belgium	1954	1. Cancer (B 18)	204
		2. Senility (B 45)	157
		3. Heart disease (B 26)	121
Denmark	1955	1. Heart disease (B 26)	201
		2. Cancer (B 18)	191
		3. Vascular lesions (B 22)	122

Table XXXVIII. The Three Leading Causes of Death (Continued)

Country	Year	Three leading causes of death Name	Rate †
Finland	1955	1. Heart disease (B 26)	202
		2. Cancer (B 18)	146
		3. Vascular lesions (B 22)	120
France	1955	1. Senility (B 45)	211
		2. Cancer (B 18)	184
		3. Other heart diseases (B 27)	155
West Germany	1954	1. Cancer (B 18)	187
		2. Heart disease (B 26)	163
		3. Vascular lesions (B 22)	161
Greece	1955	1. Senility (B 45)	182
		2. Cancer (B 18)	78
		3. Vascular lesions (B 22)	61
Hungary	1955	1. Heart disease (B 26)	147
		2. Cancer (B 18)	142
		3. Vascular lesions (B 22)	121
Iceland	1955	1. Cancer (B 18)	128
		2. Heart disease (B 26)	121
		3. Vascular lesions (B 22)	102
Ireland	1955	1. Heart disease (B 26)	324
		2. Cancer (B 18)	161
		3. Vascular lesions (B 22)	128
Italy	1954	1. Heart disease (B 26)	158
		2. Vascular lesions (B 22)	128
		3. Cancer (B 18)	124
Netherlands	1955	1. Heart disease (B 26)	158
		2. Cancer (B 18)	155
		3. Vascular lesions (B 22)	101
Norway	1954	1. Cancer (B 18)	160
		2. Heart disease (B 26)	143
		3. Vascular lesions (B 22)	131
Portugal	1955	1. Senility (B 45)	187
		2. Gastritis, etc. (B 36)	114
		3. Vascular lesions (B 22)	96
Sweden	1954	1. Heart disease (B 26)	231
		2. Cancer (B 18)	159
		3. Vascular lesions (B 22)	141
Switzerland	1954	1. Heart disease (B 26)	234
		2. Cancer (B 18)	188
		3. Vascular lesions (B 22)	136

Table XXXVIII. The Three Leading Causes of Death (Continued)

Country	Year	Three leading causes of death Name	Rate †
United Kingdom	1955		
England and Wales		1. Heart disease (B 26)	311
		2. Cancer (B 18)	206
		3. Vascular lesions (B 22)	167
Northern Ireland		1. Heart disease (B 26)	291
		2. Cancer (B 18)	160
		3. Vascular lesions (B 22)	152
Scotland		1. Heart disease (B 26)	351
		2. Cancer (B 18)	206
		3. Vascular lesions (B 22)	187
Yugoslavia	1954	1. Heart disease (B 26)	157
		2. Cancer (B 18)	121
		3. Vascular lesions (B 22)	90
Oceania			
Australia	1954	1. Heart disease (B 26)	244
		2. Cancer (B 18)	129
		3. Vascular lesions (B 22)	122
Hawaii	1954	1. Heart disease (B 26)	115
		2. Cancer (B 18)	94
		3. Vascular lesions (B 22)	66
New Zealand (European population)	1954	1. Heart disease (B 26)	241
		2. Cancer (B 18)	147
		3. Vascular lesions (B 22)	115

SOURCE: United Nations, *Demographic Yearbook, 1956* (New York: United Nations, 1956). Numbers in parentheses are appropriate ones from List B, the abbreviated list of 50 causes, International List of Causes of Death. †Rates are per 100,000 population.
Abbreviations:
Tuberculosis (B 1) = Tuberculosis of respiratory system.
Infective and parasitic (B 17) = All other diseases classified as infective and parasitic.
Cancer (B 18) = Malignant neoplasms, including neoplasms of lymphatic and haemotopoietic tissues.
Vascular lesions (B 22) = Vascular lesions affecting central nervous system.
Heart disease (B 26) = Arteriosclerotic and degenerative heart disease.
Gastritis, etc. (B 36) = Gastritis, duodenitis, enteritis and colitis, except diarrhoea of the newborn.
Other diseases of infants (B 44) = Other diseases peculiar to early infancy, and immaturity unqualified.
Senility (B 45) = Senility without mention of psychosis, ill-defined and unknown causes.

tion of the Union of South Africa, Chile, Peru, Egypt, India, and Colombia. In addition, and in descending order according to the rates, Yugoslavia, the Philippines, Costa Rica, Pakistan, Ecuador, Poland, Guatemala, Bolivia, and the Federation of Malaya all have reported rates of well over 100. It should be indicated, of course, that any tendency for birth registration to be incomplete is likely to result in an artificial inflation of the infant mortality rate, and that the high indexes for some of these countries may be due in part to this factor. In Colombia, for example, it is highly probable that the reported infant mortality rate is inflated by at least 20 per cent merely because the number of births used in the calculation of the rate is far too small.

The white population of the United States has a much lower infant mortality rate than the nonwhite population. However, the rate of 45 for nonwhites (mostly Negroes) is approximately the same as that in such countries as Greece, Finland, and Ireland; and it is substantially lower than the ones for Germany, Italy, and Spain.

These data indicate that in many of the most populous parts of the earth infant mortality rates are still very high. The deaths of young infants, though, are among those which are most easily prevented through the proper application of modern scientific knowledge in the fields of preventive medicine, the care and feeding of children, care of mothers during childbirth, sanitation, and so on. During the second half of the twentieth century, this knowledge is being widely diffused, and it is being applied to safeguard the lives of the very young. If this trend continues, as appears certain to be the case, during the decades immediately ahead the world may very well see an upsurge of population that will dwarf the increases that have taken place since 1950.

Mortality in the United States

A study of mortality in the United States does much to bring out the factors responsible for variations in the death rates and in the expectation of life generally, even though our data and procedures must be greatly improved before accurate measurements and comparisons of the levels of mortality in the various states and regions will be possible. The basic difficulty in this respect is the extremely high mobility of our population, which often accounts for deaths being charged to states to which the persons involved had been sent for their health and not to the sections of the country in which they had contracted their fatal illnesses. No recent life tables have been constructed for most of the states, but

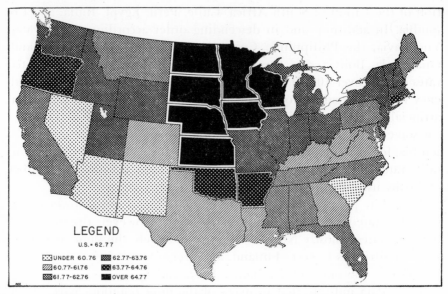

Figure 67. Variations in the computed expectation of life at birth among white males in the United States, 1939–1941.

those for 1939–1941 serve to bring out the nature of the problem. (See Figures 67 and 68.) These are based on values from the life tables, the most refined indexes of mortality that have been developed. But any measures that show the risks of life in the United States to be greatest in the states of Arizona, Colorado, and New Mexico, and least in the Plains States, obviously leave a great deal to be desired. Likewise it probably is absolutely impossible, with the data available, to secure a reliable answer to a question of what effect, if any, retirement to an area such as southern California, Arizona, the Gulf Coast, or peninsular Florida may have upon the longevity of the persons making such a move. We are unable to charge properly the deaths occurring in our population to the areas to which the debits should be given. Nevertheless the data we do have enable the demographer to explore many important aspects of mortality.

Age and the Death Rate

The close relationship between age and the death rate has already been referred to in connection with the presentation of Table XXXVII. Even in the United States, with its very low infant mortality rate, the hazards of life are great during infancy. This is especially true during

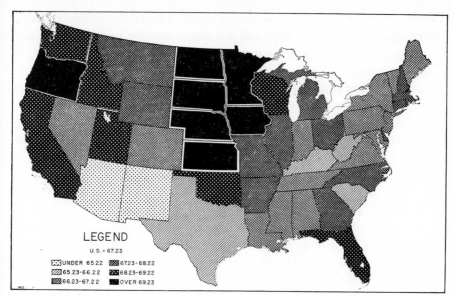

Figure 68. Variations in the computed expectation of life at birth among white females in the United States, 1939–1941.

the first hours and days of the baby's life, but the death rate then declines precipitously during the first year of life, rapidly for another two or three years, and slowly but gradually until the age of ten. During early adolescence the chances that one will lose his life during a given year are near their minimum, but by the time the person reaches fifteen the age-specific mortality rate has begun to rise perceptibly. Henceforth the trend is ever upward, although not until age fifty-five or thereabouts has been attained is the rapidity of the increase greatly accelerated. By age sixty-six, though, the risks of life are approximately equal to those encountered during infancy. Eventually, after the mark of "threescore years and ten" has been passed, the rates soar. At age eighty there is one chance out of ten that a given person will pass away before attaining his next birthday, at age eighty-nine one chance in five, at age ninety-seven one chance in three, and at age 106 one chance in two.

Sex and the Mortality Rate

That females have a longer expectation of life than males has already been indicated in connection with the analysis of the materials in Table XXXVII. All of the data for the United States are in absolute accord.

For the years 1949–1951, for example, the life tables indicate that at every age from birth to 100, and for the nonwhite population as well as the white, the age specific death rate for males was higher than the one for females. Moreover, irrespective of the manner in which the data are presented, it can be asserted with a reasonable degree of certainty that among whites and Negroes (regardless of whether they live in cities or in the open country), and in all sections of the country, the death rates of males are higher than those for females of comparable ages. (See Table XXXIX.) For this reason the mortality data should always be subdivided by sex before any other comparisons are attempted.

Race or Color and the Mortality Rate

As indicated above, from the standpoint of longevity the white population enjoys a distinct superiority over the nonwhite (mostly Negro) population. This was true in 1901, the year for which our first life tables were constructed, when the life expectation at birth of Negro males was only 34.1 compared with 50.2 for white males; and when the corresponding averages for Negro and white females were 35.0 and 51.1 years, respectively. The same pattern prevailed at every subsequent date at which the census of the population supplied the age distributions essential for making the computations, including 1950, the latest one, for which the appropriate data are given in Table XXXIX. However, it will be noted that the differential between whites and Negroes was greatly reduced in the course of the fifty years covered by our inventories of the length of life of the population. Thus, in 1901, the materials given above indicate that the life expectation at birth of white males was forty-seven per cent above that of Negro males, and that the average for the white females was 46 per cent higher than the index for colored females. By 1949–1951, though, so much more rapid had been the increase in life expectancy among Negroes than among whites, the corresponding differences for males and females had been reduced to 13 per cent and 15 per cent, respectively.

The racial or color differential is true, of course, for persons of both sexes, and it also is to be observed in every one of the nine geographic divisions used for regional compilations of the data by the U. S. Bureau of the Census. (See Table XXXIX.)

Residence and the Mortality Rate

It now is very difficult to prepare life tables and other indexes of mortality in a manner that will permit valid comparisons of mortality

Table XXXIX. Expectation of Life in the United States and in the Nine Geographic Divisions, 1949–1951, for Selected Ages, by Sex and Color

Division, sex, and color	Age 0	Age 20	Age 45	Age 65
United States				
Male	65.5	48.9	26.6	12.7
Female	71.0	53.7	30.6	15.0
White				
Male	66.3	49.5	26.9	12.8
Female	72.0	54.6	31.1	15.0
Nonwhite				
Male	58.9	43.7	23.6	12.8
Female	62.7	46.8	26.1	14.5
New England				
White				
Male	66.9	49.6	26.6	12.6
Female	72.1	54.3	30.8	14.8
Nonwhite				
Male	61.3	45.6	24.1	12.1
Female	64.0	47.9	26.4	13.6
Middle Atlantic				
White				
Male	66.2	49.0	26.0	12.2
Female	71.2	53.4	29.9	14.2
Nonwhite				
Male	59.0	43.5	23.0	11.8
Female	63.3	47.1	25.9	13.7
East North Central				
White				
Male	66.5	49.6	26.8	12.7
Female	71.9	54.3	30.8	14.8
Nonwhite				
Male	59.1	43.5	23.1	11.7
Female	62.9	46.5	25.6	13.8
West North Central				
White				
Male	67.8	50.9	28.2	13.3
Female	73.3	55.7	32.1	15.5
Nonwhite				
Male	57.6	43.0	22.7	11.7
Female	61.3	45.8	25.1	13.6

Table XXXIX. Expectation of Life in the United States and in the Nine Geographic Divisions (Continued)

Division, sex, and color	Age			
	0	20	45	65
South Atlantic				
White				
Male	66.0	49.3	26.9	13.0
Female	72.5	55.1	31.7	15.3
Nonwhite				
Male	57.5	42.2	22.5	13.0
Female	62.0	46.0	25.6	15.1
East South Central				
White				
Male	66.0	49.8	27.6	13.2
Female	71.8	54.9	31.6	15.1
Nonwhite				
Male	58.9	43.9	23.8	12.8
Female	61.8	45.9	25.6	14.1
West South Central				
White				
Male	66.1	50.1	27.7	13.4
Female	72.6	55.9	32.6	16.0
Nonwhite				
Male	60.3	45.3	25.0	13.6
Female	63.7	48.0	27.2	15.2
Mountain				
White				
Male	65.4	49.5	27.4	13.1
Female	71.9	55.1	32.0	15.7
Nonwhite				
Male	55.4	46.5	27.3	14.3
Female	58.8	48.7	29.3	15.7
Pacific				
White				
Male	66.1	49.1	26.6	12.7
Female	72.9	55.2	31.8	15.6
Nonwhite				
Male	63.6	47.5	26.2	13.2
Female	68.1	51.4	29.7	16.0

SOURCE: "United States Life Tables, 1949–1951," *Vital Statistics—Special Reports*, 41, No. 1 (1954); and "Life Tables for the Geographic Divisions of the United States," *Vital Statistics—Special Reports*, 41, No. 4 (1956).

in rural and urban areas, and this apparently is becoming more so with the passing of each decade. The mushrooming of the suburbs, the development of rural residential areas for those who work in the city, the growing tendency for farm owners and farm laborers to reside in towns and cities, the greater use of hospitals, and the rapidly increasing territorial mobility of the population all serve to complicate the work. Probably it already is almost impossible to match population counts and mortality records in a way that will make it possible to compute reliable age-specific death rates for rural residents and for those who live in urban districts. In 1900 and 1910, the task was not so involved, and the first official life tables prepared in the Bureau of the Census included separate computations for the rural and urban popula-tions.[1] These may be supplemented with fairly comparable compila-tions prepared for 1930 by the *Metropolitan Life Insurance Company*.[2] Finally, in 1943 the United States Bureau of the Census published abridged life tables for the year 1939 for the rural and urban, white and nonwhite portions of the population.[3] These, the latest for the residen-tial categories known to the present writer, were the first prepared with data in which deaths were recorded by place of residence of the de-ceased rather than by place of occurrence. For later years, however, any comparisons of rural and urban mortality in which the necessary control is exercised over the factors of age, sex, and color or race must rest upon the results of special endeavors by a few students working with the data for selected states.

From the data given in Table XL it is evident that among the white population in 1901, 1910, and 1930, rural persons, both male and fe-male, enjoyed a considerably longer expectation of life at birth, and also at age fifty, than did people living in the cities of the United States. Similar is the conclusion to be derived from the results of later efforts to determine the nature and extent of rural-urban differences in mortality.[4] Among both males and females the expectation of life has

---

[1] See James W. Glover, *United States Life Tables, 1890, 1901, 1910, and 1901–1910* (Washington: Government Printing Office, 1921).

[2] Published in the company's *Statistical Bulletin, 16* (July, 1935).

[3] Republished in "United States Abridged Life Tables, 1939: Urban and Rural, by Regions, Color, and Sex," *Vital Statistics—Special Reports, 23*, No. 15 (1947), 297–316.

[4] See the summary of these attempts in C. A. McMahan, "Rural-Urban Differen-tials in Longevity," in T. Lynn Smith and C. A. McMahan, *The Sociology of Urban Life* (New York: The Dryden Press, 1951), pp. 281–289.

been and seems to remain greater in rural than in urban areas. However, a study of the materials for 1939–1941 (the latest years for which we have somewhat satisfactory data) indicates that the age-specific death rates of the rural population were not uniformly lower than those of urban centers of all sizes. (See Figure 69.) As a matter of fact, for ages up to thirty-five the large cities made a better showing than the strictly rural areas. From thirty-five to eighty-four, however, the indexes are decidedly favorable to the rural category, irrespective of the size of the centers with which comparisons are made. On the whole, the

Table XL. Changes in the Expectation of Life of the White Population of the Original Registration Area, 1901, 1910, and 1930, by Residence and Sex

Age and class	Expectation of life		
	1901	1910	1930
At birth:			
Urban males	43.97	47.32	56.73
Urban females	47.90	51.39	61.05
Rural males	54.03	55.06	62.09
Rural females	55.41	57.35	65.09
At age twenty:			
Urban males	39.13	40.51	44.20
Urban females	41.86	43.51	47.35
Rural males	45.97	45.92	48.32
Rural females	46.09	46.86	50.37
At age fifty:			
Urban males	18.56	18.59	19.78
Urban females	20.28	20.53	22.40
Rural males	22.78	22.43	23.39
Rural females	23.54	23.27	24.77
At age seventy:			
Urban males	8.20	8.14	8.50
Urban females	8.97	8.99	9.70
Rural males	9.56	9.36	9.88
Rural females	10.10	9.76	10.43

SOURCES: James W. Glover, *United States Life Tables, 1890, 1901, 1910, and 1901–1910*, Government Printing Office, Washington, 1921; and the *Statistical Bulletin* of the Metropolitan Life Insurance Company, 16 (July, 1935). Urban in 1901 refers to cities of 8,000 or more inhabitants and in 1910 and 1930 to those with 10,000 or more residents.

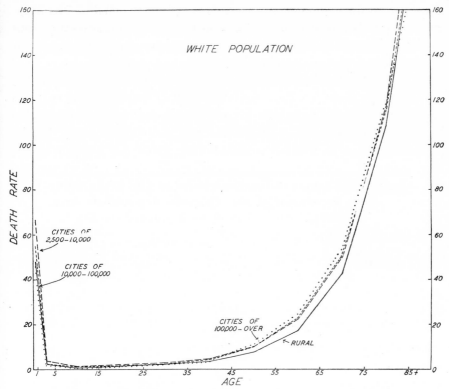

Figure 69. Age-specific death rates for the white population of the United States by size of place of residence, 1939–1941.

smallest urban places, those having less than 10,000 inhabitants, are the ones which had the highest mortality rates.

Marital Status and the Mortality Rate

That married people have lower mortality rates, or longer expectation of life, than the single, the widowed, and the divorced is rather generally known. If anyone were inclined to question this generalization, an examination of the data for the period 1949–1951, the latest comprehensive materials for the United States that will be available prior to about 1963, should remove any reasonable doubt. For these years among males and females alike, and for the nonwhite population as well as the white, at every age the death rate of those who were married was substantially below that of those who had remained single, those who were widowed, and those who were classified as divorced.[1] The second lowest position is consistently held by single persons, and highest of all are the death rates of those whose marriages have been terminated by divorces and who have not remarried.

The exact reasons for these differences are not fully known. Probably a tendency to avoid marriage on the part of those afflicted with various disabilities is part of the answer, but this could hardly explain why the single have lower mortality rates than the widowed and the divorced. A better adjustment to life on the part of the married person certainly is involved. This seems to be indicated especially by the fact that the death rates of married persons are especially low for such causes of death as syphilis, homicide, and suicide.

Regional Differences

The available data suggest that life expectation does not vary greatly from one region to another. If the comparisons are made separately for males and females subdivided by color, as is possible with the data given in Table XXXIX, the contrasts among the regions are not marked. It is true that the states in the Rocky Mountain Division rank lowest in three out of four of the comparisons involved, but caution should be used in attaching any significance to this fact. Rather, Figures 67 and 68, presented above, should be re-examined and the comments made in presenting them kept in mind. Undoubtedly, the low expectation of life in the southern part of the Rocky Mountain Division, an area famed as a health resort, is due largely to the fact the persons die in this region from diseases contracted elsewhere. All in all, it appears that the data are not sufficiently refined to enable significant regional variations in longevity, if there be any, to be determined.

Causes of Death

Since 1950 the number of deaths in the United States has averaged about 1.5 millions per year. In 1955 the total registered was 1,528,717; in 1954, 1,481,091; in 1953, 1,517,541; in 1952, 1,482,099; and so on. These figures correspond to crude death rates of 9.3, 9.2, 9.6, and 9.6, respectively, for the years indicated. An examination of the causes that

[1] See "Mortality from Selected Causes by Marital Status: United States, 1949–1951," *Vital Statistics—Special Reports,* 39, No. 7 (1956), pp. 376 ff. An analysis of earlier materials, which fully supports these conclusions, is given in Smith, *op. cit.,* p. 258.

are assigned for these deaths is another essential aspect of the study of mortality. Accordingly the most significant of abundant recent materials on the subject are presented in Table XLI and Figure 70. This table shows the rates per 100,000 population for the twenty-five leading causes of deaths in 1955. In making this compilation motor-vehicle accidents were considered as a separate category and not combined with other accidents as is the practice in the lists prepared by the National Office of Vital Statistics. This accounts for the principal differences between the indexes as they are shown in the table, and in those presented graphically in Figure 70.

Early in the second half of the twentieth century diseases of the heart are the cause of more than one-third of all the deaths occurring in the United States, and the death rate from this specific set of ailments is more than double that for any of the other causes of death. Malignant neoplasms, including neoplasms of lymphatic and hematopoietic tissues (or cancer to the layman) rank in second position, followed by vascular lesions affecting the central nervous system ("strokes"), certain diseases of early infancy, and accidents other than those in which motor vehicles are involved, in the order named. Influenza and pneumonia, motor-vehicle accidents, general arteriosclerosis, diabetes mellitus, and congenital malformations, in the order named, fill out the list of the ten most important killers.

There is a pronounced difference between the rates at which males and females are decimated by the various important causes of death. In general the rates for males are very much higher than those for females, and this is true of most of the degenerative ailments (such as heart disease and cancer), the transmissible diseases (such as tuberculosis, influenza, and syphilis), and those in which external factors are involved (such as suicide, homicide, and accidents). Even the death rates from diseases of early infancy and congenital malformations are substantially higher for males than for females, and the situation is similar with respect to the residual category of all other causes. For three of the categories in the list of twenty-five as given in Table XLI, however, the rates for women are higher than those for men. These are vascular lesions, diabetes mellitus, and benign neoplasms, respectively. In addition, for arteriosclerosis, hypertensions without mention of the heart, hernia and intestinal obstruction, and the anemias, the differences between the death rates of the sexes are too small to be considered of significance.

Table XLI. Death Rates in the United States for the Twenty-Five Leading Causes of Death, by Color and Sex, 1955

Cause of death	Rates per 100,000 population					
	Total population	White population		Nonwhite population		
		Males	Females	Males	Females	
All causes	930.4	1070.0	777.2	1131.8	876.9	
Diseases of the heart	355.8	437.9	292.4	317.6	255.8	
Malignant neoplasms	146.5	160.1	141.0	119.8	108.5	
Vascular lesions of central nervous system	106.0	102.3	106.2	117.8	121.9	
Certain diseases of early infancy	39.0	40.8	27.7	90.7	67.2	
Accidents (other than motor-vehicle)	33.5	42.3	22.3	60.7	28.7	
Influenza and pneumonia, except of newborn	27.1	27.8	21.3	57.5	40.1	
Motor-vehicle accidents	23.4	35.0	11.5	40.1	12.1	
General arteriosclerosis	19.8	20.5	20.7	14.2	11.7	
Diabetes mellitus	15.5	12.8	18.5	9.7	18.6	
Congenital malformations	12.5	13.6	11.2	14.9	11.9	
Cirrhosis of liver	10.2	14.2	7.0	9.0	6.0	
Suicide	10.2	17.2	4.9	6.1	1.5	
Chronic nephritis and other renal sclerosis	9.6	9.6	7.8	17.9	17.3	
Tuberculosis, all forms	9.1	11.2	4.1	28.4	15.0	
Other diseases of circulatory system	7.3	9.3	5.3	8.0	6.8	

Hypertension without mention of heart	6.8	6.2	5.9	13.9	12.5
Ulcer of stomach and duodenum	5.9	9.7	2.7	6.3	2.2
Hernia and intestinal obstruction	5.3	5.4	5.0	6.8	5.2
Gastritis, duodenitis, enteritis, and colitis	4.7	4.2	3.8	11.7	10.0
Homicide	4.5	3.4	1.2	36.9	9.5
Hyperplasia of prostate	3.7	7.5	. . .	7.4	. . .
Benign neoplasms and neoplasms of unspecified nature	3.1	2.7	3.2	2.8	6.3
All other infective and parasitic diseases	2.5	2.5	2.0	5.2	4.5
Syphilis and its sequelae	2.3	2.5	0.8	11.6	4.3
Anemias	1.9	1.7	1.9	3.0	2.4
All other causes	64.2	69.5	48.8	124.8	97.8

SOURCE: Compiled from data given in "Leading Causes of Death: United States . . . , 1955," *Vital Statistics—Special Reports*, 46, No. 8 (1957), 234–237.

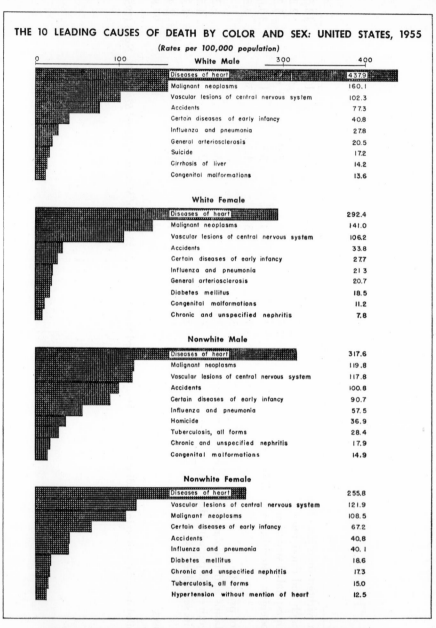

THE 10 LEADING CAUSES OF DEATH BY COLOR AND SEX: UNITED STATES, 1955

(Rates per 100,000 population)

White Male

Diseases of heart	437.9
Malignant neoplasms	160.1
Vascular lesions of central nervous system	102.3
Accidents	77.3
Certain diseases of early infancy	40.8
Influenza and pneumonia	27.8
General arteriosclerosis	20.5
Suicide	17.2
Cirrhosis of liver	14.2
Congenital malformations	13.6

White Female

Diseases of heart	292.4
Malignant neoplasms	141.0
Vascular lesions of central nervous system	106.2
Accidents	33.8
Certain diseases of early infancy	27.7
Influenza and pneumonia	21.3
General arteriosclerosis	20.7
Diabetes mellitus	18.5
Congenital malformations	11.2
Chronic and unspecified nephritis	7.8

Nonwhite Male

Diseases of heart	317.6
Malignant neoplasms	119.8
Vascular lesions of central nervous system	117.8
Accidents	100.8
Certain diseases of early infancy	90.7
Influenza and pneumonia	57.5
Homicide	36.9
Tuberculosis, all forms	28.4
Chronic and unspecified nephritis	17.9
Congenital malformations	14.9

Nonwhite Female

Diseases of heart	255.8
Vascular lesions of central nervous system	121.9
Malignant neoplasms	108.5
Certain diseases of early infancy	67.2
Accidents	40.8
Influenza and pneumonia	40.1
Diabetes mellitus	18.6
Chronic and unspecified nephritis	17.3
Tuberculosis, all forms	15.0
Hypertension without mention of heart	12.5

Figure 70. The leading causes of death in the United States, 1955. (Illustration from the National Office of Vital Statistics)

The principal causes of death for the white population also differ substantially from those for the nonwhite (largely Negro) population of the United States. Among the former the rates of the fatalities attributed to diseases of the heart, cancer, general arteriosclerosis, cirrhosis of the liver, suicide, the residual category styled other diseases of the circulatory system, and ulcers of the stomach or duodenum definitely are much higher than they are among the latter. For males only, diabetes mellitus should be added to this list. In sharp contrast, the death rates from the following causes are substantially higher for nonwhites than for whites: vascular lesions, certain diseases of early infancy, accidents in which motor vehicles are involved as well as those in which they are not, influenza and pneumonia, tuberculosis, hypertension in which no mention of the heart is included in the report, gastritis and so forth, homicide, the residual category of all other infectious and parasitic diseases, syphilis, and the anemias. For women only, benign neoplasms also should be added. The only items in the list of twenty-five for which there appear to be no significant differences between the death rates of the white and nonwhite segments of the population are congenital malformations, hernia and intestinal obstruction, and hyperplasia of the prostate.

Infant Mortality

In 1955 the infant mortality rate in the United States was 26.4, or only a little more than one-fourth of what it was in 1915, the first year for which the data needed for computing this highly important index are available. As late as 1937 infant mortality in this country was twice the 1955 level. The reduction of the infant mortality rate from 99.9 in 1915 to less than 27 in 1955 was a remarkable achievement.

Racial or color differentials in the infant mortality rate are considerable (see Figure 71), and there may be some rural-urban and regional differences as well. The fact that the rate for the white population is substantially below that for the nonwhite stands out strikingly in Figure 71. This holds true in every state in which the nonwhite population is large enough to lend significance to a comparison.

The differences between the infant mortality rates of the urban and the rural parts of the population are, of course, much more difficult to determine. However, by using a classification employed in recent reports by the National Office of Vital Statistics it is possible to indicate

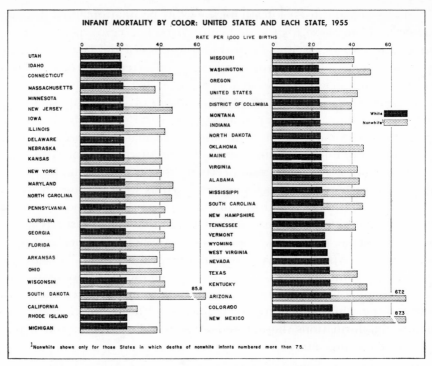

Figure 71. State-to-state variations in the infant mortality rate in the United States, by color, 1955. (Illustration from the National Office of Vital Statistics)

that there seems to be a slightly lower infant mortality rate in rural areas than in urban districts. For this purpose the Office applied the "old" definition of urban, or the one that figured in the 1920, 1930, and 1940 censuses and that was used somewhat for comparative purposes in the 1950 tabulations. In addition all counties were classified as "metropolitan" or "nonmetropolitan" and the indexes computed separately for the rural and urban portions of each. Consider the principal results for the year 1955. At that time the rate in the urban districts was 26.6, that in the rural areas 26.2, a minor difference. Moreover, although for the urban white population the index was 23.6 and that for the rural white population 23.4, among the nonwhite population the rural rate was the higher of the two, with the exact indexes being 41.9 and 44.5, respectively. If, however, the data are refined by making the comparisons separately for the "metropolitan" and "nonmetropolitan" counties, the indexes for the rural segment of the population are consistently lower than those for the urban part. Thus in the former the infant mortality rates for the urban and rural populations, respectively, are as follows: total population, 25.7 and 22.6; white population, 22.9 and 21.8; and nonwhite population, 39.8 and 37.7. And in the latter the comparable indexes are as follows: total population, 29.1 and 25.0; white population, 26.2 and 24.3; and nonwhite population, 50.1 and 45.9. Furthermore, in thirty of the forty-eight states in 1955 the reported infant mortality rates for the urban population were higher than those for the rural. Nevertheless, it should be indicated, that imperfections in the data, such as underregistration of births and failure to assign cases properly according to the residence of the mother, would have the effect of inflating the urban rates and deflating the rural. Probably the only sound conclusion to be drawn is that there either is no differential, or that the infant mortality rate in the rural districts is slightly lower than that in the urban.

The materials charted in Figure 71 seem to indicate that there are some significant state-to-state variations in infant mortality rates, but that it is difficult to combine them into a regional pattern. Thus, for the white population alone, Utah and Idaho rank at the end of the scale representing the lowest infant mortality rates, whereas their close neighbors New Mexico, Colorado, and Arizona are at the other extreme. In this case, however, the presence of sizeable Spanish-American populations in the states in the southern part of the Rocky Mountain region probably accounts for most of the difference. Similarly, in the New England division Connecticut and Massachusetts rival Utah and Idaho for the most favorable positions in the list, whereas Vermont and New Hampshire are among the states with the highest reported infant mortality rates. Likewise, the rates for the white populations of some southern states such as North Carolina, Louisiana, Georgia, Florida, and Arkansas are substantially lower than that for the nation as a whole, whereas those for Kentucky, Texas, Tennessee, and South Carolina are significantly higher. The magnitude of these differences and the factors responsible for the variations deserve much more careful study than anyone has given them to date, and this is even more true of the obviously very great variations in the infant mortality rates of the nonwhite population. At the present time there seems to be no firm indication of any significant regional differences in infant mortality in the United States.

SUGGESTED SUPPLEMENTARY READINGS

Bogue, Donald J., *The Population of the United States*. Chicago: The Free Press, 1959, chapter 9.

Burrus, John N., *Life Opportunities*. Sociological Study Series, No. 3. Oxford: Bureau of Public Administration, University of Mississippi, 1951, chapters II, III, and IV.

Hamilton, C. Horace, "Ecological and Social Factors in Mortality Variation," *Eugenics Quarterly*, 2, No. 4 (1955), 212–223.

Hitt, Homer L., and Alvin L. Bertrand, *Social Aspects of Hospital Planning in Louisiana*. Baton Rouge: Louisiana Agricultural Experiment Station and Office of the Governor, 1947, chapter I.

Landis, Paul H., and Paul K. Hatt, *Population Problems: A Cultural Interpretation* (Second Edition). New York: American Book Company, 1954, chapter 10.

McMahan, C. A., *The People of Atlanta*. Athens: University of Georgia Press, 1950, chapter XII.

National Office of Vital Statistics, "Mortality from Selected Causes, by Age, Race, and Sex: United States, 1955," *Vital Statistics—Special Reports*, 46, No. 5 (1957), 111–121.

Smith, T. Lynn, and Homer L. Hitt, *The People of Louisiana*. Baton Rouge: Louisiana State University Press, 1952, pp. 164–183.

Wrong, Dennis H., *Population*. New York: Random House, 1956, chapter 3.

Chapter 17

Mortality Trends

THE FALLING DEATH RATE which has characterized most of the world during the twentieth century should be thought of as one of the most significant items in history. This striking evidence of mankind's growing control over the forces responsible for disease and death became apparent in Sweden, the Netherlands, and Denmark shortly after 1850; and before the end of the nineteenth century the mortality data for England and Wales, Scotland, France, Germany, and Italy made it clear that expectation of life definitely was on the increase in all of these countries. Furthermore, the evidence makes it appear that, by 1900, the curves showing the average duration of life in all these portions of Europe were moving upward at an increasing rate.[1] Probably the results of improvements in education and preventive medicine were having similar results in other portions of the Western world, but the statistical data needed to establish this in a satisfactory manner are lacking.

After 1900 spectacular increases in the expectation of life took place throughout most of Europe, in Australia and New Zealand, and in the United States and Canada; and in all of these the upward trend in the average duration of life has continued unabated well into the second half of the nineteenth century. In addition since 1925 the educational, health, sanitary, and medical measures which had worked such wonders in conserving lives in these portions of Western civilization were extended to or copied by peoples elsewhere in the world. The full impact of these efforts, as reflected in plummeting mortality rates, or increasing life expectation, has been felt for the most part only in the

[1] See T. Lynn Smith, *Population Analysis* (New York: McGraw-Hill Book Company, 1948) , pp. 270–271.

Table XLII. The Increase in Expectation of Life at Birth in Selected Countries During the Twentieth Century

Country	Period	Males		Females	
		Increase (in years)	Average per year	Increase (in years)	Average per year
Union of South Africa (white population)	1921 to 1946	8.2	.27	9.1	.37
Canada	1931 to 1951	5.2	.26	7.0	.35
United States	1901 to 1950	17.6	.36	20.3	.41
India	1900 to 1945	9.8	.22	7.7	.17
Japan	1923 to 1955	21.8	.68	25.2	.79
Austria	1903 to 1950	22.8	.48	25.9	.55
Denmark	1903 to 1948	14.9	.33	13.9	.31
France	1900 to 1950	18.3	.37	20.6	.42
Netherlands	1905 to 1951	19.6	.43	19.5	.42
Norway	1906 to 1948	14.4	.34	15.0	.36
Spain	1900 to 1940	13.2	.33	17.5	.44
Sweden	1906 to 1948	14.5	.35	14.6	.35
England and Wales	1911 to 1951	14.3	.36	15.6	.39
Australia	1906 to 1947	10.9	.27	11.8	.29
New Zealand (except Maoris)	1903 to 1951	10.2	.21	11.9	.25

SOURCES: Computed from materials in the United Nations, *Demographic Yearbook, 1953* (New York: United Nations, 1953), pp. 324–341; and *Demographic Yearbook, 1956* (New York: United Nations, 1956), pp. 734–743.

years since the outbreak of the second world war. Since midcentury the trends probably have been particularly sharp.

As it is necessary to stress again and again, the data needed for adequate study of mortality trends throughout the world are far from satisfactory. This will be evident to anyone who attempts to add substantially, with comparable materials, to the facts presented in Table XLII. Even so, however, the information in this compilation serves to substantiate the statements made above. In addition one may see from these data that during the twentieth century in such countries as the United States, Denmark, France, Norway, Sweden, and England and Wales the life expectation of the male population has increased annually by about one-third of a year; and that the gain among the female population has been still greater. Only slightly less pronounced have been the rates of increase in the Union of South Africa, Canada, Australia, and New Zealand, probably because in 1900 the expectation of life in these parts of the world already was so high that additional gains were more difficult to achieve. On the other hand, in Japan and Austria, the extension of the average duration of life has proceeded even more rapidly than in the countries enumerated above, due in the case of the former undoubtedly to the fact that the starting point was so low and that the data refer only to the period since 1923. Even in India during the first forty-five years of the twentieth century, expectation of life moved upward by approximately one-fifth of a year per annum.

For two reasons the present writer believes that increases in expectation of life throughout the world are likely to be fully as spectacular during the third quarter of the twentieth century as they were during the second. First, during the most recent intercensal period in the United States and other parts of the Western world there was little or no tendency for the rate of change to be less than it was in the decades immediately before. Second, in much of Africa, Latin America, and Asia the death rates from many of the transmissible diseases still are very high, and it seems reasonable to suppose that, shortly, these causes of death will be brought under control to a degree comparable with that already achieved in many parts of the world. Consider in this connection the mortality rates per 100,000 population from a few selected causes of death as reported for years since 1950 by recent issues of the *Demographic Yearbook* of the United Nations: *tuberculosis*, 211 for the colored population of the Union of South Africa, 89 in Brazil's federal district (almost the same as the city of Rio de Janeiro), 82 in Hong

Kong, 62 in Chile, 56 in Taiwan (Formosa), 56 in Yugoslavia, and 52 in Portugal; *typhoid,* 14 in Nicaragua, 12 in Mexico, 10 in Guatemala, 9 in the Dominican Republic, and 7 in Egypt; *malaria,* 280 in Nicaragua, 210 in Guatemala, 82 in the Cape Verde Islands, 67 in Mexico, 62 in the Dominican Republic, and 43 in Jamaica; *infections of the newborn,* 80 in Guatemala, 70 in British Honduras, 54 in Mexico, 49 in Nicaragua, 43 in Colombia, and 35 in Chile; and *pneumonia,* 282 for the colored population of the Union of South Africa, 229 in Chile, 172 in Mexico, 163 in Hong Kong, 156 in Guatemala, 138 in Barbados, 111 in Taiwan, 85 in Egypt, and 84 in Yugoslavia. Were data available for China, India, and many other populous parts of the earth it is likely that even greater opportunities for saving lives through the applications of modern sanitary, health, and medical measures would be revealed. Much of this work certainly will be done before 1975. The resulting decreases in mortality probably will result in keeping the rates of natural increase so high that fear of world overpopulation will continue for several decades to come.

Trends in the United States

The general nature of mortality trends in the United States during the twentieth century, the only period for which comprehensive information is available, may be observed easily from the data presented in Figure 72. The fact that the materials have been classified according to color, further subdivided by sex, and adjusted for changes in the age composition adds greatly to the reliability of any comparisons that may be based upon them. One should be cautious about attributing too much significance to the changes since 1950, due to the fact that population projections figure in the computations for those years; and even greater precautions should be employed in the interpretation of rates that may be calculated for any subsequent years until after the 1960 census results are available and thus make it possible for one to determine more accurately the population during each year of the intercensal period.

The most striking feature of these historical series is the rather consistent manner in which the death rate fell over the entire fifty-five year period under consideration. The major exception to this is the pronounced peak corresponding to 1918, the year of the great influenza epidemic. The various other fluctuations prior to 1930 should be discounted liberally, due to the fact that the data are for the expanding

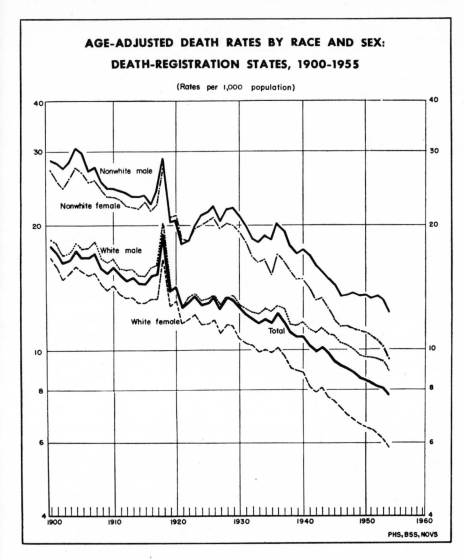

AGE-ADJUSTED DEATH RATES BY RACE AND SEX: DEATH-REGISTRATION STATES, 1900-1955

(Rates per 1,000 population)

Nonwhite male

Nonwhite female

White male

White female

Total

PHS, BSS, NOVS

Figure 72. Trends in the death rate in the United States, by race and sex, 1900–1955. (Illustration from the National Office of Vital Statistics)

death registration area. This gradually added data for the southern states and the Negro population, with somewhat different mortality patterns, to the national series, and this factor alone may very well be responsible for many of the gyrations. The 1937 peak probably is truly

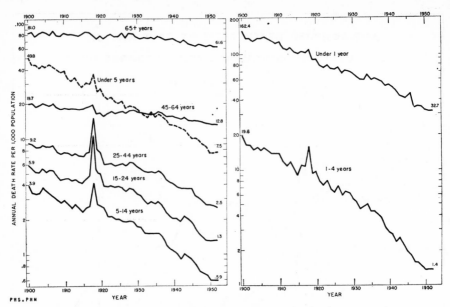

Figure 73. Trends in the death rates of principal age groups in the United States, 1900–1952. (Illustration from the U. S. Public Health Service)

indicative of a slightly higher mortality rate for the year, although the reasons for such an increase are not readily apparent. The striking feature of the chart is the sharp and consistent fall in the death rate from 1937 on except for the curve representing the mortality of nonwhite males. The fact that Negro males in increasing numbers left the areas in which they had been living and had to adjust to climate and society amid quite different surroundings than the ones to which they had been accustomed probably is largely responsible for this exception.

By consulting Figure 73 one may see at a glance the nature of the trends among eight important age groups into which the total population may be divided. From the materials presented in this illustration one should note especially that in 1952 the mortality rate of children aged one to four had been reduced to a level that was only 7 per cent as high as that prevailing in 1900, and that the one for children aged five to fourteen was only 15 per cent as high as it was at the beginning of the century. Similarly for the other age groupings represented on the chart, the 1952 death rates as percentages of those for 1900 are as follows: under one, 20 per cent; fifteen to twenty-four, 22 per cent; twenty-five to forty-four, 27 per cent; forty-five to sixty-four, 65 per cent; and sixty-five and over, 76 per cent.

Trends in mortality in the United States also may be gauged by the increase in life expectation that has taken place in this country since 1900–1902, the years for which our first life tables were constructed. Some of the most reliable and pertinent of the data, that for the white population subdivided according to sex, are presented in Table XLIII.

These materials give ample evidence of the phenomenal increase in the average length of life that took place during the first half of the twentieth century. For white males the expectation of life at birth increased from 48.2 years in 1900–1902 to 66.3 in 1949–1951, a gain of 18.1 or 37.6 per cent; and the increase for females was even greater, from 51.1 to 72.0, a change of 21.9 years or 42.9 per cent. Much of the increase was due, of course, to the saving of lives of infants and young children, but it is easy to overstress this point. It should be observed in Table XLIII that among both males and females the increase in life expectancy at age twenty and at age forty-five was considerable during the period to which the data pertain, and that there was some increase at age seventy as well.

Causes of Death

The primary factors underlying the trends in mortality are, of course, the various causes of death to which the fatalities are attributed. In studying these matters, though, it must be recognized that the changes or trends observed in the magnitude of the various specific causes are due to two sets of influences: (1) the antecedents making for an actual increase or decrease in the risks to life from any particular disease, ailment, or external cause; and (2) the changing age distribution of the population. Thus, in a period such as that between 1900 and 1940 the decreasing proportion of children in the population of the United States should have caused the total number of deaths from children's diseases to fall, even though such dangers had not been substantially reduced; and the aging of the population, such as has occurred in the United States since 1900, should increase the mortality from heart disease, cancer, cirrhosis of the liver, and other degenerative ailments even though a given person's risks from them had remained unchanged.

To facilitate the study of the trends in mortality from specific causes in the United States since 1900, Table XLIV has been prepared, and Figure 74 is reproduced. In this table the death rates for each of thirty-

Table XLIII. Trends in the Expectation of Life Among the White Population of the United States, 1900–1902 to 1949–1951, by Sex

	Average future lifetime							
	At birth		Age 20		Age 45		Age 70	
Year	Males	Females	Males	Females	Males	Females	Males	Females
1900–1902	48	51	42	44	24	26	9	10
1919–1921	56	59	46	47	26	27	10	10
1929–1931	59	63	46	49	25	27	9	10
1939–1941	63	67	48	51	26	29	9	11
1949–1951	66	72	50	55	27	31	10	12

SOURCES: Elbertie Foudray and Thomas N. E. Greville, "United States Life Tables 1930–1939 (Preliminary) for White and Nonwhite by Sex," *Vital Statistics—Special Reports*, 23, No. 13 (1947), 265; Thomas N. E. Greville, *United States Life Tables and Actuarial Tables 1939–1941* (Washington: Government Printing Office, 1946); and Monroe G. Sirkin and Gustav A. Carlson, "United States Life Tables: 1949–1951," *Vital Statistics—Special Reports*, 41, No. 1 (1954), 16–19.

Table XLIV. Specific Death Rates for Selected Causes: Death Registration States, 1900, 1920, 1940, and 1955

	Number of deaths per 100,000 population			
Cause of death	1900	1920	1940	1955
Typhoid and paratyphoid fever	31.3	7.6	1.1	0.0
Cerebrospinal meningitis	. . . .	1.6	0.5	1.1
Scarlet fever	9.6	4.6	0.5	0.1
Whooping cough	12.2	12.5	2.2	0.3
Diphtheria	40.3	15.3	1.1	0.1
Tuberculosis of the respiratory system	174.5	99.8	42.2	8.3
Tuberculosis (other forms)	19.9	13.4	3.7	0.8
Dysentery	12.0	4.0	1.9	0.3
Malaria	6.2	3.4	1.1	0.0
Syphilis	12.0	16.5	14.4	2.3
Measles	13.3	8.8	0.5	0.2
Cancer and other malignant tumors	64.0	83.4	120.3	146.5
Diabetes mellitus	11.0	16.1	26.6	15.5
Pellagra	0.0	2.5	1.6	0.0
Alcoholism	5.3	1.0	1.9	?
Intercranial lesions of vascular origin	106.9	93.0	90.9	106.0
Diseases of the heart	137.4	159.6	292.5	355.8
Bronchitis	45.2	13.2	3.0	1.9
Pneumonia and influenza	202.2	207.3	70.3	27.1
Ulcer of stomach or duodenum	2.7	3.6	6.8	5.9
Diarrhea, enteritis, and ulceration of intestines	142.7	53.7	10.3	4.7
Appendicitis	8.8	13.2	9.9	1.4
Hernia and intestinal obstruction	11.9	10.5	9.0	5.3
Cirrhosis of the liver	12.5	7.1	8.6	10.2
Nephritis	88.6	88.8	81.5	11.1
Diseases of the prostate (male only)	3.3	8.2	13.3	3.7
Puerperal causes (female only)	26.9	38.6	13.5	1.2
Congenital malformations, etc.	74.6	84.4	49.2	12.5
Senility	50.2	14.2	7.7	12.1
Suicide	10.2	10.2	14.4	10.2
Homicide	1.2	6.8	6.2	4.5
Motor-vehicle accidents	. . .	10.3	26.2	23.4
Other accidents	72.3	60.7	47.4	33.5

SOURCES: Forrest E. Linder and Robert D. Grove, *Vital Statistics Rates in the United States, 1900–1940* (Washington: Government Printing Office, 1943), pp. 258–273; and "Leading Causes of Death: United States and Each State, and Alaska, Hawaii, Puerto Rico, and the Virgin Islands (U. S.), 1955," *Vital Statistics—Special Reports*, 46, no. 8 (1957), 234–237.

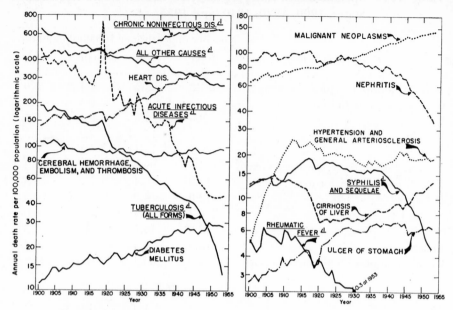

Figure 74. Trends in the death rates from specific causes, United States, 1900–1953. (Illustration from the U. S. Public Health Service)

three categories of causes are given for the years 1900, 1920, 1940, and 1955; and in this chart curves are given showing the variations between 1900 and 1953 in the death rates from fourteen groups of causes, including six groupings organized so as to equal the total for all causes. In studying these data it is well to keep in mind that the data for the years after 1925 probably are considerably better than those for the first quarter of the century.

The most striking of the changes or trends shown by these materials is the tremendous reduction in the mortality from tuberculosis. In the United States in 1900 respiratory tuberculosis alone was responsible for the death of 175 persons per 100,000 population, whereas in 1955 the corresponding index was only eight. Success in the control of this scourge was particularly rapid following 1940.

The control of acute infectious diseases also proceeded rapidly, with deaths from many once deadly bacteria being almost eliminated. The reduction in deaths attributed to influenza and pneumonia (from 202 per 100,000 population in 1900 to 27 in 1955) closely rivals the control of fatalities from tuberculosis. Typhoid fever, scarlet fever, whooping cough, diphtheria, dysentery, malaria, and measles, all responsible for sizeable numbers of deaths in 1900, had been reduced to statistically negligible proportions by 1955. Even syphilis, which as late as 1920 was assigned as the cause of 16.5 deaths per 100,000 population, figured to only one-seventh that extent in 1955.

Accompanying these accomplishments of preventive medicine and other safeguards to health, however, were substantial increases in the numbers and proportions of deaths attributed to heart disease, malignant neoplasms, ulcer of the stomach, and other ailments associated with aging. Indeed by 1955 heart disease alone was responsible for almost two-fifths of the deaths in the United States. In all of these increases, better reporting of the causes of death, and the substantial reduction in the numbers relegated to residual and poorly defined categories, probably are of some significance. Of much greater significance surely is the effect of the changing age distribution, but the fact that various revisions of the international list of causes of death figured in the tabulations makes it impracticable if not impossible to control this factor adequately. (Note in this connection the data for alcoholism and nephritis in Table XLIV. The former does not appear in the latest lists, and the data for the latter given in the table do not agree at all with those plotted in Figure 74.)

Finally, a few words about the trends in mortality from suicide, homicide, and accidents are in order. The increase in homicide, between 1900 and 1920, was due to the inclusion in the death registration area of southern states with their large Negro populations, among whom the incidence of this cause has been very prevalent.[1] Automobile accidents did not, of course, figure at all in 1900, whereas from 1925 on they have been prominent as a cause of death and even more important in the news about human fatalities. The curve representing mortality from this cause made its appearance about 1910, rose steadily to a rate of slightly more than 25 per 100,000 population in 1931, fluctuated about that level until 1941, dropped sharply during the years of the second world war, and has remained just under 25 from 1947 until the present.

[1] Charts showing the trends in the homicide and suicide rates of whites and Negroes in the United States during the period 1920 to 1940 will be found in T. Lynn Smith and Homer L. Hitt, *The People of Louisiana* (Baton Rouge: Louisiana State University Press, 1952), pp. 196–197.

The one for other accidents, on the other hand, dropped rather consistently between 1900 and 1955, except for sharp upturns in 1936 and during the second world war.

SUGGESTED SUPPLEMENTARY READINGS

Davis, Kingsley, *The Population of India and Pakistan.* Princeton, N. J.: Princeton University Press, 1951, part II.

Maclachlan, John M., *Health and the People in Florida.* Planning Florida's Health Leadership, No. 3. Gainesville: University of Florida Press, 1954, chapter 5.

Maclachlan, John M., and Joe S. Floyd, *This Changing South.* Gainesville: University of Florida Press, 1956, pp. 133–141.

Milbank Memorial Fund, *Trends and Differentials in Mortality,* Papers Presented at the 1955 Annual Conference of the Milbank Memorial Fund. New York: Milbank Memorial Fund, 1956.

Schmid, Calvin F., Earle H. MacCannell, and Maurice D. Van Arsdol, Jr., *Mortality Trends in the State of Washington.* Seattle: Washington State Census Board, 1955.

Smith, T. Lynn, and Homer L. Hitt, *The People of Louisiana.* Baton Rouge: Louisiana State University Press, 1952, pp. 183–204.

Statistical Office of the United Nations, *Demographic Yearbook, 1951.* New York: United Nations, 1951, pp. 9–17.

Stolnitz, George J., "A Century of International Mortality Trends," *Population Studies,* IX, No. 1 (1955), 24–55, and X, No. 1 (1956), 17–42.

Taeuber, Conrad, and Irene B. Taeuber, *The Changing Population of the United States.* New York: John Wiley & Sons, 1958, chapter 14.

Part Five

MIGRATION

Emigration and Immigration
Internal Migration

Chapter 18

Emigration and Immigration

MIGRATION IS THE LAST OF THE THREE factors affecting changes in the number and distribution of populations to be discussed in this volume. From a strictly demographic point of view it usually is considerably less important than births or deaths in effecting changes in the populations of nations or even of regions within a given nation. However, it frequently becomes the more important of the three primary factors involved in population changes within a given community, county, or state. Furthermore, from the standpoint of the social and economic effects upon the societies involved, the exodus of population from one area and the influx of migrants in another often greatly outweigh the influences exerted by variations in the birth rate or those in the death rate, even though the results of the changes in the vital processes should by no means be depreciated. Finally, international migration is much more a subject of expressed public policy and legal regulation than are either the fertility or the mortality of the population. This is not to say that the modern state does not assume a heavy responsibility in the control of transmissible diseases and that it does not in many other ways implement the general belief that life is better than death. Neither is it to deny that some national and state governments may maintain clinics for the dissemination of knowledge and the distribution of apparatus related to birth control. Nor is it to maintain that modern governments lack the legal enactments which make it a crime to practice infanticide or to engage in other forms of homicide. But it is to state flatly that all such attempts at direct regulation of the factors of fertility and mortality are slight in comparison with the legal provisions and the administrative machinery established to deal with immigration and emigration.

The Social Significance of Migration

Consider briefly some of the significant social and economic aspects of the movement of people from one place to another. Migration as such affects directly the physical constitutions and health of the populations involved. It has a powerful impact upon the structures and processes of the societies concerned, and it exerts tremendous influences upon the personalities of the migrants themselves. All of these are, of course, at a minimum in a nomadic society in which a wandering existence is the normal way of life; for then each group of nomads carries along with it all of the institutional accoutrements of its particular society. Consequently little social disruption is brought about because of the movement of persons in physical space, and the influences of migration upon human personalities are reduced to the minimum. Nevertheless, even under these circumstances the individuals involved must adjust to new or constantly varying physical surroundings. In addition, in nomadic societies man's devices for sheltering himself from the weather, along with all other portions of the protective shield of manmade environment or culture that the members of social groups place between themselves and the natural environment, are less highly developed and perfected than they are in more stable and sedentary groups. Hence the social repercussions of migration are at a minimum in societies where people are always on the move.

A wandering existence also sets definite limits upon the social structures that may be developed and put into use. For example, nomadic groups must necessarily be small—the limitations of securing food for man and beast dictate this. In turn, the limitation of numbers precludes the high development of specialization by tasks and industries and of any elaborate division of labor. Therefore, among such groups the economy has to be a simple one, based as a rule upon mere collecting, hunting and fishing, or herding. The elaboration of great systems of communication and transportation is impossible among people who are always on the move; a nomadic society could never develop the telephone, the telegraph, the radio, television, the superhighway, the automobile, and the aeroplane; and attempts to overcome the effects of earth's gravitational pull must take the fictionalized form represented by magic carpets or winged steeds instead of the intricate missiles, space platforms, and space ships such as are the concern of scientists and engineers during the second half of the twentieth century. Great and enduring institutions, universities, churches, and cathedrals, and many other familiar portions of the social structure of a great modern society all are made absolutely impossible by a wandering type of existence. It should hardly be necessary to say more to indicate that the role of migration is no small one, even in a nomadic society.

When a sedentary type of living is the normal situation for the bulk of the population, such migration as takes place is of even greater significance. Most important under these circumstances are the effects of migration upon societal processes and structures and human personalities. In a society where permanent settlements are the norm the movement of persons from one location to another results in the severing of the most significant social ties and bonds. Emigration entails disruption of established social structures in the communities of origin, and immigration introduces new and oftentimes conflicting ethnic and cultural groups into the social groups at the place of settlement. Therefore migration necessitates social and economic adjustments on the part of the communities in which the migrants originated, the ones to which they move, and personal and social adjustments on the part of the persons who move from one place to another. The community of origin, that into which the newcomer enters, and the migrant himself are never again the same. If the number of persons involved in the exodus or the influx forms a very large proportion of the total population, the repercussions may be paralyzing in their effects.

Tremendous are the influences of migration upon the individual and his personality. By moving from one place to another a person severs most of the ties and bonds that bound him to his old groups and gave him status in them. Through migration he sheds most of his social obligations, and through it, in turn, he is shorn of nearly all of the benefits and privileges of group association. For him position and status in the groups and classes of the new community do not come automatically, but he must find his place in them during a period of trial and testing. The migrant's status in a new community may be vastly different from what it was in the old, and the greater the role of inheritance (or caste) in establishing the person's position within the society involved, the more important this discrepancy is likely to be. Cut adrift from all his primary and interest groups, separated from his class identification, the individual must gain a place for himself in the new groups, and establish his social level at which he is to operate in the new community.

Since he is forced to abandon the role of "native" and assume that of "stranger," the process of becoming accepted and established in the new locality may be neither pleasant nor rapid.

Whenever migration involves a shift between radically different societies or cultures, and especially if a change of language is necessitated, a complete adjustment may be impossible for the migrant and even for his children. At best assimilation is a slow, difficult, and painful process. Thousands of immigrants to countries such as Argentina, Australia, Brazil, Canada, New Zealand, the United States, and Venezuela have never succeeded in becoming fully attuned to the new society. As long as they live, they bear some of the social markings of the foreigner and are unable to adapt themselves fully to the changed social surroundings. Many of them continue to live for the most part in the Old World. Frequently the effect upon the second generation is disastrous, the immigrants themselves remaining enmeshed in patterns and tensions of the old country, and the children going to all extremes in their endeavors to break away, throw off all identification with the heritage of their fathers, and to achieve full acceptance into the new. In portions of the world in which immigrants are less numerous, all of these effects upon the migrant himself and his offspring probably are even more pronounced.

Definition and Types

The verb *migrate* is given three shades of meaning in the New Merriam-Webster Dictionary as follows: (1) to move from one place to another, especially to move from one country, region, or place of abode or sojourn to another, with a view to residence; (2) to pass periodically from one region or climate to another; and (3) to transfer. In accordance with these definitions the term *migration* seems generally to be employed to refer to all movements in physical space—with the assumption more or less implicit that a change of residence or domicile is involved. Obviously the dictionary definitions and current usages are adjusted to a society in which settled living is the normal situation and in which nomadism is absent or largely lacking. In a society in which residential instability seems to be waxing, it is likely that more shades of meaning need to be developed. In sociology, where the practice of using migration and mobility (or even social mobility) as interchangeable terms is almost universal, this seems particularly essential. Additional attention is given to this point in the following chapter.

For demographic purposes it is useful to divide the subject of migration into two large parts, the first of which involves the changes of residence from one country to another and the second of which covers all kinds of migratory movements that take place within the boundaries of a given nation. The first of these is designated as *emigration,* from the standpoint of the nation from which the movement occurs, and *immigration* from the point of view of the receiving country. All of the intranational migrations conventionally are grouped together under the designation of *internal* migration. Emigration and immigration are discussed in the remaining pages of this chapter, and internal migration is the subject of the two that follow.

Sources of Data

Data on emigration and immigration leave a great deal to be desired. Despite the widespread interest in and concern about the subject, within the entire realm of population study the paucity of reliable information about international migrations of populations is matched only by the lack of comprehensive materials relating to internal migration. This state of affairs presents a curious paradox in a world which has succeeded in overcoming so many intricate problems connected with the definition, counting, and measurement of so many elusive phenomena.

The fact that the mass movement of population from one country to another was a highly important feature of world affairs during the first half of the twentieth century and well into the second half is so obvious that it hardly calls for comment. Merely to mention that approximately one out of every forty persons in the United States on January 1, 1915, had been living in his native European country on the corresponding date in 1913 is sufficient to demonstrate this point to the majority of those who will read these pages, but even an abbreviated list of recent mass dislocations of population through migration would have to include comparable movements of persons from other parts of the world to Argentina, Brazil, Canada, and Australia, to mention only four other large takers of immigrants. Even more significant to many in other parts of the world would be the uprooting of many millions of Europeans during the first world war; the flight from a Hitlerized Central Europe in the 1930's; the displacement of millions that resulted from the marching of armies, the shifts in factories, and the remaking of the maps of Europe and Asia during and immediately after the second world war;

the partition of India and Pakistan and the resulting mass migrations and transfers of population; the establishment and growth of the new nation of Israel; the flight of population from East Germany to West Germany; the Hungarian uprising and its aftermath; and the expulsion of the Dutch from the East Indies. Irrespective of whether migrations of these types are produced principally by developments in the homelands which lead to the flight of large numbers of persons from their native countries, or whether attractions in other nations are responsible for the movements, these gigantic streams of human migration are of vital concern nationally and internationally.

This is strikingly revealed through the organization of international meetings such as the conference on "The Cultural Integration of Immigrants" sponsored by UNESCO and held at Havana, Cuba, April 18–27, 1956. There for ten days the official representatives of the principal countries of emigration, those of the countries on the receiving end of the major streams of immigration, delegates from more than a dozen international agencies concerned with emigration and immigration, and social scientists representing the principal international organizations of economists, sociologists, and so on, discussed the nature, magnitude, and possible ways of easing some of the problems involved. In this conference it was abundantly clear that problems and policies relative to immigration are of basic concern to all branches of the modern state, executive, legislative, and judicial; to capital and labor alike; to church as well as to state; to those whose principal professional interest is in social welfare as well as to those engaged in manufacturing, transportation, agriculture, commerce, and banking; and to all of those who devote time to the intellectual activities connected with the social sciences, and particularly to sociologists and economists. Since national policies eventually must rest upon public opinion in the countries involved, the debates on immigration problems and policies which seem to be on the "regular agenda" of contemporary parliaments have widespread repercussions in local communities of which the nations are composed, and much of the stimulus for these debates comes as well from these same small localities.

In spite of all this, however, in most parts of the world the first steps still are to be taken towards the collection of comprehensive, reliable, informative and comparable data on emigration and immigration. It hardly is an accident, for example, that those responsible for the preparation of the *Demographic Yearbook* of the United Nations selected "natality" as the special topic to be stressed in two of the first eight issues of this indispensable compendium and have still to single emigration and immigration out for special consideration in one of the annual volumes. Indeed in the 1953, 1955, and 1956 editions of the *Yearbook* statistics on this highly important portion of demography do not figure at all. The 1948, 1949–50, 1951, 1952, and 1954 compilations do give such fragmentary materials as could be secured with respect to the following aspects of the general subject: continental and intercontinental migration (1948 issue only), major categories of departures and arrivals, emigrants by country of intended permanent residence, emigrants by age and sex, and immigrants by age and sex. In addition the 1952 volume includes data on refugees resettled by the International Refugee Organization and on refugees repatriated by this organization, for the years 1947–1951.

The 1954 edition of the *Yearbook* not only contains the most comprehensive set of materials extant to date, but it also includes an enlightening discussion of the problems inherent in the collection and collation of data on immigration and emigration, pertinent extracts from the recommendations adopted by the Population and Statistical Commissions of the Economic and Social Council, and some indications as to why the tabulations presented fail to meet the standards proposed in the recommendations. The student of population would do well to attend carefully to what is said in this volume with respect to the difficulties inherent in definitions and nomenclatures pertaining to the international movements of persons. The proposals set forth by this international agency are a far cry from those that sufficed in the days in which it could almost be assumed that data about persons debarking as third-class or steerage passengers from transoceanic vessels could be considered as statistics on immigration.

Two basic categories of compilations are included in these recommendations and in the tabulations resulting from them as contained in the 1954 issue of the *Yearbook:* (1) statistics on departures to other countries (except frontier traffic); and (2) statistics on arrivals from other countries (except frontier traffic). The first of these, in turn, should consist of four subgroups, namely, *permanent immigrants,* or residents, both nationals and aliens, leaving with intention to remain abroad for more than one year; *temporary immigrants* departing; *visitors* departing on completion of visit; and *residents,* both aliens and nationals, intending to remain out of the country for less than one year.

The second category also should be subdivided into four subgroups, as follows: *permanent immigrants,* that is nonresidents, either aliens or nationals,[1] intending to remain in the country for more than one year; *temporary immigrants,* or nonresidents intending to engage in an occupation for remuneration within the country for a period of less than one year; *visitors,* or nonresidents intending to remain in the country for less than one year and to engage in no occupation for remuneration; and *residents,* either nationals or aliens, returning after a stay abroad of less than one year. Obviously, it would be somewhat laborious, involved, and expensive to secure materials of this type even if well-trained international agents were stationed at all places of entry in order to take charge of all the bookkeeping involved. When this must be done voluntarily by all of the governments individually, working through such personnel as they station on their frontiers, and complicated by the frequently quite different sets of categories provided for on the visas required by each, the prospects do not appear very bright that satisfactory information will be readily forthcoming. Adding to the complications is the fact of the large illegal movement across international boundaries, of which the enormous influx of "wetbacks" from Mexico to the United States is merely one of the more-publicized examples. For years to come those working with international migration statistics probably will have to do the best they can to piece together fragments of information drawn from a variety of sources and highly lacking in comparability.

The best evidence that this is the case is gained from an examination of the materials on the international movements of population assembled in the 1954 volume of the *Demographic Yearbook,* which, as stated above, at the time of writing is the latest one to give any data on emigration and immigration. The five tabulations attempted were concerned with the major categories of departures and arrivals: 1948–1953, emigrants by country of intended permanent residence: 1950–1953, immigrants by country of last permanent residence: 1950–1953, emigrants by age and sex: 1950–1953, and immigrants by age and sex: 1950–1953, respectively. An examination of the most general of these, the classification of departures into permanent emigrants and other subcategories and of arrivals into permanent immigrants and other subcategories, suffices for present purposes. The only countries and terri-

[1] The United States does not include its own nationals in the immigrant category for statistical purposes.

tories of all those to be found throughout the world for which data are presented showing the number of permanent immigrants arriving for all or part of the years designated are as follows: Argentina, Australia, Austria, the Belgian Congo and Ruanda Urundi, Belgium, Brazil, Canada, Cuba, Denmark, West Germany (provisional figure for 1953, only), West Berlin, Israel, Italy, the Netherlands, New Zealand, Southern Rhodesia, Sweden, Switzerland, the Union of South Africa, the United Kingdom, and the United States. Even so, the materials for the United Kingdom pertain only to movements involving direct travel between that country and places outside Europe and the Mediterranean area, those for the United States are for travellers admitted for the first time for one year or more and former residents returning after a sojourn abroad for a year or more, those for Italy apply to Italian nationals, only, and so on. Obviously much remains to be done before comprehensive, accurate, and comparable statistics on emigration and immigration will be available even for the countries which are sending out the most emigrants and those receiving the most immigrants.

International Migrations and Their Magnitude

Great historical importance is attached to overseas movements of Europeans during the second half of the nineteenth century and the first quarter of the twentieth, especially to countries such as the United States, Canada, Argentina, Brazil, Australia, and New Zealand whose national destinies were so strongly influenced by the millions of immigrants they received.[1] More important for most contemporary demographic matters, however, are the tremendous shifts of populations from their native hearths to other lands brought about by the scrambling of national boundaries and the uprooting of millions of families produced by two recent world wars. This can best be considered by examining first the international movements of population in the interim between the first and the second world wars and second those that have taken place since the close of the latter. The tremendous dislocations of populations during the wars themselves hardly should be treated under the heading of emigration and immigration.

[1] Probably the nearest to a definitive compilation of the statistical data on emigration and immigration for this period that will ever be made is found in Walter F. Willcox, *International Migrations* (New York: National Bureau of Economic Research, Inc., 1929), 2 vols.

The Inter-War Period

In an earlier work,[1] all of the fairly reliable, available information on world immigration movements for the period between the two world wars was assembled and analyzed. Naturally the data were sadly inadequate. The most serious shortcomings were the lack of anything at all comprehensive and reliable for China, Soviet Russia, a large part of Africa, and some parts of Central and South America. However, for most of the European countries, the Union of South Africa, India, New Zealand, Australia, and much of North and South America the materials for the decade immediately preceding the outbreak of the second world war are fairly complete and reasonably accurate. The most trustworthy information is that for the years 1926 to 1936, inclusive, and the materials for this period are the ones that figure in the following discussion.[2]

Exclusive of Turkey and Russia there was an annual migration of about 1 million persons from the various European countries during the period 1926 to 1930. The onslaught of the great economic depression brought about a sharp decline in the number of persons leaving one European country for another, or for an overseas destination, and the number fell to slightly over 600,000 in 1931 and then to approximately 380,000 in 1936.

At the beginning of the period, in 1926 and 1927, some 700,000 persons annually were immigrating to these same European countries, either by leaving one of them for another or by returning to Europe from overseas. The economic depression greatly accelerated these movements, and the number of immigrants to European countries rose to above 1 million in 1930. Then the figure gradually declined until by 1936 the comparable figure was only 400,000.

The result attained by balancing European emigration and immigration during this period indicates a slight loss of people by the continent prior to 1930, an almost exact balance in 1930, an annual excess of immigrants over emigrants in 1931 and in 1932, and a return to a near balance by 1936.

Considerable significance is attached to the situation in the various countries. Italy was the source of far more emigrants than any other

[1] T. Lynn Smith, *Population Analysis* (New York: McGraw-Hill Book Company, 1948).

[2] For the detailed figures for each country see *ibid.*, pp. 302–304.

country during the eleven-year period under consideration. Between 1926 and 1936 more than 1.5 million emigrants left Italy. Poland, with 1.25 million ranks second, followed by Great Britain and Northern Ireland, France, the Netherlands, Spain, Germany, and Portugal, in the order named. The emigration from these six nations totaled 880,-768, 693,713, 476,053, 472,958, 361,439, and 317,025, respectively. On the receiving end France outranked all other European countries, it alone permitting the entrance during the eleven years of more than 1.14 million persons classified as immigrants. (Of course the admission of thousands of war refugees from Spain greatly swelled this figure.) Italy and Germany also were heavy takers, each receiving more than 1 million immigrants in the period under consideration, for which the inducements offered to get former nationals to return to their homelands by the nationalistic and belligerent dictators of these two countries must be given a considerable share of the credit. In third place is Great Britain and Northern Ireland, with 779,834 immigrants, and fourth is Poland with 735,951. Switzerland, which hardly figures in the list as far as emigrants are concerned (only 62,977 for the eleven years) is credited with taking 578,718 immigrants during the period, Spain with 503,902, Belgium with 365,303, and Portugal with 329,203.

Of most significance, of course, is the net amount of movement in these international and intercontinental exchanges of population. Of those European countries in which immigration exceeded emigration Germany led the list with a net gain of 638,736 for the period 1926 to 1936, followed by Switzerland (515,741), France (446,831), and Belgium (108,912). The country losing most heavily was Poland, with a net loss of 511,622 persons, followed closely by Italy (506,246), and then by Czechoslovakia (266,046), Yugoslavia (131,096), Great Britain and Northern Ireland (100,934), Ireland (94,914), Bulgaria (94,621), Romania (84,230), and Greece (77,059).

Unfortunately the data for most of the Asiatic countries are so inadequate that no significant conclusions may be established. The Philippine Islands, Japan, India, and Palestine, however, are exceptions to the rule, and worthwhile comments about the migration from and to each of them may be made. From the Philippines emigration was heavy in the years 1926 to 1936, totaling 326,095 for the eleven-year period. However, 360,331 immigrants were admitted during the same period, so that the balance shows an increase in population of 34,326 due to migration. From Japan likewise there was heavy emigration, or a total of 1,99,765 during the years under consideration. But for every two persons leaving one returned (a total of 103,966), and the net loss of population was only 95,799. There were 171,678 emigrants (mostly Arabs?) from Palestine in the years 1926 to 1936, inclusive. During the same period, however, a total of 222,350 immigrants was admitted by the small country. One may presume that most of these were Jews. As a result the net gain was 50,672. The flow of population from India was very large, involving almost 1 million persons classified as emigrants, but the reverse movement was slightly larger so that a population gain of 90,000 is to be credited to migration.

For Africa, only the materials for the Union of South Africa merit attention. This was an important area of absorption during the period 1926 to 1936, since it received a total of 975,505 immigrants during the eleven years. Emigration was negligible (54,161), so that the net recorded gain was 921,344.

Next let us consider those parts of the world most commonly thought of as havens for immigrants from other lands. Latin America long has been one of the principal takers of international migrants. But large numbers of persons also leave the Latin American countries, going either to other places in the New World or returning to their homelands across the seas. Fortunately, relatively good information is available for Argentina, Brazil, Chile, Mexico, Uruguay, and Venezuela, countries which contain the bulk of the Latin American population. Prior to 1930 this group of nations was receiving approximately 500,000 immigrants annually. Following 1930 the number dropped sharply to less than 300,000 per year, and then it rose to 336,000 in 1936. In 1926 nearly 240,000 persons were recorded as emigrating from the Latin American countries under consideration, and this figure rose steadily to 413,000 in 1930. The level dropped slightly during the depression years, and then rose again to 333,000 in 1936. As a net result of immigration and emigration the countries under consideration gained between 150,000 and 200,000 persons a year prior to 1930, after which the figure fell to 3,000 by 1936. The net gain for the period was greatest in Argentina (423,000), followed by Mexico (374,000), Brazil (308,000), and Uruguay (104,000). For the six countries taken together the net gain was 1,232,000.

Detailed information for the United States, which in the period immediately preceding the first world war had received up to 1.2 million immigrants in a single year (1914), are presented later in this chapter.

For comparative purposes, however, the following information is presented for the period 1926 to 1936: total immigration, 1,606,000; total emigration, 876,000; and net gain from migration, 730,000.

Sadly lacking, as far as the present writer has been able to ascertain, are comparable data for Canada, but Australia received a net immigration of more than 100,000 and New Zealand a net of about 24,000 persons during the eleven-year period under consideration.

All in all, emigration and immigration were much less important during the period between the two world wars than they were in the first fourteen years of the twentieth century. In part, and especially during the 1920's, this was due to the restrictions on immigration instituted by various countries. Later on, however, it was because of the great world-wide economic depression. Each year from 1932 to 1935, for example, the number of emigrants leaving the United States exceeded the number of immigrants.

The Period Following the End of the Second World War

For the use of the delegates to the 1956 world conference on "The Cultural Integration of Immigrants," mentioned above, the International Labor Office compiled data on the gross volume of immigration to the principal receiving countries, that is, Argentina, Australia, Belgium, Brazil, Canada, France, Israel, the United Kingdom, the United States, and Venezuela, for the years 1946 to 1954, inclusive. The information was presented in as concise and uniform a manner as possible, and where national statistics on the emigration of aliens were available, the I.L.O. gave supplementary information on net immigration. These materials, along with those on international migrations given in several issues of the *Demographic Yearbook* of the United Nations, are the sources of the statistical information presented in this section.

Between 1946 and 1954 immigration to the ten countries listed above totaled over 7 million persons, most of them of European origin. Significant numbers of immigrants coming from other parts of the world were received only by Israel, the United States, and Venezuela. In order of their importance in admitting immigrants the ten countries rank as follows: first, the United States, 1.7 million; second, Canada, 1.1 million; third, Australia, 900,000; fourth, Israel, 780,000; fifth, Argentina, 760,000; sixth, the United Kingdom, 440,000 net between 1946 and 1953; seventh, Brazil, 411,000; eighth, France, 390,000 persons, consisting of foreign workers and their families; ninth, Venezuela, almost 300,000 during the years 1950, 1951, 1953, and 1954; and tenth, Belgium, 290,000 between 1948 and 1954. The striking increase in immigration since 1946, over that in the period between the two world wars described above, is readily apparent.

By considering some of the data relative to the origins of the immigrants entering each of these countries, one may also obtain the fundamental facts relative to the countries that recently have been sending out the more significant numbers of emigrants. The 1,714,000 immigrants entering the United States in the years 1946 to 1954 is equivalent to 190,000 persons annually. Of these, the immigrants from Germany constituted the largest contingent (14 per cent), followed by those from Canada (12 per cent), those born in the United Kingdom (11 per cent), and those from Poland (10 per cent). Other large numbers came from Mexico, Italy, the West Indies and Central and South America, the Baltic countries, and the nations of eastern Europe.

During the nine years under consideration, 1946–1954, immigration to Canada averaged about 125,000 persons annually. Nearly one-third of the total originated in the United Kingdom, with Germany, Italy, the Netherlands, and Poland each contributing about 10 per cent. The only other significant numbers of Canada's immigrants came from the United States and from the Baltic countries.

Australia received approximately 100,000 immigrants annually during the nine-year period and enough more in 1955 to run the total well above 1 million. Almost one-half of these came from the United Kingdom and Ireland, with Italy contributing the second largest contingent, or 12 per cent. Another 21 per cent of the "new Australians" was made up of ex-citizens of various eastern European countries; and following 1950 there was a significant influx of persons from the Netherlands and the former Dutch colonies. After 1950 the numbers of German immigrants to Australia rose significantly, the figure for 1954 being 13,000.

In the years 1946 to 1954, inclusive, Israel and, earlier, Palestine received 787,000 immigrants, or an average of 87,000 per year. Thus the number of arrivals since 1946 considerably exceeds the Jewish population of Palestine in 1946, which was approximately 600,000. About 20 per cent of this immigration took place during the four years which followed the proclamation of the state of Israel in 1948. Approximately one-half of the immigrants came from various European countries (Romania, Poland, and Bulgaria, mainly); one-third from the

Asiatic countries of Iraq, Yemen, Turkey, and Iran; and 15 per cent from Tunisia, Algeria, Morocco, Libya, and other parts of Africa.

The volume of immigration to Argentina totaled 760,000 for the period under consideration so that the average per year is approximately 85,000. Italy alone supplied almost 0.5 million of the immigrants, or 58 per cent, and Spain 193,000, or 25 per cent. Germany was the country of origin of 2.1 per cent of the total, Poland of 2.1 per cent also, and Portugal of 1.5 per cent.

Gross immigration figures for the United Kingdom could not be determined by the International Labor Office, but on the basis of passenger statistics and other information its research workers estimated that net immigration for the years 1946 to 1953, inclusive, amounted to 440,000 persons. Of these, one-third came from Ireland and 27 per cent from Poland. The Poles figuring in the total consisted largely of the members of Poland's armed forces, almost 100,000 in number, who were resettled in the United Kingdom. Germany, Italy, and the eastern European countries were the sources of most of the other immigrants to England, Scotland, Wales, and Northern Ireland.

Brazil, which figures so importantly as a taker of immigrants during the last quarter of the nineteenth century and the first quarter of the twentieth, was somewhat slow in re-establishing the flow of population from other countries following the close of the second world war. By 1952, however, the annual intake of immigrants had risen to 85,000, and subsequently the figure remained above 70,000 per year. For the nine years under consideration the total was 411,000, or about 46,000 per year. Of these, 41 per cent came from the mother country, Portugal, 18.5 per cent from Italy, and 14.5 per cent from Spain. Germany, Lebanon, and the United States are the other countries which sent significant numbers of immigrants to Brazil during the years under consideration.

In the eight and one-half years following the close of the second world war, the period for which statistics are available, France admitted 388,000 immigrants consisting of nonseasonal workers and members of their families. This is the equivalent of approximately 46,000 persons annually. About 70 per cent of these people came from Italy, 9 per cent from Germany, and 6 per cent were from the "displaced persons" category.

During the seven years, 1948 to 1954, inclusive, Belgium received

294,000 immigrants, or some 42,000 per year. Of these, 54 per cent came from Italy, and other significant numbers came from neighboring France, the Netherlands, Germany, and Luxemburg.

Although meaningful data on immigration are not available for Venezuela for any years prior to 1950, the recent materials make it evident that this Latin American country has become a very important receiver of immigrants. The total for the four years 1950, 1951, 1953, and 1954 is 298,000 which indicates that the rate is approximately 75,000 per year. Of the immigrants arriving during these years, 27 per cent came from Italy, 21 per cent from Spain, and 7 per cent from Portugal, with persons from elsewhere in America constituting the bulk of the remainder. However, 9,800 came from the United Kingdom, 6,500 from the Netherlands, 4,500 from Germany, and 3,500 from France.

Immigration to the United States

To those who live in the Americas, immigration is a subject of more than usual interest, for to new nations in general and those of the Western Hemisphere in particular, immigration has been a basic factor in these societies' life histories. Except for the Indians, who are of minor importance numerically in the larger American nations such as Argentina, Brazil, Canada, and the United States, the inhabitants of the New World are either themselves immigrants or the descendants of persons who migrated from one of the other continents. Even in countries such as Bolivia, Chile, Colombia, Cuba, Peru, Central America, and Venezuela, the upper classes generally are composed of persons of European ancestry. The growth of population in the United States during the nineteenth century and the first quarter of the twentieth would have been much slower had there been no immigration; the ethnic composition of our people would have been quite different had we never permitted millions of immigrants to come to our shores; and the national origins and backgrounds of our inhabitants would still be changing radically had the Immigration Act of 1924 never been put into effect. Thus immigration has been so significant in the life history of our nation that it is well to consider briefly the highlights in the history of the phenomenon.

History of Immigration to the United States

The history of immigration to the United States falls rather logically into five distinct periods. The first of these embraces the years from the establishment of the first settlements to the emergence of the national state in 1783; the second, the period of free immigration, ended about 1830; the third, extending until 1882, was the period of state regulation; the fourth, beginning with the passage of the first national immigration act in 1882 and lasting until 1917 was a period of federal regulation with individual selection; and the fifth, the present stage of restricted immigration, began in 1917 when both the House and the Senate passed by two-thirds majority, over the veto of President Woodrow Wilson, the law whose purpose Wilson stated clearly was "restriction and not selection." Let us consider briefly each of these five eras in the history of immigration to the United States.

Those who came from overseas to the northern portions of the Western Hemisphere during the colonial period were in a situation vastly different from that encountered by later arrivals. They came to an unclaimed wilderness and not to an established nation with fixed boundaries, laws, well-grounded customs, and a definite status in the family of nations. Unfortunately, though, there are few reliable data concerning the number and origin of persons coming to the United States before the Revolutionary War. During this period the natural increase of population doubtless was very rapid; but on the other hand, there were large influxes of population through such important migrations as that of the Scotch-Irish during the early part of the eighteenth century. It is estimated that 20,000 of these Ulstermen left Ireland for America between 1700 and 1730, and it is known that 6,000 of them debarked in Philadelphia in the year 1729 alone. In fact it has been calculated that by 1750 they and their children comprised one-fourth of the total population of Pennsylvania.[1] Natural increase and immigration combined to produce a population of approximately 4 million at the time of the first census in 1790.

The era which began with the adoption of the federal constitution and ended about 1830 was one of free immigration. Rarely in the history of any nation has the freedom of ingress been so complete. During these years of infancy of the new nation the immigrants arriving were similar in kind and heritage to those who had preceded them. For decades there was little or no thought given to the advisability of limiting in any way the number or types of persons who should be permitted

[1] See Constance Lindsay Skinner, *Pioneers of the Old Southwest* (New Haven: Yale University Press, 1921), pp. 1–6; and John R. Commons, *Races and Immigrants in America* (New York: The Macmillan Company, 1907), pp. 31–32.

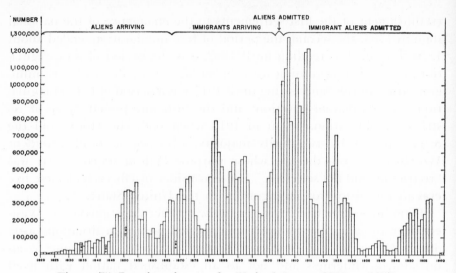

Figure 75. Immigration to the United States, 1820 to 1957.

to land. By 1830, however, enough agitation had arisen over asserted drawbacks to the system of free immigration that this year is selected as the closing one for this period in the immigration history of the period. Of the numbers of persons coming to our shores during these formative years we lack precise information. Official estimates place the number of persons admitted during the years 1783 to 1820 at 250,000, a figure thought by some to be too low.[1] From 1820 on data are available. (See Figure 75.) Even then, however, no distinction was made between visitors and those who came with the avowed intention of remaining. In any case the numbers were small and the arrival each year of a few thousand newcomers aroused little interest or concern on the part of the earlier arrivals. It was not until 1825 that the number of debarkations reached 10,000 per year. Thereafter immigration increased rapidly; and as the incoming tide swelled in volume, there arose a belief that the newcomers were partially responsible for some of the nation's pressing social and economic problems.

The regulation of immigration and emigration was not one of the functions attributed to the federal government when the constitution was adopted in 1787. Consequently, when widespread belief arose that absolutely unrestricted and unregulated immigration was undesirable,

[1] See Henry Pratt Fairchild, *Immigration: A World Movement and Its American Significance* (Revised Edition), (New York: The Macmillan Company, 1928), p. 57.

the agitation which arose was for control at the state level. Among all the factors leading to attempts by various states to control immigration none was more important than the tendency for paupers and criminals to immigrate either of their own accord or by means of subsidies supplied by those in the old countries who wished to be rid of them. As early as 1830 *Nile's Register* contained a bitter protest because the British ship *Anacreon* put off in Norfolk 168 passengers of whom more than three-fourths were said to be transported paupers. By 1838 the immigration of such indigents, large numbers of whom were duped into migrating by means of a subsidy [1] paid by the overseers in the home parishes in England, was of such moment that it was the subject of a voluminous report prepared by the then Secretary of State John Forsyth.[2] In addition competition from the immigrant workers with low standards of living, opposition to the Roman Catholic religion of the Irish who had begun swarming to the United States, and asserted clannishness on the part of the Irish and Germans all were effective in helping generate opposition to continued unrestricted immigration. They crystallized in a nativist political movement which made considerable headway in this country in the years immediately before the ones in which the conflict over slavery entered its final stages. The economic depression of 1857 followed closely by the Civil War pushed immigration problems temporarily into the background. In fact the low number of immigrants during 1862 was never again equalled until the depth of the great world economic depression in 1932. As soon as the war ended, however, the struggle over immigration policy was resumed, and in this the opposition to the Irish, widely publicized by the Molly Maguire disturbances in the coal-mining districts of Pennsylvania, and the alarm on the West Coast over the coming of the Chinese were major issues. The agitation eventually was responsible for the passage in 1882 of federal legislation which included laws excluding the Chinese and others designed to keep paupers, criminals, and those suffering from various diseases from gaining admission to the United States. By these acts the federal government definitively took control over matters pertaining to immigration and emigration, thus ushering in the fourth period in the history of migration to and from the United States.

The first epoch in the federal control of immigration was based on

[1] See on this point, Marcus Lee Hansen, *The Atlantic Migration, 1607–1860* (Cambridge: Harvard University Press, 1940), p. 281.

[2] Fairchild, *op. cit.*, p. 70.

the principal of individual selection. It began in a year (1882) in which the arrival of 788,992 immigrants, the highest to date, was recorded. But while the federal government was designing and placing into effect its immigration policy, the tide of newcomers was designed to move up to much higher levels. In 1884, Congress corrected a discrimination in favor of those arriving overland at our borders in comparison with those coming by sea; and in 1885 it was made

. . . unlawful for any person, company, partnership, or corporation, in any manner whatsoever, to prepay the transportation, or in any way to assist or encourage the importation or migration of any alien or aliens, any foreigner or foreigners, into the United States, its Territories, or the District of Columbia, under contract or agreement, parol or special, express or implied, made previously to the importation or migration of such alien or aliens, foreigner or foreigners, to perform labor or service of any kind in the United States, its Territories, or the District of Columbia.[1]

Thereafter, with debate over immigration policy annually on its regular agenda, Congress continued year after year to develop in piecemeal fashion legislation regulating immigration. Additions in 1887 and 1888 were minor, those during the last decade of the nineteenth century somewhat more substantial, and those in 1903 of considerable importance. The latter was the date when the exclusion of the mentally ill, beggars, anarchists, prostitutes, and procurers was decreed. Thereafter, year after year Congress was at the job of filling the gaps in the legislation, and it also was responding to tremendous pressures from its constituents in the states for laws that would restrict immigration. Specifically there was a widespread popular demand that immigration from southern and eastern Europe should be stopped.

The particular device proposed to achieve this goal was the literacy test. Thirty-two times between 1882 and 1917, an act establishing such a test was passed either in the House or in the Senate. Four times it was passed by both houses of Congress, only to be vetoed—in 1897 by Cleveland, in 1913 by Taft, and in 1915 and 1917 by Wilson. Finally, on February 5, 1917, over Wilson's second veto, the House and the Senate passed a bill providing for the exclusion of "all aliens over sixteen years of age, physically capable of reading, who cannot read the English language, or some other language or dialect, including Hebrew or Yiddish," but providing some exceptions for near relatives of citizens

[1] From Act of February 26, 1885, Section 1, quoted in *ibid.,* p. 113.

and for refugees from religious persecution. The final passage of this bill was a triumph for the forces advocating restriction of immigration, and it marked the end of the period of individual selection and the beginning of the fifth epoch, that of immigration restriction.

The literacy test soon proved ineffective, for after the end of the first world war, a heavy tide of immigration once more got underway. Thereupon the proponents of restriction quickly set about to secure the passage of legislation that effectively would reduce the numbers of immigrants to the United States and would limit those who did come largely to persons from the countries of northern and western Europe. The quota system, under which immigration has been controlled from shortly after the end of the first world war until the present, was put into effect temporarily by a 1921 act, and more definitively by one passed in 1924. The National Origins Plan provided for by the latter was designed to apportion a total of about 150,000 immigrants annually among the various countries in about the same proportions as natives of those nations were represented in the population of the United States in 1920. This was reworked to some extent by the Immigration and Nationality Act of 1952 under which the quotas presently prevailing were established. Roughly the formula employed allows to each country an annual quota of immigrants equal to one-sixth of 1 per cent of the number of persons born in that country who were residing in the United States in 1920.[1] There are no quotas restricting immigration of persons born in Canada, Mexico, Cuba, Haiti, the Dominican Republic, the Canal Zone, or in one of the independent countries of Central and South America; nor are there any for the spouses and children of such persons who are accompanying or following to join them in this country.

The Number of Immigrants

As has been indicated above, the data on immigration to the United States leave a great deal to be desired. Prior to 1820 no comprehensive

[1] Specifically, the total of 154,657 quota immigrants is assigned as follows: 149,667 to Europe, 2,990 to Asia (including the Philippines), 1,400 to Africa, and 600 to Australia, New Zealand, and the Pacific Isles. The European quotas, in turn, are distributed as follows: Great Britain, 65,351; Germany, 25,814; Ireland, 17,756; Poland, 6,488; Italy, 5,645; Sweden, 3,295; the Netherlands, 3,136; France, 3,069; Czechoslovakia, 2,859; the U.S.S.R., 2,697; Norway, 2,364; Switzerland, 1,698; Austria, 1,405; Belgium, 1,297; Denmark, 1,175; Yugoslavia, 933; Hungary, 865; Finland, 566; Portugal, 438; Greece, 308; Romania, 289; Spain, 250; Turkey, 225; Bulgaria, 100; Iceland, 100; and other 1,534. *Statistical Abstract of the United States, 1957,* p. 91.

Table XLV. Immigration and Emigration, United States, 1908–1956

| Year | Aliens admitted | | Aliens departed | | Migration balance † |
	Immigrant	Non-immigrant	Emigrant	Non-emigrant	
1908	782,870	141,825	395,073	319,755	209,867
1909	751,786	192,449	225,802	174,590	543,843
1910	1,041,570	156,467	202,436	177,982	817,619
1911	878,587	151,713	295,666	222,549	512,085
1912	838,172	178,983	333,262	282,030	401,863
1913	1,197,892	229,335	308,190	303,734	815,303
1914	1,218,480	184,601	303,338	330,467	769,276
1915	326,700	107,544	204,074	180,100	50,070
1916	298,826	67,922	129,765	111,042	125,941
1917	295,403	67,474	66,277	80,102	216,498
1918	110,618	101,235	94,585	98,683	18,585
1919	141,132	95,889	123,522	92,709	20,790
1920	430,001	191,575	288,315	139,747	193,514
1921	805,228	172,935	247,718	178,313	552,132
1922	309,556	122,949	198,712	146,672	87,121
1923	522,919	150,487	81,450	119,136	472,820
1924	706,896	172,406	76,789	139,956	662,557
1925	294,314	164,121	92,728	132,762	232,945
1926	304,488	191,618	76,992	150,763	268,351
1927	335,175	202,826	73,366	180,142	284,493
1928	307,255	193,376	77,457	196,899	226,275
1929	279,678	199,649	69,203	183,295	226,829
1930	241,700	204,514	50,661	221,764	173,789
1931	97,139	183,540	61,882	229,034	−10,237
1932	35,576	139,295	103,295	184,362	−112,786
1933	23,068	127,660	80,081	163,721	−93,074
1934	29,470	134,434	39,771	137,401	−13,268
1935	34,956	144,765	38,834	150,216	−9,329
1936	36,329	154,570	35,817	157,467	−2,385
1937	50,244	181,640	26,736	197,846	7,302
1938	67,895	184,802	25,210	197,404	30,083
1939	82,998	185,333	26,651	174,758	66,922
1940	70,756	138,032	21,461	144,703	42,624
1941	51,776	100,008	17,115	71,362	63,307
1942	28,781	82,457	7,363	67,189	36,686
1943	23,725	81,117	5,107	53,615	46,120
1944	28,551	113,641	5,669	78,740	57,783
1945	38,119	164,247	7,442	85,920	109,004
1946	107,721	203,469	18,143	186,210	106,837

Table XLV. Immigration and Emigration, United States (Continued)

| Year | Aliens admitted | | Aliens departed | | Migration balance † |
	Immigrant	Non-immigrant	Emigrant	Non-emigrant	
1947	147,292	366,305	22,501	300,921	190,175
1948	170,570	476,006	20,875	427,343	198,358
1949	188,317	447,272	24,586	405,503	205,500
1950	249,187	426,837	27,598	429,091	219,335
1951	205,717	465,106	26,174	446,727	197,922
1952	265,520	516,082	21,880	487,617	272,105
1953	170,434	485,714	24,256	520,246	111,646
1954	208,177	566,613	30,665	568,496	175,629
1955	237,790	620,946	31,245	634,555	192,936
1956	321,625	686,259	22,824	692,376	292,684

SOURCES: *Vital Statistics—Special Reports*, 9 (1940), 456; *Statistical Abstract of the United States, 1946* (Washington: Government Printing Office, 1946), p. 107; *Continuation to 1952 of Historical Statistics of the United States, 1789–1945* (Washington: Government Printing Office, 1954), p. 6; and *Statistical Abstract of the United States, 1957* (Washington: Government Printing Office, 1957), p. 92.
† Balance of total aliens admitted and total aliens departed.

records were kept, and from then until 1868 the statistics pertained only to aliens arriving from overseas. In 1868 the attempt began to assemble data on immigrants as such. In 1908 those entering the United States were classified as immigrant or nonimmigrant, and that practice has been continued until the present. With the year 1908 also begins the series of data pertaining to departures, with the materials recorded also divided into those for emigrants and nonemigrants.

Charted in Figure 75 are the materials for the years 1820 to 1957. This covers the entire period in which the migration of people to the United States was an important factor in our demographic processes. Observation of these materials enables one to identify the peaks and depressions in the movement of persons from abroad, with those recorded in 1855, 1874, 1908, 1914, and 1921 deserving special attention. From 1908 on, the period for which the materials are most reliable, the detailed figures also are presented in Table XLV. This table also supplies the recorded information about departures from this country, both those classified as emigrants and those counted as visitors who are leaving, along with the balance secured by subtracting the number of depar-

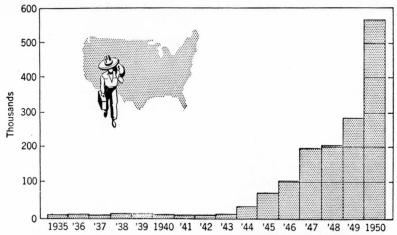

Figure 76. The magnitude of the "wetback" problem. Deportations and voluntary departures of illegal Mexican aliens. (Reproduced from "Migratory Labor in American Agriculture," Washington: Government Printing Office, 1951, p. 70)

tures from the number of arrivals. It is important to note from this table that at no time since 1924 has the number of arrivals registered exceeded by 300,000 a year the number of departures recorded. This emphasizes the point made above that the major importance of immigration in recent decades involves the social, economic, and political, rather than the strictly demographic aspects of the subject.

Before closing this section, however, it is important to indicate that these records are by no means a complete accounting of the migration of persons to the continental United States. Two additional movements of persons into the area lying between the Canadian border and the Mexican border and the Gulf of Mexico also must be noted. The first of these is the heavy influx of Puerto Ricans into New York City and other heavily populated areas of the country. Technically, this is not immigration at all, nor is the amount of such migration known. However, the 1950 census accounted for a total of 226,110 persons born in Puerto Rico who were enumerated in the continental United States, of whom 187,420 were in New York City, and the migration since then also is known to be considerable.[1]

[1] See U. S. Bureau of the Census, *U. S. Census of Population: 1950*, Vol. IV, *Special Reports*, Chapter D, Part 3, "Puerto Ricans in Continental United States," (Washington: Government Printing Office, 1953), p. 4.

Second, and probably even more important numerically, is the large flow of migrants without benefit of passport or visa across the border between the United States and Mexico. That this has reached enormous proportions is known from the numbers of such illegal entrants who have been deported (see Figure 76). It is likely, however, that co-operative efforts between Mexico and the United States designed to control the flow of this current of migration and to safeguard the conditions of work for the laborers who are given permission to enter (largely for seasonal work in agriculture) has been successful in reducing considerably the numbers of such "wetbacks" entering the United States in the years since 1950.

Immigration Policy

The immigration policies of a given country rarely are the result of careful, cool, deliberate, and systematic analysis of the problems and alternatives involved, nor are the specific provisions put into effect those that would prove most advantageous to it socially and economically. Rather the immigration policies of most nations grow out of rough and tumble struggle between political forces in an arena in which special interests of all kinds seek for what they consider to be the measures that will best serve their own ends. Some employers, for example, may use all means at their disposal to promote the adoption of immigration policies that seem to promise a more abundant supply of labor at lower wages than they otherwise would be obliged to pay. Labor organizations, on the other hand, are likely to oppose strongly proposals designed to have this effect. However, many labor leaders and members of the unions may fiercely champion measures that would permit the entry of greater numbers of people from the countries in which they or their parents originated or of the religious faith which they profess. Doctors, lawyers, dentists, and members of the other professions may personally advocate liberal immigration policies, at the very same time that their professional associations are effective in securing the adoption of provisions that made it extremely difficult, or even impossible, for highly trained immigrants to practice those particular professions. In general immigrants are welcome, provided they offer no threat of competition in the fields to which given persons or groups are occupied.

Along with these clashes of economic interests, many considerations of a cultural or religious nature are involved in the struggle. If the prospective immigrants are of a different religious faith than the majority of those in the country in question, their coming in any great numbers is likely to be viewed with alarm by the older settlers. In many countries the adoption of laws relating to the operation and control of cemeteries has proved especially effective in preventing the immigration of persons whose religious faith differs from that of the majority of those already in the country. Likewise if the suspicion arises that the newcomers will seek to preserve their language and other cultural forms, in preference to those of the country to which they are immigrating, bitterness and opposition are almost certain to arise. As a result of all of this the immigration policies arrived at through the democratic process may be far different than those that might be designed by a commission of impartial, competent, and well-informed statesmen who had only the welfare of the nation as a whole under consideration. This is probably the reason so many countries seek as immigrants primarily those in the category of agricultural laborers (the least skilled, least informed, and least organized portion of society), although any nation should shun, as it would the plague, any immigrants who would be satisfied permanently with the status of agricultural laborers.

For the reasons just indicated, a given nation may have at any particular time rather unsatisfactory answers to such problems as the following: How many immigrants shall be admitted annually? From which countries shall they come, and in what numbers and proportions? In the selection of the immigrants, which occupations and professions are to receive preference? Is there to be any restriction with respect to the localities in which the immigrants may settle and with respect to the proportions those of a given origin may constitute of the population of a given community? What restrictions, if any, shall govern the eligibility of individuals for admission from the standpoint of health, record of convictions for offenses against the law, and previous affiliations with various ideological groups? What preference, if any, shall be given those closely related to citizens of the receiving country, such as wives or husbands, children, parents, cousins, and so forth? What sponsorship, if any, shall be required for each immigrant on the part of those already citizens of the country?

SUGGESTED SUPPLEMENTARY READINGS

Bogue, Donald J., *The Population of the United States*. Chicago: The Free Press, 1959, chapter 14.

Davis, Kingsley, *The Population of India and Pakistan*. Princeton, N. J.: Princeton University Press, 1951, chapters 12 and 13.

Handlin, Oscar, Brindley Thomas, and others, eds., *The Positive Contribution by Immigrants: A Symposium Prepared for UNESCO. . . .* Paris: UNESCO, 1955.

Hutchinson, E. P., *Immigrants and Their Children, 1850–1950*. New York: John Wiley & Sons, 1956.

Kirk, Dudley, "Major Migrations Since World War II," in *Selected Studies of Migration Since World War II*. New York: Milbank Memorial Fund, 1958, pp. 11–29.

Landis, Paul H., and Paul K. Hatt, *Population Problems: A Cultural Interpretation* (Second Edition). New York: American Book Company, 1954, chapters 22 and 23.

Lawrence, Norman, *Israel: Jewish Population and Immigration*. U. S. Bureau of the Census International Population Statistics Reports, Series P-90, No. 2. Washington: Government Printing Office, 1952, chapters V and VI.

Murphy, H. B. M., and Others, *Flight and Resettlement*. Paris: UNESCO, 1955.

Phelps, Harold A., and David Henderson, *Population in Its Human Apects*. New York: Appleton-Century-Crofts, Inc., 1958, chapter 7.

Taeuber, Conrad, and Irene B. Taeuber, *The Changing Population of the United States*. New York: John Wiley & Sons, 1958, chapter 3.

Taylor, Carl C., *Rural Life in Argentina*. Baton Rouge: Louisiana State University Press, 1948, chapter IV.

Vance, Rupert B., "Prerequisites to Immigration: Elements of National Policy," in *Selected Studies of Migration Since World War II*. New York: Milbank Memorial Fund, 1958, pp. 75–88.

Willcox, Walter F., *Studies in American Demography*. Ithaca: Cornell University Press, 1940, chapter 20.

Chapter 19

Internal Migration

THE PRECEDING CHAPTER SHOULD HAVE MADE it clear that the student of population must be prepared to deal with immigration and emigration as factors in the changing number of inhabitants in a given country. In all that has to do with the changing number and distribution of population within a given nation, however, it is even more important that he have professional proficiency in handling various kinds of internal migration. This is because the role of internal migration in the increase or decrease of population in a given region, state, district, county, city, town, or minor civil division frequently is much greater than that of natural increase, whereas only in a few countries, for brief periods and under exceptional circumstances, does immigration or emigration become the principal factor in population change. In addition, poor as they are, the data on international migrations usually are better than those pertaining to the rural-urban exchange of population, state-to-state movements of persons, or any of the other varieties of internal migration. Therefore, because the poorer the data the greater is the skill one needs in order to make reasonable approximations, the student who works with population materials should leave nothing undone in order to become as conversant as possible with the theory and method that have been developed in the study of internal migrations. Finally, it should be recognized that the flow of population from areas in which the natural increase of population is rapid to those in which it is slow, such as the immense movement in the years since 1920 of persons from south of the Mason-Dixon line to sections north of it, may be the principal factor in keeping a radical redistribution of population among the regions from taking place. In brief, in all that has to do with the number, distribution, redistribution, and growth of population within a

444

country the demographer who is thoroughly conversant with the subject of internal migration will be more competent than the one who is not.

Types of Internal Migration

The varieties of internal migration are numerous, but a great deal of work remains to be done before they all may be classified into a number of clearly defined, mutually exclusive categories or types. The mere mention of some of the principal kinds of internal movements of population makes this abundantly evident.

During the nineteenth century the mass movement of people from the country to the city got underway on a large scale throughout much of Europe and North America, and in the course of the twentieth century this exodus from rural areas to urban districts has become rampant in all parts of the world. Indeed, even in the so-called underdeveloped sections of the earth, such as the twenty independent Latin American countries, many of them with huge, unoccupied areas still awaiting the fructifying effects of man's efforts, a rush of people to the cities took on great proportions before the outbreak of the second world war; and since the close of that epic struggle it continues at an accelerated pace. Indeed, since 1950 the migration of people from the country to the city well may be considered as the most important current demographic fact in that immense section of the earth's surface. As a matter of fact, throughout the entire world the phenomenal growth of cities which has taken place in the course of the last century was possible only because of the flow of population from the rural to the urban districts. It is not too much to say that the continuous migration of population from farm to city is one of the primary characteristics of Western civilization, and that this feature presently is one of those being copied most widely by societies in other parts of the world. Certainly it is the most extensive and significant of all the varieties of internal migration.

In many parts of the earth the pushing forward of the frontier still looms large in national affairs. The gradual process that in the United States edged settlement forward from the Atlantic to the Pacific in the course of two centuries, mostly in the nineteenth, has its parallels elsewhere. The westward and northwestward trend of settlement in Canada, the push to the north in Australia, the "march to the west" in Brazil, the advancement of settlement down the slopes of the eastern Cordillera and out into the heavily forested Montaña in Peru, a comparable edging down to and out on the plains at the base of the Andes in

Colombia, the surge of population from the high sierras down into the coastal plain in Ecuador, and the crowding of Argentine settlers northward into the Chaco are only a few of the important cases of contemporary expansions of the frontier. If the facts were known, undoubtedly remarkable extensions of settlement would be discovered within the boundaries of the Soviet Union.

Nor is the mass movement of people from a region, whether propelled by unbearable circumstances in their old locations or attracted by brighter prospects of a new home, to be relegated merely to the realm of history. The depopulation of the Great Plains area of the United States, so greatly dramatized by the "dust bowl" epic of the 1930's, did not end with the coming of the rains but continued through 1950 and thereafter; and the abandonment of southern plantations by hundreds of thousands of Negroes who were lured to the West Coast by jobs in war plants during the early years of the second world war has been followed by sustained heavy migrations of Negroes from the South in the decades that have followed. Such phenomena are parelleled in Brazil by the periodic flights from the terrific droughts that every ten or fifteen years make life practically impossible in a vast area in the northeastern portion of the country and by the long trek south to the cities of Rio de Janeiro and São Paulo by hundreds of thousands of northeasterners ever since the first road passable by trucks was put through from these cities to Fortaleza, on the northern coast, in 1951. Undoubtedly, these interregional movements of population in the two largest nations of the Western hemisphere could be matched with many others in various parts of the earth, and especially by interregional migrations of population in China, India, and the Soviet Union. Finally, in the United States at least, in recent decades and as the social status and financial circumstances of the aged have changed, there has developed a tremendous movement from one region to another of those in or near the retirement ages.

Nomadism is still to be reckoned with, even in countries such as the United States. At a time when civilization already is well within the atomic age, there are still in this country hundreds of thousands of persons who lead a wandering existence "following the crops." This is to say that these people are constantly on the move from one place to another in order to participate as laborers in the harvest of fruits, vegetables, and other crops. Furthermore, the high degree of specialization achieved in some industries, such as the building of bridges and other construction activities, serves to make seminomads out of large numbers of highly skilled workers. For example, the men who handle the steel-work on a new bridge over the Mississippi River at New Orleans, may find after a stay in the Crescent City of from two to three years that their company's next contract is in New England or on the Pacific Coast. Like-wise specialization and division of labor have reached the point that the technicians who instruct workers in Dallas in the use of a new machine during the first half of a year may be engaged in similar activities in Ohio in the fall.

Finally, in the agricultural districts of most countries there is always much shifting of people from one farm to another. In the United States this is particularly important in the areas in which the farms are large and in which sharecroppers or other kinds of agricultural laborers are numerous, but it also is prevalent where any considerable proportions of the farm operators are tenants or renters.

In the United States and in the Latin American countries the frag-mentary nature of the data determines to a large extent the categories into which internal migrations may be classified. Furthermore, there is little to be found in the literature that would lead one to suspect that the situation is substantially different in any other part of the world. Such sources as we do have make it possible for the student to advance our understanding of the subject somewhat by dividing these migra-tions into the rural-to-urban, urban-to-rural, state-to-state or region-to-region, and farm-to-farm varieties. Not all of these categories are mu-tually exclusive, but in this case pragmatic considerations must weigh heavily. It may be that a student with considerable ingenuity, abun-dant time, and much perseverance could with the existing data learn enough about migration from city to city to enable us to add this cate-gory to those listed above.

Problems on Which Research Is Badly Needed

From what has been said above, it should be evident that it presently is impossible to make comparative studies of the nature, types of, and relative importance of internal migration in various parts of the world. Before this can be done the last of the landmarks in population study, mentioned in chapter 2, must be reached and demographers must have had time to analyze and interpret the materials that are made availa-ble. Therefore, in lieu of an attempt to outline the nature and extent of internal migration in various countries, at this point are sketched a few of the problems in this field needing thoroughgoing attention by students of population around the world.[1] The aspects of internal migration which currently appear of paramount importance are as follows: (1) the measurement of the amount of migration to and from each of the states (departments, provinces, and so forth) , counties or comparable subdivisions, and cities of which a given nation is composed; (2) the nature of the selective processes at work in the rural-urban exchanges of population and in other types of internal migration, how these vary from time to time and place to place, and the relative importance of the factors associated with the variations; (3) the absolute and relative importance of the movement of operators and laborers from farm to farm within the various areas in a nation, and the extent to which this is associated with vertical social mobility and other social, demographic, and economic phenomena which may be regarded either as causes or effects of the shifting of families from one farm to another; and (4) the migrations of agricultural laborers, the number of persons involved and how it fluctuates, the principal routes followed and the seasonal ebb and flow of movement over each, and the social and economic effects of their migratory mode of existence, with respect both to the migrants themselves (especially the children involved) and the neighborhoods and communities through which they pass. Each of these is commented upon briefly in the following paragraphs.

At various places in this volume it has been necessary to mention that our inability to handle the migration factor adequately is the chief obstacle in the way of adequate population accounting on the community, county, and state levels. The amount of effort sociologists have put into demographic study since 1930, and the pre-eminence they have attained in the United States and elsewhere in the world as a result, make it unnecessary to say more about the necessity of being able to measure the migration to and from each significant political or administrative subdivision of a country. It should be stressed, however, that for most social scientists, as well as for people in general, the data for counties or comparable political subdivisions are by far the most useful of those

---

[1] Those who wish to consider briefly the more important currents of internal migration in a few selected countries should find helpful materials in the following works: Kingsley Davis, *The Population of India and Pakistan* (Princeton, N. J.: Princeton University Press, 1951) , chapter 14; Nathan L. Whetten and Robert G. Burnight, "Internal Migration in Mexico," *Rural Sociology*, 21, No. 2 (1956) , 141-151; and T. Lynn Smith, *Brazil: People and Institutions* (Revised Edition) , (Baton Rouge: Louisiana State University Press, 1954) , chapter XI.

gathered and published by the statistical agencies of the various countries.

The little we know about the general problem of selectivity of migration is due largely to the efforts of a few sociologists; and for some time
to come they and other demographers will need to concern themselves
with the broader as well as the particular aspects of this subject. As is
shown in chapter 13, most societies are characterized by rural-urban
differentials in fertility which result in the rural population producing
far more than its proportionate share of the oncoming generation. This
phenomenon has been pronounced in the United States all through the
nineteenth and twentieth centuries. Therefore any tendency whatsoever for migration from the country to the city to comb over the rural
population—taking the "better lives" and leaving those of less innate
ability or natural endowments—is fraught with serious consequences;
and one need not be partisan of an extreme zoological interpretation of
history in order to be convinced of its importance. Unfortunately, only
the surface has been scratched in the study of this subject, and those
who attempt researches along this line in the future will have to be
much more ingenious than those in the past have been, or it is unlikely
that any great accretions to knowledge on the matter will take place.

The few studies of the circulation of the farm population in local
areas are among the most significant contributions made in the study of
internal migration. Many more are needed, however, in various parts
of the world and with migration treated first as a dependent variable
(or effect) and then as an independent variable (or cause) in the analyses.

A report in 1951 [1] by the Commission on Migratory Labor appointed
by the President of the United States highlights the waxing importance
of a floating element in the population of the rural part of our nation.
The phenomenon is by no means confined to the United States, however, and the need for comprehensive data on the subject is patent.[2]

[1] President's Commission on Migratory Labor, *Migratory Labor in American
Agriculture* (Washington: Government Printing Office, 1951).

[2] For example, from the most ambitious attempt ever made to assemble pertinent
information on this and other aspects of agricultural labor in Asia [*Documentation
prepared for the Center on Land Problems in Asia and the Far East held in
Bangkok, Thailand, . . . 1954. . . ,* (Rome: Food and Agriculture Organization of
the United Nations, 1955)], one may glean the following. "The most significant fact
that strikes anyone attempting to discuss the conditions and problems of agricultural labour in Asia is the great lack of precise or even general information about
the subject. . . . only for India was there any data. . . ." (p. 159). This material,

Nevertheless, so great is the problem that even the task of assembling, collating, classifying, analyzing, and interpreting the fragments of information that may be available for various parts of the earth is not likely to be done unless the International Labor Office or some other agency of the United Nations or one of the great foundations, supplies all the financial and linguistic assistance necessary and makes it possible for a few of the students of population who have the requisite theoretical training and research experience to do sustained work on the subject.

Data and Indexes

As is mentioned repeatedly in this volume, every competent student of population always has uppermost in his mind the fact that there are only three primary factors influencing the changing number and distribution of the population, migration being one of them and births and deaths the other two. But, whereas for a nation such as the United States as a whole, and for the various state, county, or other subdivisions of which it is composed, it is possible to determine rather well the fertility and the mortality of the population, migration generally remains in the realm of the great unknown. Indeed, a substantial part of what is known about migration is inference based on materials derived from successive census counts of the inhabitants and a knowledge of the other two factors directly involved in the changes. For this reason currently the greatest need of contemporary population students is ways and means of getting current and reliable information about internal migration that will match the fertility and mortality data presently available to the analyst. Hence the discovery or development of adequate data and the perfection of significant indicators or indexes of migration are the primary problems confronting those interested in the general field of demography.

In the second half of the twentieth century, throughout the world, the data on migration are probably the most deficient in amount and quality of those relating to any major aspect of population study. As is well known, it was not until 1940 that the United States Census in-

---

that assembled in India's 1951 census, however, revealed the following significant dimensions of the subject. Some 44.8 million persons, or 12.6 per cent of the total population, were classed as agricultural laborers; and of these, 85 per cent were casual laborers, that is those working for less than one month for a given employer. (p. 160).

cluded a question on migration in the population schedule, and then the results obtained were hardly such as would enable one to answer most of the elementary questions about the subject. Another somewhat different attempt in 1950 yielded results that are little if any better. Specifically in 1940, persons in a sample of the population were queried about where they were residing on April 1, 1935, and in 1950 those in another sample were questioned concerning their residences on April 1, 1949. Voluminous tabulations have been published giving the results of these inquiries, and, undoubtedly, much could be learned about internal migration in the United States if they were adequately analyzed. However, because of their nature and the span covered, these materials cannot be employed, in combination with those on births and deaths and successive census counts of the inhabitants, for the purpose of drawing up a population balance sheet for a given state or county covering the decade 1930 to 1940 or that from 1940 to 1950. Nor is one even safe in assuming that the figures purporting to show the net flow of population between farms and urban and other nonfarm areas in the nation as a whole during the period 1935 to 1940 or during the twelve months preceding the 1950 census are accurate. This is because residence at the earlier date in each case is merely the person's report on where he was living five years earlier, for the 1940 materials, and one year earlier, for the later data, whereas residence at the census date was determined by the enumerator's own application of specified criteria. An analysis of the results makes it appear beyond doubt that (especially in 1940) many persons who actually had moved from farms and other portions of the fringes surrounding various urban centers to homes within the corporate limits of others were counted merely as moving from one urban center to another. The information gathered in these two attempts which does seem to be fairly reliable shows the amount of movement from one state to another during the stated periods and the absolute and relative importance of migrants (that is of persons who had moved from one county or quasi-county to another) in the populations of various states and some other subdivisions. The data secured in the 1950 census, indeed, were tabulated so as to show the numbers of persons who had moved from one house to another in the twelve months prior to April 1, 1950, and these materials were published not merely for the various regions and states but also for each of 443 "state economic areas" into which the nation has been divided for certain statistical purposes.

All of this amounts to a formidable amount of information, which, unfortunately has as yet received relatively little study. Perhaps the failure of students of population to make better use of this voluminous and expensive information is due to the fact that it is difficult or impossible to make it serve a useful purpose in connection with the demographic problems with which almost perforce they must occupy their time. It would appear that the best way of improving the migration data would be to make the question on the census schedule pertain to residence at the time of the preceding census for those who had passed their tenth birthdays and to place of birth of those under ten years of age and to ask the question of each person enumerated, similar to the procedure with respect to age, sex, occupation, and so forth. This would enable tables to be prepared for each state, county, and quasi-county showing the number of persons who had migrated to it in the interim between the two censuses. With such data at hand, along with the census counts and the materials from the registries of births and deaths, population students in all sections of the country would be in position to check fully the reliability of the information and, if the data were all correct, to determine the absolute and relative influence of each of the factors in population change. They also would be in position to estimate, with much greater accuracy than is now possible, the populations of states, cities, and counties (a service for which there is a tremendous demand in every state) in postcensus years. Of course, in many cases it probably would be found that formulas such as the following would fail to check out:

Population in 1950 plus Natural Increase,
April 1, 1950, to March 31, 1960, plus or
minus Net Migration, 1950–1960 = population in 1960.

If so, it would be obvious that something was wrong: one or more of the two census counts, the count of the number of births, the count of the number of deaths, the amount of net migration, or two or more of these items. Nevertheless this type of accounting has become imperative in the present stage of population studies, and only the migration data are needed in order to make it feasible. If such procedures reveal shortcomings in the materials presently available, they will also point the way to the necessary corrections or improvements in registration systems or enumeration techniques. As to cost, it is entirely possible that such materials could be supplied in substantially less space than was devoted to the publication of migration data in the reports of both the 1940 and the 1950 censuses.

In addition to the migration data, as such, certain other information secured in the decennial census in the United States, and likewise in the censuses of many other countries, are of great utility in the study of internal migration. Most important of these are the materials showing state-of-birth of the inhabitants in cross-tabulation with state-of-residence. For the United States such information has been secured and published in connection with every census from 1850 to 1950, inclusive.

One of our most useful bodies of data relative to internal migration in the United States is the series of annual estimates of the movement of population away from and to the farms of the nation. These data are assembled and published by the U. S. Department of Agriculture; the former Bureau of Agricultural Economics had the responsibility for the materials assembled for the years 1920 to 1949 and the Agricultural Marketing Service that for the estimates for 1950 and subsequent years. These data are secured along with and in the same manner as the facts upon which the crop estimates are prepared. This is to say that they come from thousands of farmers throughout the country who voluntarily fill in questionnaires for their own farms and those of their neighbors. For example, the estimates for 1955 are based upon information for 87,918 farms; those for 1956, 88,249 farms; and those for 1957, 94,882 farms. The materials from these sources are carefully assembled, analyzed, and weighted, so as to eliminate as many sources of error as possible. Even so, however, users are warned not to attach any great significance to variations from one year to the next because of the effects of sampling errors upon the calculations for any given year.

Much can also be learned about the geographical distribution and intensity of the movement from one farm to another through an analysis of the materials assembled each five years by the U. S. Census of Agriculture relative to the length of time farm operators have occupied the farms upon which they are located. The reports of every recent census of agriculture contain elaborate materials on this subject, but unfortunately students of population have made relatively little use of them.

As yet few indexes have been developed that are of any particular value in the study of internal migration. No doubt this is due in large part to the defective nature of the data and the fact that the attention of investigators has had to be devoted to ways of approximating or estimating the extent to which migration has been a factor in various demographic changes. Worthy of emphasis in this connection, however, is the method of estimating migration by comparing the number of persons in a certain age group at a given census, decreased by the expected mortality over an intercensal period for the specific age groups involved, with the same contingent at the next census. In the United States, for example, the number of persons aged forty to forty-four in 1940, decreased by the expected mortality of persons in these and progressively older ages over a ten-year span, may be compared with the number of persons aged fifty to fifty-four in 1950, with the difference being attributed to migration. This technique has been used by a number of students in order to add substantially to our knowledge of the currents of internal migration in the United States, their volume, and the direction in which they flow. Some of these demographers have used the life tables as the basis for computing the mortality to be expected; whereas others have maintained that the proportion by which a given contingent of the national population decreases during the course of the ten-year period in which it moves up the age ladder (as, for example, it ceases to be the group aged forty to forty-four in 1940 and becomes that aged fifty to fifty-four in 1950) is a better indicator of the importance of the mortality factor in the various parts of the nation. The former sets of computations are sometimes designated as *life table survival ratios,* and the latter as *census survival ratios.* Nowadays it seems rather well agreed that the second of these procedures is the more practicable and reliable, and it is likely that it will be relied upon rather heavily until such time as the necessary improvements are made in the collection of migration data.[1]

[1] For descriptions of the methodology and examples of the types of analyses in which it has been employed see, Gladys K. Bowles, *Farm Population—Net Migration from the Rural-Farm Population, 1940–1950,* Statistical Bulletin No. 176 (Washington: U. S. Department of Agriculture, Agricultural Marketing Service, 1956); C. Horace Hamilton, *Rural-Urban Migration in North Carolina, 1920–1930,* North Carolina Agricultural Experiment Station Bulletin No. 295 (Raleigh: North Carolina Agricultural Experiment Station, 1934); C. Horace Hamilton and F. M. Henderson, "Use of Survival Rate Method in Measuring Net Migration," *Journal of the American Statistical Association,* 39, No. 226 (1944), 197–206; Everett S. Lee, "Migration Estimates," in Everett S. Lee, Ann Ratner Miller, Carol P. Brainerd, and Richard A. Easterlin, *Population Redistribution and Economic Growth, United States, 1870–1950, I, Methodological Considerations and Reference Tables* (Philadelphia: The American Philosophical Society, 1957), pp. 15–55; Homer L. Hitt, "America's Aged at Mid-Century," in T. Lynn Smith (Editor), *Living in the Later*

Also deserving of consideration is the device of comparing the age configuration of segments of a population with that of the whole, and inferring that migration is the factor responsible for persistent concentrations or deficiencies such as the exceedingly high proportions of people in the productive ages in the urban population or the low percentage of persons in the productive ages in the rural-farm population. This, of course, entered into the discussions in chapter 6 above.[1]

The simple expedient of taking the population of a county (or other administrative unit) at a given census, adjusting the number by the natural increase (births minus deaths) for the ensuing decade, comparing the result with the population enumerated at the next census, and attributing the difference to migration eventually may become highly useful in the study of internal migration. This will only be the case, though, if birth registration is improved to the point that the number of births reported for a given county in the course of a decade is a fair approximation of the number actually born to mothers whose residences are located in that county. This definitely was not the case in the 1930's when this index was used in all seriousness as the principal basis for one of the most ambitious studies of internal migration ever made in the United States.[2]

Rural-Urban Migration

The migration of population from rural areas to urban districts during the second half of the twentieth century is taking place on a scale unparalleled at any other period of human history. However, in Western civilization the constant flow of people from the country to the city

---

Years (Gainesville: University of Florida Press, 1952), pp. 20–27; T. Lynn Smith, "The Migration of the Aged," in T. Lynn Smith (Editor), Problems of America's Aging Population (Gainesville: University of Florida Press, 1951), pp. 15–28; and T. Lynn Smith, "The Migration of the Aged," in New York State Joint Legislative Committee on Problems of the Aging, Growing With the Years (Albany: Legislative Document No. 32, 1954), pp. 69–80.

[1] Other examples are to be found in T. Lynn Smith, The Sociology of Rural Life (Third Edition), (New York: Harper & Brothers, 1953), pp. 76–80; C. A. McMahan, The People of Atlanta (Athens: University of Georgia Press, 1950), pp. 180, 190–191; and Homer L. Hitt, "Migration and Southern Cities," in T. Lynn Smith and C. A. McMahan, The Sociology of Urban Life: A Text with Readings (New York: The Dryden Press, 1951), pp. 332–334.

[2] See Carter Goodrich, et al., Migration and Economic Opportunity (Philadelphia: University of Pennsylvania Press, 1936), pp. 685–686, plate VIII-A, and passim.

has been going on for hundreds of years, and it is likely that the large-scale movement of persons from farms to cities also has been underway in other parts of the earth for centuries. As early as 1662, as indicated in chapter 2, John Graunt, "Citizen of London," concluded that there was constant and heavy migration of people from the surrounding districts to that metropolis. Thus as a result of his study of death certificates, and in a manner that would warm the hearts of modern investors in real estate, he observed "that, let the *Mortality* be what it will, the City repairs its loss of Inhabitants within two years, which Observation lessens the Objection made against the value of houses in *London,* as if they were liable to great prejudice through the loss of Inhabitants by the *Plague.*"[1] This ingenious pioneer gave details to show that in London there were many more burials than christenings, and then employed the same sort of reasoning that contemporary demographers are forced to rely upon in their studies of internal migration. Thus from the facts on fertility, mortality, and observed changes in the number of inhabitants, the founder of population study and statistics generalized that: "from this single Observation it will follow, That *London* hath decreased in its People, the contrary whereof we see by its daily increase of Buildings upon new Foundations, and by the turning of great Palacious Houses into small Tenements. It is therefore certain, that *London* is supplied with People from out of the Countrey, whereby not onely to repair the overplus difference of *Burials* above-mentioned, but likewise to increase its *Inhabitants* according to the said increase of housing."[2]

The data on fertility and mortality for the United States and other parts of the Western world also seem to demonstrate that, until very recently, cities would have dwindled away, as would have London in the sixteenth century, had the numbers of their inhabitants not been replenished constantly by migration from the rural districts. All through the nineteenth century and well into the twentieth it seems that the cities of Europe and the United States were sorts of colonies which had to be partially repopulated every year by the rural portions of these societies; and it is entirely possible that this situation still prevails in many parts of the world.

[1] The most convenient edition of Graunt's work is that edited by Walter F. Willcox, *Natural and Political Observations Made upon the Bills of Mortality by John Graunt* (Baltimore: The Johns Hopkins Press, 1939) . See p. 50.

[2] *Ibid.,* p. 52.

There are, of course, no comprehensive materials on the amount of movement from rural districts to urban centers in most parts of the world. Nor are we likely to have such information in the near future. By comparing the rates of natural increase in rural and urban areas and the growth of population in country and city, one is enabled to establish a firm basis for the conclusion that there is a heavy movement of people from the farms and villages to the urban districts. This proposition also gains substantial support from an analysis of materials assembled by the censuses of many countries showing state or province of birth in cross-tabulation with place of residence, especially where such information is classified separately for some of the principal cities, or in countries such as the United States, Brazil, Mexico, and Venezuela, in which the limits of the nation's capital city are roughly comparable to those of the federal district in which it is located. For example, the present writer has made such an analysis of the information for the Latin American countries, Kingsley Davis has reached similar conclusions by studying the materials for India and Pakistan,[1] and Irene Barnes Taeuber has demonstrated in similar ways the importance of the migration from the rural districts to towns and cities in Japan.[2]

For the United States for the years 1920 to the present the annual estimates made by some of the divisions of the U. S. Department of Agriculture are available. By analyzing them we can obtain considerable understanding about the rural-urban exchange of population in this country over a period of almost forty years. To begin with it is well to know the annual flow of migrations from farm to nonfarm areas and vice versa. Accordingly, Table XLVI was prepared. It will be observed that shortly after the close of the first world war, approximately 1 million persons left the farms for villages, towns, and cities in the course of a year. Probably the movement had been even greater during the war years, but of this we cannot be sure. With the onslaught of the economic depression in the rural sections of the country, which began early in the 1920's, the number of departures from farms rose to more than 2.25 millions per year, and it remained above 2 million annually until the impact of the great industrial depression about 1931, when it fell

[1] Kingsley Davis, *The Population of India and Pakistan* (Princeton, N. J.: Princeton University Press, 1951), pp. 114–115 and 134–137.

[2] "Population and Labor Force in the Industrialization of Japan, 1850–1950," in Simon Kuznets, Wilbert E. Moore, and Joseph J. Spengler (Editors), *Economic Growth: Brazil, India, Japan* (Durham, N. C.: Duke University Press, 1955), pp. 316–359.

Table XLVI. Annual Estimates of the Number of Persons Moving to and from Farms in the United States, 1920 to 1956

Year	Number moving (thousands) From farms	Number moving (thousands) To farms	Net movement from farms (thousands)
1920	896	560	336
1921	1,323	759	564
1922	2,252	1,115	1,137
1923	2,162	1,355	807
1924	2,068	1,581	487
1925	2,038	1,336	702
1926	2,334	1,427	907
1927	2,162	1,705	457
1928	2,120	1,698	422
1929	2,081	1,604	477
1930	2,046	1,985	61
1931	1,762	1,918	†156
1932	1,219	1,826	†607
1933	1,433	970	463
1934	1,310	783	527
1935	1,624	825	799
1936	1,553	719	834
1937	1,533	872	661
1938	1,368	823	545
1939	1,522	819	703
1940	1,254	696	558
1941	2,035	822	1,213
1942	2,940	824	2,116
1943	2,053	995	1,058
1944	1,180	816	364
1945	1,530	1,691	† 161
1946	1,458	1,062	396
1947	2,633	900	1,733
1948	1,463	1,112	351
1949	2,262	931	1,331
1950	1,660	564	1,096
1951	693	598	95
1952	2,309	425	1,884
1953	1,686	561	1,125
1954	635	544	91

Table XLVI. Annual Estimates of the Number of Persons Moving to and from Farms in the United States (Continued)

| Year | Number moving (thousands) | | Net movement from farms (thousands) |
	From farms	To farms	
1955	753	497	256
1956	2,695	459	2,236

SOURCES: Agricultural Marketing Service, *Farm Population—Migration to and from Farms, 1920–54*, AMS-10 (Washington: U. S. Department of Agriculture, 1954); and Agricultural Marketing Service, *Farm Population Estimates* for 1955, 1956, and 1957, respectively, AMS-80 (1955), AMS-80 (1956), and AMS-80 (1957) issued by the U. S. Department of Agriculture in 1955, 1956, and 1958.

The data for the years 1940 to 1953, inclusive, exclude movements to and from the armed forces. The materials for the years 1954 to 1956 pertain to the periods between April 1 of the years stated and April 1 of the following year.

† Net movement to farms.

to a level of approximately 1.2 million for 1932. From then until 1940 the yearly total remained around 1.4 million but as the defense and then the war programs became the dominant features of national life the movement from farms rose sharply to an all-time high of 2.94 million in 1942. (An additional 859,000 farm men and women were inducted into the armed services that year.) Migration of civilians from the farms also exceeded 2 million in 1943, after which it dropped considerably until, following the end of the war and demobilization, it moved up to another peak of 2,633,000 during 1947. Since that year the fluctuations have been considerable, with the lows of 693,000 in 1951 and of 635,000 in 1954, and the highs of 2,309,000 in 1953 and 2,695,000 in 1956 deserving special mention. For the thirty-seven year period the total of the estimated departures from farms amounts to the staggering sum of 64,045,000.

There is, of course, also a large movement of persons from nonfarm to farm territory. This has failed to amount to as much as 600,000 per year in the years since 1950, but it averaged almost 1 million annually during the four years immediately after the second world war and was 1,691,000 in 1945. Between 1922 and 1932, also, it was well over a million per year, and during the depth of the great economic depression (1930 to 1932) it was almost 2 million per year.

The net effect of the movement from the land into villages, towns, and cities was a loss of farm population during each of the thirty-seven years except in 1931, 1932, and 1945. This annual net movement from the farms has been particularly heavy since the close of the second world war, even though during some years such as 1951 and 1954 it was very small. In 1956 alone the total amounted to almost 2.25 million, the highest in the series and considerably above the previous record of 2,116,000 in 1942. In 1952, also, almost 2 million more people moved away from the farms than there were migrants in the opposite direction, and during both 1950 and 1953 the comparable totals were well over 1.6 million. During the thirty-seven years for which the materials are available, the farms contributed a net total of 25,868,000 persons to the nation's villages, towns, and cities. This is allowing each person arriving on farms to offset one of the departures; qualitatively this may not be justified, at least in the economic sense, for many of those who move to farms may already have passed the prime of life, whereas the great majority of those leaving the farms are just on the threshold of productive life.

The numbers and proportions of the farm population who migrate to villages, towns, and cities varies greatly, of course, from one area to another. Materials showing the ratio between the number of migrants during the decade ending in 1950 and the rural-farm population enumerated that year, for the economic areas of the various states, are presented in Figure 77. Strikingly apparent is the very heavy movement of people away from the farms of Louisiana, Oklahoma, the eastern two-thirds of Texas, the southern half of Arkansas, the western third of Mississippi, the central and southeastern two-thirds of Alabama, all of Georgia except the northern quarter, the central portions of South Carolina, and eastern Kentucky. Most of these districts are ones in which the farming areas are densely populated, so that the numbers of persons who participated in the exodus are large. Heavy rates of migration from the rural-farm areas also occurred in large sections of New Mexico, Arizona, Colorado, North Dakota, and Montana, but in these cases the numbers involved were much smaller. On the other hand, in a broad belt of territory extending from Maine to Iowa, including the entire state of New Jersey, and in the Pacific States, with the exception of southeastern Washington, the migration from the farms between 1940 and 1950 was comparatively light.

During the years 1920 to 1940 the natural increase of the farm population of the United States was high enough to allow for this heavy migration from the land and still maintain numbers on the farms. Thus

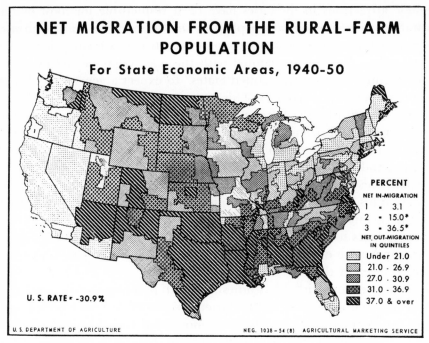

Figure 77. Net migration of persons from farms 1940–1950 as a percentage of the rural-farm population aged ten years and over in 1950. *Apparent rates of net in-migration are a result of problems arising from urban-rural definition changes between 1940 and 1950 and probably should not be considered reliable. (Illustration from the Agricultural Marketing Service, U. S. Department of Agriculture)

the enumerated rural-farm population was 31,393,262 in 1920, 30,157,-513 in 1930, and 30,216,188 in 1940. Since 1940, however, the large movement of persons from the farms has meant the partial depopulation of the rural areas, or one might say that this migration took away not only all of the natural increase but part of the "seed stock" as well. By 1950 the rural-farm population had fallen to 23,048,350, and by April 1, 1957 to 20,396,000.

The factors responsible for the mass movement on a world-wide scale of population from the agricultural districts into towns and cities also deserves comment, even though the task of identifying these and determining their relative importance is still largely to be done. In the United States it is generally assumed, and probably correctly, that economic attractions in the cities have been responsible for most of the rural-urban migration taking place in this country. In sharp contrast, Kingsley Davis [1] describes the economic situation in Indian villages that would lead "anyone acquainted with the mass flight of farmers from the blighted areas in the United States" to expect a general exodus of population from the villages. This does not occur, however, because the glitter of city life, the faster pace, the greater opportunities, and the broader social horizons seem to mean little to the villager. The peasant goes to the city merely to work, is not accompanied by his wife and family, and desires to remain only as long as it is necessary. "To the peasant the city is simply a bit of hell which fortunately is not eternal." [2] This analysis not only emphasizes the strictly economic nature of the factors responsible for the movement of people, mostly males, from villages to urban centers in India, but it also serves to emphasize the importance of social and cultural factors in drawing persons from the country to the city in the United States.

In connection with his studies of rural-urban migration in Latin America, the present writer has attempted to identify the broad general forces responsible for the mass movement to urban centers presently underway and also to set forth the influences of media responsible for specific persons deciding to abandon their home communities and neighborhoods for new ones in the towns and cities. The broad social changes in process in most Latin American countries which, in the last analysis, are the factors or forces responsible for the tremendous currents of migration presently flowing from the rural districts to the urban, were identified as follows: (1) the development and extension of modern means of communication and transportation, both those that link one country with another, and those that unite the various parts of a given country; (2) the first steps in the development of what may eventually become a system of universal education in each of the countries; (3) greatly increased contacts between Latin American societies and those in other parts of the Western world, and especially with those in which relatively strong middle-class standards and values and a high degree of industrialization have combined to produce exceptionally high levels and standards of living; (4) great social ferment among the masses, among the descendants of those who for centuries were so docile and tractable in the hands of the aristocratic elements of Latin

[1] *Op. cit.,* p. 135.
[2] *Ibid.,* p. 136.

American society; (5) the enactment in all of the Latin American countries of large bodies of social legislation relating to hours of work, minimum wages, security of tenure, paid vacations, severance pay, and so forth, all of which have been much more effective in urban districts than in rural, thus helping to broaden the differentials in working conditions in the two; (6) the growing conviction on the part of political and other leaders that industrialization offers the most promising solutions for a host of the acute and chronic problems with which their countries must deal; (7) the onslaught in some of the countries, and particularly in Colombia since 1947, of extended periods of serious internal strife which have caused hundreds of thousands of rural people to seek safety for their lives in towns and cities; and (8) some fundamental changes in the nature and functions of Latin American cities. In turn the following were set forth as being important in a long list of immediate influences or media which cause specific individuals to transfer their residences from rural areas to urban districts: (1) word-of-mouth reports and letters describing the advantages of life in the city which some earlier migrants take back or send back to their friends and relatives in the rural communities; (2) the location of almost all secondary schools in towns and cities, which induces many a large landowner to move his family to one of them so that the children may continue their education; (3) the "scouring" of the countryside by high-born city women in search of servants for their mansions; (4) temporary transfer by the absentee landlord of a few of his retainers, male and female, from one of his estates to his palatial home and grounds in a state or national capital; (5) recruitment in the rural districts of workers for construction and other projects in which foreign and national companies are engaged; (6) the glib promises made to the girls they meet in the farming districts by the young Lotharios who pilot the trucks, busses, and automobiles from the cities over the newly opened trails and roads throughout the back country; (7) the advice and counsel of the urban-reared or trained schoolteacher to the youths of the neighborhood in which she is employed; and, (9) at least in Paraíba, Ceará, and other parts of northeastern Brazil, the glowing pictures of city life painted by the truck drivers who are engaged in transporting families and their possessions, often as many as fifty persons per load, over the long, rough, and hot road to Rio de Janeiro and São Paulo. These are, of course, only examples of some of the dimensions that may be added to the study of rural-urban migration by observation and analysis of the materials for many of the so-called underdeveloped sections of the world.

SUGGESTED SUPPLEMENTARY READINGS

Bogue, Donald J., *The Population of the United States.* Chicago: The Free Press, 1959, chapter 15.

Bowles, Gladys, *Farm Population—Net Migration from the Rural-Farm Population, 1940–50,* Agricultural Marketing Service Statistical Bulletin No. 176. Washington: Government Printing Office, 1956, pp. 1–14.

Davis, Kingsley, *The Population of India and Pakistan.* Princeton, N. J.: Princeton University Press, 1951, chapters 14 and 15.

Heeren, H. J., ed., *The Urbanization of Djakarta.* Djakarta: University of Indonesia, Institute for Economic and Social Research, 1955.

Hitt, Homer L., "Peopling the City: Migration," in Rupert B. Vance and Nicolas J. Demerath (Editors), *The Urban South.* Chapel Hill: University of North Carolina Press, 1954, chapter 4.

Landis, Paul H., and Paul K. Hatt, *Population Problems: A Cultural Interpretation* (Second Edition). New York: American Book Company, 1954, chapter 20.

Lee, Everett S., Ann Ratner Miller, Carol P. Brainerd, and Richard A. Esterlin, *Population Redistribution and Economic Growth, United States, 1870–1950, I, Methodological Considerations and Reference Tables.* Philadelphia: American Philosophical Society, 1957, pp. 1–99.

Mauldin, W. Parker, and Donald S. Akers, *The Population of Poland.* U. S. Bureau of the Census International Population Statistics Reports, Series P-90, No. 4. Washington: Government Printing Office, 1954, chapter V.

McMahan, C. A., *The People of Atlanta.* Athens: University of Georgia Press, 1950, chapter XIII.

Petersen, William, "A General Typology of Migration," *American Sociological Review,* 23, No. 3 (1958), 256–265.

Royal Commission on Agriculture and Rural Life, *Movement of Farm People.* Report No. 7. Regina, Saskatchewan: The Queen's Printer, 1956, chapters V and VI.

Smith, T. Lynn, *The Sociology of Rural Life* (Third Edition). New York: Harper & Brothers, 1953, chapter 9.

Smith, T. Lynn, and Homer L. Hitt, *The People of Louisiana.* Baton Rouge: Louisiana State University Press, 1952, pp. 224–230.

Taeuber, Conrad, and Irene B. Taeuber, *The Changing Population of the United States.* New York: John Wiley & Sons, Inc., 1958, chapter 5.

Tarver, James D., "Bureau of the Census Data on the Selectivity of Migration from Farms," *Rural Sociology,* 22, No. 2 (1957), 162–163.

Chapter 20

Internal Migration (Continued)

MUCH CAN BE LEARNED ABOUT THE NET result of the interchange of population among the various states of the United States by an analysis of the state-of-birth data in the reports of the various censuses from 1850 to the present. The same is true through study of comparable materials assembled in recent censuses in other countries, such as those for India which were analyzed by Davis,[1] those for Mexico which have been studied by Whetten and Burnight,[2] and those for Brazil which have been utilized by Giorgio Mortara and other Brazilian scholars, as well as by the present writer.[3] Of course, these data give us no information, other than that of the state of birth and the state of residence, on the movement of persons from one state to another. The thousands of persons born in Illinois who spent most of their lives in Iowa and then moved to California as they neared the retirement ages are shown only as moving from Illinois to California, and Iowa does not figure one way or the other in the tabulations. Likewise, in Brazil the thousands of persons born and reared in the northeastern portion of that great country who made the long migration into the Amazon Basin during the attempt during the period of the second world war to rejuvenate rubber production in the area in which it originated and then later found their way to the south are shown merely as born in Ceará or one of the other northeastern states and residing in the Federal District, the state of São Paulo, or one of the other states.

[1] Kingsley Davis, *The Population of India and Pakistan* (Princeton, N. J.: Princeton University Press, 1951), pp. 108–109.

[2] Nathan L. Whetten and Robert G. Burnight, "Internal Migration in Mexico," *Rural Sociology,* 21, No. 2 (1956), 141–151.

[3] T. Lynn Smith, *Brazil: People and Institutions* (Revised Edition) (Baton Rouge: Louisiana State University Press, 1954), pp. 248–254.

State-to-State Migration

The manner in which state-of-birth and state-of-residence data may be used to chart the interchange of population between states over a sixty-year period, and thereby reveal the direction and intensity of important currents of internal migration that have been taking place within a nation, is illustrated excellently in the comprehensive series of maps prepared by Charles J. Galpin and T. B. Manny.[1] Consider, in this connection, the series of maps for California, New York, and Kentucky presented in Figures 78, 79, and 80.

The data on the interstate exchanges of population assembled in the 1940 census of population in the United States also may be used to determine the extent to which each state in the nation was sending out and receiving migrants during the five year period ending April 1, 1940. (See Figure 81.) More recently, the materials on the migrations occurring in the course of the twelve months preceding the 1950 census, and made available for analysis in 1956,[2] can serve as a basis for testing with comprehensive quantitative data many important propositions having to do with interstate migrations. For example, Hitt found that these data indicated that the eleven states in the southeastern region received more migrants from the other regions during the twelve months under consideration than they had sent to the other regions.[3] This is in sharp contradiction to conclusions for the periods 1940 to 1950 and 1950 to 1954 obtained by Maclachlan[4] as a result of a careful analysis of estimates of migration to and from each state prepared by the U. S. Bureau of the Census. Only two possibilities seem satisfactory as an explanation of the differences: (1) the twelve months ending April 1, 1950, may have been a period in which the interstate movement of population was quite different from that occurring between 1940 and 1950 and between 1950 and 1954; or (2) since the number of migrants in the census estimates is the residue that remains after the figure on natural

[1] *Interstate Migrations among the Native White Population as Indicated by Differences between State of Birth and State of Residence* (Washington: U. S. Department of Agriculture, 1934) .

[2] U. S. Bureau of the Census, *U. S. Census of Population: 1950*, Vol. IV, *Special Reports*, Part 4, Chapter B, "Population Mobility—State and Economic Areas," (Washington: Government Printing Office, 1956) .

[3] Homer L. Hitt, "Migration between the South and Other Regions, 1949 to 1950," *Social Forces*, 36, No. 1 (1957) , 9–16.

[4] John M. Maclachlan, "Recent Population Trends in the Southeast," *Social Forces,* 35, No. 2 (1956) , 149.

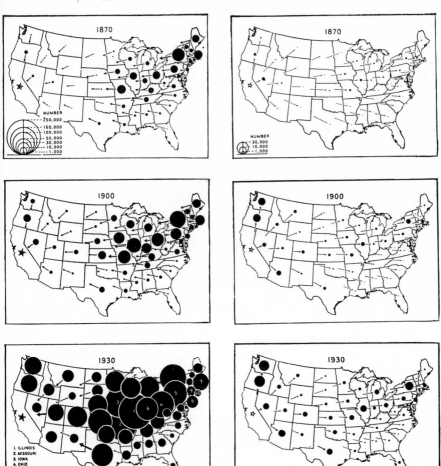

Figure 78. Native white migrants to California, by state of birth, and native white migrants from California, by state of residence, 1870, 1900, and 1930. (Reproduced from Galpin and Manny, "Interstate Migrations Among the Native White Population as Indicated by Differences between State of Birth and State of Residence," (Washington: U. S. Department of Agriculture, Bureau of Agricultural Economics, 1934, pp. 104–105)

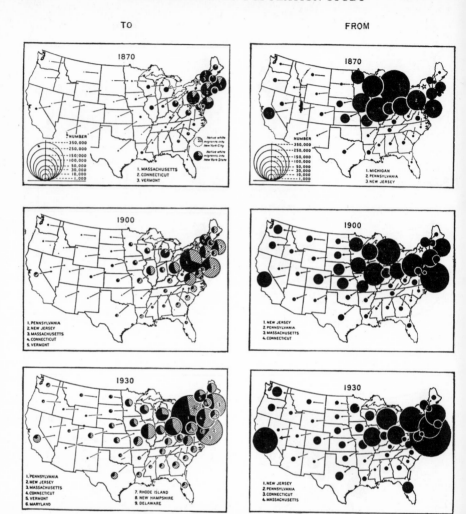

Figure 79. Native white migrants to New York, by state of birth, and native white migrants from New York, by state of residence, 1870, 1900, and 1930. (Reproduced from Galpin and Manny, "Interstate Migrations," loc. cit., pp. 20–21)

increase has been subtracted from the total change in the number of inhabitants, were the estimates of the population of a given state, such as North Carolina or Florida, in a postcensal year, such as 1954, too low, the estimate of the migration to that state also would be too low.[1]

[1] Hitt, *op. cit.*, p. 16.

TO   FROM

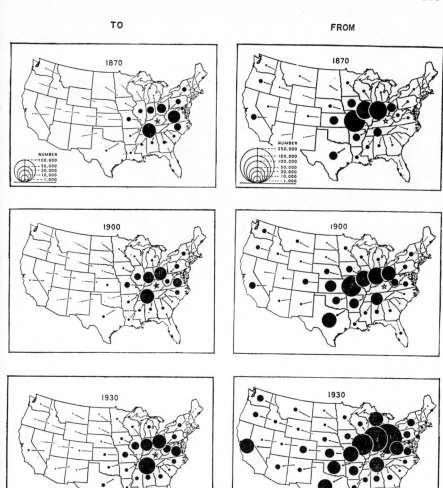

Figure 80. Native white migrants to Kentucky, by state of birth, and native white migrants from Kentucky, by state of residence, 1870, 1900, and 1930.

The fact that the Bureau of the Census in 1957 revised upwards its estimates of the population of Florida makes it appear likely that the second alternative is at least a partial explanation of the discrepancy. It should be remembered, though, that the reliability of conclusions based upon the migration data for a single year gathered from a sample of the population in connection with the 1950 census may be open to

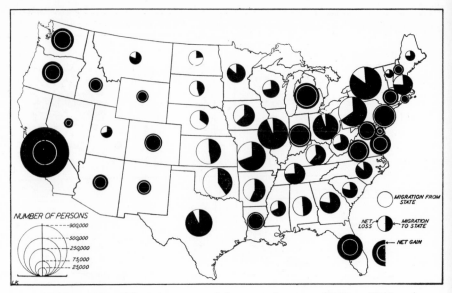

Figure 81. Migration to and from each state, 1935 to 1940.

serious question. This probably will occur to many of the readers of these pages as they study the nature and implications of the statements, in the following paragraphs, summarizing some of the materials on interstate migrations assembled in the 1950 enumeration.

As a basis for such study and reflection, Table XLVII was prepared. It shows merely the net migration to or from each of the states and the District of Columbia during the twelve months prior to April 1, 1950, according to the materials gathered and published in connection with the seventeenth census of the United States. Figures are given separately for the total, the white, and the nonwhite populations. Some of the results are hardly in line with expectations, nor with conclusions based upon other materials covering longer periods. That Texas and Florida received during the period under consideration many thousands more migrants from other states than they sent to other parts of the Union is hardly open to question. But that each of them had a net gain in population due to migration during the year approximately double that for California hardly seems possible. Yet the data indicate that, during the twelve months preceding April 1, 1950, Texas was the largest gainer of population through net migration from other portions of the United States, followed closely by Florida, and that California

Table XLVII. Net Interstate Migration in the United States During the Twelve Months Ending April 1, 1950, by Color

State	Net migration Total	White	Nonwhite
New England			
Maine	−8,125	−7,860	−265
New Hampshire	−5,090	−4,840	−250
Vermont	−1,345	−1,260	−85
Massachusetts	−12,970	−12,775	−195
Rhode Island	−2,400	−2,390	−10
Connecticut	−5,120	−4,690	−430
Middle Atlantic			
New York	−66,955	−63,995	−2,960
New Jersey	+8,250	+7,890	+360
Pennsylvania	−41,540	−39,520	−2,015
East North Central			
Ohio	−8,390	−7,945	−445
Indiana	+5,620	+4,500	+1,120
Illinois	−23,790	−21,910	−1,880
Michigan	−2,200	−5,385	+3,185
Wisconsin	−5,340	−5,300	−40
West North Central			
Minnesota	+745	+605	+140
Iowa	−1,725	−1,905	+180
Missouri	−11,410	−11,115	−295
North Dakota	−4,155	−4,270	+115
South Dakota	+695	+325	+370
Nebraska	−2,875	−2,655	−220
Kansas	−1,095	−830	−265
South Atlantic			
Delaware	−500	−655	+155
Maryland	+32,075	+30,200	+1,875
District of Columbia	−24,585	−25,825	+1,240
Virginia	+22,020	+22,100	−80
West Virginia	−8,780	−8,415	−365
North Carolina	+1,545	+1,220	+325
South Carolina	−5,865	−2,125	−3,740
Georgia	+400	+5,185	−4,785
Florida	+66,350	+58,395	+7,955
East South Central			
Kentucky	−13,640	−13,365	−275

Table XLVII. Net Interstate Migration in the United States (Continued)

State	Net migration		
	Total	White	Nonwhite
Tennessee	+12,155	+9,135	+3,020
Alabama	−15,570	−11,300	−4,270
Mississippi	−10,650	−5,670	−4,980
West South Central			
Arkansas	−17,520	−16,550	−970
Louisiana	+4,135	+3,130	+1,005
Oklahoma	+3,815	+3,670	+145
Texas	+68,885	+65,790	+3,095
Mountain			
Montana	+750	+825	−75
Idaho	+1,625	+1,750	−125
Wyoming	+780	+175	+605
Colorado	+10,665	+10,330	+335
New Mexico	+11,095	+11,120	−25
Arizona	+2,530	+2,090	+440
Utah	−555	−480	−75
Nevada	+830	+885	−55
Pacific			
Washington	+2,260	+2,005	+255
Oregon	+10,005	+9,895	+110
California	+34,960	+31,815	+3,145

SOURCE: Data assembled from U. S. Bureau of the Census, *U. S. Census of Population: 1950*, Vol. IV, *Special Reports*, Part 4, Chapter B, "Population Mobility—States and Economic Areas" (Washington: Government Printing Office, 1956), pp. 32–33.

was a very poor third. Next in order came Maryland and Virginia, both produced in large measure, no doubt, by the mushrooming of the suburbs of Washington, D. C.

If one turns his attention to the heavy losers of population through net migration, as evidenced by the data in Table XLVII, there appears little reason to question New York's right to first place or Pennsylvania's right to second. It requires a bit more credulity, however, to believe that the District of Columbia actually ranked third in this respect. More reasonable are the positions of Illinois and Arkansas, in fourth and fifth places, respectively.

If the white population is considered separately, the five states showing the largest increases for the year due to net migration are the same and they rank in the same order as those given above for the total population. Likewise New York, Pennsylvania, the District of Columbia, Illinois, and Arkansas, in the order named, were the ones losing most heavily by net migration to other parts of the nation. Quite different, however, is the list of heavy gainers and losers of population during the year produced by net migration of the nonwhite population. Among the states on the receiving end of such a movement Florida far outranked all the others, followed by Michigan, California, Texas, and Tennessee, in the order named, but all receiving approximately the same number. Among those sending more nonwhite migrants to other parts of the nation than they received from them, Mississippi led the list, closely followed by Georgia and Alabama, and with South Carolina and New York occupying the fourth and fifth positions, respectively. Did more Negroes and other nonwhite persons actually leave New York for other parts of the United States between April 1, 1949, and April 1, 1950, than moved in the opposite direction?

In general the materials in Table XLVII would indicate that a given state either lost or gained both whites and nonwhites through migration during the period under consideration. However, the exceptions to this rule merit attention. As the materials in this compilation show, the states that might be thought of as exchanging nonwhites for whites through migration are Virginia, Georgia, Montana, Idaho, New Mexico, and Nevada, with the numbers involved being substantial for Georgia. On the other hand, those exchanging white persons for nonwhites, that is receiving a net migration of Negroes and other nonwhites and sending out more whites than they got from elsewhere, are Michigan, Iowa, North Dakota, Delaware, and the District of Columbia, with the numbers being substantial in the cases of Michigan and the District of Columbia.

Before leaving the analysis of these materials, those which resulted from the second and most recent attempt to collect migration data as such in connection with the decennial census of population in the United States, it is interesting to note what they show with respect to the magnitude of the net flow of population between various states (including the District of Columbia). For this purpose the appropriate tabulations were analyzed for the purpose of identifying all the cases in which the interchange between two given states had resulted in a net movement of 5,000 or more persons from the one to the other during the twelve months under consideration. This endeavor indicated that

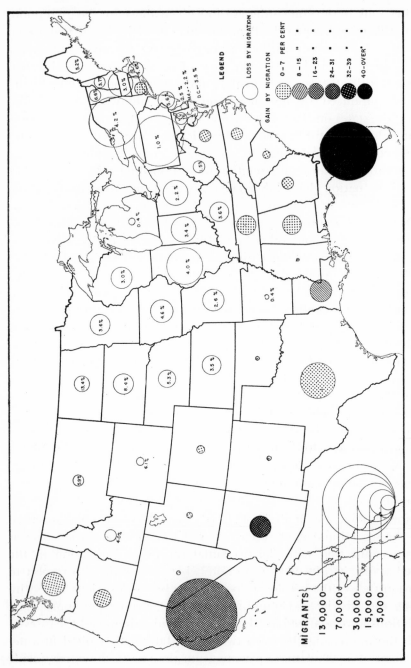

Figure 82. Estimated net gains and losses of persons aged sixty-five and over in 1940 by inter-state migrations during the decade 1940–1950, by states.

the net movement of 20,010 persons from the District of Columbia to Maryland heads the list, with one of 18,050 from New York to New Jersey ranking as a close second. A net migration of 16,230 from New York to Florida ranks third; one of 7,735 persons from New York to California, fourth; and one of 7,470 from Oklahoma to Texas, fifth. Other cases in descending order are as follows: from Georgia to Florida, 7,310; from Louisiana to Texas, 7,075; from Arkansas to Texas, 7,060; from Illinois to California, 6,945; from the District of Columbia to Virginia, 6,300; from California to Texas, 6,275; from Pennsylvania to New Jersey, 5,700; from Pennsylvania to Florida, 5,605; from Ohio to Florida, 5,435; and from California to Oklahoma, 5,135.

One particularly interesting aspect of the subject of state-to-state migrations is the movement from one section of the nation to another of persons near or in the retirement ages. Since comprehensive data on this subject are not directly available from the census compilations, except for the five years ending April 1, 1940, estimates of the amount of migration on the part of the aged population during the decade 1930 to 1940 were made as follows: (1) the population aged fifty-five and over in 1930 of each state was decreased by 39.9 per cent, the national average, in order to determine how many persons sixty-five and over there would have been in 1940 had there been no migration from one state to another; and (2) this figure was compared with the enumerated population in the ages sixty-five and over in 1940 and the difference attributed to migration. The same method later was used to estimate the migration between 1940 and 1950 of those who figured in the age group sixty-five and over in the 1950 census, and these were then mapped to show the absolute and relative gains and losses in the various states attributable to migration. (See Figure 82) Comparison of the materials for the two decades demonstrated that the currents of migration of elderly persons were about the same between 1940 and 1950 as they had been during the preceding ten years, except that the volume had greatly increased. Apparently there were 130,000 more persons aged sixty-five and over in California in 1950 than would have been the case had there been no migration during the decade ending that year; and for Florida the corresponding number is 66,400. In each case the figure is more than double the one for the years 1930 to 1940. As may be seen from Figure 82, Texas, Washington, and Louisiana are the other states to which the largest numbers of those in or near the retirement ages are attracted. On the relative basis, however, Florida is the one in which migrants make up the highest proportions of the state's elderly population, followed by Arizona, California, Louisiana, and Texas, in the order named. Also readily determined from the data presented in this illustration are the absolute and relative losses for the states, a majority of all those in the nation, from which elderly persons were resorting to the states on the Pacific Coast, Arizona, the Gulf States, and peninsular Florida.[1]

Farm-to-Farm Migration

The milling around of the farm population, especially in some sections of the country, is a third important variety of internal migration. Fortunately, for the United States a considerable amount of reliable data that may be used in studying this phenomenon is readily available in the reports of the agricultural censuses that are taken each five years. The significant information on the shifting about from one farm or plantation to another is that secured from the tabulations of the question on the farm schedule which asks for the "year when you began to operate *this* farm." The answers usually are tabulated to show for each color and tenure category the numbers of farm families who had been occupying their farms for less than five years, five to nine years, ten to fourteen years, and fifteen years or more.

For the United States as a whole, the average period of farm occupancy in 1950 was about thirteen years, or, the average year of occupancy for all farm operators was 1937. Full owners had been on their farms for an average of sixteen years, part owners for fourteen years, and tenants for only six years. Furthermore, the varying proportions of these tenure categories and other factors caused the index to vary greatly from one part of the nation to another. (See Figure 83.) Especially striking is the extremely short average period of occupancy in the plantation sections of the South, particularly in the Mississippi delta from Kentucky to Louisiana, where large proportions of all farm families are sharecroppers and where January 1 tends to be "moving day." In these sections the milling around of the farm population reaches excessive proportions;[2] but the data indicate that a great deal of shifting

[1] For more details on this subject see Smith, "The Migration of the Aged"; and Homer L. Hitt, "The Role of Migration in Population Change Among the Aged," *American Sociological Review*, XIX, No. 2 (1954), 194–200.

[2] Many excellent studies have been made of the excessive amount of shifting from farm to farm that goes on in the plantation districts of the southern part of the United States. Some of the best early work on this subject is that by Alfred H. Stone,

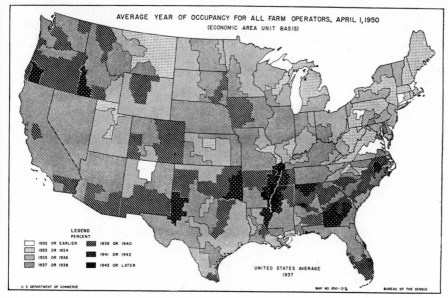

Figure 83. Variations in the length of time farm operators
had been occupying their farms in the United States, 1950.
(Illustration from the U. S. Bureau of the Census)

also goes on in much of Oregon and in parts of Washington, California, Iowa, and several other states. Most stable of all are the farm families in northern Virginia and in portions of Pennsylvania, Connecticut,
and Massachusetts.

One of the phases of farm-to-farm migration in which society as a
whole must be most concerned is that involving migratory agricultural
laborers. Prior to the second world war persons who "followed the"

"Plantation Experiment," *Quarterly Journal of Economics*, XIX (February, 1905),
271–275. Later important contributions in the long list that might be compiled are
Rupert B. Vance, *Human Factors in Cotton Culture* (Chapel Hill: University of
North Carolina Press, 1929), pp. 134–135, 151–154, *passim;* Charles S. Johnson,
Shadow of the Plantation (Chicago: University of Chicago Press, 1934), pp. 25–27;
B. O. Williams, "Mobility," in T. J. Woofter, Jr., and associates, *Landlord and
Tenant on the Cotton Plantation*, Research Monograph V (Washington: Works
Progress Administration, 1936), chapter VIII; Max R. White, Douglas Ensminger,
and Cecil Gregory, *Rich Land—Poor People*, Research Report 1 (Indianapolis:
Farm Security Administration, 1938), p. 4, *passim;* and Homer L. Hitt, *Recent
Migration into and within the Upper Mississippi Delta of Louisiana*, Louisiana
Agricultural Experiment Station Bulletin No. 364 (Baton Rouge: Louisiana
Agricultural Experiment Station, 1943).

Figure 84. The major currents of migratory farm laborers in the United States about 1938. (Illustration from the Bureau of Agricultural Economics, U. S. Department of Agriculture)

crops," farm laborers for whom being always on the move was a way of life, numbered between 200,000 and 350,000 according to the estimates of the most noted authority on the subject, Paul S. Taylor,[1] or an even million as estimated by the President's Commission on Migratory Labor.[2] It is believed that the number fell to about 600,000 during the war years, and then increased once more to more than a million.[3] Taylor charted the principal currents of this floating population (see Figure 84) as they were in 1938, but as far as the present writer has been able to determine no comprehensive attempt has been made in recent years to determine the direction and flow of the migratory streams. The report of the President's Commission cited above does specify that the "Texas-Mexicans" once shifted about mostly "within Texas and from Texas into the Mountain and Great Lake States. But recently its migrancy has increased both in scale and in the area through

[1] "Migratory Farm Labor in the United States," *Monthly Labor Review,* 44, No. 3 (1937) , 537–549.

[2] *Op. cit.,* p. 1.

[3] *Ibid.*

which it moves." Furthermore it indicates that "in the past two decades, there has developed another clearly identified migratory group
made up almost exclusively of Negroes who have their home base in
Florida. Many of these are ex-sharecroppers or their descendants from
other Southern states. They spend the winter in Florida and in the
spring and summer follow a northward course along the Atlantic shore
reaching through the Carolinas, Virginia, New Jersey, New York, and
even into Maine." [1] The conditions under which they work and live
frequently produce reverberations in the nation's press, and when
disasters strike, such as the repeated severe freezes in Florida during
the winter of 1957–1958, the distress among the workers and their families serves to call attention to some of the ways in which the large-
scale organization of agricultural enterprises is disadvantageous to the
general welfare. Then little support for the unemployed workers comes
from the employers' profits in earlier years, the community's facilities
are overtaxed, and the chief burden of tiding the workers over a difficult time falls upon state and national agencies.

In truth migratory laborers are a social class apart from the settled
communities amid which they move. Forced to dig and pick the crops
of others, poorly paid, frequently laid low by disease and infirmities,
usually lacking shelters that meet the minimum standards of protection and decency, forever on the move, its members are never an accepted part of any community. Working in one crop today, another
tomorrow, this rural proletariat alone makes possible the seeming efficiency of many large commercial agricultural operations, and it accounts for the most serious relief problems of many towns and cities. In
the words of the President's Commission on Migratory Labor:

Migratory farm laborers move restlessly over the face of the land, but they
neither belong to the land nor does the land belong to them. They pass
through community after community, but they neither claim the community as home nor does the community claim them. Under the law, the domestic migrants are citizens of the United States, but they are scarcely
more a part of the land of their birth than the alien migrants working be-
side them.

The migratory workers engage in a common occupation, but their cohe-
sion is scarcely greater than that of pebbles on the seashore. Each harvest
collects and regroups them. They live under a common condition, but
create no techniques for meeting common problems. The public acknowl-

[1] *Ibid.*, pp. 2–3.

edges the existence of migrants, yet declines to accept them as full members of the community. As crops ripen, farmers anxiously await their coming; as the harvest closes, the community, with equal anxiety, awaits their going.

. . . .

Migrants generally are easily identified as outsiders. Their faces are those of strangers and, for many of them, differences of color and other physical characteristics serve as badges of identification. Their heavily laden cars or trucks, packed with beds, cooking utensils, and furniture are easily distinguished from those of campers on vacation. Even their work clothes by material, style, or cut seem to indicate an outside origin. All along the way are those who take advantage of the migratory worker's helplessness. Professional gamblers, prostitutes, and peddlers of dope follow the work routes to obtain, each in his own way, a share of the migrant's money.

Residents tend to separate migrants from themselves in domicile and law, in thought and feeling. They assign special places to migrants seeking shelter, or leave them to go where their poverty and condition force them. Here they encamp in tents or simply under canvas supported by a rope strung between two trees or from the side of the car to the ground. They sleep on pallets, or on bedsprings or folding cots which some of them carry. Where rains are frequent during work season they find shelter in crude shacks. On farms they use what shelter their employers may provide.

The lines of segregation are further sharpened, particularly for Negroes, Mexicans, and Puerto Ricans by differences of skin color, stature, and language. For several years the Mexican Government declined to allow its citizens to go to Texas under the Mexican–United States International Agreement because of the flagrant social discriminations under which they had to live.[1]

The Selectivity of Migration

How do those who migrate compare with those who do not? Do those who leave the country for the city differ in significant ways from those who remain in the communities in which they were born? What distinguishing characteristics, if any, are possessed by those who participate in the back-to-the-land movement? Those who move from one state to another? Those who follow the crops? In a word, does migration select persons with any particular set of bio-social attributes or qualities?

These questions are of considerable moment, even though there generally is much more speculation than fact in the answers presented. Consider, for example, the implications of rural-urban migration if it

[1] *Ibid.,* pp. 3–4.

should be that there are any particular features or qualities, especially those having to do with innate or inherited characteristics, which distinguish the migrants from the ones who stay at home. That like tends to produce like is a biological generalization known to all. Therefore if those who migrate are more intelligent than the other members of their families, or if in any other way they tend to be the "cream of the population" or the "better lives," the substantial differences in the rates of natural increase in city and country are fraught with serious implications for the societies concerned. But in spite of the significance of the subject, it is still one of the portions of demography in which the glib phrase is most likely to take the place of the tested fact. To find in the sociological literature statements similar to the following is easy:

> No doubt rural decline from this cause has occurred sporadically for thousands of years, but it assumes acute forms in the United States because the double pull of city and frontier, propagated by schools and newspapers, has worked on our old rural population like a cream separator. In New England there are rural counties which have been losing their best for three or four generations, leaving the coarse, dull, and hidebound. The number of loafers in some slackwater villages of the Middle States indicates that the natural pacemakers of the locality have gone elsewhere to create prosperity. In parts of southern Michigan, Illinois, Wisconsin, and even as far west as Missouri, there are communities which remind one of fished-out ponds populated chiefly by bull-heads and suckers.[1]

More difficult to find, however, are reports of studies in which various possibilities have been tested with substantial and reliable quantitative data.

Before considering the specific characteristics for which migration may or may not be selective, it is well for one to have in mind that the type of migration involved no doubt has much to do with the attributes of the migrants. One could hardly expect the migrants who fled the "dust bowl" during the 1930's to have the same characteristics as the ones moving from California to Texas and Oklahoma in 1949, nor is it likely that those leaving the farms for the cities resemble in most respects those moving in the opposite direction. Again the characteristics of the migrants are almost certain to differ as the incentives to migration vary. For example, the highly remunerative jobs that attracted hundreds of thousands of Negroes from the cotton belt to the West

[1] Edward Allsworth Ross, *The Outlines of Sociology* (New York: Century Company, 1924), pp. 23–24. Reprinted by permission.

Coast during the second world war probably called forth persons with characteristics substantially different from those of persons who left the same area as a result of the tensions produced by the attempts to desegregate the schools of the various southern states.

Race

In countries such as the United States, Brazil, or Soviet Russia, in which sharply different racial and ethnic groups make up substantial portions of the population, the extent to which the various racial or ethnic elements participate in the various forms of migration is of considerable importance. In the United States this long was true in the South, where most students of population accepted as axiomatic that an essential element in any demographic analysis was the subdivision of the data according to race. It attained national importance after the flood of Negro migration into northern cities during the first world war, the heavy migration of Negroes to the West Coast during the second world war, and the sustained movement of Negroes from the South to other parts of the nation from 1946 on.

For decades following his political emancipation the Negroes remained for the most part in the same districts where they had lived as slaves. But as education gradually emancipated their minds, and as information they trusted about alternatives came to them from venturesome relatives and friends who had migrated to the North, Negroes by the hundreds of thousands began abandoning the farms of the southern region. To demonstrate this one merely needs to show that the Negro population is urbanizing more rapidly than the white, and this in turn is easily done. In 1910 only 27 per cent of the Negroes were classified as urban in comparison with 48 per cent of the white population. By 1940 the Negro population was 49 per cent urban, the white population 58 per cent, and by 1950 the corresponding percentages had risen to 62 and 63 per cent, respectively. Obviously since 1910 the tremendous flow of population from the rural districts to the urban centers has been selective of Negroes.

In view of the foregoing data, it is not surprising that Negroes recently have been participating in interstate movements of population to a much greater extent, relatively, than have white people. Even as early as 1930, 25.3 per cent of the nation's Negroes were enumerated in a different state from the one in which they had been born, whereas for native whites the corresponding percentage was only 23.4. Exactly comparable data are not available for 1950, but at the time of this census 29.2 per cent of the nonwhite population (of which the overwhelming proportion is Negro) were living in a state other than the one in which they were born in comparison with 25.1 per cent of the native white population.

Age

At most times and in most places voluntary migration is largely a phenomenon of youth. The bulk of the persons who abandon the farming districts of a nation for its towns and cities, the larger proportions of those who leave one country in order to become citizens of another, and most of those who transfer their residences from one state to another are less than twenty-five years of age. They leave the communities in which they were born and reared for the city, the new homeland, or another state just at the time their playmates and former schoolmates are marrying and establishing homes of their own. Of course, these statements need some qualifications. Populations torn from their homes by war, those fleeing from oppression in their native lands, and those driven out by famine include persons of all ages. Also, in all probability, a considerable share of the migrants from city to country are middle-aged or beyond, individuals born in the rural districts who have spent their most productive years in the city and who return to the land to spend their remaining years. Moreover, in the United States, at least, in recent decades increasingly large numbers and proportions of those nearing or in the retirement ages have left the sections of the country in which they lived and worked throughout their productive years to establish new homes in southern California, Arizona, all along the Gulf Coast, and in peninsular Florida.

That immigrants and migrants from farm to city are young, most of them in late adolescence or early adulthood, long was generally agreed upon by those who had given most study to the subject. Hart, Sorokin, Zimmerman, Thomas, and McMahan, who made exhaustive examinations of the available materials, all arrived at this conclusion. Hart found, for example, that three-fourths of the immigrants to the United States came to this country before attaining the age of thirty, and that more than one-fourth of them were less than twenty when they arrived. He also discovered that migrants from the farms to the city were even younger than the immigrants, more than half of them being less than twenty.[1] The results of many studies summarized by Sorokin and Zimmerman,[2] Thomas,[3] and McMahan,[4] are all in agreement.

As indicated above, information presently available seems to indicate that those in the more advanced ages are participating to an increasing extent in the various types of internal migration within the United States. Figure 82, presented above, indicates that the state-to-state movement of those who have passed their sixty-fifth birthdays is by no means to be ignored. Furthermore, estimates indicate that in 1950 there were almost a million fewer persons aged sixty-five and over on the farms of the United States than would have been the case had there been no migration during the decade 1940 to 1950.[5]

Sex

Migration is also highly selective for sex, but again the nature of the selection depends largely upon the type of migration involved. If it is one in which long distances are spanned, such as immigration, the migration of Negroes from southern farms to cities in the North or on the Pacific Coast, or the movement from northeastern Brazil to São Paulo or Rio de Janeiro, males usually greatly outnumber females. On the other hand, if the migration covers a short distance only, as is the case with most of the movement from farms to towns and cities, females usually participate in the exodus in much greater numbers than males. These conclusions are in agreement with the detailed information presented in chapters 6 and 7 on the differences between the sex composition of urban and rural populations. They are also consistent with the results of the various studies which are summarized in the works of Sorokin and Zimmerman, Thomas, and McMahan cited above.

The sex ratio (number of males per hundred females) is probably

---

[1] Hornell N. Hart, *Selective Migration,* University of Iowa Studies No. 53 (Iowa City: University of Iowa, 1921), p. 32, *passim.*

[2] Pitirim A. Sorokin and Carle C. Zimmerman, *Principles of Rural-Urban Sociology* (New York: Henry Holt and Company, 1929), pp. 540–544.

[3] Dorothy Swaine Thomas, *Research Memorandum on Migration Differentials* (New York: Social Science Research Council, 1938), pp. 11–54.

[4] C. A. McMahan, "Selectivity of Rural-to-Urban Migration," in T. Lynn Smith and C. A. McMahan, *The Sociology of Urban Life* (New York: The Dryden Press, 1951), pp. 334–340.

[5] T. Lynn Smith, "The Changing Number and Distribution of the Aged Population," *Journal of the American Geriatrics Society,* III, No. 1 (1955), 12.

the most useful index yet devised for studying the sex selectivity of migration. In evaluating the import of this statement, the population student should remember that (1) the sex ratio at birth can be determined accurately from registration statistics, (2) specific death rates show that at nearly all times and in nearly all places the death rates of females of all ages are lower than those of males, and (3) the data frequently are available for color and nativity groups so that the influences of immigration can be largely eliminated. Therefore, it is possible to determine quickly in a general way and precisely by more painstaking methods the fact of considerable sex selectivity in the various types of internal migration. For example, it is easily demonstrated that the migration of native whites from the rural to the urban districts of the United States includes many more women than men. The sex ratio at birth among native whites in this country is approximately 106. In 1900, 1910, 1920, 1930, 1939–1941, and 1949–1951, among the white population at all ages the expectation of life for females was higher than that for males. Yet, after the movement of tens of millions of persons from the farms to the cities of the United States, the sex ratios among native whites in 1930 were 96 in the urban population and 112 in the rural-farm population; and in 1940 and 1950 the comparable indexes were 95 and 112, and 94 and 111, respectively. The predominance of females among the migrants from the farms to the city is the only hypothesis that fits all these facts. Where societal arrangements are radically different from those in the United States, however, such as in India, rural-urban migration seems to result in the transfer from farm to city of much higher proportions of males than females.[1]

In addition to the low sex ratios prevailing in nations that have lost heavily by emigration and the high sex ratios among the foreign born populations of such countries as Argentina, Australia, Brazil, Canada, and the United States, there is much other evidence that long-distance migration usually is highly selective of males. One of the more convenient bodies of such information is that relating to Negroes in the United States which shows that males once made up the bulk of the Negro populations of northern cities, that sex ratios of Negroes in southern cities are very low, and that the heavy migrations of Negroes from the South have even greatly depressed the sex ratios in the rural parts of the region. These facts are strictly in accord with the

[1] See Kingsley Davis, *op. cit.*, pp. 139–141, *passim*.

principle that males greatly predominate among those who migrate long distances.

An interesting exception to this rule, however, is encountered in the study of migration to the federal district (essentially the same as the City of Rio de Janeiro) from other parts of Brazil. For the decade 1940 to 1950, there was a very heavy influx of migrants from nearby states, among whom females greatly out-numbered males, and another one from the northeastern states, thousands of miles away, in which males were much more numerous than females. As a matter of fact, in the extremely heavy movement of people to the national capital from the state of Paraíba, whose migrants and their music set Rio de Janeiro agog, the newcomers included almost three times as many males as females. All of this was strictly in line with expectations. But in the migrations from the most distant parts of Brazil, such as those from the territory of Acre, and the states of Amazonas, Pará, Mato Grosso, and Maranhão, the sex ratios were very low, with the actual indexes ranging from fifty-five males per hundred females for Amazonas to a comparable figure of seventy-five for Maranhão. These are even lower than sex ratios among the migrants from the nearby states of Rio de Janeiro and Minas Gerais, which were seventy-eight and seventy-six, respectively. As an hypothesis to explain this departure from the rule, it is suggested that the employees of the federal government who are sent to the uttermost parts of Brazil as civil servants consist largely of young, unmarried men. In their distant posts not a few of them marry local girls and start their families. When opportunity affords they return to the nation's capital, along with their brides. When state-of-birth and state-of-residence data alone are available for use in estimating internal migrations, the men involved do not figure as migrants, but their wives do.

Other Traits or Characteristics

Most of the popular interest in the selectivity of migration centers upon the question of whether the "best" or the "worst" and the most intelligent or least intelligent elements of the population are selected by migration. Dr. E. A. Ross, in the quotation given above, accepted and stated in lucid terms the prevailing assumptions concerning the selectivity popularly supposed to be in operation. It is extremely difficult, however, to discover comprehensive, objective studies that would lend support to such generalizations. It is probably best to conclude that we know practically nothing about the subject.[1]

[1] For summaries of such studies as have been made, most of them several decades ago, see Sorokin and Zimmerman, *op. cit.*, pp. 558–583; Thomas, *op. cit.*, 93–125; McMahan, *op. cit.*, pp. 334–340; and T. Lynn Smith, *Population Analysis* (New York: McGraw-Hill Book Company, 1948), pp. 364–368.

SUGGESTED SUPPLEMENTARY READINGS

Anderson, Walfred A., *The Characteristics of New York State Population,* Cornell University Agricultural Experiment Station, Bulletin No. 925, Ithaca (1958), pp. 50–54.

Bogue, Donald J., and Margaret Jarman Hagood, *Subregional Migration in the United States, 1935–40, Volume II, Differential Migration in the Corn and Cotton Belts,* Scripps Foundation Studies in Population Distribution, No. 6. Oxford, Ohio: Scripps Foundation, 1953.

Bogue, Donald J., Henry S. Shyrock, Jr., and Siegfried A. Hoermann, *Subregional Migration in the United States, 1935–40, Volume I, Streams of Migration Between Subregions.* Scripps Foundation Studies in Population Distribution, No. 5. Oxford, Ohio: Scripps Foundations, 1957.

Burnight, Robert G., *100 Years of Interstate Migration—1850–1950.* Storrs Agricultural Experiment Station Bulletin 330. Storrs, Conn.: College of Agriculture, University of Connecticut, 1957.

Hamilton, C. Horace, "Educational Selectivity of Rural-Urban Migration: Preliminary Results of a North Carolina Study," in *Selected Studies of Migration Since World War II.* New York: Milbank Memorial Fund, 1958, pp. 110–122.

Hitt, Homer L., "Migration between the South and Other Regions, 1949 to 1950," *Social Forces,* 36, No. 1 (1957), 9–16.

Landis, Paul H., and Paul K. Hatt, *Population Problems: A Cultural Interpretation* (Second Edition). New York: American Book Company, 1954, chapter 21.

Maclachlan, John M., and Joe S. Floyd, *This Changing South.* Gainesville: University of Florida Press, 1956, chapter 4.

McMahan, C. A., "Selectivity of Rural-to-Urban Migration," in T. Lynn Smith and C. A. McMahan, *The Sociology of Urban Life.* New York: The Dryden Press, 1951, pp. 334–340.

President's Commission on Migratory Labor, *Migratory Labor in American Agriculture.* Washington: Government Printing Office, 1951.

Ramsey, Charles E. and Walfred A. Anderson, *Migration of the New York*

State Population. Cornell University Agricultural Experiment Station, Bulletin No. 929. Ithaca, 1958.

Smith, T. Lynn, *Brazil: People and Institutions* (Revised Edition). Baton Rouge: Louisiana State University Press, 1954, chapter XI.

Smith, T. Lynn, and Homer L. Hitt, *The People of Louisiana,* pp. 205–224.

Tarver, James D., *Population Change and Migration in Oklahoma, 1940–50.* Oklahoma Agricultural Experiment Station Bulletin No. B-485. Stillwater, 1957.

Thornthwaite, C. Warren, *Internal Migration in the United States.* Philadelphia: University of Pennsylvania Press, 1934.

Vance, Rupert B., and Nadia Danilevsky, *All These People: The Nation's Human Resources in the South.* Chapel Hill: University of North Carolina Press, 1945, chapters 9 and 10.

Thomas, Dorothy S., "Age and Economic Differentials in Interstate Migration," *Population Index,* 24, No. 4 (1958), 313–325.

Thompson, Warren S., *Growth and Changes in California's Population,* part III. Los Angeles: The Haynes Foundation, 1955.

Part Six

GROWTH OF POPULATION

Chapter 21

The Growth of Population

GROWTH OF POPULATION [1] IS THE SECOND most important subject in the entire realm of demography or population study. From the standpoints of general interest, theoretical significance, and utility or application, matters having to do with the number and distribution of the inhabitants are the only ones that may be thought of as exceeding in importance those which constitute the subject of population growth. In this volume the treatment of this subject has been postponed until the three primary factors that may be involved (fertility, mortality, and migration) in the changing number of the inhabitants have all been examined.

The study of the growth of population falls naturally into two parts: an analysis and description of changes that already have occurred and the attempt to project or forecast what the population of a given area or territory will be at stated dates in the future. In our present state of knowledge no very high degree of dependability may be placed upon efforts made in connection with the second of these; and the longer the period for which the forecasts or projections are made, the greater will be the unreliability of the estimates. Even for short periods in the future, unless one can foretell with a high degree of accuracy the numbers of births that will take place in ensuing years, the projections or predictions quickly get out of line with reality. If, on the other hand, the experts making the projections merely supply the reader with various sets of computations based upon different assumptions with respect to the future course of births (or deaths and migrations as well), the

---

[1] Changes in the number of the inhabitants of a given area naturally may involve decreases as well as increases in population. For convenience, though, the present writer follows rather conventional procedures and uses the expression "growth of population" to denote this entire subject.

results are of still more dubious value. Such a procedure merely transfers the responsibility for making the most reasonable inferences with
respect to the subject from the ones who have at their disposal all of
the available facts and who supposedly have studied thoroughly all aspects of the problem to those who do not have access to many of the
data and who may have given little or no previous attention to the
problems involved. If those engaged professionally in such studies are
unable to judge the respective probabilities of the various alternatives,
what reason is there to suppose that the ordinary reader will be able to
do so?

There likewise are two basic approaches used in studies of population growth. One of these attempts to take into account the absolute
and relative importance of the three factors that may be involved and
to base all conclusions upon a knowledge of births, deaths, and migrations. The other would explain and predict variations in the numbers
of people on the earth or any of its respective parts in terms of the
workings of some inexorable mathematical law. Most of the so-called
mathematical "laws" of population growth appear to be merely excellent illustrations of jumping to a conclusion that something actually
occurred in a given way simply because it might have happened in that
manner, or of reasoning out a possible connection between two phenomena and then gradually coming to the stage of asserting that they
are in fact related. Approaches of the latter kind are afforded no space
in this volume.

World Population Growth

As was indicated in chapter 3, even at the middle of the twentieth
century the total population of the earth was not known with any degree of precision. Nevertheless current knowledge relative to the populations of various sections of the world is vastly superior to that available a hundred years ago. This means, though, that statements relative
to the absolute and relative increases in world population, even those
pertaining to happenings during the last century, or indeed changes
during the twentieth century, are in a considerable part mere conjec-
ture. For earlier periods there is no likelihood that any fairly accurate
knowledge ever will be attained.

If one wishes to consider world population trends during the eighteenth and nineteenth centuries (and there is little scientific basis for
any earlier estimates), the materials assembled by the French *Mini-*

stere du travail et de la prévoyance social probably are as satisfactory as any. This authority arrived at the figure of 750 million as the number of inhabitants of the earth in 1761 and of 1.15 billion as that in 1861. The estimated increase in the population of the various continents during this hundred-year period are as follows: Africa, from 80 to 100 million; America, from 20 to 70 million; Asia (including Oceania), from 520 to 700 million; and Europe, from 130 to 280 million.[1]

In order to set forth the more significant facts on this subject as simply and concisely as possible, Figure 85 is presented. Plotting population (the dependent variable) on a logarithmetic scale, as is done in this illustration, has two advantages: (1) it enables one to keep the diagram within reasonable dimensions; and (2) since any variable that is increasing at a constant rate results in a straight line when it is plotted on a semilogarithmic basis, it permits one to tell at a glance from a diagram such as this whether the rate of increase is holding its own, falling off, or increasing. Especially is the comparison of trends in the various continents facilitated by the use of this device. The student is again warned, however, against placing any considerable degree of confidence in the data for the eighteenth and nineteenth centuries which were used in the preparation of this chart.

Only a few comments are called for in discussing the trends portrayed in Figure 85. The phenomenal growth of population on the North American continent is the most striking feature of world history in the course of the last 200 years. Since 1900 the South American continent also has commanded attention by the rapidity with which its inhabitants have been multiplying, and, indeed, the twentieth century is one in which the rate of population growth in that continent is unmatched by that of any other major portion of the world. The populations of Asia and Europe continue to increase, thus adding each year many millions of additional people to the earth's total, even though the rates of increase are comparatively low. In Oceania, on the other hand, the rates are high, but the absolute numbers involved are not large. If the curve for Africa is starting to rise to parallel the trends on the other continents, as the data in Table XLVIII seem to indicate actually is happening, another very potent factor is being added to those currently producing a rapid upsurge in world population.

The most reliable information on world population trends in the

[1] *Statistique internationale du mouvement de la population,* Vol. II (Paris: Imprimerie Nationale, 1913), p. x.

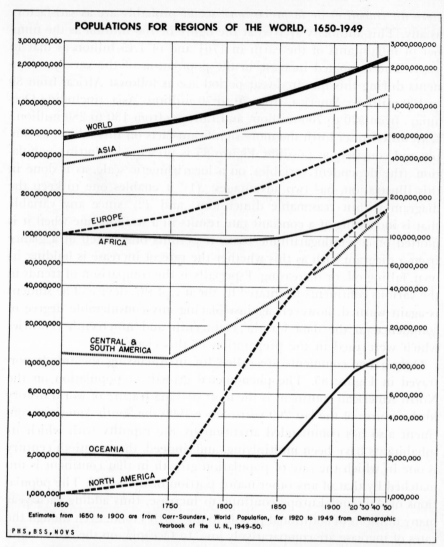

POPULATIONS FOR REGIONS OF THE WORLD, 1650-1949

Estimates from 1650 to 1900 are from Carr-Saunders, World Population, for 1920 to 1949 from Demographic Yearbook of the U. N., 1949-50.

PHS, BSS, NOVS

Figure 85. Three centuries of population growth in the major world divisions. (Illustration from the U. S. Public Health Service)

opening years of the second half of the twentieth century is contained in Table XLVIII. Not until about 1964, when the bulk of the data from censuses taken in 1960 and 1961 become available, will it be possible for another somewhat reliable assessment of the situation to be

Table XLVIII. Estimates of the Annual Growth of Population in Major World Regions, 1951–1955

Regions	Population at midyear, 1955 (millions)	Annual growth 1951–1955	
		Millions	Rate
The world	2,691	42.6	1.6
Africa			
Northern Africa	78	1.5	2.0
Tropical and southern Africa	145	2.8	2.0
America			
Northern America	183	3.0	1.7
Middle America	58	1.4	2.6
South America	125	3.0	2.5
Asia			
South west Asia	73	1.4	2.0
South central Asia	499	6.3	1.3
South east Asia	185	3.0	1.7
East Asia	724	13.3	1.9
Europe			
Northern and western Europe	137	0.8	0.6
Central Europe	134	1.2	0.9
South Europe	138	1.4	1.0
Oceania	15	0.3	2.2
U.S.S.R.	197	3.2	1.7

SOURCE: United Nations, *Demographic Yearbook, 1956* (New York: United Nations, 1956), p. 2. The figures for Asia and Europe are exclusive of the data for the U.S.S.R.

made. The student of population should bear in mind that by 1955 the earth's inhabitants already numbered almost 2.7 billions, that each succeeding year has added about 43 million persons to this total, and that at the end of the year there are approximately 1,016 persons alive for each thousand in existence at its beginning. Other interesting and significant details of current world population trends, on the absolute basis, are as follows: well over one-half of the annual increase in world population is taking place in Asia, most of it in east Asia whose "teeming millions" already have produced the greatest overcrowding the earth has ever seen; all of Europe, the Soviet Union omitted, is adding each year to the world total, only slightly more persons than are the United States and Canada together, or as is being done by the nations occupying the South American continent; and the annual increase of population in South America and that in the United States and Canada is almost as large as that in the U.S.S.R.

The rate of population growth is most rapid in the various Latin America countries, or in Middle America and South America in terms of great world regions, followed by Oceania, Africa, and southwest Asia. It is lowest in northern and western Europe, where the index is only slightly more than one-third as high as that for the earth as a whole, followed most closely by the rates for Central Europe and southern Europe. Interestingly enough the index for the Soviet Union and that for the United States and Canada are equal, and both of them are barely higher than that for members of the human race collectively.

The Growth of Population in Selected Countries

The practice of taking a census of population at regular intervals has been so limited and the changes in national boundaries so frequent and extensive that it is difficult to obtain successive accurate counts of population for various nations. These in turn are essential in order to study the growth of population in the different important sections of the earth's surface. Therefore any extensive and exact comparative analysis of the growth of population throughout the countries of the world is impossible. Nevertheless, for a considerable number of selected countries some data that are of value may be presented. (See Table XLIX.) In choosing the materials to be presented in this form, first consideration was given to making the coverage of nations or territories having a million or more inhabitants as complete as possible for a recent intercensal period. Therefore, a considerable number of countries are included, even though comparable materials for the early portion of the twentieth century are lacking. Wherever possible, though, the table contains the annual rate of increase for an intercensal period early in the present century as well as the most recent one near its middle.

It is interesting to note that on the basis of the census counts on which these rates are based (and it should be emphasized that all estimates have been excluded), Venezuela is the nation with the highest rate of population growth in the world.[1] Between 1941 and 1950 the number of inhabitants in that world-famous producer of petroleum in-

[1] Because of the special circumstances involved, Israel is omitted from consideration in this connection.

Table XLIX. Rates of Population Growth in Selected Countries During Intercensal Periods Early in and Near the Middle of the Twentieth Century

Country	Intercensal period	Annual rate of growth	Intercensal period	Annual rate of growth
Africa				
Algeria	1901–1906	2.0	1948–1954	1.6
Egypt	1907–1917	1.3	1937–1947	1.8
Tunisia	1911–1921	0.8	1936–1946	2.2
Union of South Africa	1904–1911	2.1	1946–1951	2.1
North America				
Canada	1901–1911	2.9	1941–1951	1.7
Costa Rica	....	..	1927–1950	2.3
Cuba	1907–1919	2.9	1943–1953	2.1
Dominican Republic	....	..	1935–1950	2.5
El Salvador	1901–1930	1.2	1930–1950	1.3
Honduras	....	..	1945–1950	2.7
Mexico	1900–1910	1.1	1940–1950	2.7
Panama	1911–1920	3.2	1940–1950	2.9
Puerto Rico	1899–1910	1.5	1940–1950	1.7
United States	1900–1910	2.0	1940–1950	1.4
South America				
Argentina	....	..	1914–1947	2.2
Brazil	....	..	1940–1950	2.4
Chile	1907–1920	1.1	1940–1952	1.5
Colombia	....	..	1938–1951	2.2
Venezuela	1920–1926	3.5	1941–1950	3.0
Asia				
Ceylon	1901–1911	1.4	1946–1953	2.8
Formosa	1920–1925	1.8	1935–1945	2.4
India [1]	1901–1911	0.7	1931–1941	1.4
Israel	....	..	1931–1948	8.7
Japan	1920–1925	1.3	1935–1940	1.1
Korea	1920–1925	2.4	1940–1944	1.4
Malaya, Federation of	1911–1921	2.2	1931–1947	1.6
Pakistan	....	..	1941–1951	0.8
Philippines	1903–1918	1.9	1939–1948	1.9
Thailand	1911–1919	1.4	1937–1947	1.9
Turkey	....	..	1945–1950	2.2

Table XLIX. Rates of Population Growth in Selected Countries (Continued)

Country	Intercensal period	Annual rate of growth	Intercensal period	Annual rate of growth
Europe				
Albania	....	..	1930–1945	0.7
Austria	1900–1910	1.1	1939–1951	0.3
Belgium	1900–1910	1.0	1930–1947	0.3
Bulgaria	1900–1905	1.5	1934–1946	0.8
Czechoslovakia	1900–1910	0.7	1930–1947	−0.9
Denmark	1901–1906	1.1	1945–1950	1.1
Finland	1900–1910	1.0	1930–1940	0.7
France	1901–1906	0.2	1936–1946	−0.3
Germany	1900–1910	1.4	1946–1950 [2]	2.1
Hungary	1900–1920	0.5	1941–1949	−0.2
Ireland	1901–1911	−0.3	1946–1951	0.0
Italy	1901–1911	0.9	1936–1951	0.7
Netherlands	1899–1909	1.4	1930–1947	1.2
Norway	1900–1910	0.6	1946–1950	1.0
Poland	....	..	1946–1950	0.9
Portugal	1900–1911	0.9	1940–1950	0.9
Romania	....	..	1941–1948	−0.2
Spain	1900–1910	0.8	1940–1950	0.7
Sweden	1900–1910	0.7	1945–1950	1.1
Switzerland	1900–1910	1.3	1941–1950	1.1
United Kingdom				
England and Wales	1901–1911	1.0	1931–1951	0.5
Northern Ireland	1901–1911	0.1	1931–1951	0.5
Scotland	1901–1911	0.6	1931–1951	0.3
Yugoslavia	1921–1931	1.5	1948–1953	1.4
Oceania				
Australia	1901–1911	1.7	1947–1954	2.5
New Zealand	1901–1906	2.8	1945–1951	2.4
U.S.S.R.	1926–1939	1.2	....	..

SOURCE: United Nations, *Demographic Yearbook, 1955* (New York: United Nations, 1955), Table 4.

[1] Pre-partition India.
[2] Western Germany.

creased at the rate of 3 per cent per annum. It was closely rivaled in this respect by Panama, for which the rate as established by the comparison of two well-done censuses of population taken in 1940 and 1950 was 2.9 per cent per year. Ceylon is in third position, with a rate of 2.8, followed by Honduras and Mexico, each with an index of 2.7. The Dominican Republic and Australia, countries in which the rate of population growth was 2.5 per cent per year during the latest intercensal period, were tied for sixth position; and Brazil, Formosa, and New Zealand, all with rates of 2.4 per cent per annum, complete the list of the ten countries, for which satisfactory data are available, in which the growth of population is most rapid. In addition, eight other countries have experienced recent increases in population that were above 2 per cent per year. These are Costa Rica, 2.3; Tunisia, 2.2; Argentina, 2.2; Colombia, 2.2; Turkey, 2.2; the Union of South Africa, 2.1; Cuba, 2.1; and West Germany, 2.1.

There are four countries listed in Table XLIX in which population decreased during the most recent intercensal period, although the falling off in the number of inhabitants was slight in each case. All of them (Czechoslovakia, France, Hungary, and Romania) are European countries, the intercensal period in each case involves the years of the second world war, and in some of them at least there may be some question relative to the extent to which boundary changes have been adequately taken into account. In addition, the Republic of Ireland showed no significant change in population between 1946 and 1951, the dates of the censuses involved.

European countries also constitute twelve of the other thirteen countries in the list in which the rate of population growth near the middle of the twentieth century was less than 1 per cent per annum. Pakistan is the one non-European country to figure in this category. With the exception of West Germany mentioned above, among all the countries of Europe only Denmark, the Netherlands, Norway, Sweden, Switzerland, and Yugoslavia figure among the group in which the rate of population increase is 1 per cent per annum or higher.

Twelve of the twenty Latin American countries are among the states for which data are given in Table XLIX. It is interesting to note that in addition to rating first and second among the nations in rate of population growth, as noted above, ten of the twelve also are in the group of eighteen countries in which the rate is 2 per cent per annum or higher. El Salvador, from which thousands of persons emigrate each year to neighboring Honduras, and Chile are the only two of these Latin American countries in which the annual rate of increase is less than 2 per cent. Therefore it should be evident to all that what is happening to the populations of Mexico and Central America, the three republics that are located in the Greater Antilles, and South America is of mounting importance in world affairs. Some of the materials for them may be used to illustrate the need for more concerted efforts to get indexes that are comparable for the various parts of the earth. In this connection it is essential that the period of time involved in the comparisons be the same for each of the nations under study and that estimates as reliable as it is possible to make be used for the years and countries for which census data are lacking. In Table L are given the results of the efforts designed to determine the absolute and relative increases of population in the twenty Latin American countries between 1940 and 1950, with materials for the United States and Puerto Rico included for comparative purposes; and in Figures 86 and 87 the changes in the Latin American countries are mapped to facilitate observation and comparison.

One should note that even for this important part of the Western Hemisphere, an area in which much effort of representatives of all the Latin American countries and the United States was expended in connection with the 1950 census of the Americas, nineteen of the forty population figures for the twenty Latin American countries are estimates rather than census counts. Even so, no attempt was made to compensate for variations in census dates so that exactly ten years would be involved in the period between 1940 and 1950. (In Brazil, for example, the 1940 census was taken as of September 1, whereas the 1950 census was taken as of July 1. The elapsed time between the two was therefore only nine years and ten months instead of a full ten years.) It is believed that the data are not sufficiently reliable to justify such refinements. In the case of Uruguay, for which no census has been taken since 1908, and for one of the years involved in the cases of Cuba, Guatemala, Bolivia, Chile, Colombia, and Ecuador, the present writer has preferred to use estimates he himself has made rather than those supplied in the *Demographic Yearbook* of the United Nations.

The increase of 24.8 per cent during the decade in the population of the twenty Latin American republics taken collectively, which represents the sum of these computations, corresponds to an annual rate of 2.4 per cent per annum. This in turn compares with current rates of

Table L. Increase of Population in Latin American Countries, 1940 to 1950

Country	Population		Increase 1940–1950	
	1940	1950	Number	Per Cent
North America	35,811,623	42,202,766	9,391,143	26.2
Costa Rica	619,000 [1]	800,875	181,875	29.4
Cuba	4,566,000 [1]	5,500,000 [2]	934,000	20.5
Dominican				
Republic	1,674,000 [1]	2,135,872	461,872	27.6
El Salvador	1,633,000 [1]	1,855,917	222,917	13.7
Guatemala	2,500,000 [2]	2,790,868	290,868	11.6
Haiti	2,600,000 [2]	3,097,304	497,304	19.1
Honduras	1,107,859	1,368,605	260,746	23.5
Mexico	19,653,552	25,791,017	6,137,465	31.2
Nicaragua	835,636	1,057,023	221,387	26.5
Panama	622,576	805,285	182,709	29.3
South America	87,603,821	108,769,450	21,165,629	24.2
Argentina	14,169,000 [1]	17,189,000 [1]	3,020,000	21.3
Bolivia	2,600,000 [2]	2,704,165	104,165	4.0
Brazil	41,236,315	51,976,357	10,740,042	26.0
Chile	5,023,539	5,750,000 [2]	726,461	14.5
Colombia	9,076,000 [1]	11,000,000 [2]	1,924,000	21.2
Ecuador	2,600,000 [2]	3,202,757	602,757	23.2
Paraguay	1,111,000 [1]	1,341,333	230,333	20.7
Peru	6,207,967	8,521,000 [1]	2,313,033	35.4
Uruguay	1,870,000 [2]	2,050,000 [2]	180,000	9.6
Venezuela	3,710,000 [1]	5,034,838	1,324,838	35.7
Latin America	123,415,444	153,972,216	30,556,772	24.8
United States	131,669,275	150,697,361	19,028,086	14.5
Puerto Rico	1,869,255	2,205,398	336,143	18.0

SOURCES: data are from official census enumerations unless otherwise indicated.
[1] United Nation's estimate.
[2] Author's estimate.

about 0.9 per cent for the earth as a whole, 1.2 per cent in Soviet Russia, and 1.4 per cent in the United States.[1]

When the twentieth century opened there were only about 43 million inhabitants in all of the Latin American countries taken together.

[1] The figure for the U.S.S.R. is derived from the "allowances" in the 1953 issue of the *Demographic Yearbook* for the population of that important country in the world population total. It is more likely to be too high than too low.

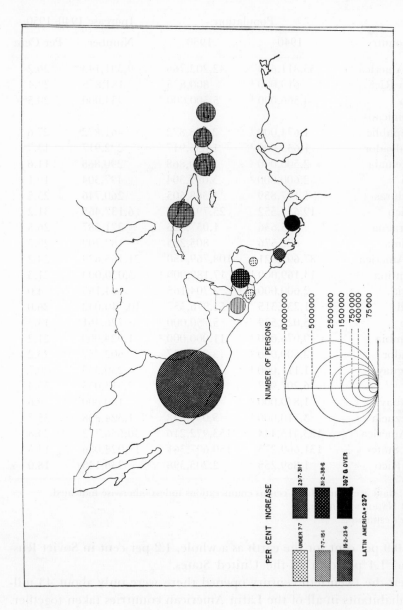

Figure 86. Absolute and relative increases of population in Mexico, Central America, and the island republics, 1940 to 1950.

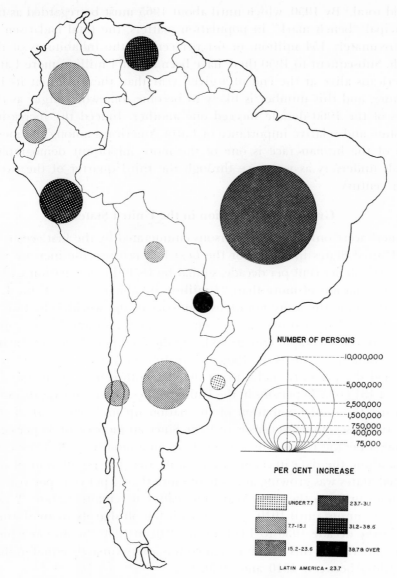

NUMBER OF PERSONS

--------- 10,000,000

--------- 5,000,000

--------- 2,500,000
--------- 1,500,000
--------- 750,000
--------- 400,000
--------- 75,000

PER CENT INCREASE

UNDER 7.7		23.7-31.1	
7.7-15.1		31.2-38.6	
15.2-23.6		38.78 OVER	

LATIN AMERICA = 23.7

Figure 87. Absolute and relative increases of population in the various countries of South America, 1940 to 1950.

As well as can be determined, this was only about 2.7 per cent of the world total.[1] By 1950, which until about 1965 must be regarded as the principal "bench mark" in population matters, the total had risen to approximately 154 million, or 6.4 per cent of the inhabitants of the earth. Subsequent to 1950 there have been about 4 million more Latin Americans alive at the end of a given year than there were at its beginning, and this number is likely to become somewhat larger as the years of the 1960 decade succeed one another. Indeed the increasing absolute and relative importance of Latin Americans among the members of the human race is one of the more important demographic trends underway as we move through the third quarter of the twentieth century.

Growth of Population in the United States

There were only 3,929,214 persons enumerated by the first census of the United States in 1790. For the next half century the increase was well over 30 per cent per decade, so that by 1850 the new nation with a total population of more than 23 million inhabitants (see Table LI) ranked among the more populous countries of the world. The rate of growth fell sharply during the second half of the nineteenth century, but even so it was rapid enough to bring the total population of the nation to almost 76 million by 1900. Thereafter the annual rate of growth declined sharply until 1940, when the sixteenth census enumerated a total of 131,669,275 persons in the United States, and then rose abruptly to bring the total population of the nation up to 150,687,361 at the time of the seventeenth census in 1950. Since an increase of 30 per cent during a decade is only slightly less than an annual rate of 3 per cent per annum, the data in Table LI indicate that the population of the United States was growing at a rate of more than 3 per cent per year at all times prior to the Civil War. Thereafter it remained above 2 per cent per annum until 1910, after which it fell off sharply to an all-time low in the decade 1930 to 1940. From 1940 to 1950 the rate at which the population of this nation increased was approximately equal to that prevailing between 1910 and 1920.

From Figure 88 one may see at a glance how the nation's four principal regions compare with respect to population growth from the time of the respective divisions first figured in the census of population until

[1] T. Lynn Smith, *Population Analysis* (New York: McGraw-Hill Book Company, 1948), p. 372.

Table LI. The Growth of Population in the United States, 1790 to 1950

Year	Number of inhabitants	Increase over preceding census (per cent)
1790	3,929,214	. . .
1800	5,308,483	35.1
1810	7,239,881	36.4
1820	9,638,453	33.1
1830	12,866,020	33.5
1840	17,069,453	32.7
1850	23,191,876	35.9
1860	31,443,321	35.6
1870	38,558,371	22.6
1880	50,155,783	30.1
1890	62,947,714	25.5
1900	75,994,575	20.7
1910	91,972,266	21.0
1920	105,710,620	14.9
1930	122,775,046	16.1
1940	131,669,275	7.2
1950	150,697,361	14.5

SOURCE: U. S. Bureau of the Census, *Census of Population: 1950*, Vol. I, *Number of Inhabitants* (Washington: Government Printing Office, 1952), p. 3.

1950. Particularly interesting is the closeness with which the curve representing the South corresponds to that for the Northeast, although after 1870 the former moved forward along a higher level than the latter, and after 1930 the differential widened considerably. The curve for the North Central States is striking because of the steepness with which it rose from 1800 to 1880—the period of settlement in this region—and the comparatively low rate of growth from 1890 to 1950. Most rapid of all has been the population growth in the West, and from the nature of past trends one might anticipate that the number of inhabitants in this region would equal those in each of the three other sections before the end of the twentieth century.

The rates at which the various states of the nation have grown during recent decades also is of considerable interest to all students of population in the United States. In order to make this information available

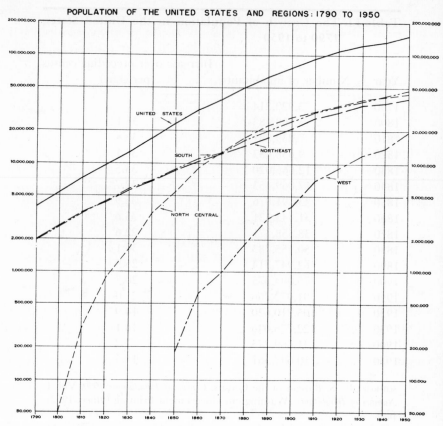

POPULATION OF THE UNITED STATES AND REGIONS: 1790 TO 1950

Figure 88. Growth of population in the United States, 1790 to 1950, by regions. (Illustration from the U. S. Bureau of the Census)

in simple, compact form, Figures 89 and 90 are presented. These two maps also serve to illustrate the sharply different mapping techniques that are used by various demographers for the purpose of portraying population changes in the several parts of the nation. As is evident from Figure 90, the present writer prefers to show simultaneously the magnitude of the changes (as represented by the varying sizes of the circles) and the relative increase or decrease (as shown by the degree of shading). This is done so that "area bias" may be eliminated, that is, so that the reader will not have to consult another map or a table in order to evaluate to some degree the relative importance of changes in two states, such as California and Nevada or North Carolina and Wyoming. Six degrees of shading is also preferable as in Figure 90, instead of four used in Figure 89, and also it is preferable to make the limit separating two of the classes near the middle of the distribution correspond exactly to the national average. The latter device enables the reader to see at a glance which of the states have grown more rapidly and which less rapidly than the nation as a whole.

The decade 1930 to 1940 was characterized by rapid increase of the population in California and some other parts of the West, in Florida, and in and around the nation's capital; and by a substantial loss of population throughout the Great Plains. Much the same pattern of change prevailed between 1940 and 1950, except that the growth of population was much more rapid and also more widespread throughout the West and Southwest, in Florida, and in the District of Columbia and the neighboring states. Likewise, for this decade, the substantial rates of increase of population in Michigan and adjacent states also strike the attention. On the other hand, the loss of population in the Great Plains area was not as general as it was between 1930 and 1940, but Arkansas and Mississippi also figured in the list of states in which the population declined. A full interpretation of all the changes during these two decades would, of course, entail a detailed study of the impact of our rapidly changing economic, social, political, and military system, and that is far beyond the scope of this volume.

Population Estimates

One cannot proceed very far in the study of any given population before population estimates of one kind or another must figure in his analyses. Most of the estimates that are needed, however, fall into two sharply distinct categories, namely *interpolation* and *extrapolation*. The first of these is comprised of the calculations designed to show the most reasonable population figures to use for years or other units or points in time which fall between two dates on which census counts of the number of inhabitants have been taken. Examples of such estimates are those for the United States as a whole, or any one of its parts, for such years as 1842, 1914, and 1948. Such information is in demand for a myriad of purposes, including the computation of birth rates, death rates, and many other indexes which the student of population himself must use. The second category is made up of estimates which seek to determine reasonable approximations of what the population of a given area is or was at dates subsequent to the latest census counts,

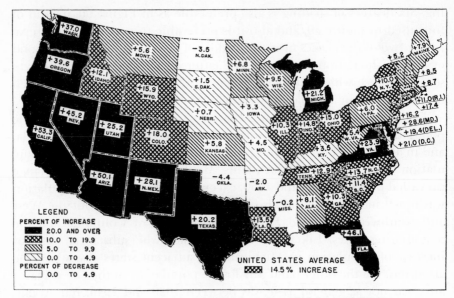

Figure 89. Percentage increase or decrease in population in
the United States, 1940 to 1950, by states. (Reproduced from
U. S. Bureau of the Census, "U. S. Census of Population:
1950," Vol. II, part 1, p. 3)

along with those which seek to forecast what it will be at specified times
in the future. Since planning for the future in all fields of activity—
educational, industrial, military, community, and so on—is quite un-
realistic unless the numbers of persons who will be involved is known,
there always is a strong demand for population estimates of this second type, especially for those pertaining to the future. There is a growing tendency to designate as population *projections* these attempts to
forecast future populations.

The need for estimates of current populations is patent, and the student of population must accept the responsibility of making calculations that are as reasonable as possible. As is the case with respect to
intercensal years, he himself must have such figures for use in connection with his studies of fertility, mortality, and other demographic matters. The extent to which a demographer should engage in population
forecasts, predictions, or projections, however, is a more debatable matter. As has been shown throughout this volume, the birth rate, the
death rate, and migration (the three primary factors in population

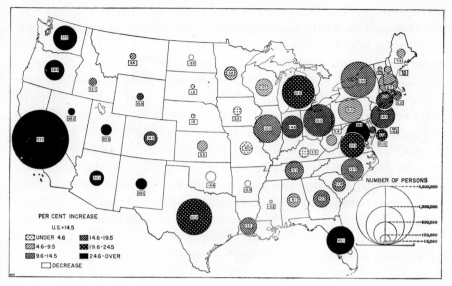

Figure 90. The absolute and relative changes in the populations of the various states, 1940 to 1950.

change) are influenced directly by a host of factors such as war, the business cycle, advancements in the medical and sanitary sciences, changes in the educational accomplishments of the population, and so on. Therefore unless someone is prepared to supply him with knowledge of what is to be expected along these lines, that is, with respect to the independent variables which are responsible for changes in population (the dependent variable), the present writer is unwilling to spend very much time and effort in population forecasts or projections of any type. Especially is he unwilling to engage very extensively in any such mental gymnastics which presuppose an ability to foretell the numbers of births that will occur in future years—and fertility usually is the major component in population change.

Interpolation

Two methods, the arithmetic and the geometric, are generally relied upon for purposes of interpolation, and there appears to be little need for additional ones unless the intercensal period involved is very long. The arithmetic method involves the assumption that the annual increment remains constant or that the population increases or decreases by a given amount during each of the years in the period between two censuses. Therefore the procedures involved are very simple. One merely has to determine the total amount of change, divide this change into as many equal parts as there are years in the intercensal period, and attribute one of these parts to each of the years. (See Table LII.) Thus, if one wished to use this method for the purpose of estimating how many inhabitants there were in the United States on April 1, 1942, a date corresponding closely to that of general mobilization for the second world war, he would proceed as follows. Subtract 131,669,275, the population enumerated in 1940, from 150,-697,361, that given by the 1950 count, to obtain 19,028,086, or the gain for the decade. Dividing this total increase by ten, the number of years in the intercensal period, gives 1,902,809 per year; and adding two such amounts, one for the year ending April 1, 1941 and another for that ending April 1, 1942, to the 1940 population gives 135,474,893 as the estimate needed. The weakness of this method is that it allows for an annual increase on the part of the 131,669,275 persons alive at the beginning of the first year of the decade which is as great as that attributed to considerably more than 148 million persons in the population at the beginning of the tenth year of the interval. The longer the intercensal period, the more serious this defect becomes. However, if the rate of increase of the population is falling off, the arithmetic method generally is to be recommended.

The geometric method of interpolation rests upon the assumption that the rate of population growth is constant throughout the period involved. Unless the rate of growth is declining, it generally is to be preferred over the arithmetic method. If the annual rate of growth is constant, it can be determined from the formula: $\log (1 + r) = \log P_1 - \log P_0/N$, in which P_1 equals the population at the end of the period, P_0 the population at the beginning of the period, N the number of years included, and r the annual rate of increase. Applying this formula to the data for the United States for the period 1940 to 1950 gives these results:

$$\log (1 + r) = \frac{\log 150,697,361 - \log 131,669,275}{10}$$

$$= \frac{8.17810 - 8.11950}{10}$$

$$= 0.005860$$

$$1 + r = 1.013586$$

$$r = 0.013586 \text{ or } 1.3586 \text{ per cent}$$

Table LII. Estimates of the Population of the United States for Each Year, 1940 to 1950, According to the Arithmetic and Geometric Methods

| | Number of inhabitants on April 1 | |
| | | |
Year	Arithmetic method	Geometric method (Annual rate = 1.3586 per cent)
1940 *	131,669,275	131,669,275
1941	133,572,084	133,458,134
1942	135,474,893	135,271,296
1943	137,377,702	137,109,092
1944	139,280,511	138,971,856
1945	141,183,320	140,859,928
1946	143,086,129	142,773,651
1947	144,988,938	144,713,374
1948	146,891,747	146,679,450
1949	148,794,556	148,672,237
1950 *	150,697,361	150,697,361

* Census figure.

If the rate of population increase is low and if the intercensal period is short, it makes very little difference whether the arithmetic or the geometric method of interpolation is used. This is readily evident from the materials in Table LII showing the calculations by each of these methods of the population of the United States for each year between 1940 and 1950. In this case, and even though the rate of increase for this country between 1940 and 1950 was fairly rapid, the maximum difference is of the order of 324,000 for the year 1945, the midpoint in the intercensal period.

As was indicated above, the annual increments are all equal (in the amount of 1,902,809 persons) when the arithmetic method is employed. The geometric method, on the other hand, gives an increase of only 1,788,859 for the first year of the decade, followed by steadily rising increments until the figure for the last of the ten years is 2,025,124. If the estimates so made are to be used in the computations of such indexes as the birth rate or the death rate, it is well for one to bear in mind that interpolation by the arithmetic method gives a slightly larger population than the geometric method for every one of the years in an intercensal period.

Extrapolation

If fairly adequate data on births, deaths, and migrations are available, the student would do well to make use of them in the preparation of any postcensal estimates of population that he may be called upon to make. If these essential data are lacking, however, the arithmetic and the geometric methods may be used as a basis for computing probable populations for a short period following any given census. It should be stressed, though, that such estimates should be used with the greatest of caution, and that they should not be relied upon if information on fertility, mortality, and migration are available for use in making the necessary computations. For illustrative purposes the estimates presented in Table LIII were prepared; along with them are given the estimates for the comparable years prepared by the personnel of the U. S. Bureau of the Census and published by that responsible agency.

An examination of the materials so assembled makes it readily apparent how rapidly the results obtained by using the arithmetic method of extrapolation come to differ substantially from those secured by employing the geometric method. In the case of extrapolation, however, it should be noted that, if the population is increasing at all, the geometric procedure yields a higher estimate for every year than the arithmetic method. Even more important is the fact that, in the course of only a few years, either of these methods of extrapolation may give results radically different from those which will result if fairly accurate knowledge of the number of deaths, a less satisfactory inventory of the births, and a crude approximation of the amount of migration are used by skilled persons as a basis for preparing estimates of the population. If in a country such as the United States, even the geometric method of estimating the population for the years immediately following a census results in less than eight years in a figure that is 5 million less than the one based upon a knowledge of the primary factors involved, what degree of confidence may one place upon the results obtained for the various parts of the nation and for other parts of the world? Furthermore, the figure of 172,790,000, the estimate of the population of the United States as of January 1, 1958, may very well be too low. All of this points to the need for great caution in placing very much reliance upon any estimates of population for postcensal years or any forecasts of what the number of inhabitants of a given area will be at some date in the

Table LIII. Estimates of the Population of the United States, 1950 to 1958, According to the Arithmetic and Geometric Methods, with Estimates Prepared by the U. S. Bureau of the Census Included for Comparative Purposes

Year	Arithmetic method	Geometric method (Annual rate = 1.3586 per cent)	Estimate by the U. S. Bureau of the Census [1]
1950	150,697,361 [2]	150,697,361 [2]	150,552,000
1951	152,600,170	152,744,735	153,072,000
1952	154,502,979	154,819,925	155,790,000
1953	156,405,788	156,923,309	158,434,000
1954	158,308,597	159,055,269	161,115,000
1955	160,211,406	161,216,194	163,956,000
1956	162,114,215	163,406,477	166,805,000
1957	164,017,024	165,626,517	169,800,000
1958	165,919,833	167,876,719	172,790,000

[1] Data are from U. S. Bureau of the Census, *Current Population Reports: Population Estimates*, Series P-25, No. 173, February 17, 1958. The figures are for January 1 of each year.
[2] Census year.

future. The more removed the date from that of a fairly accurate census, the greater the amount of error in the figures involved. Since, as was indicated above, the number of inhabitants of a given area is a dependent variable which is directly influenced by such independent variables as fluctuations in the business cycle, wars and internal disturbances, progress or the lack of it in the medical and sanitary sciences, and so on, it could not be otherwise. There seems to be little reason for believing that population forecasting or the making of population projections will ever become an exact science.

The Use of the Death Rate in Making Estimates of Population

For some purposes and in many situations a fairly reliable current estimate of the population in the years following a census may be based upon a knowledge of the death rate and of the trends in it. This procedure is especially useful in making population estimates for such areas as states or large cities, or for evaluating the estimates that others make for such units. It is not very accurate if the population involved is a small one. One using this method assumes that the changes in the death rate are not capricious, that for any large population the annual fluctuations are small, and that the trend is fairly constant and gradual. Hence if one makes the supposition that the change in the death rate is very slight, or that it is moving in a given direction to a stated degree, for any year in which the number of deaths in a city or state is known, the population is easily estimated from the formula for the death rate. One needs merely to solve for the one unknown, that is, the population, in the formula:

$$\text{Death rate} = \frac{\text{Number of deaths}}{\text{Population}} \times 1,000$$

As a check, comparable procedures based upon the formula for the birth rate may be used.

SUGGESTED SUPPLEMENTARY READINGS

Beegle, J. Allan, and Donald Halsted, *Michigan's Changing Population.* Michigan Agricultural Experiment Station Special Bulletin 415. East Lansing, 1957, pp. 4–11, *passim.*

Bogue, Donald J., *The Population of the United States.* Chicago: The Free Press, 1959, chapter 26.

Coale, Ansley J., and Edgar M. Hoover, *Population Growth and Economic Development in Low-Income Countries: A Case Study of India's Prospects.* Princeton, N. J.: Princeton University Press, 1958.

Geisert, Harold L., *World Population Pressures.* Washington: George Washington University, 1958.

Glass, D. V., *Population Policies and Movements in Europe.* Oxford: Clarendon Press, 1940.

Hitt, Homer L., "Population Movements in the Southern United States," *Scientific Monthly,* 82, No. 5 (1956), 241–246.

Landis, Paul H., and Paul K. Hatt, *Population Problems: A Cultural Interpretation* (Second Edition). New York: American Book Company, 1954, chapter 2.

Maclachlan, John M., and Joe S. Floyd, *This Changing South.* Gainesville: University of Florida Press, 1956, chapters 1 and 2.

Meyers, Paul F., and Arthur A. Campbell, *The Population of Yugoslavia.* U. S. Bureau of the Census International Population Statistics Reports, Series P-90, No. 5. Washington: Government Printing Office, 1954, chapters I, III, and IX.

Phelps, Harold A., and David Henderson, *Population in Its Human Aspects.* New York: Appleton-Century-Crofts, Inc., 1958, part I.

Schnore, Leo F., "Components of Population Change in Large Metropolitan Suburbs," *American Sociological Review,* 22, No. 5 (1958), 570–573.

Smith, T. Lynn, *Brazil: People and Institutions* (Revised Edition) . Baton Rouge: Louisiana State University Press, 1954, chapter V.

Smith, T. Lynn, "Current Population Trends in Latin America," *American Journal of Sociology*, LXII, No. 4 (1957) , 399–406.

Smith, T. Lynn, and Homer L. Hitt, *The People of Louisiana*. Baton Rouge: Louisiana State University Press, 1952, chapter XIV.

Taeuber, Conrad, and Irene B. Taeuber, *The Changing Population of the United States*. New York: John Wiley & Sons, Inc., 1958, chapter 1.

Thompson, Warren S., *Population and Progress in the Far East*. Chicago: University of Chicago Press, 1959, chapters I and XVIII.

Conclusion

IT IS NEITHER NECESSARY NOR DESIRABLE to conclude a volume such as this with an elaborate summary of its contents. The usefulness of this book to the student of population would be enhanced little if any by a detailed restatement of the more significant facts, procedures, principles, and relationships already set forth. Indeed, these are all more easily understood and more fully appreciated in the specific contexts in which they have been given where they are closely supported by the data on which they are based. It is in order, however, to make a few general comments relating to the current situation and prospects of population study.

Since about 1930 at least three significant tendencies or trends have been underway in the field of population research and teaching in the United States and other parts of the world. Probably these have been more noticeable in the teaching than in the research aspects, due no doubt to the fact that a broadening of interests on the part of those doing research work in the field of demography eventually resulted in modifications in the subject matter of courses. In any case, in contrast with the situation during the first quarter of the twentieth century, since about 1930 the following tendencies have been rather pronounced: (1) the emphasis on "population problems" has ceased to dominate the field, and concern with the normal or nonpathological aspects of the subject have become for the most part the chief concern of those teaching population courses and doing research in demography; (2) whereas as late as 1925 the major attention of most of those engaged in population study was with the numbers of people, during recent decades more and more attention has been given to the characteristics of the population and to the factors involved in population change; and (3) closely related to the second tendency, there seems to have been a marked decrease in the once rather widespread tendency to apply supposed general mathematical laws of population growth and decline and an upsurge of endeavor to understand and account for population changes through a knowledge of the three primary factors involved, namely, fertility, mortality, and migration. In the preparation of this textbook an effort has been made to keep all of the sections of this volume attuned to these three important current developments and trends.

It is hoped that the specific manner in which the various aspects of population study have been developed in this volume has made it apparent to the beginning student that the field already is a scientific discipline of creditable standing. The frame of reference, or the systematized arrangement of all the topics and concepts involved in the study of population, from those relating to the study of the number and distribution of the inhabitants to those connected with mortality, fertility, and migration, is a substantial one. Thousands of persons working during many centuries have contributed to building it, and throughout the entire world there is remarkable agreement in theory and practice with respect to its principal elements.

The facts that are ready for use by all those engaged in population study, and especially the quantitative data available to all because of the many censuses that have been taken and the lengthy and detailed records that have been kept of births, deaths, and migrations, are of an order of magnitude undreamed of in most other portions of social science. Each decade the ingenuity of the men and women concerned with population study brings these data, many of them assembled over a hundred years ago, to bear in testing ideas or hypotheses of immediate practical or theoretical concern. Furthermore every year that passes enables those in charge of censuses and registers of vital statistics throughout the world to enrich substantially with new compilations of population data the invaluable store already in existence.

In addition to its well-established and systematized frame of reference and its rich store of facts, the field of population study includes a host of analytical devices and techniques that are of prime utility. Over the decades population students have devised and tested a host of such methods or techniques that are extremely useful in the organization, analysis, and interpretation of demographic facts, relationships, and trends. Many of these are statistical in nature, ranging from the simple, direct, and conclusive varieties of tabulation or subsorting, which the plenitude of data make possible, to highly involved correlation procedures. Many of the devices are graphical. Indeed it may be said with some degree of certainty that the manipulation of population data has been one of the principal sources of the improvements in graphical devices that have taken place during the last three decades. Many of the tables and charts used in this volume were, of course, designed by the author himself, but others were selected from a wide variety of sources. They deserve special study solely from the standpoint of the methods of analysis and presentation presently readily available to those working with demographic data.

The general field of population theory has not been overlooked in the preparation of the specific sections and chapters which make up this book. Generalizations about demographic matters that are based upon careful observations and are in agreement with all the known facts, tested hypotheses, and established relationships between two or more attributes or variables are rapidly accumulating. Such inductions are the warp and woof of scientific theory in any field of knowledge. In this volume almost every section has dealt with some aspect of population theory, and in all cases an endeavor has been made to have conclusions reached confronted with the relevant facts, previously established relationships, and verified hypotheses. Because they have survived such exacting and searching tests, they merit the careful consideration of those concerned with population theory in particular or social theory in general.

Population facts and principles also are the keys to an understanding of many existing social conditions and current social changes. Therefore throughout this volume there are many suggestions of the manner in which a demographic factor, as an independent variable, is involved in many social and economic matters of public interest. The relation of population facts and relationships in the proper planning of health, welfare, business, educational, agricultural, industrial, and a host of other public policies is so obvious that further comment is unnecessary. However, the impression should not be left that interest in them is limited to those concerned with public problems. Private organizations, enterprises, and individuals, too, make much use of reliable population information when they are laying plans for the future. Apparently this becomes the case increasingly as the years go by and as we increase substantially our knowledge about the number, distribution, characteristics, vital processes, migration, and growth of the population.

Finally, a word should be said about population policies, or the public and private measures designed to get and maintain the kind of population that is desired, from the standpoints of number, quality, and distribution. Only a little thought is necessary in order to determine that the formulation and execution of such policies hardly are, or can be, the sole or even the main responsibility of those engaged in the study of population as such. A state or national policy with respect to birth control, the limitation of immigration, measures designed to extend the expectation of life, or the encouragement or discouragement of migration between urban and rural areas—to mention only a few of the possible issues—involve knowledge and interests far beyond the special province of the demographer. Nevertheless, in all of these matters there is no substitute for the facts, and the student of population is the one most likely to possess the knowledge and skill needed in order to assemble many of the most pertinent facts with respect to the topic involved. Therefore, it is not surprising that the general body of fact and theory that has been developed in the field of population study finds many of its most important applications in connection with population policies as such.

SUGGESTED SUPPLEMENTARY READINGS

Bogue, Donald J. (Editor), *Applications of Demography: Composition and Distribution of the U. S. Population in 1975*. Scripps Foundation Studies in Population Distribution, No. 13. Oxford, Ohio: Scripps Foundation, 1957.

Burch, Guy Irving, and Elmer Pendell, *Population Roads to Peace and War*. Washington: Population Reference Bureau, 1945.

East, Edward M., *Mankind at the Crossroads*. New York and London: Charles Scribner's Sons, 1926.

Francis, Roy G. (Editor), *The Population Ahead*. Minneapolis: University of Minnesota Press, 1958.

Krotki, K. J. (Editor), *The Population of Sudan*. Khartoun: Philosophical Society of Sudan, 1958, pp. 20–39, *passim*.

Landis, Paul H., and Paul K. Hatt, *Population Problems: A Cultural Interpretation* (Second Edition). New York: American Book Company, 1954, chapter 26.

Hauser, Philip M. (Editor), *Population and World Politics*. Glencoe, Illinois: Free Press, 1958.

Phelps, Harold A., and David Henderson, *Population in Its Human Aspects*. New York: Appleton-Century-Crofts, Inc., 1958, chapter 21.

Ross, Edward Alsworth, *Standing Room Only?* New York: The Century Co., 1927.

Smith, T. Lynn, and Homer L. Hitt, *The People of Louisiana*. Baton Rouge: Louisiana State University Press, 1952, chapter XV.

Spengler, Joseph J., and Otis Dudley Duncan, *Population Theory and Policy: Selected Readings*. Glencoe, Ill.: The Free Press, 1956.

Taeuber, Irene B., *The Population of Japan*. Princeton, N. J.: Princeton University Press, 1959, chapters XVI–XVIII.

Vance, Rupert B., and Nadia Danilevsky, *All These People: The Nation's Human Resources in the South*. Chapel Hill: University of North Carolina Press, 1945, part V.

Vogt, William, *Road to Survival*. New York: William Sloane Associates, Inc., 1948.

Whelpton, P. K. (Interview with), "Too Many People in the World?" *U. S. News & World Report*, July 13, 1956.

Whitney, V. H., "Some Interrelations of Population and Atomic Power," *American Sociological Review*, 21, No. 3 (1956), 273–279.

Exercises

CHAPTER 1: The Scope and Method of Population Study

1. Consult a recent issue of *Population Index* and set down in written form the principal headings used in classifying population materials in this comprehensive annotated bibliography.
2. Outline the basic elements of the scientific method as it is applied in population study.
3. Study carefully the table of contents of this volume, and then indicate which of the subjects included must be studied largely through use of materials gathered in population censuses and which must be studied for the most part by use of data from various registration systems.
4. List five ways in which population materials may be applied in social and economic planning.
5. In what way is demography or the study of population related to the following disciplines: biology, economics, political economy, sociology, and geography?
6. Give in your own words a definition of demography.
7. Is it wise to place the study of the growth of population at the end of a volume such as this? Explain.
8. Why are fertility, mortality, and migration the only *primary* factors influencing the number of inhabitants and the distribution of the population?
9. Select a city, county, or state and then examine the reports of the latest U. S. census of population and determine specifically the items of information that are available for it.

CHAPTER 2: Important Landmarks in the Development of Population Study

1. Write a paper of 500 words criticizing or defending the proposition that the history of demography or population study should begin with the work of John Graunt.

2. Indicate why the census of the United States may be called a political accident and why the year 1790 should figure as one of the landmarks in the development of population study.
3. Consult J. D. B. DeBow's *Compendium of the Seventh Census,* and then write a 500-word exposition setting forth its importance for the student of population.
4. Consult *Studies in American Demography* by Willcox and *Population Analysis* by Smith, and then write a brief history of the development of mortality statistics in the United States.
5. Of what significance for the study of population was the publication of the first issue of the *Demographic Yearbook* in 1949?
6. What must be done before students of population will have available for their use the necessary statistics about internal migration?
7. Compile a short bibliography of the demographic works of one of the following authors: Walter F. Willcox, Warren S. Thompson, Rupert B. Vance, Irene B. Taeuber, Kingsley Davis, P. K. Whelpton, Frank Lorimer, Frank W. Notestein, Robert R. Kuczynski, Joseph J. Spengler, Louis I. Dublin, Philip M. Hauser, and William F. Ogburn.
8. Revise the list of landmarks in the development of population study, as given in chapter 2 of this volume, deleting those that are not entitled to a place in such a list and adding others that are.
9. Should the elements of genetics be included in a course on population? Explain.

CHAPTER 3: The Number and Geographic Distribution of the Population

1. Indicate in your own words the meanings of the following concepts: census, density of population, center of population, *de jure,* minor civil division, census tract, township, incorporated center, enumeration, and population.
2. Why is the determination of the number and distribution of the inhabitants the most important single task in population study?
3. Why is the tabulation of census data by small and homogeneous subdivisions of counties and municipalities, territorial units having boundaries that are easily identified and stable, of such tremendous significance in the study of the distribution of the population?
4. Discuss briefly the more important reasons why we do not know rather accurately how many people there are on earth at the present time.
5. Set forth briefly the more important facts about the present distribution of population in the United States.

6. Using the data from the most recent census publications and the techniques which you think most appropriate, construct a map showing the distribution of population in the county in which you reside.

7. How do the estimates of population in current use in a nation, state, or city at the beginning of a census year usually compare with the results of the population counts made by the census in the course of the year?

8. What is the present population of the state in which you live?

9. Indicate why it is inaccurate to assume that each inhabitant of the United States has one and only one usual place of residence.

10. What is the correlation between the size of the states of the United States as measured in terms of area and size as indicated by the number of inhabitants? And what implications, if any, does this have for the mapping of demographic data for the nation?

CHAPTER 4: Rural or Urban Residence

1. How do the definitions of urban and rural categories employed by the United States Census compare and contrast with those used in the following countries: England, Canada, Mexico, Cuba, Australia, Sweden, France, Brazil, and India?

2. Indicate specifically how the "new" definitions of urban, rural-nonfarm, and rural-farm employed in the 1950 census of the United States differ from those used in 1940 and 1930.

3. Is the practice of the U. S. Census in making the urban-rural classification of the population a primary one in most of its tabulations a sound procedure? Why or why not?

4. Suggest ways in which the residential classification used by the U. S. Census might be improved.

5. Why is it that definitions of urban and rural that are highly satisfactory for statistical purposes would be entirely inadequate for more theoretical sociological purposes, and vice versa?

6. How may one determine the degree of urbanity or rurality of various states, counties, or other civil divisions?

7. Which is the most urban state in the United States? Which the most rural? Explain.

8. In what ways, if at all, is one's personality affected by the fact that he resides in a highly urban, a strictly rural, or a suburban environment?

9. Who is the typical American: the resident of a large city? the one who lives on a farm in the open country? or the person whose home is in one of the "Middletowns" or "Littletowns" spread about throughout the nation? Explain.

CHAPTER 5: Race, Color, Ethnic Stock, and Nativity

1. Consult the 1956 issue of the *Demographic Yearbook* of the United Nations, and then write a 500-word paper on the present status of racial, color, and ethnic classifications of the populations in the censuses of five countries selected by the instructor.
2. What are the basic procedures of the U. S. Census in classifying the population according to color, race, and nativity?
3. Is the practice of the U. S. Census in making the color and racial classification of the population a primary one in most of its tabulations a sound procedure? Why or why not?
4. Why is it that definitions of white and Negro that are highly satisfactory for statistical purposes would be entirely inadequate for more theoretical anthropological purposes, and vice versa?
5. How does the relative importance of the native white, the foreign-born white, and the Negro populations vary throughout the United States?
6. Describe recent changes in the distribution of the Negro population in the United States.
7. To what extent are the foreign-born portions of the population of the United States concentrated in the urban districts?
8. From the series of maps given in chapter 5, indicate the sections of the United States in which the immigrants of each nationality have made their largest contributions to the nation's civilization and culture.
9. Compare and contrast the race and nativity make up of the population of the United States in 1950 with that prevailing in 1850.
10. In which states is the Negro population still concentrated in the rural districts and in which is it concentrated in the cities?

CHAPTER 6: Age Composition

1. What similarities would you expect to find between the age-sex pyramid for a predominantly rural state in the South such as Mississippi, and that of Italy? Why?
2. Give a critical appraisal of the method used in the text for the purpose of scoring populations with respect to the accuracy of age reporting.
3. Construct an age-sex pyramid for the population of a given country, city, or state, and then identify the factor or factors responsible for each "scar" or irregularity it exhibits.
4. Discuss in some detail the social and economic significance of the "aging" of the population in the United States that has taken place since 1900.
5. Construct a diagram (similar to those given in Figures 44 and 45) showing the extent to which the population of a given state contains more or less than its pro rata share of each age group from zero to four to seventy-

five and over in the nation's population. What factors are chiefly responsible for the surpluses and deficits?

6. Why do cities located in the western portions of the United States have relatively high proportions of aged persons whereas most cities in the South have relatively low proportions?

7. Using the data in Table VIII construct a scatter diagram showing the relationship between educational status (the independent variable, or X, as measured by the percentage of illiteracy) and the index of correctness in age reporting (the dependent variable or Y).

8. Those supplying the age data for India to the United Nations have not given the counts assembled from the census tabulations. Rather they supplied estimates showing the number of persons in each year of age as determined from the "smoothed" frequency distribution of the age data. In 1951, however, the percentage of illiteracy among those of ten years of age and over was 82.1. On the basis of the chart prepared in the preceding exercise, estimate the index of accuracy in age reporting that would be secured if the original data were available for use in the computations. (Note: use a thread or a straight edge to determine approximately the line $Y = a + bX$ which best fits the points plotted in exercise 7, and from the appropriate point on this line, estimate the score for India.)

CHAPTER 7: Sex Composition

1. How may one explain the high sex ratios that prevail in the populations of Alaska, Cuba, Argentina, India, and Israel, and the low sex ratios in those of Austria, Germany, Portugal, Spain, and the United Kingdom?

2. Using the latest census data, determine the sex ratios for the white and Negro populations of the six largest cities in your state. Compare these findings with the sex ratios among the rural-farm population of six of the most rural counties in your state. What factors have produced these differences?

3. Why is the sex ratio of the Negro population so much lower than that of the native white population?

4. Other things remaining equal, what will be the effect upon the sex ratio of a population of (a) a fall in the birth rate, (b) an increase in the expectation of life, (c) a strong current of immigration, and (d) the arrival of large numbers of migrants from distant portions of the country itself.

5. How may one determine that the S-shape of the curve showing sex ratios by age is due to the understatement of women's ages rather than the overstatement of men's ages?

6. Why is the sex ratio high among children of less than ten years of age? Why is it low among those aged sixty-five and over?

7. Is the high sex ratio in the western portions of the United States and the comparatively low sex ratio in the South likely to persist for several decades to come? Explain.

8. Identify the factors responsible for the fall in the sex ratio of the population of the United States from 106.0 in 1910 to 98.6 in 1950.

CHAPTER 8: Marital Condition

1. With data from the 1955 and later issues of the *Demographic Yearbook* of the United Nations construct charts similar to Figure 49 showing the marital status of the population of four countries which are selected by the instructor.

2. The data make it evident that women are much more likely than men to remain single throughout life. Write a 500-word paper in which you (a) identify the factors responsible for this difference and (b) describe the principal social consequences of the differential.

3. Discuss the reasons for and the social significance of the fact that widowers are much more likely to remarry than are widows.

4. Describe in your own way how the marital status of a population changes as age advances.

5. How does the marital status of the white population of the United States compare with that of the Negro population?

6. How does the maldistribution of the sexes in the United States hinder marriage and affect mate selection.

7. As the expectation of life of a population increases, what changes take place in the proportions of widows and widowers in the country concerned?

8. In what ways does the marital status of the urban, the rural-nonfarm, and the rural-farm populations differ?

9. In 1950 the percentages of married persons among those fourteen years of age and over in the United States were as follows: urban males, 64.9; urban females, 63.8; rural-farm males, 64.0; and rural-farm females, 70.9. Does this mean that urban men are more likely and urban women less likely to marry than men and women who live on farms? Explain.

10. For census purposes exactly who should be included in and who excluded from the married category?

CHAPTER 9: Occupational Status

1. Of what importance is one's occupation in the determination of one's personality?

2. How does the category of the "economically active" population differ from one country to another?
3. Why is it that in the United States both the total number of persons employed and the index of unemployment generally rise during the month of June?
4. How may the occupational statistics be employed by urban sociologists in the study of city functions?
5. Describe the principal occupational trends in the United States since 1900.
6. How does the relative importance of each of the major industry groups in the city or county in which you reside compare with the national average?
7. Which portions of the United States are most dependent upon agricultural activities? Which upon manufacturing? And which upon trade and commerce?
8. Look up the concepts of "organic" and "mechanistic" social solidarity as developed by Emile Durkheim. How are these related to occupational specialization and industrial division of labor?

CHAPTER 10: Educational Status

1. Under what circumstances is it preferable to use each of the following indexes of educational status: the percentage of illiterates in the population of ten years of age and over; the median years of schooling attained by the adult population; and the percentage of high school graduates among the adult population?
2. Sometimes a given state or county will rank fairly high if the percentage of high school graduates is used as the index of educational status and low if the median years of schooling is employed. Of what important social phenomenon is this indicative?
3. As a general rule, how does the educational status of women compare with that of men? Under what circumstances is the situation reversed?
4. Indicate how the educational status of the population varies throughout the world, and evaluate the position of the United States in this respect.
5. In which portions of the United States is the educational status of the population the highest? The lowest? Explain.
6. How does the educational status of Negroes in the United States compare with that of whites? With that of populations in other selected parts of the world?
7. Analyze the factors that are responsible for the very high educational status of the urban white population in the southern states.
8. Use the latest census data to compare the educational status of the popu-

lation of Illinois with that of the population of Mississippi, making sure that you are not merely using a cumbersome method of showing that the former is much more urban and contains a far lower proportion of Negroes than the latter.

CHAPTER 11: Measuring the Rate of Reproduction

1. What conditions must be met before one is justified in using the birth rate as a measure of the fertility of a population?
2. What are the advantages and disadvantages of the fertility ratio as a measure of fertility?
3. Suppose you wish to compare the rate of reproduction of the population of the United States at intervals over the period 1850 to 1950. What index of fertility will you use? Explain.
4. Consult the appropriate pages in *Studies in American Demography* by Walter F. Willcox and *Population Analysis* by T. Lynn Smith, and then write a 500-word paper dealing with Dr. J. S. Billings' efforts to measure the birth rate in the United States and to determine its trend.
5. Who was responsible for developing the fertility ratio as a measure of the rate of reproduction? Trace the development of its use.
6. Of what value is the net reproduction rate in the study of fertility?
7. Why should one not employ the fertility ratio for comparisons of the rates of reproduction of the native-born and foreign-born white populations? What changes in census tabulations would be necessary to obviate this difficulty?
8. Consult the volumes of *Vital Statistics* published by the National Office of Vital Statistics and determine the categories of population for which birth statistics are available for the county in which you live; and consult the publications of the U. S. Bureau of the Census and determine the categories for which fertility ratios may be computed.

CHAPTER 12: Fertility Levels

1. How does the present rate of reproduction in the United States compare with that in such countries as Japan, France, Great Britain, India, Argentina, Brazil, and Mexico?
2. Compute the fertility ratios for representative urban and rural counties of the state in which you reside. How do these compare with the indexes for the urban and rural-farm populations of the United States as a whole?
3. From the data in Table XXVI make a list of the countries in which you judge that the actual level of fertility is rather accurately depicted by the reported crude birth rates.

4. In which sections of the United States are the actual birth rates the highest? The lowest? Nearest the average for the nation as a whole?

5. Describe the manner in which the net reproduction rate of the white population varies throughout the United States.

6. What factors probably account for the fact that Utah and New Mexico have the highest rates of reproduction in the nation irrespective of the indexes used in making the comparisons?

7. Why is the level of reproduction of the population in the District of Columbia the lowest in the United States?

8. Since the birth rates of the populations in various parts of the world were no higher at the middle of the twentieth century than they had been in 1900, why is it that since 1950 so many people have been concerned about the "population bomb" or "population explosion"?

9. How does a serious war affect the birth rates of the populations in the nations taking part in it?

CHAPTER 13: Differential Fertility

1. If one reasoned from Malthusian theory, what relationship between socio-economic status and the birth rate would he postulate? How would this compare with the actual results of a study in a country such as the United States in which some measure of economic position (such as the rent or rent equivalent of the home) was correlated with an index of the number of children in the family?

2. As the proportion of Negroes in the population increases in the various parts of the United States, what happens to the birth rate or other index of the rate of reproduction?

3. Discuss the validity and implications of the following statement: "Every refinement introduced into the presentation of data on the net reproduction rate in the United States tends to emphasize the importance of the rural-urban differential in fertility and to minimize racial and regional differences in the rate of reproduction."

4. Of what biological and social significance is the sharp rural-urban differential in fertility that has prevailed in the United States for many decades?

5. Compute fertility ratios for the white and Negro portions of the urban, rural-nonfarm, and rural-farm populations of your state. Basing your judgment upon these indexes, which differential is the greater, that between the races or that between the rural and urban segments of the population?

6. As the United States urbanized swiftly between 1850 and 1935, the birth rate of the population fell rapidly; and in 1930, 1940, and 1950, in this

country, the birth rate decreased rapidly as one passed from the most highly urbanized and industrialized sections of the nation to the most remote of the agricultural areas. How, then, may one account for the fact that between 1930 and 1947, a period in which the urbanization of the nation was proceeding very rapidly, the birth rate ceased to fall and then rose abruptly?

CHAPTER 14: Fertility Trends

1. Prepare a chart showing the trends in the rate of reproduction of the population of your state over the hundred year period 1850 to 1950. How do the fluctuations that occurred in this state compare with those in the nation as a whole?
2. Is the birth rate in most parts of Latin America likely to fall much during the next decade? That in China? In Russia? In Japan? In Germany? Explain.
3. Outline some of the social effects of the rise in the birth rate in the United States that took place between 1935 and 1950.
4. To what extent may one predict the trend in the birth rate a decade ahead from a knowledge of the trends during the preceding twenty-five years?
5. Give as much detail as you can about the falling birth rate of the population of the United States during the period 1830 to 1930.
6. Following 1935, how did the trend in the rate of reproduction of the urban population of the United States compare with that of the rural-farm population?
7. Prepare a chart showing how the changes since 1930 in the fertility ratios of the Negro population compare with the changes in those of the white population.
8. Prepare an annotated bibliography of fifteen items on the subject of current trends in the rate of reproduction of the population of the United States.

CHAPTER 15: The Measurement of Mortality

1. What data must one have for the making of a life table, and precisely what steps are involved in constructing one?
2. What are the *pros* and the *cons* with respect to the use of the crude death rate as the index on which is based a comparative study of the mortality in different countries and among various segments of a nation's population such as the white and the Negro, the rural and the urban, and so forth?

3. How is the infant mortality rate computed? How does it differ from the death rate of children of less than one year of age? And why is this index so important as an indicator of the social and economic well being of the people involved?
4. Of what value is the *International List of Causes of Death?*
5. Why is the coverage secured in the registration of deaths usually more complete than that secured in the registration of births?
6. Is the expectation of life at birth in a given state an accurate indicator of healthfulness in that state? Explain.
7. If you were to undertake the construction of life tables for the population of your state, precisely which years out of the decade would you select for such purposes? Explain.
8. Note in any life table to which you have ready access that the expectation of life at age one is higher than that at birth. How is this possible?

CHAPTER 16: Mortality Levels, Differentials, and Causes

1. How does the death rate of females of all ages generally compare with that of males? In what places and under what circumstances is this situation sometimes reversed?
2. In what parts of the world are current mortality rates the highest? In which areas are they the lowest? And in which other countries is the expectation of life at birth most closely comparable with that of the population of the United States?
3. How does the expectation of life at birth of the Negro population of the United States compare with that of the white population? With that in various Latin American countries and the Mediterranean countries of Europe?
4. In countries such as the United States and Canada, how do the mortality rates of the rural populations compare with those of the urban populations?
5. In which states of the United States is the expectation of life at birth of the white population the highest? In which is it the lowest? What conclusion, if any, does this lead you to with respect to the validity of such a measure for the purpose of comparing health and morbidity in one state with that in another?
6. Assemble the available mortality data for the county in which you live. To what extent may you use this information to compare the mortality of the population in your county with that of the people in the state as a whole?
7. From the *Vital Statistics* published annually by the National Office of Vital Statistics, determine the ten leading causes of death in the state in

which you live. How do these compare or differ from the list for the nation as a whole?

8. Determine the infant mortality rate for the county or city in which you live. How does this compare with that for the state as a whole? And what are the probable reasons for any differences observed?

CHAPTER 17: Mortality Trends

1. The changes in the death rate in the United States since 1920 are best described as a "trend," those in the birth rate as "fluctuations." Explain why this is the case.

2. Between 1900 and 1950 the expectation of life at birth of the white population of the United States rose from about fifty years to approximately sixty-nine years. Is there any possibility that a comparable increase will take place between 1950 and the year 2000? Explain.

3. Write a short paper (not over 1,000 words) on the social significance of falling death rates throughout the world during the period since 1925.

4. What relationship, if any, is there between the trends since 1900 in fatalities from diseases of the heart on the one hand and those from tuberculosis, typhoid fever, scarlet fever, and other transmissible diseases on the other?

5. In the long-continued increase in the expectation of life of the population of the United States, what has been the effect of (a) the decreasing infant mortality rate, (b) the prolongation of life for those seventy years of age or over, and (c) the urbanization of the nation?

6. To what extent is the current rapid increase in world population due to changes in the mortality rate, and to what extent has it been produced by changes in the birth rate?

7. Re-examine the data in Table XXXVIII, and then make a list of the countries in which you expect substantial reductions in the death rate to take place prior to 1965.

8. How do the trends in the expectation of life of the white population compare with those of the nonwhite (Negro) population? If the same relative rates of change are maintained subsequently to 1950, about when should the expectation of life at birth for the two come to be equal?

CHAPTER 18: Emigration and Immigration

1. The 1956 issue of the *Demographic Yearbook* of the United Nations carried an estimate of 2,579,000 for the population of Uruguay in 1954 and one of 2,615,000 for 1955. The same source publishes birth rates for the

country of 18.8 per thousand population for 1952 and 12.2 for 1955, and a death rate of 7.7 for 1952 and also 1953. (The birth rate and death rate for 1954 are not given.) Assume, however, that the 1954 rates were at the 1952 levels, and then estimate the amount of net immigration to the country that would have had to occur during 1954 in order to make the figure on increase of population during the year a reasonable one.

2. Under what circumstances may a stream of immigration that is negligible from the standpoint of population increase have profound social and economic consequences for a country?

3. Make a list of the countries which have been the principal sources of emigrants in the years since 1900, and make another showing the countries which have been most important as receivers of immigrants.

4. Into what five periods may the history of immigration to the United States be divided?

5. Describe the manner in which the composition of the immigration stream to the United States changed, decade by decade, between 1850 and 1950.

6. What elements, groups, organizations, and so forth favor rather free immigration of Mexicans to the United States? Which ones are opposed?

7. In what ways are a nation's immigration policies determined?

8. What has been the fate of the millions of "displaced persons" who were found in Central Europe at the close of the second world war?

9. In what ways was the Immigration Act of 1924 modified and changed by the McCarran-Walter Act?

10. How important is immigration as a factor in population change?

CHAPTER 19: Internal Migration

1. What are the principal varieties of internal migration? And from what sources may one secure pertinent information about each of them?

2. What difference, if any, is there between migration and social mobility? Is one justified in referring to migration as territorial social mobility? Explain.

3. Prepare an annotated bibliography of ten items on the subject of rural-urban migration.

4. Of what value for the study of internal migration are the U. S. Census tables showing state of birth cross-tabulated with state of residence?

5. What is the role of rural-to-urban migration in the maintenance and growth of towns and cities?

6. To what extent is the United States becoming a nation of nomads? Explain.

7. How do the "factors" and "media" related to rural-urban migrations in

Latin American countries, as set forth in the text, compare with those presently of importance in the United States?

8. Why are the data on migration the most deficient of all those required in population study?

9. Suppose you require information on the movement of people to or from the county in which you live. Precisely what data would you be able to obtain from the various publications of the United States Census of population?

10. How does the relative importance of farm-to-city migration vary from one part of the United States to another?

CHAPTER 20: Internal Migration (Continued)

1. How does the residential stability of the farm population in the state in which you reside compare and contrast with that of the farmers in other parts of the United States?

2. Describe the principal regional interchanges of population which took place in 1949 (the year to which the 1950 census data apply).

3. Of what value to society in general is the movement of the farm population from one farm to another?

4. How does the residential stability of the farmers in the "cotton belt" compare with that of those in the "corn belt"?

5. In what ways is the migration from rural to urban areas selective?

6. What differences, if any, are there between the migrants who move long distances and those who move short distances?

7. Give some of the social characteristics of migratory farm laborers.

8. Are Negroes more migratory than white people? Explain.

9. Write a paper approximately 1,000 words in length outlining the principal migrations of the Negro population of the United States in the period 1915 to the present.

10. How may charts showing age and sex distributions of the population be used to make inferences with respect to recent migrations to or from the population under consideration?

CHAPTER 21: The Growth of Population

1. About how many people will there be in the United States in 1970, and where will the center of population be at that time?

2. Why is it extremely difficult or impossible to trace the growth of population in most countries from the time the national state emerged until the present?

3. Should the growth of population be considered for analytical purposes as an independent variable or a dependent variable? Explain.

4. Using semilogarithmic paper prepare a chart on which you compare the growth of population since 1900 in the county in which you live, the state in which it is located, and the United States as a whole.

5. Set forth what appear to you to be the social correlates of a rapid growth of population, and also those of a decreasing population.

6. Prepare a chart on which you show the growth of population in your state from 1900 to the present, along with extrapolations, both arithmetic and geometric, until the year 1970.

7. What is the present population of the state in which you reside?

8. Note the percentage increase in the population of the United States during each intercensal period from 1790–1800 to the present time, and comment upon the principal causes of the variations which occurred from one decade to another.

9. In recent decades what has been the absolute and relative importance of fertility, mortality, and migration (immigration or emigration) in accounting for changes in the numbers of inhabitants in the following countries: Canada, India, France, the United States, Japan, and Brazil?

CONCLUSION

1. What is the general nature of population theory? And how does the method by which it is produced differ, if at all, from theory in the fields of zoology, astronomy, geology, philosophy, and psychology?

2. What tested hypotheses derived from the empirical study of population materials may legitimately be designated as theories?

3. What should be the role of population experts in the development of national population policies?

4. Set forth what appear to you to be the most important ways in which population facts and principles may be applied in connection with social problems and social and economic policies and planning.

5. What are the major features of the population policy of the United States? And, what facts, fears, and forces have enabled each of these to prevail?

6. Indicate at least six demographic principles or relationships that should be included in the subject matter taught in the introductory courses in sociology and economics.

7. What are the principal population problems of the United States at the present time?

8. How do the population problems of Japan compare with those of Brazil?

Author and Source Index

537

Subject Index

541